Considering the anthropological ideas of Britain between 1885 and 1945, this book explores the relationship between social scientific ideas and behavior. Professor Kuklick shows how the descriptions British anthropologists produced about the peoples of exotic cultures can be translated into commentaries on their own society. Read as such, the anthropology of the period covered by the book represents an appeal for a society that rewards individuals on the basis of talent and achievement, not inherited status; a brief for a society that is committed to caring for those whose circumstances have denied them the capacity to care for themselves; and a plea for tolerance of cultural diversity, based on observation of a range of ways of life that satisfy human needs and desires. The book also shows how anthropological insight informed consideration of specific problems – for example, the rights of women, the Irish, and all colonized peoples.

The savage within

The savage within

The social history of
British anthropology, 1885–1945

HENRIKA KUKLICK

CAMBRIDGE
UNIVERSITY PRESS

Published by the Press Syndicate of the University of Cambridge
The Pitt Building, Trumpington Street, Cambridge CB2 IRP
40 West 20th Street, New York, NY 10011-4211, USA
10 Stamford Road, Oakleigh, Melbourne 3166, Australia

© Cambridge University Press 1991

First published 1991
First paperback edition 1993

Printed in the United States of America

Library of Congress Cataloging-in-Publication Data is available.

A catolog record for this book is available from the British Library.

ISBN 0-521-41109-2 hardback
ISBN 0-521-45739-4 paperback

Contents

Acknowledgments

I have accrued many debts during the course of working on this book. For financial support, I am grateful to the Spencer Foundation, the American Philosophical Society, and the American Council of Learned Societies. I am much obliged to those unsung heroes of scholarship, the staffs of the various archives I have used. I have been fortunate to work in the Department of History and Sociology of Science at the University of Pennsylvania, where my colleagues have provided me with an environment both supportive and stimulating. Many people have suffered preliminary drafts of portions of my manuscript. In particular, for their advice, assistance, and encouragement, I am indebted to Mark Adams, Gila Berkovitch, Jenny Coates, Paul Coates, Richard Gillespie, Elizabeth Hunt, Julie Johnson, Patricia Johnson, David van Keuren, Roy MacLeod, Jack Pressman, Charles Rosenberg, Helen Rozwadowski, Lyn Schumaker, George Stocking, Sarah Tracy, and last, but hardly least, Marya Kuklick.

Abbreviations

ASA	Association of Social Anthropologists
BAAS	British Association for the Advancement of Science
CAS	Colonial Administrative Service
CRC	Colonial Research Council Papers, London School of Economics
CSSRC	Colonial Social Science Research Council
HP, CU	Haddon Papers, Cambridge University Library
IAI	International African Institute Manuscript Collection
ICS	Indian Civil Service
IMC/CBMS	International Missionary Council, Conference of British Missionary Societies, Joint Archive, School of Oriental and African Studies
LSE	London School of Economics
MP, LSE	Malinowski Papers, London School of Economics
MP, YU	Malinowski Papers, Yale University
NAG	National Archives of Ghana
NIIP	National Institute of Industrial Psychology
OUODP	Oxford University Overseas Development Project, Rhodes House
PRO	Public Record Office, Great Britain
RAI	Royal Anthropological Institute
RF	Rockefeller Foundation Archives
TNA	Tanganyika National Archives
UCL	University College, London

Chapter 1
Through the looking glass

When Daniel Gookin observed the Massachusetts Algonquins in 1674, he saw "as in a mirror or looking glass, the woful, miserable, and deplorable estate that sin reduced mankind unto naturally."[1] His was a conventional European view: technologically unsophisticated, preliterate peoples were living in humankind's primeval condition, innocent of the repressions necessary to civilization. This image has persisted in the Western mind, although its lineaments have varied considerably, as historical experiences have altered assumptions about human nature. For centuries, European observers of exotic peoples have found their understanding of their own impulses both challenged and confirmed. This study will explain the sources and consequences of self-examination framed in ethnographic terms. For this purpose, it considers the anthropological thought of Britain from the late nineteenth through the middle of the twentieth centuries.

To identify technologically unsophisticated peoples as the untutored children of the human race is not necessarily to imply that their lives are deficient in any but material satisfactions – which may be seen as obstacles to spiritual perfection. Observers' judgments have depended on their understanding of the course of human history. According to the biblical narrative Gookin believed, human beings became naturally depraved with the Fall from God's grace; the strictures of civilized society developed from morally imperative efforts to suppress mankind's ineradicable base drives. Almost as important in the Western tradition is the antithetical conception of human beings as creatures who are in their natural state essentially good. Consider, in contrast to Gookin's views, those advanced by his near-contemporary John Locke, whose model of natural man relied on information about the very peoples observed by Gookin, who was first superintendent of the Indians of Massachusetts. Locke also saw the "pattern of the first ages" in Native American Indian societies. But his natural men were not Gookin's "brutish barbarians." They were exemplary – enjoying "comfortable, safe, and peaceable living" conditions, effected

---

[1] Quoted in James Axtell, *The European and the Indian* (New York, 1981), 308.

through voluntary cooperation. They were not oppressed by the social institutions of civilized society – which were created when populations expanded beyond the numbers easily sustained in their habitats – which defined and perpetuated inequities of wealth and power.[2]

The disagreement between Locke and Gookin suggests all of the essential elements of this book. Like the later figures I shall discuss, both men expected ethnographic evidence to answer basic questions about the conduct of human affairs: What is fundamental human nature? How effective may social conditioning be in molding human behavior? What social organization most effectively shapes human beings into moral creatures? And both men were able to draw the lessons they wanted from the material at their disposal. This is not to say that ethnography is merely a pretext for projective fantasy. Whatever their interpretative disagreements, observers of a given society frequently agree about its salient traits – as Gookin and Locke did. Nevertheless, their interpretations cannot be treated as superficial glosses covering material that in its unvarnished state contributes to the growing body of knowledge about cultural variation. For our purposes, interpretation must be the principal focus, since this is the feature of ethnographic accounts that gives them practical implications.

This is the heart of the matter. Data make sense only when they are interpreted with theories, and theories are always, as the philosopher's maxim has it, "*underdetermined* by facts."[3] Moreover, no matter how rigorous are the methods used to compile and analyze evidence, decisions about the practical implications of evidence are always problematic. The limits of the possible can be only vaguely approximated through calculations of the frequencies of the probable, and the practical actor is concerned with what might be and what ought to be, not with what currently is. This was clear in 1893 to T. H. Huxley (1825–95), a man of formidable scientific accomplishments who figures in this book because he was central to the organization of anthropology as a discipline, and it is clear today to scholars committed to combatting racism and sexism.[4]

The constructions Gookin and Locke placed on their ethnographic

[2] Ibid.; and see John L. Myres, "The Influence of Anthropology on the Course of Political Science," *University of California Publications in History* 4 (1916): 31–3; John Locke, *Of Civil Government, Second Treatise* (Chicago, 1955 [orig. 1689]), 78, 88.
[3] For example, Mary Hesse, "Theory and Value in the Social Sciences," in C. Hookway and P. Petit, eds., *Action and Interpretation* (Cambridge, 1978), 1.
[4] T. H. Huxley, "Evolution and Ethics," the Romanes Lecture for 1893, in *Evolution and Ethics and Other Essays* (New York, 1902), 46–116. For one contemporary consideration of these issues see Helen Lambert, "Biology and Equality: A Perspective on Sex Differences," in Sandra Harding and Jean O'Barr, eds., *Sex and Scientific Inquiry* (Chicago, 1987), 125–45.

Observations of a young naturalist in the South Seas: a watercolor painted by Thomas Huxley in the Louisiade Archipelago in 1849 while he was serving on the H. M. S. *Rattlesnake*.

evidence implied altogether different courses of action. Whereas Gookin expected civilized men to recognize their moral duty to impose European ways on depraved savages, Locke expected his fellow citizens to emulate the virtues of natural men, creating a polity that restored original freedoms. Their disagreement exemplifies a general pattern – that interpretative differences are often products of observers' social circumstances. Given Gookin's official role, it is not surprising that his position rationalized systematic erosion of Indian rights in colonial America. Given American revolutionaries' objectives, it is not surprising that they found in arguments such as Locke's useful justifications for their cause. American colonists could invoke whichever image of Native Americans suited their immediate purposes. Settlers eradicated Native Americans' way of life through measures ranging from cultural modification to genocide. Yet they made the American Indian into an icon of the revolution, representing his love of liberty and fierce independence as the essential American spirit.[5] That

5 For description of the ways in which revolutionary ideologues such as Benjamin Franklin and Thomas Jefferson took Native American norms and institutions as exemplary, see Bruce E. Johansen, *Forgotten Founders* (Ipswich, Mass., 1982), 71, 108. For analyses of the context-dependent variation in settler behavior toward Native Americans, see Axtell, *The European and the Indian*; and Bernard Sheehan, *Savagism and Civility* (Cambridge, 1975).

the population of early America put ethnographic evidence to various ideological uses does not mark it as exceptionally confused or dishonest; like that of any society, it was pursuing diverse goals and incorporated groups and individuals acting at cross purposes.

Early America presents a pattern of use of ethnographic information that has been repeated time and again. The problem of this book is to explicate this pattern. In it, I ask a fundamental question for historical sociologists and social historians: What relationships obtain among ideas, experiences, and action? The cast of characters who will appear are appropriately seen as the figures neither of textbook sociology nor of textbook history: neither as creatures whose conduct is so completely conditioned by upbringing and material interests that any departures they make from expected patterns are consequences of programing error; nor as virtually free-willed creatures who endure one test of character after another, negotiating sequences of irreproducible situations.[6] That is, they performed creatively within circumstantial limitations, making decisions that seemed sensible to them, using ethnography as an aid to understanding the constraints and possibilities of their lives.

I offer no elaborate justification for my conceptualization of social actors. I do not wish to bore the reader either with the scholarly ceremony of invoking myriad previous works that set precedents for this one, or with personal revelations of the experiences that shaped my views. I only observe that mine is the model of the person that seems plausible to intellectuals (and others) in the late twentieth century. That we think of ourselves in terms of this model – as acting within bounded possibilities, choosing among the options available to us using the standards of our culture (or subculture) – substantiates this book's thesis. Our self-image has been shaped in many ways by comparative cultural evidence and, indeed, has antecedents in the anthropology of the period I shall discuss. That is one of the reasons this book has its particular substantive focus – because the period it treats was critical for the development of contemporary, self-critical sensibility.

The peculiarities of the British

The anthropological ideas treated in this book deserve particular attention, and not just because they left a lasting legacy. The history of anthropology

---

[6] The classic description of textbook "sociological man" is that of Dennis Wrong, "The Oversocialized Conception of Man in Modern Sociology," *American Sociological Review* 26 (1961): 184–93. Allan Megill has defined textbook "historical man" in his "Disciplinary History and Other Kinds," a paper presented to the University of Iowa conference on "Argument in Science: New Sociologies of Science/Rhetoric of Inquiry," 9–11, October, 1987.

in Britain permits specification of the elements of culture, power, class, and institution in the development of a specialized intellectual enterprise. That is, anthropologists were specimen members of a developing intellectual class, whose positions on national issues reflected their social status at any given moment, and whose capacity to alter the events of their time was a function of intellectuals' changing role. Moreover, their enterprise was central to the national debates of the period covered by this book, for during it Britain first reached the heights of her imperial power and then determined to divest herself of her colonies – and anthropologists were as likely to condemn as to condone colonialism. Because anthropologists initially undertook to understand all of the world's peoples, not just the subjects of the Empire, they also advanced their findings in support of various policies within Britain. The practical interests of British anthropologists thus represent the full range of problems apparently illuminated by evidence about exotic peoples. And the purposes to which anthropology was put demonstrated not only the convictions of the intellectuals who developed it but also the plausibility of anthropologists' observations to a considerable audience.

Britain has been peculiar among industrialized nations in having both a flourishing intellectual culture and an underdeveloped university system. Many of her leading intellectuals have not been cloistered scholars, but men and women positioned to implement their ideas in practical terms. Among the causes they prosecuted in the late nineteenth century was the elevation of academic standards in the universities of Oxford and Cambridge, requiring both structural and curricular reforms: university regulations had to change so that merit criteria alone would determine careers of students and faculty; and courses had to be broadened, particularly in the sciences – including anthropology – in order to satisfy the nation's needs for trained workers. But anthropology long remained one among several intellectual activities conducted largely outside academe. While it did, anthropological ideas were elaborately linked to social practices in a fashion without parallel since.

Anthropologists' work reflected Britain's loss of the self-confidence it once enjoyed as the first industrialized nation and economic leader of the world. In the last quarter of the nineteenth century, Britain became only one among a number of world powers. Its rate of economic growth had declined, and it had lost international ground in volume of industrial production and national income, most notably by contrast to Germany and the United States. The vast expansion of British colonial holdings, especially in Africa, was undertaken in pursuit of new markets in which the nation would have competitive advantages functionally equivalent to those it had lost in her old ones. Britain's cultural superiority also figured in arguments for colonialism: the process of colonial conquest was seen as a vehicle for strengthening national character; and colonial rule was celebrated as a peacekeeping and civilizing mission – despite reports from the colonies replete with descriptions of the unfortunate consequences of colonialism for subject peoples.

Witnesses to Britain's difficulties at home and abroad, anthropologists were by no means alone in their efforts to explain them. But they were peculiarly situated observers of their society by virtue of their social backgrounds and intellectual associations. Largely drawn from the classes that had benefited from the liberalizing effects of economic growth – practitioners of old and new professional occupations, industrialists, members of dissenting religious groups (or hostile to organized religion) – they were obliged to contemplate the relationship between individual initiative and social forces. Moreover, because pre–World War I anthropologists tried to explain all varieties of societies, they were confronted with irreconcilable elements in Britain's self-image – self-doubt in many aspects of its domestic affairs and pretensions to cultural superiority in justification of its colonial ventures.

Without some level of public agreement about the value of knowledge about the nonindustrialized world, anthropology would never have emerged as a recognizable field of study. If language is an index to popular understanding, anthropology had a recognizable identity by 1805; in that year, the first published use of the word "anthropologist" to denote the occupant of a specialized role appeared in the *Edinburgh Review*, a journal of the cultivated upper middle class. As an organized enterprise (impossible without enthusiasts in sufficient numbers to sustain learned societies and support publication of journals and monographs), anthropology grew throughout the nineteenth century. Not until 1884, however, was the field accorded recognition indicative of its acceptance as a pursuit for genuine scholars and men of position. In that year, the first university post in anthropology in Britain was created for E. B. (Sir Edward) Tylor (1832–1917), a readership at Oxford (later converted to a professorship for him alone); and the British Association for the Advancement of Science at last conceded that the field was entitled to a section of its own, Section H.

Throughout its formative years, anthropology was conceived as useful scholarship. Its intellectual roots drew upon classics, biblical studies, and philosophy, but it is best appreciated as a type of natural history, one species of a class of knowledge – also including geology, botany, zoology, and geography – that could be used to manage the nation's resources of people and land. Before the British Association gave the field its own section, it housed anthropology with several varieties of natural history, and many of the figures treated in this study pursued anthropology along with other interests of this species. Because anthropologists were generally neither leisured gentlemen nor academics but men of affairs (and a very few women), they expected their scholarship to inform the decisions of their daily lives.

The expectations of the scholars and practical men who created anthropology may be gathered from their own testimony. Their hopes for the utilitarian potential of science were virtually boundless. Their optimism was best expressed by John Stuart Mill, whose *Principles of Political Economy*, first published in 1848, was throughout the latter half of the century the single most influential analysis of the relationship between social institutions and individual behavior. Scientific knowledge was advancing so rapidly, Mill wrote, "as to justify our belief that our acquaintance with nature is still in its infancy." Furthermore, as soon as scientific principles were discovered, they were put to practical use: the electromagnetic telegraph, for example, "sprang into existence but a few years after the establishment of the scientific theory which it realizes and exemplifies." The growth of knowledge was but one aspect of the general trend toward human improvement. Manufacturers could adopt "the most delicate processes of the application of science" because of the elevation of the working classes; they had "no difficulty in finding or forming, in a sufficient number of the working hands of the community, the skills requisite for" their industrial innovations.[7] Mill articulated a faith in progress in general and in science in particular that was to dim in the future; indeed, its diminution is central to the narrative of this book. But this faith was critical to the development of enterprises such as anthropology.

Throughout the years covered by this study, leading anthropologists frequently advertised their field's practical value. Tylor often termed anthropology the "reformer's science," the findings of which would enable the "great modern nations to understand themselves, to weigh in a just balance their own merits and defects, and even in some measure to forecast . . . the possibilities of the future."[8] Bronislaw Malinowski (1884–1942), the preeminent anthropologist in Britain during the interwar period, likewise insisted that comparative cultural evidence compelled "intelligent and even drastic reform" of Western society.[9] Certainly, academics must

---

[7] On the influence of Mill's *Principles of Political Economy*, see A. W. Coats, "The Historicist Reaction in English Political Economy, 1870–1890," *Economica* [n. s.] 21 (1954): 144. Coats's argument itself rests on nineteenth-century observers, particularly Herbert Somerton Foxwell, writing in 1899. The quotations from Mill come from *Principles of Political Economy* (London, 1862 [orig. 1848]), Vol. II, 259.

[8] E. B. Tylor, "Introduction" to Friedrich Ratzel, *The History of Mankind* (London, 1896), v.

[9] Bronislaw Malinowski, "Parenthood – The Basis of Social Structure," in V. W. Calverton and Samuel D. Schmalhausen, eds., *The New Generation* (New York, 1930),

cast their popular appeals in this mold. If Malinowski's sometime student
E. E. (Sir Edward) Evans-Pritchard (1902–73) had not assured his radio
listeners in 1950 that anthropological findings "have obvious significance
for the understanding... of any society, including our own," could he have
expected them to stay tuned?[10]

Though anthropology increasingly became an activity dominated by
professionals – figures who made careers of anthropology in universities
and museums – even in the 1930s the professional community was so
small that anthropology's audience was composed largely of amateurs.
Nineteenth-century anthropologists published in specialist journals, to
be sure, but they placed some of their most important contributions in
general publications that were founded during their lifetimes – and the very
existence of which denoted the recent growth of the educated public.
They addressed the readers of such periodicals as the politically centrist
Nineteenth Century, the utilitarian *Westminster Review*, and, perhaps most
important, the *Fortnightly Review*, which was in the latter third of the
century "the acknowledged mouthpiece of advanced, free-thinking radicalism."[11] In the twentieth century, anthropologists have addressed a
narrower audience. Nevertheless, as late as the interwar years they aired
their theoretical disputes in public.[12] And they wrote their academic books
so that they would be interesting and intelligible to general readers as well
as to specialists.[13]

They were addressing a receptive audience, however. Few anthropologists gathered a readership as large as that of J. G. (Sir James) Frazer
(1854–1941), a sometime classicist who spent virtually his entire adult life
within the protected environment of Trinity College, Cambridge. But the
remarkable public response to Frazer's work demonstrated that anthropology could exert a powerful hold on the popular imagination. Particularly

---

168. And note that he wrote in an introductory note to this essay that "although this
   article is written in simple language and without any display of learning... it is more
   than a mere popular exposition of established views. It is the first full statement of my
   theory of kinship, the result of over twenty years' work on a subject to which I have
   devoted most of my attention" (p. 112).

[10] E. E. Evans-Pritchard, "Social Anthropology," reprinted in *Social Anthropology and
   Other Essays* (New York, 1962 [originally London, 1950]), 108.

[11] John Gross, *The Rise and Fall of the Man of Letters* (New York, 1970), 66.

[12] One such debate that aired in public during the interwar period centered on the merits
   of diffusionist versus functionalist anthropology. The diffusionists, in particular, sought
   popular support in their efforts to win disciplinary supremacy. For one attempt to make
   this debate accessible to a general audience, see G. Elliot Smith, B. Malinowski, H. J.
   Spindler, and A. Goldenweiser, *Culture: The Diffusion Controversy* (London, 1928).

[13] See Raymond Firth, "An Appraisal of Modern Social Anthropology," *Annual Review of
   Anthropology* 4 (1975): 4.

The popular appeal of J. G. Frazer and of images of supposedly irrational peoples: the cover of *The Illustrated London News* for February 4, 1911. The caption reads, "Sympathetic Magic: Killing an Unfaithful Wife in Effigy, Australia." The text below observes, "To quote Mr. J. G. Frazer's "The Golden Bough": 'Perhaps the most familiar application of the principle that like produces like is the attempt which has been made by many people in many ages to injure or destroy an enemy by injuring or destroying an image of him ...' "

in the era of World War I, disillusioned intellectuals found the objective correlatives to their feelings of despair in his eternal images of dying kings and parched fields. Hundreds of readers were moved to write to him that his work had opened their eyes and changed their lives, and the sales of his most popular book, *The Golden Bough*, were by any standards extraordinary.[14] By the interwar period, a fair percentage of leading anthropologists were emigrants to Britain from the Empire Dominions or other countries, who encouraged their colleagues to attend to intellectual developments outside Britain. But anthropologists had to adapt to the local

[14] Robert Ackerman, *J. G. Frazer: His Life and Work* (Cambridge, 1987), 3, 256–7.

intellectual ecology, not the least because they were dependent on a general
audience concerned with issues of national interest.[15]

After World War II, however, professional anthropologists were able
to write largely for themselves, and that is why this study ends at that
point. Research funds grew, and, most important, were allocated on
academic anthropologists' recommendations. The business of anthropologists became the training of other anthropologists to occupy professional
posts and the writing of arcane analyses to impress colleagues. Anthropologists presented a collective front to the outsiders on whom they ultimately
depended, but regarded with near-hostility – an attitude prefigured during
the interwar years. They assured their patrons that research funds would
be spent in pursuit of immediately useful knowledge, while privately determining their own research agendas. Adopting language unintelligible to
laymen, professionals became preoccupied with apparently purely technical
matters – such as the stylistic niceties of representing varieties of kinship
structures.[16] Earlier, leading academic anthropologists had resisted such
developments, as Malinowski did in a 1930 article tellingly entitled "Must
Kinship Studies Be Dehumanised by Mock Algebra?"[17]

The era of professional domination of British anthropology can fairly be
said to have begun in 1946 with the foundation of the Association of Social
Anthropologists (ASA). Unlike the previously dominant anthropological
society, the Royal Anthropological Institute (RAI) of Great Britain and
Ireland (founded in 1871 as the Anthropological Institute), which effectively welcomed all who wished to join, the ASA restricted its membership
to those who had Ph.D.s in anthropology or equivalent accomplishments.
At its foundation, the ASA was very small, enrolling roughly twenty people.
In contrast, the RAI had at this time approximately six hundred members
(still but a fraction of anthropology's general audience). Professional
dominance of the field was not yet complete, but it was certain.

---

[15] There has lately been some debate over the nature of emigré influence on British
scholarship, anthropological and other. It seems safe to conclude that whatever
significance their ideas had in their countries of origin, the emigré scholars' schemes
were welcomed in Britain because they could be reconciled with indigenous ones, not
the least because the emigré scholars took some pains to adapt them to their new
surroundings. See, for example, Ernest Gellner, "Malinowski Go Home," *Anthropology
Today* 1, No. 5 (October 1985): 5–7; Paul H. Koch, "No Utopia: Refugee Scholars in
Britain," *History Today* 35 (November 1985): 53–6. For the saga of a refugee scholar
whose adaptive efforts proved relatively unsuccessful, see A. P. Simonds, *Karl
Mannheim's Sociology of Knowledge* (Oxford, 1978).

[16] This point is made and illustrated effectively in J. A. Barnes, *Three Styles in the Study of
Kinship* (Berkeley, 1971).

[17] B. Malinowski, "Must Kinship Studies Be Dehumanised by Mock Algebra?" *Man* 30
(1930): 256–7.

It is worth looking briefly at the consequences of this development, since the distinguishing features of the prewar anthropological community are highlighted by comparison. After the war there remained a popular audience eager to learn from ethnography whether humankind is naturally violent or peaceable, selfish or altruistic, egalitarian or hierarchical. If persons eager to achieve eminence in academic anthropology would not address their concerns (because those who wrote for the public would lose professional status), others not so motivated were prepared to write popular works. To be sure, since World War II anthropologists have been willing to broadcast their views in the mass media, and the occasional study has engaged the attention of both academics and general readers – but for reasons peculiar to each group.[18]

Indeed, popular anthropology has become a nearly distinctive genre. It is not merely academic work simplified and translated for a general audience. Its interpretation presents special problems posed by any form of popular culture; its readers are not joined in deliberate effort to reach collective agreement, so they respond to it in idiosyncratic fashion.[19] To be sure, the motives of its audience often seem self-evident. Works dealing with inherent sex differences, say, surely appeal to persons concerned with problematic gender roles. And the readers' ability to find meanings in a text not intended by the author is hardly unique to our time: Frazer did not intend to convey the feelings of despair his readers derived from his work, although it seems unlikely that he would have captured their attention had they not once shared the faith he sustained – the expectation that human society could be perfected through the exercise of reason. What has changed is the shape of the population of popular anthropology's writers and readers. Its writers today are not a cohesive group whose ethos we can see emergent from collective experience, and its readers do not express in publicly accountable ways the lessons they learn from it.

I do not wish to suggest that academic anthropologists were removed to a high intellectual plane, on which the concerns of the world around them did not intrude. No academic professionals are so removed, even those whose work is largely speculative. Smith does not persuade Jones through

---

[18] The best illustration of the disjunction between popular and professional interpretations of anthropological analysis is found in the debates over Margaret Mead's analysis of Samoan culture provoked by Derek Freeman, *Margaret Mead and Samoa* (Cambridge, Mass., 1983). See Ivan Brady, ed., "Speaking in the Name of the Real: Freeman and Mead on Samoa," *American Anthropologist* [n.s.] 85 (1983): 908–47. The debates among anthropologists in this instance cross national boundaries – indicating another significant feature of contemporary anthropology.

[19] For an analysis of popular culture that makes this point see Janice A. Radway, *Reading the Romance* (Chapel Hill, N.C., 1984).

the rigor of her logic and the wealth of her documentation alone, but must frame her argument in terms that Jones has learned to trust on the basis of his everyday experience. Anthropologists are no different from other academics; they hold notions of common sense that are functions of the general habits of their culture, the historical memories of their generation, and the experiences peculiar to their social milieux. Post–World War II British anthropologists have shared with other members of their society assumptions of the very diffuse sort that permeate any culture, assumptions recognizable in both scholarship and behavior. But if we want to specify the relationships between anthropology and practical action, we have to look to the pre–World War II period.

The decline of anthropology's popular relevance dates from its fragmentation into discrete subfields. During the first half of the twentieth century, anthropologists became convinced that human racial and cultural variation were entirely independent of each other, and that therefore members of existing simple societies were not living physical and behavioral fossils of the earliest humans. Their conclusions entailed a strict division of labor among social anthropologists, physical anthropologists, and archaeologists. Earlier anthropologists had usually concentrated on one of the discipline's areas (and each subfield was informed by somewhat different premises), but whatever their focus anthropologists had assumed that their findings contributed to an understanding of the human species in all of its aspects. Physical and social anthropology were practically distinct before World War I, but after the war anthropologists became more insistent that race did not determine culture – not the least because they became aware of the political abuses that could be rationalized on the grounds of scientific racism.[20]

When the lines of filiation joining all varieties of humankind seemed clear, general readers could understand anthropology as an enterprise that elucidated their innate impulses and traced the origins of their society. Indeed, the public responded enthusiastically to the last anthropological effort to integrate archeological, physical, and cultural research: the work of the diffusionists, who were in their heyday roughly from 1910 to 1930.[21]

---

[20] For one discussion of the highly elaborated division of intellectual labor that obtained in anthropology by the 1930s, see John L. Myres, "Anthropology, Pure and Applied," *Journal of the Royal Anthropological Institute* 61 (1931): xxvi–xxviii.

[21] The space given to reports of the diffusionists' claims in *The Times*, for example, was considerable. Dangerous though it is to infer public interest from media coverage, we are probably justified in doing so here. See, for one illustration, the relatively long article published by G. Elliot Smith, "Asiatic Influence in Mayan Art: A New Discovery," *The Times*, 14 January, 1927, pp. 13–14, 16. And see the similarly extensive space allotted to the same story in a more popular periodical: G. Elliot

During the 1930s, however, most anthropologists agreed that the diffusionists' synthesis did not hold. To be sure, some specialized anthropological work still fascinated general readers – especially paleontological findings about the origins of the human species and archaeological investigations of ancient settlements. And social anthropology still offered the British public entertainment and enlightenment: illustrations of alternative ways of life possible for humanity; cautionary tales about the pleasures and pitfalls of societies organized in various fashions; messages of tolerance for diversity; and analyses of the impact of colonialism on subject peoples – a matter of considerable concern in an era in which the vast majority of British subjects were the peoples of the Empire.[22]

But nonspecialist readers of ethnography did not depend on scholars. If they wished to be entertained as well as to be reassured of the merits of their own way of life, they might prefer to turn to travelers' accounts. These offered thrilling reports of explorers' physical heroism in the wilds of the Empire – and represented a form of pornography that could be openly admitted to polite households, describing behavior forbidden in Western society "with a particularity of detail."[23] In the nineteenth century, such accounts had provided material for "armchair" anthropologists – theorists who did not collect evidence themselves. When anthropologists took to the field at the turn of the century, they stressed scientific regularities far more than exotic curiosities, so the change in their research methodology also contributed to the differentiation of their work from that directed toward a popular audience.

There remained, however, a practical sphere in which anthropologists maintained that they could offer explicit guidance: the colonial Empire. Like their predecessors, anthropologists of the interwar period pressed colonial officials to acknowledge the need for their advice. Ironically, anthropologists withdrew from public affairs just when state demand for their services was most intense. Britain was particularly eager to employ anthropologists in the post–World War II period, when officials hoped that

Smith, "The 'Elephant Controversy' Settled by a Decisive Discovery," *The Illustrated London News*, 15 January, 1927, pp. 85–7, 108.

[22] See, for examples, the interpretations given scholarly books in the popular press. E. H. G., "Red Paint, Scarification, and Human Bones: 'Medicine' in the Andamans," a review of A. R. Brown (later Radcliffe-Brown), *The Andaman Islanders*, in *The Illustrated London News*, 21 September, 1922, p. 161; "The Evil Eye: Attack, Defense – and Cures!" a review of Edward Westermarck, *Ritual and Belief in Morocco*, in *The Illustrated London News*, 22 January, 1927, p. 132.

[23] The quotation is from "Civilisation the Destroyer," a review of Tom Harrisson, *Savage Civilisation*, in *The Illustrated London News*, 23 January, 1937, pp. 144–5. The breathless tone of this review is typical.

anthropologists would help develop viable strategies for turning colonies into independent nations. But leading anthropologists then protested that true scientists do not do commissioned research. Officials such as Lord Hailey, a retired member of the Indian Civil Service who was the first head of the Colonial Research Council, were exasperated. Anthropological expertise was so vital to colonial development, said Hailey in 1946, that if the anthropologist would not supply colonial regimes with necessary assistance, "we must find someone calling himself by a different name who will do so."[24]

The cleavage between post–World War II professional anthropologists and practical men had a social structural manifestation: the disappearance of routine personal contacts between them. As contemporary data indicate, if social scientists and policymakers are joined in working relationships – perhaps because they meet together regularly for some shared purpose, or perhaps because standard career patterns involve regular circulation of personnel from one group to another – their worldviews can become nearly indistinguishable.[25] Relationships of this sort had been encouraged when the important organizational loci of anthropological work had been ecumenical groups such as the RAI and Section H, rather than exclusively professional groups such as the ASA. They had been deliberately fostered through the efforts of an anthropological entrepreneur such as Malinowski, who during the interwar period held seminars at the London School of Economics that were famous because they involved people from as many of the social groups found in the colonies as Malinowski could attract. Most important, such relationships were products of the prewar occupational environment.

To appreciate how different was the anthropologists' social milieu in the late nineteenth and early twentieth centuries, consider again the extraordinary career of J. G. Frazer. His social network reveals the range of associations anthropologists of his day could form in the course of their scholarly activities. Indeed, the diversity of Frazer's friends is especially remarkable because he was the quintessential armchair scholar, rarely venturing from his study. He himself had little taste for practical action (including academic politics). But because he associated with men of affairs, he assumed as they did that all worthwhile scholarship had some

---

[24] Lord Hailey to E. W. Smith, 22 April, 1946. Hailey Papers, in OUODP.
[25] For examples of such a situation, see Derek B. Cornish and Ronald V. Clarke, "Social Science in Government: The Case of the Home Office Research and Planning Unit," in Martin Bulmer, ed., *Social Science Research and Government* (Cambridge, 1987), 166–96; and Stuart S. Blume, "Social Science in Whitehall: Two Analytic Perspectives," in Bulmer, ed., 77–93.

practical value. And many of his friends were not content with mere speculation about the uses of anthropology.

Summary characterizations of just a few members of Frazer's network indicate that in his day commitment to the scholarly life did not entail (and in fact precluded) today's intellectual specialization. James Ward, professor of moral philosophy at Cambridge and one of the first Britons to take seriously German psychophysical research, discussed all manner of intellectual matters with Frazer during the forty-five years of their close friendship; it was Ward who introduced the then-classicist Frazer to anthropology, urging him to read Tylor's *Primitive Culture*. The closest friend of Frazer's life, William Robertson Smith, tried as a heretic by the Free Church of Scotland because he embraced the German "higher criticism" in his biblical scholarship, commissioned and actively guided Frazer's earliest anthropological efforts in his capacity as coeditor of the *Encyclopaedia Britannica*. Charles Darwin's cousin, (Sir) Francis Galton (1822–1911) – the pioneer statistician, founder of eugenics, general polymath, and, like Frazer, a Trinity man – was Frazer's mentor and patron. As president of the Anthropological Institute in 1885, Galton chaired the scholarly meeting at which Frazer presented his first anthropological paper, addressing an audience that included the sociologist Herbert Spencer, to whom Frazer acknowledged a lifelong intellectual debt. With some assistance from Frazer, A. C. Haddon (1855–1940) transformed himself from a zoologist into an anthropologist and tempted Frazer to join the 1898 Cambridge Anthropological Expedition to Torres Straits, the venture that revolutionized British anthropology because it demonstrated that anthropologists who did their own ethnographic research could take the rigorous scientific standards of the laboratory into the field.

Furthermore, Frazer's friends exercised power not only in learned but also in public circles. Hoping to enlarge scientists' national role, they acted to remedy "the very inadequate manner in which the progress of Science and the labour and opinions of our scientific men have been recorded in the weekly press" – to quote the manifesto of *The Reader*, founded in 1864 under the coeditorship of Spencer, Galton, and Norman Lockyear, another pillar of mid-Victorian science; although this publication was short-lived, its progenitors resuscitated their creation in the journal *Nature*, which still flourishes.[26] Some members of Frazer's network were scientific statesmen, sitting on commissions established by learned societies and by the government to collect and evaluate expert testimony on matters of national

---

[26] Quoted in Karl Pearson, *The Life, Letters and Labours of Francis Galton* (Cambridge, 1924), Vol. 2, 67–8.

interest. Galton played this role, sometimes in the company of (Sir) Michael Foster, the quintessential scientist-statesman, who was the teacher of Haddon and Ward, as well as of other important scientists. Leader at Cambridge of an innovative school of physiology, Liberal Member of Parliament from 1900 to 1906, Foster figured in an episode in academic politics in which Frazer was prevailed upon to play an uncharacteristically active part: the successful campaign to create a post in anthropology at Cambridge for Haddon. Some of Frazer's friends held local government offices, as did the solicitor Sidney Hartland (1848–1927), who was selected to give the first lecture in the annual series established in Frazer's honor in 1922.

A network so articulated had its uses. More than once Frazer was rescued from financial desperation through the efforts of (Sir) Edmund Gosse, an eminent author and critic well connected to wealthy patrons. Gosse's most significant contribution to Frazer's financial security was the arrangement of an act of political patronage – the award in 1905 of a Civil List pension, conferred by Parliament upon recommendation by the prime minister. And Frazer himself could exercise influence through his friends. When, during World War I, his protégé Malinowski faced the prospect of interruption of his fieldwork in the Trobriand Islands because as a Polish national he was subject to the treatment accorded enemy aliens, Frazer was able to help Malinowski to remain at work. The Trobriands were within the jurisdiction of J. H. P. (Sir Hubert) Murray, lieutenant-governor of Papua (earlier British New Guinea), and Murray was the older brother of Frazer's friend Gilbert Murray, an Oxford classicist of anthropological bent; at Frazer's request, Gilbert urged his brother to lend his support to Malinowski's cause.[27]

This episode illustrates an important integrative feature of Frazer's social milieu: kinship relations. Through friendship, he was linked to members of the endogamous new class that emerged in Britain during the course of the nineteenth century – that class Noel Annan has termed the "intellectual aristocracy." Members of this group were themselves conscious of the kinship ties that bound them. When, for example, Galton surveyed the habits and parentage of 180 distinguished scientists for his *English Men of Science*, first published in 1874, he noted that two-thirds of them came

---

[27] Ironically, J. H. P. Murray took an intense dislike to Malinowski, and unsuccessfully tried to prevent him from doing later research in the Trobriands. I owe a good deal of this information to Ackerman, *J. G. Frazer*. On Malinowski's relationship with Australian officials, see D. J. Mulvaney and J. H. Calaby, *"So Much That Is New"*: *Baldwin Spencer, 1860–1920* (Melbourne, 1985), 322–4.

from thirteen families.[28] The brothers Murray, children of a prominent Australian official, did not belong to the British intellectual aristocracy, but their career choices nevertheless fit the pattern Annan has identified as characteristic of the children of these families. Imbued with an ethos of service, hostile to traditional aristocratic privilege, and determined to create a society governed by a natural aristocracy of talent, this class was "wedded to gradual reform of accepted institutions and able to move between the worlds of speculation and government," and it sent its children into the world as educators and public servants.[29] The son of a Glasgow pharmacist, Frazer did not have a pedigree that included Darwins, Huxleys, Wedgwoods, Hodgkins, or Stracheys. But members of this group recognized talent such as his when they saw it. Moreover, the government recognized the contributions of the intellectual aristocracy and their adopted kin, conferring upon them knighthoods in abundance. During the years covered by this study (if not necessarily others), this title is a reliable index to meritocratic status, reserved for those who had earned it by making some contribution to the national welfare.[30]

Members of the intellectual aristocracy were present in the anthropological community in significant numbers through the turn of the century. Their direct descendants – such as Malinowski's student Audrey Richards (1899–1984) – and persons eminently qualified for adoption – such as E. R. (Sir Edmund) Leach (1910–89), the student of Malinowski's students – became prominent anthropologists after World War II, but by that time their social type was relatively rare in the discipline. Their scarcity was another factor that contributed to anthropology's changing social role, along with the discipline's differentiation into subfields and its professionalization. Of course, these trends were linked. The process of professionalization that made subdisciplinary specialization a viable career option and permitted anthropologists to become a self-referential population also made status in the community more dependent on scholarly accomplishment alone. The prestige attached to possession of a proud family name – even a name glorious because of the family's tradition of achievement – was devalued in professionalized academic circles.

For example, no academic post was found for Gregory Bateson (1904–80), a scion of the intellectual aristocracy as the son of the distinguished geneticist William Bateson (who refused a knighthood). Perhaps it was the

[28] Francis Galton, *English Men of Science* (London, 1970 [orig. 1874]), pp. 40–64.

[29] N. G. Annan, "The Intellectual Aristocracy," in J. H. Plumb, ed., *Studies in Social History* (London, 1955), 244. For the argument that the reformist orientation of this class disqualifies it as a genuine intelligentsia, see M. S. Hickox, "Has There Been a British Intelligentsia?" *British Journal of Sociology* 37 (1986): 200–8.

[30] Lawrence Stone and Jeanne C. Fawtier Stone, *An Open Elite?* (New York, 1984), 261.

confidence born of his lineage that gave the son the audacity to propose himself for the William Wyse professorship in Anthropology at Cambridge when he was only thirty.[31] To be sure, Bateson's nonincorporation into the British university system was an overdetermined phenomenon, the product of a range of personal choices he made and, in particular, of the sort of anthropologist he was (so long as he remained an anthropologist). Class considerations had hardly disappeared from British academic judgments, but had they been more important, a position might have been found for Bateson despite his intellectual eccentricities.

The moral tone of anthropology was set by the personal attitudes of the new class of people whose status was based on achievement. The barely qualified optimism of late-nineteenth-century anthropology bespeaks its writers' experience. Because they themselves were the beneficiaries of historical trends, they represented the course of history in positive terms, using evidence about simple societies to mark the distance Western culture had traveled. True, their faith in progress, and in the importance of the intelligentsia to its direction, was tried by the onset of the depression of 1873–96. Britain's previous prosperity had been a source of special pride to one portion of the intelligentsia, the political economists, who had credited themselves with articulating the rational principles that had guided national development. The crisis of confidence in economics was critical by 1877, when the British Association for the Advancement of Science entertained a formal motion that Section F (Economic Science and Statistics) be eliminated because its methods and findings were unscientific.

The motion to exclude Section F, which was proposed by Francis Galton, signaled a repudiation of classical formalism in social science. Economists responded to the challenge to their accustomed habits by invoking cultural phenomena, arguing that economic behavior was shaped by conditions peculiar to specific times and places. Some economists looked for inspiration to figures in the anthropological community such as Galton's friend H. J. S. (Sir Henry) Maine (1822–88). Indeed, the new economic orthodoxy, articulated at the turn of the century by the Cambridge professor Alfred Marshall, embodied the same hopes anthropologists expressed: one, that policy-relevant generalizations could be developed from careful analysis of behavior patterns characteristic of specific historical periods; two, that lawlike regularities could be observed

---

[31] See the letter from Bateson to A. C. Haddon, January 18, 1935, in HP, CU, Env. B. Bateson at least had the decency to acknowledge in this letter that Radcliffe-Brown was a better candidate for the job than he. The position went to J. H. Hutton (1885–1968), a former member of the Indian Civil Service who had no particular intellectual or genealogical distinction.

in the general trend of human history, which demonstrated that human beings were growing ever more moral with time; and, most important, three, that conflicts among social classes were disappearing as material conditions were improving.[32] It is not surprising that academic economists conveyed this message, for they, like anthropologists, had experienced positive benefits from historical changes. The point is that Britain's international decline required the reforming intelligentsia to describe their historical mission in rather qualified terms. (Under these terms, however, the prestige of inductive sciences such as anthropology was elevated.)

By the era of World War I, the new intelligentsia had lost its faith in the inevitability of progress, having lost its belief that improvements in material standards of living brought in their train improvements in the moral standards of the population. One herald of their changed view was a quantitative analysis of known information about the world's cultures, *The Material Culture and Social Institutions of the Simpler Peoples*, produced in 1915 by the sociologists L. T. Hobhouse, G. C. Wheeler, and M. Ginsburg, using a refined version of the method of correlating cross-cultural distribution of traits pioneered by E. B. Tylor (who called his correlations "adhesions").[33] By 1916, anthropologists were describing their enterprise in new terms. It no longer seemed possible to identify anthropology as a manifestation of the capacity for rational analysis – and action – peculiar to modern peoples.

Hence, anthropology's mission was redefined as an open-ended quest for the attributes of the good life – which was no longer assumed to be identical to the life of Britons in some foreseeable future state. The Oxford classicist-anthropologist J. L. (Sir John) Myres (1869–1954) then found the discipline's antecedents in ancient times. When the ancient Greeks began to explore the Mediterranean region in the seventh and sixth centuries B.C., he wrote, their exposure to surprising ways of life prompted them to ask the questions still essential to anthropological inquiry:

> [Is] there, for example, among all the various regions and aspects of the world, any real earthy paradise, ... where without let or hindrance

---

[32] Historians have devoted some attention to examining the general shift in economists' mood from self-congratulation to defensiveness and to Marshall's role in promulgating a new economic paradigm in particular. See Coats, "Historicist Reaction," 143–53. See also Gerard Koot, "English Historical Economics and the Emergence of Economic History in England," *History of Political Economy* 12 (1980): 174–205; John Maloney, *Marshall, Orthodoxy, and the Professionalisation of Economics* (Cambridge, 1985), esp. 7–10, 145; G. Steadman Jones, *Outcast London* (New York, 1984 [orig. London, 1971]), 4–11.

[33] L. T. Hobhouse, G. C. Wheeler, and M. Ginsburg, *The Material Culture and Social Institutions of the Simpler Peoples* (London, 1915).

the good man may lead the good life? Is there an ideal diet, an ideal
social structure, or in general an ideal way of life for men, or are all
the good things of this world wholly relative to the persons, the places,
and the seasons where they occur?[34]

In practice, anthropologists had considerable difficulty effecting complete suspension of the belief that material conditions and moral virtues
were related. Indeed, post–World War I anthropologists' judgment of this
relationship was frequently the opposite of their forbears'. But because
they restricted their attention to contemporary peoples living in materially
simple conditions, they could avoid the issue of this relationship entirely, or
touch on it only obliquely. Although they occasionally betrayed signs of
being less than thoroughly convinced by their own arguments, they wished
to represent all cultures as valuable in their own terms, each possessed of a
moral code that could guide its adherents to a life rich in possibilities for
personal development and satisfaction.

The story foretold

The chapters to follow in this book describe how by stages the moral
message of British anthropology shifted: from optimism to despair, when
viewed from one perspective; from xenophobia to tolerance when viewed
from another. In the remainder of this chapter, I set forth the major
historical changes that occurred during the period covered by this study,
which affected all sectors of British society. In later chapters, I consider
the relationship between specific social circumstances and anthropological
ideas, but here I present summary characterizations of successive anthropological views as responses to the national experience.

Chapter 2 deals with the rise of the meritocratic ideal and its manifestation in the character of the anthropological community. A series of national
decisions had made the realization of a meritocratic society seem possible.
If the intellectual aristocracy could "be said to have had a Bill of Rights,"
Annan observes, "it was the Trevelyan–Northcote report of 1853 on
reform of the civil service, and their Glorious Revolution was achieved
in 1870–1 when entry to public service by privilege, purchase of army
commissions and the religious tests were finally abolished."[35] Growing
government commitment to an expanded secularized educational system
was expressed not only in the 1871 Universities Test Act, which permitted
dissenters of all creeds to participate in the teaching, administration, and

---

[34] Myres, "Political Science," 4.
[35] Annan, "Intellectual Aristocracy," 247.

government of Oxford and Cambridge, but also in the 1870 Education Act, which laid the foundations of a state-supported system of primary education. With educational opportunity, reformers reasoned, the ever-larger portion of the population granted the franchise would be prepared to exercise it sensibly, and Britain would more efficiently use its resources of talented people to reinvigorate its economy. To be sure, the beneficiaries of educational changes were but a fraction of the population; not until the 1944 Education Act instituted universal secondary schooling did members of the working classes have even remotely reasonable prospects of being able to ascend the higher rungs of the educational ladder.[36] Nevertheless, the state had fostered the growth of a specialized academic class.

The rise of the meritocratic ideal was but one feature of the restructuring of the British class system, which the evolutionist anthropologists I consider in Chapter 3 were endeavoring to understand. They wanted to know what relationships properly obtained between superior beings such as themselves – educated men – and the persons they somehow equated with inferior "primitive" peoples – children, women, the mentally disordered, and the "dangerous classes." Political reforms gave these questions palpable urgency. No political historian would dispute that the 1880s ushered in an era of redistribution of political power, and of class-based politics. The Third Reform Bill of 1884 and the Redistribution Act of 1885 enlarged the electorate considerably, and the House of Commons elected in 1886 was the first in which the majority of Members of Parliament were not drawn from the landed elite. Socialist ideology took institutional form in the Social Democratic Federation, founded in 1881. The cause of women's rights was advanced by the 1882 Married Women's Property Act, which gave women financial independence from their husbands.

These changes were to contribute to a heightened consciousness of class cleavages, and to increased class conflict, but it is important to stress the

---

[36] For one illustration of the argument for expanded educational opportunity as essential to the national interest, see the report of the Royal Commission on Secondary Education, chaired by Lord Bryce between 1893 and 1895, which stated that "the more highly organised our civilisation becomes, the more imperative grows the need for [university trained] men ... the greater the necessity for recruiting their ranks with the best blood and brains from all classes of society." Quoted in Gillian Sutherland, *Ability, Merit and Measurement* (Oxford, 1984), 109. The gap between the ideal and the real was considerable, however. To wit, by the last decade of the interwar years the fraction of working-class children of appropriate age who attended university was less than 1 percent. In the next decade, this group sent just over 1 percent to university, and in the decade after that just over 2 percent. In these decades, the children of the upper middle classes were, respectively, eight times, thirteen times, and ten times more likely to go to university. See A. H. Halsey, A. F. Heath, J. M. Ridge, *Origins and Destinations* (Oxford, 1980), 188.

peaceable manner in which much structural reform was accomplished. Witnesses to an era of relatively untroubled improvement, beneficiaries of an era of economic growth in which social mobility increased and some social barriers fell, the evolutionist anthropologists who grew to maturity in the second quarter of the nineteenth century translated their own experience into universal law. Surveying the world's cultures, looking, for example, at variations in family structures and religious practices, men such as E. B. Tylor had no doubt that the monogamous family and an austere Christianity (or a godless rational morality) represented the triumph of virtue over primitive habits. But they also imputed to peoples everywhere the impulses that gave progressive direction to history, extrapolating a model of the development of societies everywhere from their understanding of the natural dynamics of individual growth (ignoring processes of decay).

The generation of anthropologists born in the third quarter of the nineteenth century, whose influence peaked around World War I, are described in Chapter 4. Their world was very different from that of the evolutionists. They lived in a state relatively weak in international competition, beset by conflicts at home, and obliged to recognize the limits of its people's ability to care for the sick, the aged, and the unemployed by charity alone. In the last decades of the nineteenth century, the laboring classes had gained an improved standard of living, but their share of the national wealth had diminished. From the 1880s, organizing socialist and trades union groups, workers mobilized large-scale industrial unrest and protests which culminated in the General Strike of 1926. The South African War of 1899–1902 focused fears that the urban conditions in which most Britons lived fostered physical and moral degeneration – for the army rejected many potential recruits as physically unfit, and those it selected were hard pressed to defeat an Afrikaner population they outnumbered.

Although a government committee (which heard testimony from anthropologists) determined that the army applicants had been an unrepresentative group – able-bodied potential recruits had not volunteered because the lively wartime economy created employment opportunities at home – anxieties about the state of the population inspired a spate of social legislation, including provisions for child welfare as well as unemployment and health insurance for adults. Especially after the turn of the century, the wealth of the privileged classes was tapped to finance expanded state services through such mechanisms as graduated income taxes and death duties. Not surprisingly, the House of Lords initially refused to pass Lloyd George's redistributive "People's Budget" of 1909, occasioning a constitutional crisis. And, between 1910 and 1928, as Britain slowly changed from a nation with one of the most restricted electoral rolls in

Europe to a nation with full adult suffrage, constitutional reforms followed militant protests – witness the violent tactics adopted by suffragettes during the first two decades of the century.

Moreover, Britain's participation in international conflicts affected its domestic life. A significant number of citizens took exception to the South African War, both because they sympathized with Boer aspirations and because they found the military's tactics unconscionable; their attitudes helped shape the decision to grant the Union of South Africa virtual independence in 1910. In this period, Britain's colonial subjects everywhere were beginning to mount notable protests against subordinate status. Sometimes these protests were at a safe remove from British society itself – for example, the agitation in India that obliged Britain to make its first major concession to colonial nationalism, the Government of India Act of 1919. Within Britain, however, the issue of Home Rule for Ireland, first mooted in unsuccessful legislation in 1886, became a touchstone of divisions in national politics and provoked both violence from Irish nationalists and in 1914 an unpunished mutiny by officers of His Majesty's army; in 1922 Britain attempted to resolve the still-intractable problems of her oldest colony by partitioning it, granting one portion independence as the Irish Free State – a tactic no more successful in effecting peace in Ireland than it was to prove later in India and Palestine. Finally, one cannot underestimate the impact on the national consciousness made by the horrors of World War I.

The generation who lived through these changes regarded human nature as fundamentally irrational, and considered individual and social degeneration as just as natural as progress – a view that made one of their most notable members, Haddon's younger colleague W. H. R. Rivers (1864–1922), the leading proponent of Freudian ideas in Britain. Like their predecessors concerned to explain human history, they developed a model of human adaptation that was closer to Darwin's than the evolutionist's scheme: varieties of social organization were random mutations, which survived if they suited peoples' circumstances – withstanding the process of natural selection. Civilized peoples were inherently no more rational and moral than were those of simple societies. If the West had in certain respects achieved a manner of living undeniably superior to that of simple societies, it had done so by repressive measures that lowered the quality of human relations. This generation's views were articulated most clearly by the diffusionists, but they were shared by anthropologists who did not identify with the diffusionist school.

The anthropologists who in the post–World War I period created the functionalist school were born in the last quarter of the nineteenth century or the first years of the twentieth. Some were old enough to have adult memories of the social tensions of the prewar years. A. R. Radcliffe-Brown (1881–1955), for example, who receives joint credit with Malinowski for founding the functionalist school, was a mature man at the war's end. Most of the members of this school were the founders' students, and they were obviously younger persons, including such figures as Evans-Pritchard, eighteen years old in 1920. Young functionalists witnessed the British class conflicts and colonial nationalist movements sustained since before the war, as well as events that definitively disconfirmed the belief that the bearers of Western civilization could manage their affairs rationally: the catastrophe of the Great Depression and the rise of Nazism.

Functionalists also observed the transformation of the British economy during the interwar period; largely as a consequence of direct government action, it changed from one of the least to one of the most controlled national economies. The ideology of economic individualism seemed to have been forever laid to rest by effective government regulation, which increased dramatically first during World War I and again during World War II. Prices and output were controlled, labor disputes were mediated, town and country planning was instituted, and special attention was given to depressed areas; such industries as electricity, iron, coal, and steel were virtually nationalized. Many citizens came to regard state provision of welfare services as an inalienable right – as Churchill's Coalition found when it was brought down as soon as World War II ended in Europe, at least in part because many believed that Churchill was not fully committed to the goals of the 1942 Beveridge Report, which mandated the National Health Service, full employment, and family allowances.

The enlarged role of the state bespoke a view of the individual that functionalist anthropologists translated into theoretical terms which framed their analysis of every society – a view predicated on the assumption that individual behavior was best described as the product of social condition-ing. The dynamics of individual personality structure, so important to all of their predecessors, were to the functionalists practically irrelevant to the operation of social processes; they were qualitatively distinct phenomena to which anthropologists were not obliged to attend (although some func-tionalists did). And being thoroughly disabused of the notion that human beings had made meaningful progress, functionalists dispensed with history in their analyses. Their studies elucidated the systematic relationships that joined all of the elements of any given culture into a coherent whole – a "going concern," as they often said, which could be judged only on its own terms, rather than assessed by any general standard of social perfection.

The functionalists were not the first anthropologists to go into the field, but they were the first to make field research an indispensable feature of anthropological inquiry, and they were able to do so because during the interwar period they found reliable patrons to support their expeditions, as I describe in Chapter 5. Their research was conducted largely in Africa, because their patrons expected their findings to prove useful to colonial officials then developing administrative structures there. Much of the territory of Britain's African empire was acquired at or after the turn of the century, some as part of the spoils of World War I. Anthropological assistance was considered particularly important in the effort to govern those peoples over whom British authority was especially tenuous, and was also expected to prove useful in consideration of the very small percentage of Africans who migrated to the outposts of Western capitalism in the colonies: Could they adapt to industrial norms? Would the traditional societies they had left collapse in their absence?

Functionalist anthropologists reassured colonial officials that indigenous polities maintained order even in the absence of political institutions recognizable to European eyes, and that indigenous peoples were capable of adjusting to change. But their work proved of little use to colonial rulers concerned to determine how traditional African political institutions could be manipulated to serve the purposes of the British regime – the objective of "Indirect Rule," the administrative approach favored by colonial officials. Instead, the bureaucracies of British Colonial Africa found most useful the anthropological evidence collected by the civil servants they employed, whose approach represented a peculiar variant of evolutionist anthropology developed to serve administrative needs. Indeed, the financial security that functionalist anthropologists gained from their appeal to colonial patrons permitted them to do research decreasingly relevant to colonial administrators' requirements.

If, in the later years of the interwar period, anthropologists could turn away from immediate practical problems, they could not secede from their culture. They continued to consider the most fundamental issues of social order: the constitution of legitimate political authority, the processes and consequences of social change, the rights and duties of the individual. In Chapter 6, I treat the anthropology of the whole period covered by this study as a continuous debate over these issues, a debate framed in the terms of a tradition of political argument traceable to the early modern period (at least). Viewed in these terms, anthropology has nearly always constituted a vehicle for liberal political thought.

Finally, in Chapter 7, I consider the relation of the situations in which anthropological knowledge is produced to both its content and the uses to which it is put. Clearly, the enterprise of anthropology was shaped by the colonial situation. Indeed, it was once fashionable to argue that the theories of anthropology represent nothing more than types of imperialist ideology:[37] The discipline's academic constitution rests on a division of the world's peoples into higher and lower cultures, the latter the recognized province of anthropological inquiry – peoples whose identification as "primitives" has reflected their subordinate status in the geopolitical order. Yet, even if we grant the premise that anthropology was born of the colonial situation, we are obliged to recognize that the permutations of the colonial situation admit of highly variable relationships between the representatives of cultures in contact, and that these relationships can foster self-doubt as well as arrogance. How else can we explain contemporary anthropologists' drive to redefine their craft? To be sure, they work in a world in which all of the certainties of the imperialist age have disappeared. But from encounters with exotic peoples Western observers appear to have learned something about themselves and others. Thus, from the material of this book, we ought to learn something about the production of social knowledge.

[37] For a review of the literature that makes this argument, see Peter Forster, "Empiricism and Imperialism: A Review of New Left Critique of Social Anthropology," in Talal Asad, ed., *Anthropology and the Colonial Encounter* (London, 1973), 23–38.

Chapter 2
Scholars and practical men

The professionalization of anthropology was not an isolated phenomenon. It was but one manifestation of the changed occupational structure – indeed newly defined class system – of nineteenth-century Britain. Critical to the reordered social hierarchy was the elevated valuation placed on formal, specialized knowledge, which assumed new importance in the determination of individuals' fortunes. Modifications in the social order testified to the diffusion of meritocratic values – to the belief that individuals' wealth, status, and power should reflect the worth of their achievements rather than the social standing of their parents. As direct beneficiaries of the enhanced market value of expertise, anthropologists were among the ideologues of meritocracy; throughout the years covered by this study, they drafted briefs for meritocratic values – at first defended as the basis of social progress and at last as fundamental to social harmony.

To wit, during the nineteenth century, specialized knowledge became critical to advancement in high-status occupations traditionally termed "professions" – the elite branches of medical and legal practice – as well as in the civil service and the Army. Such enterprises as engineering and architecture gained elevated prestige as they rationalized their handicraft methods in scientific terms. University credentials became more valuable in the occupational marketplace, and in consequence the university system expanded and changed in character. And university reformers undertook to professionalize scholarship, determining that the advance of knowledge required that individuals be able to make lifelong, remunerated careers developing their specialized expertise – just as independent professionals did.

The university system expanded with the foundation of the heterogeneous group of colleges constituting the University of London in and after 1828, and with the later establishment of institutions in Wales and the major English provincial cities. The new foundations offered instruction in marketable skills, catering to the middle-class segment of the student population, previously the acknowledged clientele of the older Scottish and Irish universities. The ancient universities of Oxford and Cambridge, which had offered explicitly vocational education only for clergymen, were obliged to grant some legitimacy to the values animating university proliferation. Competing to attract students who sought practical education – Cambridge perhaps more successfully than Oxford – the universities added new courses to their curricula and justified instruction in utilitarian terms. If Britain's altered university system still served only a small fraction of the population, and employed very few scholars, its growth testified to the changing role of the man of knowledge – and to the increased importance of education in individuals' upward mobility.[1]

To be sure, the new classes did not gain power unopposed. There was considerable disagreement about the legitimacy of their claims, and about what sort of formal knowledge was socially useful. There were defenders of the classical curriculum that had been designed to make gentlemen into "educated amateurs"; they argued that training in the classics provided mental discipline precisely because it developed skills of no direct utility, fostering general faculties of reason that could be exercised in any situation. The reforming intelligentsia, who explained social progress as the result of the application of scientific method to the rationalization of all human affairs, countered that courses based on scientific principles were the proper preparation for every type of "brain work." Vocational instruction could provide "a more truly liberal education than the high classic," argued T. H. Huxley, inculcating both habits of abstract reason and standards by which to assess practical alternatives.[2]

---

[1] The university student population grew dramatically from the turn of the century. Only 20,000 persons were attending university in 1900, but by the 1924–5 academic year 42,000 persons were enrolled in university, and there were 50,000 university students in 1938–9. These students were, of course, a small, albeit growing fraction of the eligible age group, respectively, 8 percent, 1.5 percent, and 1.7 percent for the above years. See A. H. Halsey, "Higher Education," in Halsey, ed., *Trends in British Society Since 1900* (London, 1972), 195–6, 206; and Michael Sanderson, *The Universities in the Nineteenth Century*, (London, 1975), 19–20.

In the last two decades of the nineteenth century, Cambridge was distinguished by its concessions to practicality in its scientific course offerings: half of the veterans of its natural science tripos went into medicine; it introduced an engineering tripos in 1892; and by 1900 nearly one-third of Cambridge's honors graduates were in natural or mechanical sciences, whereas at this time Oxford graduated only roughly one-tenth of its honors students in the sciences. See Janet Howarth, "Science Education in late-Victorian Oxford: A Curious Case Of Failure?" *The English Historical Review* 102 (1987): 342.

[2] T. H. Huxley, "On Medical Degrees," an address delivered at the University of London, January 1888; in the Huxley Papers, American Philosophical Society. Men such as Huxley were engaged in debunking a tradition of classical learning that encompassed not only the humanities but also the deductive sciences – as opposed to the progressing, inductive sciences Huxley defended. Instruction in the eternal habits

Opposed to both the defenders of the classics and of scientifically designed education were the self-styled "practical men," who denied the utility of any sort of formal knowledge. Educated amateurs and brain workers alike did, after all, see merit in formal instruction per se: no matter how they conceived the relation between education and the capacity to exercise sound judgment, they agreed that a student's examination results predicted his future career performance. Practical men represented useful knowledge as a congeries of craft skills, which defied codification because they were acquired piecemeal from experience of the unpredictable realities of daily occupational life. The most successful practical men were entrepreneurial industrialists, who resisted the incursion of technical experts into their enterprises.[3]

The classically trained educated amateur, the brain worker, and the practical man have been durable popular British stereotypes, and their very persistence demonstrates the accuracy of the social observation that defined them. To be sure, historical actors rarely behaved as ideal types. The educated amateur muddling through novel tasks often rationalized his conduct in the language of the practical man, the more especially as the mystique of practical experience burgeoned during the nineteenth century. Those concerned to strengthen the university in the late nineteenth century used both old and new justifications for formal knowledge, and were wont to bolster their peculiar disciplinary causes with unexpected claims, scientists disavowing utilitarian ends and humanists embracing the scientific method.

In the reform of the elite professions of medicine and law, however, the ideology of the brain worker clearly prevailed over that of the educated amateur. Once these occupations had been reserved for educated amateurs, who gained admission to the professional ranks by displaying their gentlemanly graces, acquiring whatever technical skills they needed after they began to practice. By the end of the century, aspirant professionals were not permitted to take clients until they had mastered the specialized knowledge on which occupational craftsmanship was formally based. The actualities of professional recruitment and reward practices did not match

of reasoning apprehended by the ancients – exemplified by Euclidian geometry – was particularly stressed in the traditional curriculum of Cambridge. See, for example, Joan L. Richards, "Projective Geometry and Mathematical Progress in Mid-Victorian Britain," *Studies in History and Philosophy of Science* 17 (1986): 297–325.

[3] On the "educated amateur" versus the "practical man," see D. C. Coleman, "Gentlemen and Players," *Economic History Review* [ser. 2] 26 (1973): 92–116. The term "brain worker" enjoyed less currency, but it is a term the intellgentsia used to describe themselves. See, for example, Donald A. MacKenzie, *Statistics in Britain, 1865–1930* (Edinburgh, 1981), 26–36 and passim.

the ideal, but professional reforms still had powerful symbolic significance: They demonstrated to a population of which anthropologists were members that the values they cherished were realizable.

Viewed in the aggregate, both the changes effected in traditional professions and the transformation of the role of the university don represented convergence toward a common career pattern and ethos. In these restyled occupations – as well as new ones – an ideology emerged that still figures in professional conduct. That is, practitioners of each of these occupations demanded the right to self-regulation on the basis of their exclusive command of particular expertise. Professionals assured their institutional and individual employers that peer review procedures were the best mechanisms for screening aspirant practitioners and maintaining high occupational standards, since only trained specialists were competent to evaluate one anothers' work. And professionals expected to receive the perquisites of high status in exchange for the valuable services they performed for society.

The claimants to professional authority were rather diverse. Their work required very different kinds of esoteric knowledge. Dependent on organizations as dissimilar as the hospital and the university, rendering services to clients as disparate as patients and students, they enjoyed occupational authority and autonomy in unequal measure. Accorded varying degrees of social prestige, they came from somewhat different social strata. In sum, diverse occupational groups were not equally successful in realizing the proverbial equation between knowledge and power. Nor could they have been: in any social situation, established power relationships influence the identification of knowledge as such. If I were here attempting to measure the power and status individuals enjoyed by virtue of their memberships in groups as diverse as university dons or physicians, I would certainly stress the differing consequences of professional reforms for various occupations. Instead, I have chosen to stress the pattern common to these reforms, since it reflects a broadly based, essentially middle-class cultural ideal.[4] This is a choice dictated by my objective in this chapter: I wish to present successive generations of the anthropological population as

---

[4] The best analysis of the phenomenon of professionalization in Britain as it was effected in and affected the practice of the traditional professions remains W. J. Reader, *Professional Men* (New York, 1966). On engineering see R. A. Buchanan, "Institutional Proliferation in the British Engineering Profession, 1847–1914," *Economic History Review* [ser. 2] 38 (1985): 42–60. Arthur Engel, *From Clergyman to Don: The Rise of the Academic Profession in Nineteenth-Century Oxford* (Oxford, 1983), demonstrates that the professionalization of academe redefined the occupation of the don in the ancient university in a fashion very like the redefinition of the occupation of a practitioner of one of the learned professions. On the transformation of Cambridge, see Sheldon Rothblatt, *The Revolution of the Dons* (New York, 1968). For the professionalization of scientific work, in particular, see Gerald L. Geison, *Michael Foster and the Cambridge*

specimen social types, whose successive career patterns reflected broad social changes.

Anthropologists' personal experiences of occupational changes shaped their analyses of societal order, and their work appealed to a wide audience because it confirmed the perceptions of a significant segment of society. I cannot overemphasize this point: when anthropologists assumed that the moral basis of a society derives from its division of labor, they were hardly unique, for this assumption was granted wide currency both before and after the period covered by my study. Therefore, an account of anthropologists' career histories is more than a narrative of the institutionalization of a specialized discipline – although it is that. It is also a vehicle for understanding how individuals derive intellectual generalizations from their shared experiences.

In this chapter, I proceed with increasing specificity in analyzing the emergence of those social types represented in the anthropological community. I review (however generally) historical trends established in the late eighteenth century – the period remembered by the parents of the oldest of our subjects. I examine the development of a range of professions, since these were the occupations pursued by many members of the anthropological community during the years in which anthropology was largely an amateur enthusiasm; amateurs foresaw a future in which anthropologists would have remunerated occupations similar to their own. Their forecasts were not entirely accurate, and I describe anthropologists' unsuccessful efforts to create a career structure for themselves nearly independent of the university. Of course, anthropology eventually became a thoroughly academic enterprise, and I examine the changes in the university that made it hospitable to anthropology. Finally, I analyze the careers of members of the anthropological community, documenting historical generalizations with a survey of individuals' life histories. For this purpose, I use biographical data available for members of the Royal Anthropological Institute (RAI). The membership records compiled by the institute provide the best evidence available for approximating the anthropological community's population of professional practitioners and amateur enthusiasts.

Meritocratic ideals and class identities

Contemporary historians see changes in the British class structure much as nineteenth-century anthropologists did. They were consequences of the

School of Physiology (Princeton, 1978); Roy M. MacLeod, "The Support of Victorian Science: The Endowment of Research Movement in Great Britain, 1869–1900," *Minerva* 9 (1971): 197–230; Frank M. Turner, "The Victorian Conflict Between Science and Religion: A Professional Dimension," *Isis* 69 (1978): 356–76.

growth of a truly national culture, which was beginning to emerge long before the nineteenth century, not in the least because of political changes (such as the Act of Union, which joined Scotland to England in 1707). National integration can be recognized from a variety of indices: from the creation of a nearly uniform national price structure for transportable foodstuffs and goods by the middle of the eighteenth century; to the creation of a significant number of Scottish and Irish peers, who made the House of Lords a national body from the end of the eighteenth century; to the adoption by late eighteenth-century botanists of Latin terminology for plants, replacing (at least in learned circles) the idiosyncratic vernacular terms used by farmers and other ordinary folk.[5] By the middle of the nineteenth century, a unifying communications network had been created, completed during a frenzy of railway construction between 1835 and 1847. The diminution of local cultural variations extended to the judgment of individuals, permitting the specification and elaboration of a national class hierarchy, within which professionals occupied middle- and upper-middle-class niches. National integration thus fostered the meritocratic ethos of professionalism, which is antithetical to any sort of localism, enjoining practitioners to offer every class of client services of the same high standard.

Of course, a true meritocracy has never been realized, either in Britain or elsewhere. A range of personal characteristics that individuals do not choose to have – from such traits as ethnicity or sex, to the advantages (or disadvantages) they acquire by virtue of their families' social positions, and even to such qualities as degrees of physical attractiveness – have continued to affect individuals' fortunes along with the efforts they make to acquire variously marketable skills. Moreover, meritocratic social norms may be more apparent than real, as historians and sociologists of education have taken pains to explain. Entry into high-status occupations may seem meritocratic because it is contingent on negotiation of educational courses, yet education may be irrelevant to occupational practice. Because children of the privileged classes have relatively easy access to education, the formal credentials they acquire may in truth only serve to legitimate their succession to social positions equivalent to those of their parents, whereas children from less fortunate families gain the credentials they need to be allowed to prove themselves only by dint of exceptional talent, discipline, and luck.[6]

<hr>

[5] E. J. Hobsbawm, *Industry and Empire* (Harmondsworth, Middlesex, 1977 [orig. 1969]); Michael W. McCahill, "Peerage Creations and the Changing Character of the British Nobility, 1750–1850," *The English Historical Review* 96 (1981): 259–328; Keith Thomas, *Man and the Natural World* (New York, 1983), 87.

[6] The literature of this type is enormous. For one survey see Randall Collins, *The*

Furthermore, when accomplished individuals manage to accomplish a genuine (not merely apparent) change of status, they may by action and example negate the values crucial to their ascent. In Britain, in particular, social critics have been wont to mourn the fragility of the meritocratic ideal, observing that it is sustained within families for only a few generations. They have intoned a lament set in formulaic terms by the middle of the nineteenth century: national economic development has been retarded because the upwardly mobile have raised their sons to be gentlemen, to despise the values and behavior responsible for their parents' successes. So raised, these children have withdrawn from the commercial enterprises that had generated their family fortunes, and have imprudently invested the profits of industry in the pursuit of elegantly leisured lives (or worse, have managed their family businesses with conspicuous disregard for capitalist realities).[7]

This conventional lament is more significant as an indicator of changed cultural values than as historical analysis, however. Recent historians have tended to assign relatively little weight to gentlemanly values among the factors figuring in Britain's decline as an industrial power, and have suggested that the disdain for industry and trade promulgated in the mid-nineteenth century by the public schools ("private" schools in American parlance) was not a traditional aristocratic attitude but the ethos of teachers who catered to the aspiring middle classes.[8] To be sure, public schools products absorbed this ethos, and meritocratic standards did not displace all others in Britain. Nevertheless, supposedly gentlemanly values would not have been widely denounced as socially dysfunctional if a significant portion of the population had not in fact benefited from increasing acceptance of meritocratic standards, as was obvious to late-nineteenth-century reformers. For example, when examinations replaced patronage as the basis for entry into the Indian Civil Service (ICS) in 1853 – a change that preceded the reform of the Home Civil Service in 1870 – men from quite

---

Credential Society (New York, 1979). I would not argue, as researchers such as Collins have done, that professional education is virtually irrelevant and that useful skills are all acquired after formal training ceases and work begins.

[7] For a recent example of these jeremiads in scholarly form – significant because of the vast public attention it has received – see Martin J. Weiner, *English Culture and the Decline of the Industrial Spirit, 1820–1980* (Cambridge, 1981).

[8] See, for example, Donald N. McCloskey and Lars Sandberg, "From Damnation to Redemption: Judgements on the Late Victorian Entrepreneur," *Explorations in Economic History* 9 (1971): 89–108; D. C. Coleman and Christine MacLeod, "Attitudes to New Techniques: British Businessmen, 1800–1950," *Economic History Review* [ser. 2] 39 (1986): 588–611; Harold Perkin, *The Rise of Professional Society* (London, 1989), 119.

humble backgrounds were able to secure posts in India; in 1875 a survey of ICS men recruited by examination showed that 30 percent of them were of lower-middle-class – or even lower-class – origins. In the Home Civil Service, entry by examination meant that the top posts were no longer monopolized by sons of the upper class.[9]

Evidently, the meritocratic ideal has been crucial to the expansion and growing power of the middle class. Particularly in the nineteenth and twentieth centuries, this class has pointed to its superior endowments of talent and discipline in justifying its claims to greater influence in the direction of societal affairs. As every history student knows, the rising middle class can be identified throughout the ages, but its motives and aspirations have nevertheless changed in the relatively recent past. The foundations of social order seemed quite different to members of the middle class – and others – at the beginning of the eighteenth century than they did at the century's end, as is evident from such specimens of popular culture as Daniel Defoe's widely read novel, *Robinson Crusoe*, first published in 1719. Defoe's hero, living in the "middle state," behaves as middle-class people still do: he regulates his life of disciplined labor by the clock and the calendar, and believes that whatever satisfactions his life holds will result from his own efforts. Yet Crusoe's story permits us to see change as well as continuity in the mobile social world of the late eighteenth century.

To wit, Crusoe does not consider himself responsible for his mode of existence, except insofar as he recognizes that his attempts to escape his destiny have brought him grief. Divine providence has ordained that he will follow his father in occupying the middle state. His fate is demonstrably inescapable: after a shipwreck casts him on an uncivilized island, he laboriously reconstructs alone the life he abandoned at home. By the end of the eighteenth century, however, divine providence no longer seemed sufficient justification for individuals to reconcile themselves to lives identical to those of their parents. Instead, they understood social rank to be a consequence of individuals' achievements, and gauged rank from occupation, income, and consumption patterns. As P. J. Corfield has put it, "Power was resynthesized into active terms of acquisition, production, display; rather than inheritance, formal title, and ancient lineage."[10]

---

[9] Reader, *Professional Men*, 93–5; Perkin, *The Rise of Professional Society*, 91.

[10] P. J. Corfield, "Class by Name and Number in Eighteenth-Century Britain," *History* 72 (1987): 61. Some would argue that the concepts of class were developed by late-eighteenth century political economists and thereafter diffused through the populace; see, for example, Steven Wallech, "'Class Versus Rank': The Transformation of Eighteenth-Century English Social Terms and Theories of

Indeed, the distinction between inherited privilege and earned recognition was blurred in the late eighteenth century, when hereditary peerages were conferred on men who had been outstanding state servants.[11] In sum, the expectation that the satisfactions of one's life should be the products of one's own efforts had been generalized beyond the occupants of the "middle state."

Persons of all classes were affected by the redefinition of social rank. The various social classes became conscious of themselves as such. For example, only during the late nineteenth and early twentieth centuries did the working class adopt those features of its life-style usually thought to be traditional – denoted by the consumption of fish and chips, the male insignia of the flat cloth cap, the patronage of the music hall, and so on – as well as develop the practical tools of its political interests – the trade union and the Labour party.[12] The agricultural depression that began in 1873 effected a division between the gentry and the great landowners – who usually had other income, derived from such sources as mines, urban property, and company shareholdings – the latter joining in self-conscious alliance with capitalist millionaires to form what one historian has termed "the new plutocracy."[13] And during the course of the nineteenth and early twentieth centuries, the power of the monarchy was eroded, as the exercise of political power became contingent on the consent of the electorate and the base of the political order was slowly broadened to include all adults (whose rights to the responsibilities of citizenship became theirs by birth rather than earned through the accumulation of property). Royal rituals were elaborated and codified as the monarch became a purely symbolic figure – simultaneously the emblem of national (and imperial) unity and the mouthpiece of the popularly elected government.[14]

When anthropologists contemplated these broad social changes, it is no wonder that they characterized them as manifestations of general laws of historical development. In particular, anthropologists were concerned to justify the emergence of the middle classes, to which they belonged. In the national mind, middle-class identity came to be denoted by a range of

---

Production," *Journal of the History of Ideas* 47 (1986): esp. 418–31. Evidence provided by social historians, however, suggests that such men as Adam Smith and David Ricardo articulated notions already realized in social practice.

[11] Peers created in and after the last quarter of the eighteenth century included distinguished military commanders, judges, and diplomats, not only (as had earlier been the case) great landowners. See McCahill, "Peerage Creations," 259–84.

[12] Hobsbawm, *Industry and Empire*, 162–5.

[13] Perkin, *The Rise of Professional Society*, 27, 67.

[14] J. C. Hesterman, *The Inner Conflict of Tradition* (Chicago, 1985), 202. And see my *The Imperial Bureaucrat* (Stanford, 1979), 44–5.

traits, but two interrelated components of middle-class status assumed great significance during the nineteenth century: specialized expertise as a property of respected rank, and formal credentials as the hallmark of expertise. The very notion of the specialist gained popular currency in the first third of the nineteenth century, as language use indicates. The first recorded uses of the words "expert" and "technician" to denote persons occurred in 1825 and 1833, respectively.[15] Initially, however, specialized expertise was not thought the defining property of a high-status occupation. The first recognizable professional group, the apothecaries (pharmacists), authorized by the passage of the Apothecaries Act of 1815 to examine and license practitioners through the Society of Apothecaries, was considered little superior to tradesmen.[16] And during the first half of the nineteenth century, persons of the better classes remained convinced that no man could simultaneously pursue his occupational interest and advance the world's knowledge; "paid careers sullied the pursuit of truth."[17]

In the 1840s, however, the years in which the oldest of our subjects were growing to maturity, things began to change. Both the social customs and practical skills required for high position were increasingly seen as susceptible to formal codification and instruction. The sons of the rising classes were taught to think of themselves as the pillars of society by a vastly expanded system of public schools; the growth of the public schools figured in university reforms, since they provided employment to the university-educated. At the same time, a multitude of etiquette books flooded the market, instructing the daughters of upwardly mobile families in correct behavior.[18] Public schooling became a standard feature of upper-middle-class socialization, as university attendance was to become later. And the elite professions began to reformulate their recruitment and training procedures.

Such professional changes as were mooted at midcentury were not fully realized until the last quarter of the century, however. The Inns of Court were able to make examinations compulsory in 1872, but they had attempted to effect this reform two decades earlier. In 1852 the Inns of Court had created five readerships, and had hastened to set up a commission which recommended in 1855 that formal instruction and examination be mandatory for those called to the Bar – a judgment endorsed by, among other people, H. J. S. Maine, who had relinquished his post

[15] Elliot Freidson, *Professional Powers* (Chicago, 1986), 13.

[16] Reader, *Professional Men*, 51.

[17] James Secord, "The Geological Survey of Great Britain as a Research School, 1839–1855," *History of Science* 24 (1986): 227.

[18] Hobsbawm, *Industry and Empire*, 82.

as Regius professor of civil law at Cambridge after taking up one of the readerships. And, though a parliamentary act created the "registered medical practitioner" in 1858, it was not until the Medical Act of 1886 that the physician, now authorized to practice any branch of medicine anywhere in the United Kingdom, belonged to an occupational group with un-differentiated achievement standards and monopolistic control over craft practice.[19] Professionals could now claim that their intellectual property was as important an economic element as land and capital – a position first articulated by the Fabian Society, founded in 1884. The 1880s witnessed the beginning of a boom in professional organizations, in the foundation of occupational associations intended to secure professional status for their members.[20]

Clearly, the last quarter of the nineteenth century witnessed institutional changes designed to realize middle-class, meritocratic ideals – changes that anthropologists and other members of the intelligentsia described as expressions of progressive historical forces.[21] It hardly seemed coincidental that reform of the traditional professions followed closely upon the elim-ination of patronage from the civil service and the army, as well as the removal of religious tests from the ancient universities. And there were other indications of changed cultural standards at this time. The success of the *Dictionary of National Biography*, founded and edited by members of the intellectual aristocracy, marked a triumph for the belief that status and achievement should be closely related, if not inextricable; listings in the *DNB* were sanctioned by the educated public, consulted by the editors through the medium of the *Atheneum*, a weekly literary and scholarly review.[22] Moreover, middle-class self-consciousness engendered a distinc-tive life-style at the turn of the century – the "rapid rise of the old school tie and the even more sudden rise of the golf club."[23]

The reforms of the ancient universities and of the professions were as much independent expressions of a general cultural impulse as inter-dependent developments. Reconstructed professionals were not obliged to take formal instruction at university. (Indeed, a link with the universities had been broken; under the old dispensation, a Fellow of the Royal

---

[19] Reader, *Professional Men*, 57, 67f.
[20] See Perkin, *The Rise of Professional Society*, 132, 85–6. Perkin points out that between 1880 and 1914 thirty-nine professional associations were founded; there had been only seven qualifying associations in 1800, and between 1800 and 1880 only twenty more were founded.
[21] For a useful survey of the ideology of this class, see G. R. Searle, *The Quest for National Efficiency* (Oxford, 171).
[22] John Gross, *The Rise and Fall of the Man of Letters* (New York, 1970), 25.
[23] Eric Hobsbawm, *Workers* (New York, 1984), 200.

College of Physicians in London, at the pinnacle of the then three-level division of medical labor into physicians, surgeons, and apothecaries, had to have a degree from Oxford or Cambridge, although its function was to certify his social status, since its subject was unspecified.) Nor did the reform of the Indian and Home Civil Services depend on altered university curricula. Although applicants for elite civil service appointments were expected to be university men, they sat a competitive examination that supposedly tested general habits of mind by assessing their command of whichever stipulated standard academic subjects they elected to present – of which the only remotely vocational one was the classical languages of India. (ICS probationers were required to study Indian law, languages, and history, however, and diverse institutions of higher education did appoint persons to offer courses that would meet the approval of the secretary of state for India.)[24]

Nevertheless, university reforms transformed scholarly careers, making them akin to professional ones. The changes effected in Oxford and Cambridge deserve particular notice, since these universities were the recognized leaders of higher education. Through the 1860s, critics charged that education was a nearly incidental component of the activities of the ancient universities. They were in reality social "club[s] for the young men of the nobility and gentry", observed the Frenchman Hippolyte Taine, institutions to which T. H. Huxley avowed he "should not dream" of sending any son of his whom he intended for a career in "any branch of manufacture" because they inculcated utter contempt for utilitarian pursuits.[25] And in the unreformed ancient universities, fellowships were generally reserved for unmarried clerics, for whom university positions were usually antecedent to careers made outside academe. For those whom the universities appointed in extraordinary capacities, such as the future Sir Henry Maine, the strictures of academic obligations were hardly confining, although they might specify the number of lectures to be delivered and days to be spent in residence at the university.[26] While a Cambridge professor between 1847 and 1854, Maine spent most of his time in London as a writer of the higher journalism, working for the *Morning Chronicle* and the *Saturday Review*. Evidently, the universities' critics judged them accurately.

Not the least of the reasons for the social exclusivity of Oxford and Cambridge was their refusal to succumb to pressures to permit religious dissenters to take degrees until 1854 and 1856, respectively. The univer-

---

[24] Reader, *Professional Men*, 93–102.

[25] These are both quoted in Coleman, "Gentlemen and Players," 100, 106.

[26] Philippa Levine, *The Amateur and the Professional* (Cambridge, 1986), 153.

sities' regulations reinforced upper-class social norms, for even very wealthy nonconformists were barred from assimilation into the ruling elite unless they chose to join the established church. Because dissenters figured prominently in the manufacturing classes, religious discrimination was an element in the hostility of these classes to the ancient universities – indeed to formal education in general, since established religion was incorporated into nearly every variety of primary and secondary schooling. And dissenters loomed large in the scientific community; religion was therefore also a factor in the conduct of much scientific inquiry outside the universities (although many of the families prominent in the scientific life of nineteenth-century Britain abandoned their nonconformist religion).[27] Moreover, data available for the student body of Oxford, at least, indicate that the sheer cost of university attendance excluded all but the prosperous. In the second quarter of the nineteenth century, the university's tuition and standard of student social life together required financial expenditure that was by absolute standards greater than that exacted at any other time in its history.[28]

Comparable data are lacking for Cambridge, but it enjoyed a reputation as an institution somewhat less aristocratic and more intellectual than Oxford. It permitted nonconformists to matriculate, and during the second quarter of the nineteenth century its honors and positions were allocated in increasingly meritocratic fashion (although dissenters were not permitted to compete for them).[29] Even after the universities' regulations changed, the belief persisted that the social atmosphere of Cambridge was different from that of Oxford. In 1874, for example, J. G. Frazer's father, a devout member of the Free Church of Scotland, directed his son to go to Cambridge because he would not have him exposed to the high Anglicanism of Oxford.[30] To be sure, Cambridge had its peculiarities of intellectual climate, which were conducive to flourishing scientific activity from the end of the nineteenth century. Indeed, Cambridge-trained anthro-

---

[27] See, for example, A. H. Halsey, *Change in British Society* (Oxford, 1978), 46. On the religious assimilation of the families of British men of science, in particular, in the second half of the nineteenth century, see Victor L. Hilts, *A Guide to Francis Galton's "English Men of Science"* (Philadelphia, 1975), 30.

[28] Lawrence Stone, "The Size and Composition of the Oxford Student Body, 1580–1909," in Stone, ed., *The University in Society* (Princeton, 1974), 62–3.

[29] See John Gascoigne, "Mathematics and Meritocracy: The Emergence of the Cambridge Mathematical Tripos," *Social Studies of Science* 14 (1984): 547–84; Susan Faye Cannon, *Science in Culture* (New York, 1978), 29–31; and Rothblatt, *The Revolution of the Dons*, 29–47, 64–5.

[30] Ackerman, *J. G. Frazer* (see chap. 1, n. 14), 15.

pologists figure prominently in this book. But the social composition of its
student population overall probably differed little from that of Oxford.

With the elimination of religious tests for their students in the 1850s and
for their faculties in 1871, however, the ancient universities' mission was
redefined in secular terms. Oxford and Cambridge remained committed to
training the national government and financial elites. And they sustained
the ideal of liberal education that has been so often associated with inherited privilege (although the ideal is not necessarily invalidated by the
identity of its proponents) – the belief that scholarship was a means to the
general intellectual development of young persons whose adult careers
might have no direct relation to their degree subjects. Nevertheless, the
universities effected structural and curricular reforms, responding to
pressures to make their operations more meritocratic and their courses
more practical. Sons (and some daughters) of the professional, commercial,
and industrial middle classes joined the children of clergymen and landed
gentry in their student populations. The vast majority of Oxbridge men
now made careers in business, administration, or the professions.[31]

Moreover, the secularized ancient universities altered the recruitment
base and career pattern of their faculties. Dissenters, who figured prominently probably out of all proportion to their numbers in the early anthropological community, could obtain conventional university appointments.
Indeed, the first occupants of full-time teaching positions in anthropology
at Oxford and Cambridge were from nonconformist backgrounds: E. B.
Tylor, the son of a prosperous Quaker brass founder, and A. C. Haddon,
the son of a Baptist businessman of perpetually uncertain finances and
diverse commercial interests. Relieved of the obligation to take Holy Orders
and remain unmarried, the universities' faculties could now anticipate
lifelong careers. They could undertake to mold themselves into what the
Cambridge philosopher Henry Sidgwick termed the "new school" of professors, who considered themselves "as much bound to teach and write
as any salaried functionary is bound to discharge the duties for which
he is paid."[32] Perhaps it was a sign of the times that when H. J. S.
Maine returned from government service in India to serve as Oxford's first
Corpus professor of jurisprudence between 1869 and 1878, he worked
up several of his series of lectures into published books, including works
of legal anthropology utilizing his knowledge of India such as *Village
Communities in the East and West* (1871), *Lectures on the Early History of
Institutions* (1876), and *Dissertations on Early Law and Custom* (1883).

The new school of professors was often committed to the ideal of

---

[31] Sanderson, *The Universities in the Nineteenth Century*, 18.
[32] Quoted in Rothblatt, *The Revolution of the Dons*, 170.

useful knowledge, and the new courses they taught were framed accordingly. For example, the history tripos inaugurated at Cambridge in 1873 bore the imprint of (Sir) John Seeley, Regius professor of modern history between 1869 and 1895, for whom the study of history could "pursue a practical object," preparing students for careers in government (and approximately one-fifth of the recipients of First or Second Class Honours degress during Seeley's regime became politicians or civil servants). Practical history was "scientific in its method" – which it could be only if it were written by academics instead of by "men of letters and novelists"; it emphasized the relatively recent past; and it stressed political matters, "explaining the relation of the individual to the state or government."[33] In these sentiments Seeley was joined by E. A. Freeman, who became his opposite number at Oxford in 1884, who may be best remembered for his dictum that "history is past politics and politics present history"[34] University innovators, convinced that scientific method made scholarship practical, could also be persuaded that fields of uncertain scholarly quality – let alone practical value – could become legitimate university subjects if they were approached scientifically. Thus, when in 1885 Oxford selected its first professor of English, who would lead its new Honours School of English Language and Literature, it chose a philologist and thereby chose to develop a scientific course instead of the mooted alternative program of study of English literary traditions.[35]

Toward the professionalization of anthropology

In sum, changes effected during the last quarter of the nineteenth century indicated that the time was ripe for the development of anthropology as a university subject. Its claims to scientific status were certainly greater than those of such disciplines as history or English – which rested on methodology alone – since at the time even those anthropologists concerned entirely with cultural analysis assumed that natural scientific investigations of human behavior had some (however remote) bearing on their work. Moreover, the litany of justifications for anthropological study resembled that used to great effect in defending the study of history: anthropological evidence aided both self-understanding and practical

---

[33] The quotations are all Seeley's. See Deborah Wormell, *Sir John Seeley and the Uses of History* (Cambridge, 1980), 119–122, and passim.

[34] Quoted, for example, in C. J. W. Parker, "The Failure of Liberal Racialism: The Racial Ideas of E. A. Freeman, *The Historical Journal* 24 (1981): 826.

[35] Engel, *From Clergyman to Don*, 239–40.

Hal. being painted

Thomas Huxley drew himself in an act of participant observation – having cosmetics applied by a "native acquaintance." This was probably painted in Rockingham Bay in 1848. The caption is in his wife's handwriting.

decision making. But members of the anthropological community in the late nineteenth century looked both to the universities and to government as possible future employers. Indeed, they had good reason to believe that anthropology was more likely to become the basis of a remunerated occupation under government sponsorship than within the university. Many of them had not been to university. As men active in worldly affairs, they saw anthropology as a technical skill, akin to the skills necessary for the practice of medicine or law, and practitioners of the learned professions secured training and certification outside the university. They knew that anthropologists could not have careers identical to those of traditional professionals, since anthropologists would never be able to contract for their services with individuals qua individuals. If they could persuade the state that it required their services, however, they could expect it to create an integrated network of institutions embodying all of the stages of professional careers; thus schools would provide training and employment, and government agencies and museums would generate practical knowledge and support research.

There was a recognizable precedent for the objective of developing anthropology as a government-supported occupation: the midcentury professionalization of geology, a discipline with close ties to anthropology, which was the first scientific field in Britain to develop a career structure. All of the elements of a geological career were integrated by the Geological Survey Act of 1845, which expanded the existing Geological Survey by authorizing completion of a comprehensive survey of the British Isles, unified administration of the survey and its associated museum within the Office of Woods and Forests, and linked to the museum the Royal School of Mines, which was finished in 1851. (The school was to become the Imperial College of Science and Technology in 1907, after reintegration with its offshoot, the Royal College of Science, established in 1872.) These achievements were possible because geologists were able to persuade government figures of the utility of their knowledge. The entrepreneurial head of the survey, Henry De la Beche, stated their case: geological research could increase the nation's wealth and improve its health. Geologists could discover valuable mineral deposits, and determine which places in Britain were unhealthy by virtue of their natural drainage systems.[36]

An interlocking directorate joined the institutions of geology and anthropology. A conspicuous figure in this directorate was T. H. Huxley, whose career as a naturalist began with his service on the HMS *Rattlesnake* from 1846 to 1850, during which he observed the peoples of the Pacific and their habitat.[37] From 1854, Huxley worked for the Geological Survey in various capacities. Indeed, he disdained at least one offer of employement at a major university – from Oxford in 1881 – because he felt he exercised more influence while teaching under the auspices of the survey.[38] And Huxley was committed to the organization of anthropology as a recognized enterprise: while he was president of Section D (Biology) of the British Association in 1866, a department for anthropology was created within the section; while he was president of the Ethnological Society of London

---

[36] See Secord, in "The Geological Survey of Great Britain," esp. 232, 247.
[37] See Julian Huxley, ed., *T. H. Huxley's Diary of the Voyage of H. M. S. Rattlesnake* (London, 1935), esp. 154–71.
[38] Geison, *Michael Foster*, 157–8.

between 1868 and 1870, he oversaw the negotiations that reconciled the factions of anthropologists who had been divided between that society and the Anthropological Society of London. The two groups merged to form the Anthropological Institute, and Huxley served on its governing council until his death. Huxley's contemporaries judged the creation of the institute a quantum leap forward for anthropology as a scholarly discipline.[39]

Individuals did not join both geological and anthropological societies merely because they were fond of organized sociability, legitimated with a cultural gloss. Geology and anthropology were linked intellectually. As Huxley put it, social research was a natural offshoot of the evolving disciplines of natural history, "the application of methods of investigation adopted in physical researches to the investigation of the phenomena of society."[40] Indeed, one branch of anthropology – archaeology – made geology's stratigraphical method its own, whereas in the nineteenth century the other branches of the discipline used geology's analysis of the historical development of the earth's strata as a model for their own accounts. And anthropologists considered their knowledge no less valuable to the state than geology: Britain required their services to deal effectively with those conflicts that derived from racial and cultural variation that arose both in the colonies and at home. No wonder that anthropologists imitated the geologists' occupational strategy. Their most conspicuous effort to prosecute this strategy – the attempt to secure government support for an "imperial bureau of ethnology" ideally patterned after the Geological Survey – was unsuccessful. But it is significant because it reflected anthropologists' vision of their enterprise in the era during which they campaigned for the bureau – between the last decade of the nineteenth century and the eve of World War I.

The campaign was initiated by A. C. Haddon, who was the bureau's persistent advocate. In 1896, however, figures of greater eminence in the scientific community joined the campaign under the auspices of the British Association for the Advancement of Science. The association's effort was led by prominent anthropologists – including such professionals as E. B. (later Sir Edward) Tylor and C. H. (later Sir Hercules) Read (1857–1929), as well as such leading amateur scientists as (later Sir) John Evans (1823–1908) and Sir John Lubbock (1834–1913). Read was the keeper

[39] E. W. Brabrook, "Anniversary Address," *Journal of the Anthropological Institute* 25 (1896): 388; E. B. Tylor, "Professor Huxley as an Anthropologist," *Fortnightly Review* 64 (July–December 1895): 311. The definitive account of the foundation of the Anthropological Institute is George W. Stocking, Jr., "What's in a Name? The Origins of the Royal Anthropological Institute (1837–1971)," *Man* [n. s.] 11 (1971): 369–90.

[40] T. H. Huxley, "Science and Culture," a lecture delivered in 1880, in *Science and Education* (Akron, Oh., 1893), 158.

of British and medieval antiquities at the British Museum. Evans and Lubbock were pillars of late-nineteenth-century gentlemanly science, both active in numerous scholarly and civic associations, recipients of titles from the Crown, Fellows of the Royal Society, trustees of the British Museum, and presidents of the British Association (in 1897–8 and 1870, respectively). All four of these men also served as presidents of the Anthropological Institute: Lubbock (its first President) in 1871–3; Evans in 1877–9; Tylor in 1879–81 and 1891–3; and Read in 1899–1901 and 1917–9. None of them had been to university, although Tylor was then an Oxford professor (as a Quaker, Tylor could not have matriculated at Oxford until he was twenty-two). For men of this era, then, there was no necessary connection between university training and scientific eminence, and an institutional base for anthropology outside the university seemed entirely appropriate.

When we consider Evans's and Lubbock's careers, we appreciate the considerable prestige they brought to the cause of the imperial bureau. Evans's fortunes derived from the spread of education and the democratization of politics in nineteenth-century Britain: he was a partner in a paper-making firm founded by his uncle, which prospered by developing a process to manufacture paper suitable for use by mass-circulation newspapers. Although he had entered his firm directly after leaving the grammar school of which his father was headmaster, Evans distinguished himself in antiquarian and archaeological scholarship, as well as in geological studies – some of which proved useful in his business. And he was an industrial spokesman, a sometime president of both the Paper Makers' Association and the Society of Chemical Industry. His career was a testament to the opportunities for upward mobility available to men of his generation.

Lubbock's pedigree joined the "intellectual aristocracy" with the financial aristocracy of the City (itself joined by marriage to the old landed aristocracy).[41] His father, the third baronet in the family line, was a neighbor and friend of Charles Darwin, who became an informal tutor and friend to the son as well. Obliged to leave Eton at the age of fourteen to join the family banking firm because his father's partners were in poor health, Lubbock became a man of accomplishments so numerous and diverse that they can barely be indicated here. He was the youngest member of the "X Club," a dining society of eight men that also included Herbert Spencer

---

[41] The biographical material on John Evans and John Lubbock is for the most part derived from conventional sources of biographical information (see n. 63). On Lubbock, in particular, see also Annan, "Intellectual Aristocracy" (chap. 1, n. 29), 282; and V. Cassis, "Bankers in English Society in the Late Nineteenth Century," *Economic History Review* [ser. 2] 38 (1985): 215–19. For more information see Appendix 2.

and Thomas Huxley, which conspired to exercise extraordinary influence in the scientific community during the last third of the nineteenth century.[42] Lubbock was an effective promoter of science teaching for school children and working men, Britain's leading popular science writer in the 1880s, the instigator of major reforms of banking practices, and a Liberal MP from 1870 to 1900. Elevated to the peerage in 1900, Lubbock chose to become Lord Avebury, a title denoting prehistoric megaliths he had studied and saved from destruction.

Under British Association and later also Anthropological Institute auspices, a number of petitions were presented to the government for the creation of an imperial bureau of ethnology. The bureau was variously mooted as a subsidiary of the recently formed Imperial Institute (Haddon's initial preference), the Colonial Office, the British Museum (the British Association's preference), or the Anthropological Institute (the institute's preference). Wherever it was to be housed, the bureau was to serve dual objectives: to increase scientific knowledge by recording those varieties of human behavior that were rapidly disappearing at home and abroad; and to assist colonial administrators by interpreting the values and customs of those peoples who had come under British domination. The bureau's proponents saw these as related objectives, since they recognized that colonialism was responsible for the obliteration of customary practices among subject peoples.

Anthropologists anticipated that their prospective patrons were less likely to subsidize scientific research per se than to support immediately practical investigations, and they pointed out that the colonial regime in India had already found ethnographic information extremely useful. They found precedents for their proposal in the colonial policies of the United States and the Netherlands: in the United States, men previously employed in government-sponsored geological and geographical surveying had secured official support for the Bureau of American Ethnology in 1879; and in the Netherlands systematic training in anthropology was provided for colonial administrators. Indeed, anthropologists asserted that colonial regimes could not function effectively without their assistance. Typical of their arguments was Haddon's injunction to colonial officials to attend to the cherished practices of subject peoples: if officials unwittingly violated traditional custom, their subjects would revolt; and officials seeking to improve the lives of colonized peoples required their subjects' cooperation – which could be secured only if officials' proposals appealed to local values.

---

[42] The other members of the club were George Busk, Edward Frankland, Thomas Archer Hirst, Joseph Hooker, and John Tyndall. See J. Vernon Jensen, "The X Club: Fraternity of Victorian Scientists," *British Journal for History of Science* 5 (1970): 63–72.

When bureau advocates addressed government officials, they tried to be politically astute. They took advantage of current events to underscore the urgency of their cause; as presidents of the Folk-Lore Society and the Anthropological Institute, respectively, Sidney Hartland and A. C. Haddon used the South African situation to justify their joint petition to the government in 1900. They repeatedly reassured officials that the cost of anthropological expertise was minimal relative to its benefits, as did (Sir) Michael Foster when he presented a petition to the government in his capacity as president of the British Association in 1899, and did (Sir) William Ridgeway (1853–1926), Disney professor of archaeology at Cambridge, when he presented a petition in his capacity as president of the Anthropological Institute in 1909. In response to these entreaties, officials happily allowed that in principle anthropology ought to prove useful to colonial administrators, but they did not fund an imperial bureau of ethnology. The British Museum's trustees approved the creation of an ethnological bureau within Read's department, but Read was never provided funds sufficient to realize the original plan. For a time, a few ethnographic reports were forwarded to his department through official channels, but it hardly became the intellectual directorate of the diverse colonial services.[43]

The imperial bureau of ethnology was not realized because there was a considerable gap between the ideology and practice of the colonial Empire. Anthropologists were not alone among British scientists in assuming the colonies to be a receptive market for their skills (and hence a testing ground for reforms to be effected at home). From the pronouncements of a significant group of colonial ideologues, scientists drew the logical conclusion that their services were desired. As Michael Worboys has observed, imperialist statesmen used science as a "metaphor ... of what Empire might become"; they prescribed an Empire administered according to the "ethos, methods, and organization of science."[44] To these states-men, government decisions reached by scientific reasoning transcended

---

[43] See J. L. Myres, "The Science of Man in the Service of the State," Presidential Address to the Royal Anthropological Institute, *Journal of the Royal Anthropological Institute* 59 (1929): 38–42. For illustrations of Haddon's arguments in favor of the imperial bureau see a paper he presented to the 1914 meeting of the British Association at Sydney, "The Study of Native Culture in Relation to Administration," HP, CU, Env. 4067; and Haddon, *The Practical Value of Ethnology* (London, 1921), 33–55. A description of the campaign for the bureau that pays particular attention to Haddon's role is in David K. van Keuren, "Human Science in Victorian Britain: Anthropology in Institutional and Disciplinary Formation, 1863–1908," unpublished Ph.D. thesis, University of Pennsylvania, 1982.

[44] Michael Worboys, "The British Association and Empire: Science and Social Imperialism, 1880–1940," in Roy MacLeod and Peter Collins, eds., *The Parliament of Science* (Northwood, Middlesex, 1981), 182.

political partisanship; they were administrative judgments that were in the best interests of the polity as a whole.

This ideology was not confined to the exclusive corridors of power, for colonial officials of every rank imagined themselves above the partisan politics that impeded progress in British society, representing their decisions as administrative rather than political. Moreover, in certain particulars the operation of the Empire seemed to realize the meritocratic standards fundamental to the scientific ethos. Witness the consequences of reform of the selection procedures of the Indian Civil Service, which created opportunities for persons from humble backgrounds who were diligent brain workers (or "examination wallahs" as they were somewhat pejoratively termed in service idiom). Even in the Colonial Administrative Service, which recruited by interview rather than examination, men of undistinguished origins were able to prove themselves worthy of promotion to positions of power quite probably far more eminent than they could have achieved at home.[45]

Nevertheless, the economic constraints under which the colonies operated discouraged the employment of technical experts of any kind – not just anthropologists. Each of the colonies was supposed to be self-supporting, and in consequence each had funds sufficient to pay only a small staff, composed largely of generalist administrators – "political officers" in colonial parlance. Though the recruitment procedures of the diverse colonial services varied, they all expected political officers to be "educated amateurs" who could behave in the field as "practical men," performing all but the most specialized of government functions. Indeed, the field staff of the Empire almost invariably characterized whatever technical advice they were offered as insufficiently grounded in the practical realities of their particular situations.

Haddon's vision of anthropology's potential use in colonial administration proved more compelling to the rulers of the Empire Dominions. Save for his lobbying efforts among South African and Australian officials, the career of his student Radcliffe-Brown would certainly have been different; Radcliffe-Brown became in turn the first occupant of professorships created at the universities of Cape Town in 1921 and Sydney in 1925, in

---

[45] The CAS recruited men by interview rather than examination, and its recruitment staff thought that the classes who sent their sons to public schools and Oxbridge provided the natural rulers of the Empire. Nevertheless, unless the men I studied who administered the Gold Coast were altogether different from the members of the CAS elsewhere, men from humble backgrouds were quite successful in the CAS – just as they were in the ICS, as we saw earlier. See my *Imperial Bureaucrat*, 27–31, 95–6. On the intolerance for politics in any form among colonial rulers, see John E. Kendle, *The Round Table Movement and Imperial Union* (Toronto, 1975), 9, 172–3, 253–5.

each of which he was responsible for training officials to govern indigenous peoples.[46] More important, Haddon had considerable influence on the administration of the Australian territory of Papua. The social circle in which Haddon moved at home and the contacts he made with Australian officials from the time of his first field research in 1888 brought him into a close working relationship with J. H. P. Murray, who during his long tenure as the chief political officer of Papua (titled lieutenant-governor) was an enthusiastic supporter of applied anthropology. The Haddon Papers at Cambridge are full of letters from Murray soliciting Haddon's advice about the work done by the administrators of Papua, and especially by the anthropologists Murray employed: E. P. Chinnery, F. E. Williams, and W. C. Armstrong, the last an especially promising pupil of Haddon's who became an economist after Haddon failed to secure him a permanent anthropological post at Cambridge.

But Papua did not become a locus for applied anthropology until its administration was transferred from Britain to Australia in 1906. Because it was a territory removed from the country's areas of European settlement, its officials were able to develop an aboriginal policy considered far more "soft" than that followed in other Australian jurisdictions of aboriginal administration – a policy that predisposed its practitioners to accept anthropological advice (and set goals very different from those set in British colonial territories).[47] Papuan government anthropologists were as respected as any colonial anthropologists in British scholarly circles, but in the aggregate colonial anthropologists suffered a considerable loss of prestige after academics began to do their own fieldwork in the first decades of the twentieth century.

A single branch of Haddon's academic lineage seemed capable of securing government support within the British Empire. One of his associates in the Torres Straits Expedition, C. G. Seligman (1873–1940), was invited in

---

[46] In South Africa, however, Radcliffe-Brown's pedagogic efforts were not very successful, particularly by contrast to the teaching done by ethnologists in the Afrikaans universities. During his tenure at Cape Town he apparently attracted only five students beyond the first year and one M.A. student. See Robert Gordon, "Apartheid's Anthropologists: The Geneology of Afrikaner Anthropology," *American Ethnologist* 15 (1988): 539, 550.

[47] The anthropologists employed in Papua took great pains to insist that their views on colonial policy were very different from those that prevailed among the officials of British colonies. Their educational policy, for example, was assimilationist rather than separatist; see, for example, F. E. Williams, *Native Education: The Language of Instruction and Intellectual Education*, Territory of Papua Anthropology Report No. 9 (Port Moresby, 1928). On the peculiarities of Papuan administration, see Mulvaney and Calaby, *"So Much That Is New"*, 314–15.

1906 by the government of Ceylon to undertake research there with his wife, Brenda Z. Seligman (1883–1965), an anthropologist in her own right. In 1909, the Seligmans went to the Sudan with official sponsorship, and C. G. Seligman's students E. E. Evans-Pritchard and S. F. Nadel (1903–56) were later to produce studies commissioned by the Sudan administration.[48] But the colonial government of the Sudan was eccentric in behavior and constitution; with its sovereignty formally shared by the Egyptian Khedive and the British Crown, its affairs reluctantly and indifferently supervised by the Foreign Office, it was by far the first colonial regime to see virtue in anthropological instruction for its staff, inviting Oxford and Cambridge to develop courses for them in 1908, and it was uniquely generous in its patronage of professional anthropology.

After C. G. Seligman became professor of ethnology at the London School of Economics in 1913, he was employed to give a smattering of instruction to those future members of the Colonial Administrative Service who elected to take the optional three-month course offered them in London until 1924. Subsequently, the course was made mandatory, extended to a year, and moved to Oxford and Cambridge. But the director of recruitment for the service made these changes largely because he hoped to attract more Oxbridge men – not because he determined that colonial service probationers required more extensive training in anthropology and allied subjects.[49] In sum, Haddon's campaign had won only very small victories. Though colonial officials were to grow more enthusiastic about anthropology, the discipline never attained the status Haddon and others had envisioned – as the systematic basis for enlightened colonial administration.[50]

By the time of World War I, however, the members of the anthropological community were collectively promoting a different occupational strategy. They now envisioned the university as their appropriate institu-

---

[48] In the oral tradition of contemporary British anthropologists, it is said that Seligman and Evans-Pritchard denied that their work was of any value to colonial officials. See Adam Kuper, *Anthropology and Anthropologists: The Modern British School* (London, 1983), 103–4. From the historical record, however, this seems too sweeping a generalization.

[49] Indeed, the social experience of a year at Cambridge or Oxford was considered more valuable for the colonial cadet than the formal instruction he received, and a man who devoted much time to his studies was apt to be reprimanded for doing so. See my *Imperial Bureaucrat*, 26.

[50] For one comparative analysis of the practices of different colonial regimes, see Lennox A. Mills, "Methods of Appointment and Training in the British and Dutch Colonial Civil Service," *American Political Science Review* 33 (1939): 465–72. And see Sir Ralph Furse, *Acuparius* (London, 1962), 235.

tional base. As they gained security in the universities, they gained respect from colonial officials. By World War II, anthropologists' professional identity had become uncompromisingly academic; they were able to promise the government figures who then offered them funds that the research they undertook in the name of pure science would eventually prove useful, while disdaining (or assigning relatively little prestige to) the applied research projects officials were eager to have them undertake.

This development seemed highly unlikely at the end of the nineteenth century, when the universities were barely tolerant of anthropology, as J. G. Frazer wrote to his friend Sidney Hartland in 1895. Hartland had evidently urged Frazer to campaign for the creation of teaching posts in anthropology at Cambridge (which contributed only a small fellowship income to Frazer's support). Frazer responded:

> As for stirring up Cambridge to appoint a professor of anthropology, I fear that I must confess to never stirring up anybody to do anything.... The University and colleges are miserably poor, and their scanty incomes are necessarily devoted to far more important objects, such as giving feasts, keeping up gardens and chapel services, and maintaining hundreds of Fellows and Masters of Colleges in idleness. Or rather I should say that these are the prime objects to which the Colleges devote their energies, and that the small surplus which is left over when these essentials have been provided for is handed over to the University to be by it applied to the subordinate object of promoting science and learning. This small surplus is not sufficient to endow a professorship of anthropology.[51]

Cambridge was not to create a professorship in anthropology until 1932, and the first two occupants of the William Wyse chair were not academically trained men but retired members of the Indian Civil Service – T. C. Hodson (1871–1953) and J. H. Hutton (1885–1968). A. C. Haddon, who began lecturing at Cambridge in 1894, had a (barely remunerated) lectureship created for him in 1900, and from 1909 to his retirement worked as a reader. Anthroplogy's reception at Oxford was much the same. To be sure, Oxford had preceded Cambridge in creating a post in anthropology for E. B. Tylor in 1884. But in 1895 Tylor's proposal for a degree course was defeated through the efforts of a curious coalition of theologians, classicists, and natural scientists – "Scribes, Pharisees, and Saducees" to the wags.[52] Tylor was conceded anthropology as a "special subject" for a natural science degree, but no student ever took this option since it had to be taken in addition to the full roster of subjects required for

---

[51] Quoted in Ackerman, *J. G. Frazer*, 148.
[52] Myres, "The Science of Man," 42.

the degree. And Oxford was not to create an endowed professorship in anthropology until 1937, when it appointed Radcliffe-Brown; Tylor's successor, R. R. Marett (1866–1943), retired as a reader.

Such evidence might seem to indicate that anthropologists were right to judge the universities especially hostile to their discipline. But anthropology was only one among new fields apparently slighted by the universities. In truth, at the end of the century, Oxford and Cambridge were resistant to any sort of innovation because they were suffering from a loss of prosperity. The colleges' incomes were derived largely from agricultural investments, and the enthusiasm they had manifested for change around the time of the passage of the Universities Tests Act diminished immediately thereafter with the onset of the agricultural depression in 1873. To be sure, there are significant exceptions to the generalization that the ancient universities' conservatism was a simple function of reduced resources. Some Oxford colleges were fortunate to have substantial holdings in nonagricultural property, and enjoyed increased prosperity at the end of the century. And the organizational structure and curricular tradition of Cambridge permitted it to create distinguished science programs at this time, most conspicuously in physics, although it was even more dependent on agricultural investments than Oxford was.[53]

In fact, the universities accepted anthropology more readily than other aspirant disciplines. Indeed, Oxford was prepared to finance anthropology during the agricultural depression, if not to make it an undergraduate degree subject. Though its original appointment of E. B. Tylor was a condition of General Pitt-Rivers's deed of gift of the artifacts that formed the nucleus of the anthropological museum that bears his name, the university took the unprecedented step of creating Tylor's readership and spent an extraordinary sum – over £10,000 – on the museum building.[54] Consider the ancient universities' reluctance to establish positions in other human sciences: a professorship in psychology was not created at Oxford until 1947; sociology was not given a professorship at Cambridge until 1960. Because the proponents of English at Cambridge did not adopt the strategy of their counterparts at Oxford who embraced a scientific definition of their subject, they were frustrated by the identification of English study as dilettantish – a course for men unable to stand the rigors of classics, or, perhaps even worse, for women – and did not gain full

---

[53] Geison, *Michael Foster*, 111–112; Engel, *From Clergyman to Don*, 204–56; Howarth, "Science Education" 334–67.

[54] Howarth, "Science Education," 339; T. R. Penniman, "General Pitt Rivers," *Man* 46 (1946): 73.

acceptance of their subject until 1926.[55] It is worth noting in passing that anthropology never suffered by being made a feminist issue; anthropological evidence could be used by both advocates and opponents of feminism, and in the universities feminists found strong supporters among such anthropologists as A. C. Haddon, and staunch opponents among such pillars of the anthropological community as William Ridgeway.[56]

Moreover, university politicians were not competing for scarce resources in isolated institutional environments. They were also responding to outside pressures – in particular, those brought to bear by learned circles that, at least in the late nineteenth century, were nearly independent of university influence and enjoyed the prestige traditionally accorded gentlemanly amateurism rather than professionalism. Recall that the British Association for the Advancement of Science created a separate section for anthropology in 1884, and consider again the contrast between the recognition accorded anthropology and other human sciences; psychology gained its own section in 1921, and sociology its own section in 1960.

In sum, however dismal anthropology's prospects appeared in the universities in 1895, the next three decades were to bring steady growth in its acceptance as a subject suitable for both undergraduate and postgraduate degree study. Benchmarks in the discipline's academic institutionalization were the creation of Oxford's School of Anthropology in 1906 and Cambridge's Board of Anthropological Studies in 1908. In 1907 the first chair in social anthropology in any British university was created for J. G. Frazer at the University of Liverpool. (Because Frazer could not tolerate Liverpool, he returned to his beloved Cambridge after only one session.) Not coincidentally, it was in 1907 that the Anthropological Institute finally received a Royal Charter, after years of repeated submissions. By 1923, a British Association Committee was able to report that eleven universities provided some sort of anthropological instruction.[57]

---

[55] Wolf Lepenies, *Between Literature and Science: The Rise of Sociology* (Cambridge, 1988), 176–7.

[56] T. E. B. Howarth, *Cambridge Between Two Wars* (London, 1978), 35, 132.

[57] We should note some other benchmarks in the academic institutionalization of anthropology. At Oxford, in 1899 the "Research Degree" statute allowed the submission of an anthropological thesis for a B.Litt. or B.Sc. degree; in 1905 the postgraduate course for the Diploma in Anthropology was instituted. At Cambridge, it became possible to earn a Diploma in Anthropology by submitting a thesis in 1908 (an opportunity particularly attractive to anthropologically active colonial officials); in 1913 anthropology was allowed as part of the examination tripos. At the University of London, a lectureship in ethnology was established in 1904; in 1912 it became possible to earn a B.A. Pass degree and a B.Sc., Pass or Honours degree in anthropology; in 1922 anthropology became a subject for the B.A. Honours degree.

The utilitarian justification for anthropology only partially accounted for its acceptance. The legitimation of the discipline must be considered a product of three factors. First, it was promoted by some of the most prominent figures in the scientific community, whose recognition of anthropology as truly scientific gave it intellectual respectability. Second, although colonial officials bristled when scientists presumed to tell them how to do their jobs, they themselves eventually resolved that the managers of Empire could profit from anthropological instruction and turned to the universities to provide it; the universities happily satisfied market demand, and indicated that they regarded anthropology as vocational training by appointing a number of retired colonial officials to teach it. Third, anthropology became part of the repertoire of the conventionally cultured educated person – an area of expertise like English domestic architecture, say, or the modern novel – a subject university students were expected to master at some minimal level regardless of the formal courses they took.[58] In short, anthropology became part of the curriculum because it could serve all of the purposes of the university, which does (and should) not exist for the sole purpose of certifying individuals as competent practitioners of useful skills; anthropologists contributed to high- and upper-middle-brow culture, and also conveyed information that could be put to practical use.

Nevertheless, for anthropologists, unlike undergraduates, their discipline became the basis of a standardized career. Provided with an assured employment base in the universities, they could delimit a distinctly professional sphere within the anthropological community, occupied by persons working as anthropologists whose positions were reserved for those with academic credentials who had survived the anthropological rite of passage of fieldwork. In the emergence of thoroughly academic anthropology, the developments of greatest consequence occurred during the interwar period at the University of London – the site of university innovation in diverse fields, not just in anthropology. When British universities began to grant Ph.D.s in the 1920s, the vast majority of degrees in anthropology were conferred by London on students trained at University College (UCL) and the London School of Economics (LSE). Only lately has the Ph.D. become an essential credential for all aspiring British academics, but practitioners of such novel disciplines as anthropology needed the degree to secure university appointments in the post–World War II period.

Sheer force of numbers permitted London-trained persons to dominate academic anthropology. By the end of World War II, twelve Ph.D.s had

[58] See Howarth, *Cambridge Between Two Wars*, 131.

been trained by the UCL program housed within the department of anatomy; there they were supervised by the distinguished anatomist (Sir) Grafton Elliot Smith (1871–1937), an Australian whose initial British academic affiliation was with Cambridge, who was appointed professor of anatomy at London in 1919, and by the Cambridge-trained W. J. Perry (1887–1950), who was made reader in cultural anthropology in 1924. In the same period, twenty-four Ph.D.s were trained at the LSE in a department graced by two professors, C. G. Seligman and Bronislaw Malinowski, the latter of whom was elevated to a professorship in 1927. The UCL program took an early lead in producing Ph.D.s. By 1927, when the first degree was conferred on an LSE student, UCL had trained four men. The first UCL product, the Rev. E. O. James, proved one of its most distinguished; earning his degree in 1925, he retired as university professor of the history and philosophy of religion at UCL. The LSE's first Ph.D. recipient, the Australian R. W. (Sir Raymond) Firth (b. 1901), made an outstanding career in anthropology, retiring as professor of anthropology at the LSE.

Indeed, the LSE was considerably more successful in training persons for academic careers than was UCL. The most eminent anthropologist whose Ph.D. was conferred after training at UCL was the Australian A. P. Elkin (1891–1979), who took his degree in 1927 and returned home (where Elliot Smith's voice remained powerful in scientific circles). But Elkin then retrained by undertaking fieldwork under the (remote) supervision of Radcliffe-Brown, who had secured his Sydney professorship with the aid of a recommendation from Elliot Smith. In time, Elkin assumed the Sydney chair (and like Radcliffe-Brown devoted much of his time to training colonial officials).[59] Indeed, Elkin was one of only two London Ph.D.s trained at UCL who were able to become academic anthropologists – both working in universities outside Britain. A critical element was missing from the early careers of virtually all of the UCL students: the

[59] See Mulvaney and Calaby, "*So Much That Is New*" (see chap. 1, n. 27), 407. Elkin was the first recipient of the Rockefeller Foundation-financed fellowships for anthropological field research that Radcliffe-Brown secured through the Australian National Research Council during the latter's five-year stay as the University of Sydney's first professor of anthropology. In theory, Radcliffe-Brown was Elkin's supervisor. But Elkin had almost no contact with Radcliffe-Brown. From the field, Elkin regularly sent Radcliffe-Brown reports of his findings; but the best evidence he had that they were read was the fact that Radcliffe-Brown incorporated them, sometimes verbatim, in his own work. After Radcliffe-Brown left Australia, he was replaced in an acting capacity by Raymond Firth; and after Firth himself returned to the LSE to teach, Elkin assumed the professorship. See A. P. Elkin, "A. R. Radcliffe-Brown, 1880 [sic]–1955," *Oceania* 26 (1956): esp. 240, 245.

funding necessary to support field research, which for these early Ph.D.s
was undertaken after completion of a thesis based on library research
rather than antecedent to the completion of the degree. Students in the
more prestigious LSE department were able to secure research funds
(and/or the department gained prestige as its students won research
grants). Three-quarters of the LSE Ph.D.s were able to make careers
as academic anthropologists (and two of those who did not worked as
academics in related fields).

The number of Ph.D.s trained at the LSE is indicative of the renown
its department enjoyed in the interwar period. In fact, this number is
an inadequate measure of the department's professional influence at the
time. Candidates for Ph.D.s in anthropology at other universities came to
Malinowski's famous seminars, as did persons with Ph.D.s in other fields
who shifted into anthropology. Altogether, those persons trained at the
LSE exercised near-monopolistic control of post–World War II anthropology. Symbolic of their professional dominance were the appointments of
E. E. Evans-Pritchard as professor of social anthropology at Oxford in
1946 and of Meyer Fortes (1906–83) as professor at Cambridge, the latter
succeeding in 1950 the second of the retired Indian Civil Service men
who had been the previous occupants of the William Wyse chair. Evans-
Pritchard had earned his degree at the LSE in 1928; and while Fortes had
come from South Africa to study psychology at UCL, receiving his Ph.D.
in 1928, he had subsequently become an anthropologist with the help
of financial support from the Rockefeller Foundation and intellectual
stimulation at the LSE.

Yet even those fledgling anthropologists whose prospects seemed
brightest in the interwar period were embarking on an uncertain career
path, as the novelist Barbara Pym observed when she reviewed the files
from the 1930s of the International African Institute (IAI) – to which she
had access as the assistant editor of its journal, *Africa*. The IAI (founded in
1926 as the International Institute for African Languages and Cultures)
became the agent of transmission of most of the research monies available
to young anthropologists in the interwar period. The creation of an international group of missionaries, colonial officials, and academics (but British
based and dominated), the IAI was supported by commercial interests,
colonial governments, the Carnegie Corporation, and, most important, the
Rockefeller Foundation; and it awarded the funds at its disposal after
consultation with colonial governments, which plumped for potentially
useful projects (and would not tolerate within their jurisdictions anthropologists they judged would somehow disturb their control over their
subjects). Provided with the funds necessary to do the research that would
prove that they were capable scholars, the recipients of IAI monies were as

certain of future professional success as young anthropologists could be in the interwar years.

The funding criteria of the IAI favored social anthropologists, who thus became an especially privileged segment of the anthropological community. Yet, as Pym noted, the lot of fellowship recipients was not a happy one. Their employment prospects were unclear, they suffered physical discomfort and financial insecurity in the field, and their patrons subjected them to unwonted scrutiny.[60] The Ph.D.s trained at the LSE were awarded IAI funds, yet only six of them were able to become academic anthropologists in Britain; to be sure, fifteen of them had come from abroad to study, and several chose to go home rather than leaving Britain because of lack of opportunity there. Still, the tribulations of anthropologists trained in the interwar period did not compare to those of their professional predecessors. Consider Radcliffe-Brown's career: recognized in the 1920s as a leading figure in the field, he was obliged to work abroad until 1937, when at the age of fifty-six he was appointed professor of social anthropology at Oxford.

But post–World War II anthropologists were sufficiently secure in their professional roles to restrict membership in the Association of Social Anthropologists (ASA) to persons with Ph.D.s in anthropology (or equivalent accomplishments). The ASA was an exclusive group; in 1946, its charter members could fit comfortably into a seminar room. True, in the antecedent era, anthropology's leaders were also a small group of people who knew one another – Huxley, Lubbock, Tylor, Galton, Haddon, Frazer, Malinowski, and so on. Postwar anthropologists were distinct from their predecessors in several respects, however. Prominent among them were foreigners, several of them of Jewish extraction. (But despite the frequency of anti-Semitism in polite British circles – even among relatively liberal academics – men of Jewish ancestry had managed to become prominent members of the anthropological community in the previous era.)[61] They included a relatively large number of women – almost all of whom had impeccable British social credentials – who did not attain the most prestigious of academic posts. The post–World War II anthropological community turned inward, toward investigation of esoteric academic problems, and the social marginality of many of its members may have figured in this shift. The professionalized nature of the anthropological

---

[60] See her diary entry of April 29, 1970, in *A Very Private Eye: An Autobiography in Diaries and Letters by Barbara Pym*, edited by Hazel Holt and Hilary Pym (New York, 1984), 256.

[61] For one illustration of the anti-Semitism of a generally liberal intellectual, see C. J. W. Parker, "The Failure of Liberal Racialism," 840–1.

community was probably just as important to its changed outlook as was its social composition – if not more important.

Anthropologists were no different from other professionalized scholars, whose deficient sense of social responsibility was deplored by Karl Pearson (1857–1936), the statistician who was the first occupant of the chair in eugenics at the University of London funded by Francis Galton and was prominent in anthropological circles, honored by both the RAI and Section H. Pearson was himself a social activist, who frequently extrapolated policy recommendations from his research. And in 1924 he lamented that scientists of his type were becoming extinct. When scientific inquiry was transformed into just "one of the professional roads to a living," he said, its practitioners were wont to disregard "the meaning of science for the national welfare."[62]

Scholarly lives

Turning to the task of producing a collective biography of members of the anthropological community between 1885 and 1945, I begin with tedious but necessary explanations – to justify my decision to define the population of anthropologists as equivalent to the membership roles of the Royal Anthropological (RAI) – and specification of my process of data selection. Although I have summarized my information in quantitative form, my data should be understood as indicative of general patterns, rather than as exact measures. They confirm and supplement generalizations made earlier in this chapter.

A collective biography of the RAI is relatively easy to compile, since its journal published complete lists of the society's officers, council members, and Ordinary Fellows. I assume that the institute's membership in the years 1883, 1893, 1900, 1910, 1920, 1930, and 1938 was characteristic of the group as constituted during the entire period covered by this study. (The somewhat irregular intervals at which I examined the population of the group result from the journal's practices; complete membership lists were not published in every year.) For each year selected, I compiled data about all of the institute's officers and council and about a random sample of fifty Ordinary Fellows, using diverse sources of biographical information.[63] We can safely assume that the institute's officers and council

---

[62] Pearson, *Galton* (see chap. 1, n. 26), Vol. II, 54.

[63] I have used many sources of biographical information: *American Men and Women of Science* (New York, 1973); *International Directory of Anthropological Institutions*, W. L. Thomas, Jr., and Anna Pikelis, eds. (New York, 1953); *Dictionary of Scientific Biography*, Charles C. Gillispie, ed. (New York, 1970–); *Dictionary of National Biography* (London,

The Master

Professor Conway

Mr H. T. Francis	The University Registrary
The Master of Emmanuel	Mr E. S. Hartland
Professor J. W. Mackail	Professor Bradbury
Sir Joseph Larmor, M.P.	The President
The Most Rev. the Archbishop of Armagh	Sir T. Clifford Allbutt, K.C.B.
Professor Ridgeway	Dr L. C. Purser
Sir Arthur J. Evans	Rev. Canon Foakes-Jackson
Mr Charles Whibley	The Master of Downing
Archdeacon Beresford Potter	Professor Prior

Dr Gaskell

Professor Punnett	Mr Gaselee
Mr Stagg	Canon Scott
Rev. H. F. Stewart	Mr J. D. Anderson
Mr J. F. Cameron	Mr O. L. Richmond
Mr Birtwistle	Mr Z. N. Brooke
Mr Gallop	Mr A. B. Cook
Mr M. S. Thompson	Professor Ure
Mr S. A. Cook	Mr F. W. Green
Dr Seligmann	Mr Brindley

Dr Haddon

Professor Beresford Pite

Mr Mollison	Rev. Dr Barber
The Bursar	Professor Seward
Dr Rouse	Col. Edwards, C.B.
Professor Mawer	Major Tremearne
Mr H. J. White-Jervis	Rev. J. G. Clark
Mr Riches	Mr S. C. Cockerell
Rev. R. F. Cobbold	The Manchester Guardian
Rev. Prof. W. E. Barnes	Dr Rivers
Professor Lewis	Mr Tillyard
Professor Chadwick	Professor Housman

Professor Rapson

Professor Macdonald

Dr W. Wright	The Times
Dr Duckworth	Dr Michell
Mr Minns	Mr Dunlop
Mr E. Harrison	Mr Hutchinson
Mr Sheppard	Dr Searle
Mr Gow	The Daily News
Mr Abbott	Mr Gomme
Mr Wace	The Standard
The Morning Post	Mr Hasluck

Mr E. C. Quiggin

The social world of the anthropologist who became a prominent figure at the end of the nineteenth century: the seating plan of a birthday dinner for Sir William Ridgeway, Disney Professor of Archaeology at Cambridge, given at Gonville and Caius College, Cambridge, July 31, 1913.

were members of anthropology's guiding elite. The Ordinary Fellows were a more disparate lot: fledgling practitioners, committed anthropologists not then prominent in the society's leadership; and the more enthusiastic members of anthropology's general audience.

Happily, my equation of the membership of the RAI with the population of anthropology's most active producers and consumers is defensible as well as convenient, for there is considerable overlap between the institute's membership and that of other anthropological societies. An interlocking directorate joined the leadership of the institute and Section H of the British Association for the Advancement of Science (BAAS), the only other learned body devoted to all varieties of anthropological research – social/cultural analysis, physical anthropology, and archaeology. To wit: in every cohort I studied, nearly as many members of the governing body of the RAI had at some time been president of Section H (roughly a quarter to a third) as had been at some time president of the institute (roughly a third to two-fifths).[64] Moreover, in any given year, a considerable proportion of the institute elite (from a half to four-fifths) were active members of a range of anthropological societies other than the RAI – including Section H as well as specialized groups devoted to archaeology, antiquities, and folklore.[65] The leaders of specialized societies were almost invariably active in the RAI.

Section H engaged persons with a more casual interest in anthropology than joined the institute. Because the British Association staged its yearly meetings in provincial cities (including the outposts of Empire), it attracted many who attended only those meetings held in their city – who were entertained by papers of local interest, such as reports on archaeological excavations around Birmingham or on racial diversity in Canada. Moreover, the BAAS not only engaged dabblers in anthropology but also recognized provincial leaders more readily than the RAI. G. Elliot Smith, for example, was elected president of Section H in 1912, while he was professor of anatomy at Manchester University, but did not join the institute

1882–); *International Directory of Anthropologists*, M. Herskovits and B. Ames, eds. (Washington, D.C., 1950); *International Encyclopedia of the Social Sciences*, David L. Sills, ed. (New York, 1968, 1979); *Minerva: Handbuch der Gelehrten Welt* (Strassburg, 1911–). *Social Scientists Specializing in African Studies* (Paris, 1963), The Colonial Office and India Office Lists, *Who's Who*, and *Who Was Who* are also useful, and obituaries can be found in *Folk-Lore, Man, Nature*, and *The Times*. One also acquires much biographical information as an incidental by-product of research on various topics. I am indebted to David K. van Keuren for considerable assistance in gathering biographical information.

[64] Table A1.1, Appendix 1.
[65] Table A1.2, Appendix 1.

council until 1922, after taking up his UCL chair. Of course, members of anthropology's general audience were found outside the BAAS. They also enrolled as Ordinary members of the RAI. But because many of them were persons of no particular distinction (scholarly or otherwise), my data on them are fragmentary.

Informative though extensive information on anthropology's general audience might be, we are nevertheless more concerned with the field's most committed figures. The London-centered persons who dominated the RAI were anthropology's discipline builders and influential supporters: persons attached to the colleges of the University of London, employees of the British Museum, academic physicians doing physical anthropology at the Royal Colleges of Physicians and Surgeons, members of Oxford and Cambridge colleges, and amateur scholars drawn from various occupational groups. Only because these figures had ties to diverse networks of power were they able to define anthropology as an important enterprise, and to mobilize support for it.

The RAI was never a large organization, its membership hovering around the three-hundred mark in the late nineteenth century and growing to the six-hundred range in the interwar period. Nevertheless, its elite exercised influence through an elaborated social network, participating in an extraordinary range of societies. From the late nineteenth century through the middle of the twentieth, members of this group belonged in substantial numbers to organizations of diverse types – civic and (non-academic) professional, natural historical, biomedical, and other social scientific societies (categories determined from the clusters of association memberships characteristic of individuals). Moreover, anthropologists were also active in organizations so diverse as to defy systematic classification: other learned societies; provincial groups with catholic intellectual interests; and religious, artistic, fraternal, or explicitly recreational groups. I have not attempted to summarize this feature of anthropologists' activities. In sum, the RAI elite were persons committed to participation in organizations per se, dedicated to the reasonable proposition that intellectual and social changes are most efficiently effected by individuals acting in concert with others (a proposition that emerged in several guises in varieties of anthropological theory).

Some changes in the characteristics of anthropology as an organized enterprise are evident from the patterns of RAI members' organizational affiliations alone. Around World War I, members' participation in societies devoted to other varieties of natural history declined, as each type of natural history – including anthropology – assumed a distinct identity. And also around World War I, anthropologists belonged in especially large numbers to biomedical societies, indicative of the emphasis the discipline then placed on solving problems stressed by physical anthropologists: specification of the parameters of human racial variation, and disaggregation of the elements of race and culture in interpretation of human behavioral variation.[66]

It was not until the late 1930s that most of the members of the institute were professionals – individuals who earned their living as anthropologists. Nevertheless, the publication records of the officers and council members from the late nineteenth century indicate intense commitment both to the anthropological enterprise and to the scholarly life in general. From the beginning, virtually all of the professionals published in anthropology, although they also published outside the field, even in the late 1930s. Their publications reveal that in the nineteenth century the amateurs active in the RAI did not identify themselves primarily as anthropologists. Around World War I, however, the amateurs began to produce more anthropological works than other sorts of scholarship. Most importantly, however, throughout the years covered by this study the publication rate of most members of the institute elite – whether amateur or professional – was respectable even by the standards of modern research universities' faculties.[67]

It might be argued that the RAI was not representative of the anthropological community throughout the entire period covered by this study, that its founders might have constituted an intellectual vanguard but by the middle of the twentieth century its stalwarts were intellectually reactionary. Certainly the constitution of the RAI prevented drastic changes in its leadership at any time. This is not surprising, given that the institute's structure was created by men who believed that nature decreed a gradual course of evolution for all human institutions (and for everything else of this world). Many people figured among the institute's elite for decades. Witness the continuity in the composition of the society's officers and council. In 1893, 55 percent of the members of this group had been among it in 1883. This pattern was sustained in subsequent years. The percentages of members of the institute elite who had served in this capacity for a decade or more were 47 in 1900, 47 in 1910, 44 in 1920, 41 in 1930, 59 in 1938, and 53 in 1945. Moreover, the institute's elite were an aging group: their median age, 51 in 1883, had advanced to 58 by 1930.[68]

During the interwar period, many of the younger members of the anthropological community perceived the RAI as a retrograde force. Theirs was the argument that justified the philanthropic choices of the Rockefeller

[66] Table A1.2, Appendix 1.
[67] Table A1.3, Appendix 1.
[68] Table A1.4, Appendix 1.

Foundation at this time: just after the war, the foundation had given generously to both the RAI and the diffusionist anthropologists at UCL, but it subsequently cut its support of the institute and eliminated its support of diffusionism, allocating the bulk of the monies it distributed to British anthropologists to the functionalists based at the LSE. This decision literally favored the younger generation. An older group of students found the outlook and method embodied in the diffusionist program congenial. The population of Ph.D.s trained at UCL during the interwar period had a median age of 41 in 1930, while the corresponding group from the LSE had a median age of 26.

The Rockefeller Foundation's judgment was not accurate, however. Deliberately organized as a society in which anthropologists of every persuasion could work together, the RAI was in truth remarkably ecumenical. It remained hospitable to all anthropological factions, despite the considerable animosity that sometimes obtained among them – as it did between the diffusionists and the functionalists. Its leadership included both of the men who became professors of anthropology at the LSE: the nonfunctionalist C. G. Seligman, first elected to the council in 1905, and the functionalist Bronislaw Malinowski, first elected in 1926. And around the time that their London appointments were made, the UCL diffusionists became members of the RAI leadership: W. J. Perry joined the council in 1926, as Elliot Smith had done earlier. When the functionalist Radcliffe-Brown returned to Britain, he immediately assumed a prominent role in the institute, and served as its president from 1939 through 1941.

Moreover, the RAI welcomed the young functionalists trained at the LSE – no matter what their social antecedents were. Many of them joined, and participated actively, as the minutes of the society's meetings show. The intellectual products of the LSE were added to the RAI Council early in their careers. In 1930 Evans-Pritchard joined it (while he was still in his twenties), and in 1933 Firth did so. In 1935 the council included Lucy Mair (1901–86), who took her Ph.D. in economics at the LSE, became Malinowski's assistant, and retired as professor of applied anthropology at the LSE. In 1936 the council included Audrey Richards, who had taken her Ph.D. in 1930 and retired as reader in anthropology at Cambridge. Of these, all but Mair served as presidents of the institute after World War II. To be sure, with the exception of Firth, all of the LSE anthropologists who became prominent in the RAI in the 1930s had British upper-middle-class pedigrees. Nevertheless, when the institute elected young functionalists to its council, it demonstrated its concern to recognize every significant faction in the anthropological community.

Obviously, anthropology's militant sectarians were occasionally frustrated by the RAI's broad church tradition – as were the agents of Rockefeller

Foundation patronage, who were reluctant to give much support to the institute because they wished to be certain that their funds would not be distributed to the undeserving. But the institute's founders had constituted a society that realized their evolutionist model, which rendered tolerance for diversity as the natural order of things. Their creation was an organization committed to absorbing all possible agents of intellectual change, some of which would prevail for unanticipated reasons, an organization that has indeed persisted because it has been able to adapt to a changing intellectual ecology. The institute's founders believed that when individuals competed for recognition under free-market conditions – able to effect all manner of social exchanges without prejudicial restraints on trade – persons of intellect and achievement would receive the rewards they deserved.

In the lifetimes of the institute's founders, traditional restraints on social exchanges had been relaxed, although certainly not eliminated. And anthropologists' successes were to them proof positive of the merits of their views. The considerable public recognition they earned is visible from indices of two sorts: measures of the esteem in which they were held by the scientific community, and evidence of the respect they had won from a larger population. Indices of the first sort are election to the presidency of the British Association and to fellowship of the Royal Society (which Francis Galton also treated as a "pass examination" for inclusion in the scientific elite).[69] One index of the second sort is election to the Atheneum – the London club organized by and for distinguished scientific and literary authors and prominent artists. Another is the receipt of honors conferred by the Crown; recall that knighthoods conferred after 1860 denoted public recognition of some sort of achievement. To be sure, not all of the men offered various public honors accepted them. Francis Galton, for example, twice declined to serve as president of the British Association.[70] But such behavior was unusual. Because the recipients of virtually all the honors I have noted (save election to the Atheneum) were bound to be memorialized in prominently placed obituaries, the data I have accumulated on anthropologists' public recognition are particularly reliable.

It is significant that in their recognized achievements the members of the anthropological elite surpassed their fathers. Only four had fathers who had been given titles: two baronetcies and two knighthoods. One of these men, John Evans's son Arthur (1851–1941), who used his father's wealth to finance a distinguished career of archaeological research that included the discovery of Mycenean remains at Knossos, earned his own knight-

---

[69] Galton, *English Men of Science*, 4.
[70] L. S. Hearnshaw, *A Short History of British Psychology, 1840–1940* (New York, 1964), 57.

Table 2.1 *Distinctions achieved by RAI elite members*

	1883	1893	1900	1910	1920	1930	1938
Fellow of the Royal Society (%)	41	41	37	36	22	19	16
British Association president (%)	17	16	12	8	3	6	3
Given titles (%)	24	27	27	28	19	22	9
Atheneum member (%)	41	34	25	22	22	9	13
Biography unknown (No.)	6	7	5	3	2	3	1
Officers and council (total No.)	29	32	32	36	32	32	32

hood.[71] Only two of the men who figure in Table 2.1 received titles that were not knighthoods. They were John Lubbock and Richard B. Martin (1838–1916), the latter a financier and sometime MP active in the institute at the turn of the century, who was made a baronet in 1905. Comparable data on the Ordinary Fellows of the institute indicate what we would expect: they were a less distinguished lot than the society's elite.[72]

These data substantiate a generalization made earlier: the remarkable prominence of members of the anthropological community in learned and national circles before World War I assisted the legitimation of anthropology as a scholarly enterprise. They also suggest that as the discipline became increasingly professionalized after the war, its practitioners were more likely to achieve renown within their own specialized circles – and less as members of a national intelligentsia. My markers of public recognition produce a composite picture, since they indicate membership in groups of varying selectivity, denote recognition that came at different points in individuals' careers, and were awarded for various reasons. Persons were usually elected to the Royal Society in early middle age, coincident with the consolidation of their professional reputations, whereas those who were knighted, or the very few who served as presidents of the British Association, received these honors at the ends of their careers. Moreover, titles were conferred by the Crown for different reasons. Some were awarded to members of the anthropological community who were

[71] The others were Sir Cuthbert Peek (1855–1901), son of Sir Henry Peek, first baronet; R. R. Marett, son of (Sir) Robert Marett, and Sir Richard Carnac Temple (1850–1931), son of Sir Richard Temple, first baronet.
[72] Table A1.5, Appendix 1.

both distinguished scholars and public servants, such as John Lubbock. Others were given to men such as Harry Johnson (1858–1927), who was active in the exploration, pacification, and administration of Britain's colonies in east and central Africa and, although enjoying participation in learned societies, and a prolific author, received recognition as a public figure. Throughout the period covered by this study, the vast majority of anthropologists who received knighthoods did so in recognition of their scholarly achievements. But on the eve of World War II, there were no men among the RAI leadership who had been outstanding public servants. The precipitous decline in the percentage of knights among the institute's elite at this time indicates that anthropology had become a cloistered academic subject; in consequence of the withdrawal of public figures from anthropological circles, the discipline's academic practitioners were less in the public eye.[73]

Since anthropologists' careers demonstrated that public recognition would come to those who labored hard in the service of high ideals – the national welfare and scientific truth – it is hardly surprising that anthropologists' analyses celebrated the middle-class virtue of individual achievement. Moreover, data on the family backgrouds of members of the institute's officers and council indicate that anthropologists were of the classes whose social position depended on achievement. Those whose antecedents can be identified were largely of upper-middle-class and middle-class origins, with fathers who worked in a professional capacity or in commercial activity. The anthropologists whose fathers' occupations are unknown were quite possibly of rather more humble origins than the

---

[73] We can see the pattern of accumulation of rewards from the careers of some of our subjects. John Lubbock was elected to the Royal Society at twenty-four, became president of the British Association at forty-seven, and was elevated to the peerage at sixty-six. E. B. Tylor became a Fellow of the Royal Society at thirty-nine, and was knighted at eighty. Arthur Keith (1866–1955), a physical anthropologist employed by the Royal College of Surgeons, became a Fellow of the Royal Society at forty-seven, a knight at fifty-five, and president of the British Association at sixty-one. W. E. LeGros Clark (1895–1971), a physical anthropologist who eventually became professor of anatomy at Oxford, was elected to the Royal Society at forty, knighted at sixty, and served as president of the British Association at sixty-six. Social anthropologists born in the twentieth century were less likely to be elected to the Royal Society than their predecessors (although it had embraced such men as Frazer, whose contempt for efforts to reduce cultural phenomena to epiphenomena of physiological psychology was no less than that of the functionalists, as Ackerman tells us (see his *J. G. Frazer* 227). Nevertheless, they did receive knighthoods, and did so late in life, as was common; Evans-Pritchard, for example, was knighted at sixty-nine, and Raymond Firth at seventy-two. Parenthetically, of these men the only Atheneum members are Tylor and Firth.

Table 2.2. *Fathers' occupations of RAI officers and council*

	1883	1893	1900	1910	1920	1930	1938
Professional class (physicians, barristers/ solicitors,clergymen, military officers,engineers, schoolmasters,civil servants, architects,pharmacists, academics)	7	7	8	9	9	9	9
Commercial class (manufacturers; businessmen)	3	5	5	4	5	2	2
Financiers	4	3	2	3	0	0	0
Titled gentlemen	2[b]	2[b]	2[b]	2[b]	0	2	1
Miscellaneous[a]	1	1	1	2	2	1	1
Unknowns	13	15	15	17	17	18	19
Total officers and council	29	32	32	36	32	32	32

[a] In 1883, a handwriting instructor; in 1893, an untitled man of independent means; in 1900, a farmer; in 1910, a handwriting instructor and a farmer; in 1920, a handwriting instructor and a farmer; in 1930, a farmer; and in 1938, a farmer.
[b] In each of these columns, John Lubbock's father, a baronet, is counted twice–as a titled gentleman and a financier.

others; individuals themselves volunteered the information printed in such volumes as *Who's Who* and professional directories, and it seems appropriate to impute some conscious intention to obliterate the past on the part of the several men who concealed their own fathers' occupations while broadcasting the distinguished antecedents of their wives, or revealed nothing at all about their family connections.

Presuming that the data on roughly half of the RAI elite are adequate to plot general trends, we can judge that over time anthropology recruited an increasing proportion of its practitioners from professional families (see Table 2.2). As anthropology was itself professionalizing over time, this pattern suggests that both amateur and academic members of the anthropological community were increasingly likely to have careers that resembled those of their fathers. In 1883, half of the men whose fathers we can identify had careers of roughly the same type as their fathers'. For men born at the turn of the century, the lineaments of class became more

Table 2.3. *Professional scholars among the RAI officers and council*

	1883	1893	1900	1910	1920	1930	1938
Anthropologists	2	5	8	11	11	12	19
Natural scientists	4	4	4	3	2	1	4
Academic physicians	4	6	3	6	5	4	2
Other academics	1	0	1	5	5	2	1
Total	11	15	16	25	23	19	26

Table 2.4 *Occupations, RAI officers and council*

	1883	1893	1900	1910	1920	1930	1938
Professional scholars (employed by universities and museums)	11	15	16	25	23	19	26
Professional class (nonacademic physicians, barristers/solicitors, engineers, military officers, home and colonial civil servants, clergymen, accountants, schoolmasters)	8	6	7	9	8	9	2
Commercial class (manufacturers and businessmen)	3	1	2	0	1	1	0
Financiers	4	4	1	2	0	0	0
Political figures[a]	3	2	1	2	0	1	0
Leisured gentlemen	1	4	3	0	1	2	2
Women[b]	0	0	0	0	0	2	1
Miscellaneous[c]	1	1	0	0	2	2	1
No information	4	4	5	1	1	2	2
Total, officers and council	29	32	32	36	32	32	32

[a] Members of Parliament and politically active peers.

[b] Women of no known occupation, presumably either independently wealthy or supported by others.

[c] In 1883, a journalist; in 1938, a journalist; in 1920, an author and an industrial psychologist; in 1930, an author and a diplomat; and in 1938, an author.

restrictive. By 1938, over three-quarters of the members of the RAI elite were pursuing careers equivalent to those of their fathers.

From data on the occupations of the RAI elite themselves (Tables 2.3 and 2.4), it is evident that by the beginning of the twentieth century the anthropological enterprise was dominated by professional scholars, although until the interwar period the appointments they held were largely in fields other than anthropology. Clearly, there was more enthusiasm for anthropology in academic circles than a tabulation of the number of university positions in anthropology alone suggests. Nevertheless, amateurs remained a significant force in anthropology through the 1930s. Certainly, those members of anthropology's audience best placed to affect national decisions – political and financial figures – were an inconsequential component of the anthropological community after the turn of the century. But men from the professional classes remained a significant bloc in the institute's leadership until the eve of World War II. My samples of the institute's Ordinary Fellows may be unrepresentative (even though gathered by random sampling), but they suggest that those persons were a more diverse – and far less academic – lot than the society's leaders; the Ordinary Fellows did include a fairly sizable number of persons working in the colonies as missionaries or officials, however, and their interest in anthropology was obviously work-related.[74]

Many members of the anthropological community changed occupations during the course of their lifetimes, and I have recorded all of their occupations in my tables (see Tables 2.3 and 2.4). By so doing, I can identify a steadily declining tendency for individuals to shift from one occupation to another, a trend briefly interrupted around the 1930s, when a number of anthropologically oriented colonial officials found employment in the universities (then responding to the colonial services' new attitudes to anthropology). The careers of members of the anthropological community – whether as anthropologists or as practitioners of other occupations – exemplify a general social trend: the increasingly standardized pattern of middle-class lives.

Additional corroboration for the generalization that individual career patterns were becoming increasingly conventionalized is provided by available evidence on the higher education and/or vocational training of our subjects. Over time, they were less likely to move as students from one university to another, as Frazer and Haddon had done, for example; both took degrees at Cambridge, but Frazer took his degree first at Glasgow whereas Haddon's higher education began with evening classes at King's

---

[74] Table A1.6, Appendix 1.

College, London. And over time our subjects were less likely to guard against failure in one occupation by acquiring the credentials of another – to read law, say, as Frazer did.[75]

Conventionalized career patterns also meant diminishing opportunities for unconventional social types. To wit, although the percentage of persons on the RAI Council who had attended Oxford or Cambridge remained roughly the same in our specimen populations from 1910 onwards, the percentage of men who had prepared for one of these universities at an elite public school grew steadily.[76] These data explain an apparent paradox: while educational opportunities were expanding as a result of the new secondary schools created by the 1902 Education Act and the scholarship system instituted in 1907, it was popularly believed that it became harder for poor boys to go to Oxbridge after World War I.[77] The young person who would exploit expanded educational opportunities had now to set on a standardized course of upward mobility at a relatively young age.

As anthropology professionalized, its work became far less interesting to an amateur audience. By 1938, the leadership of the RAI was almost entirely composed of academics, and the bulk of its Ordinary Fellows were either academics or persons working in the colonies. Data available (at least for the RAI elite) on anthropologists' participation in all manner of other societies indicate this trend. Before the 1930s, roughly one-third of the amateurs among the elite belonged to societies concerned with civic affairs and/or public policy.[78] Obviously, they were a minority bloc in the discipline's leadership, but they were a very substantial minority. Evidently, while professional anthropologists were turning toward esoteric problems, the sorts of persons who had figured prominently in their general audience were drawing the conclusion that anthropology had little practical value – and perhaps also that it did not address general cultural issues.

[75] Table A1.4, Appendix 1.
[76] The public schools they attended were Charterhouse, Cheltenham, Dulwich, Eton, Edinburgh Academy, Haileybury, Harrow, Lancing, Marlborough, Merchant Taylor's, Radley, Rossall, Rugby, St. Paul's, Sherbourne, Tonbridge, University College School, Uppingham, Westminster, and Winchester. These schools did not carry equivalent social cachet, but they were all exclusive by whatever measures scholars of the social character of the public schools have used. The literature on the public schools is enormous. I have found especially useful J. R. deS. Honey, *Tom Brown's Universe* (New York, 1977), esp. 238–95. The fractions of elite public school products among the Oxbridge man were, for 1883, 4/5; 1893, 4/7; 1900, 6/9; 1910, 10/16; 1920, 7/10; 1930, 12/14; 1938, 10/13. On the 1938 council was a female Cambridge graduate, Lucy Mair, who went to St. Paul's Girls School.
[77] Perkin, *The Rise of Professional Society*, 165; Howarth, *Cambridge Between Two Wars*, 66.
[78] Table A1.2, Appendix 1.

The increasing remoteness of anthropology from general concerns was a function of both its growing dependence on the university and the steadily narrowing focus of its practitioners. Men born in the second quarter of the nineteenth century, such as E. B. Tylor and John Lubbock, required no university credentials to achieve considerable intellectual renown, and their scholarly interests were often highly diverse. Men born in the third quarter of the century, such as A. C. Haddon, W. H. R. Rivers, and J. L. Myres, rarely rose to prominence in the anthropological community unless they were academically employed, and in order to secure academic positions they needed either university or medical training. Yet the persons of this generation had diverse anthropological – and other scholarly – interests. Haddon, with a First Class Honours degree in natural science from Cambridge, moved from zoology into anthropology, undertaking both physical and social anthropological research and serving occasionally as the curator of Cambridge's Museum of Archaeology. Rivers, trained as a physician, worked in physiology, psychology, psychiatry, sociology, folklore, and social anthropology. Myres, with a First in classics from Oxford and eventually Wykeham professor of ancient history there, did archaeology, taught geography and classical literature, and wrote some notable essays on the history of anthropology which described social influences on the development of the discipline.

Prominent anthropologists born in the last quarter of the nineteenth century were highly specialized scholars. Consider the careers of three members of the RAI Council in 1938, by contrast with those of their teachers. A. R. Radcliffe-Brown, undertaking his first fieldwork in the Andaman Islands under the guidance of Haddon and Rivers, originally intended to describe both the physical and social characteristics of the Islands' inhabitants, but later abandoned his anthropometric research and became strictly a social anthropologist. V. Gordon Childe (1892–1957), a student of Arthur Evans and Myres at Oxford and eventually a professor of archaeology at the University of London, confined his scholarship to archaeology and prehistory (although he was unusually sensitive to the concerns of other sorts of anthropologists). G. M. Morant (1899–1964) was a student at the University of London of the polymath Karl Pearson. Throughout his career, Morant investigated physical anthropological problems. Unlike older anthropologists, these men ventured outside the world of academic research only when given specific commissions. Radcliffe-Brown was required to train colonial officials, and Morant was for a time employed by the Royal Air Force School of Aviation Medicine.[79]

---

[79] For brief biographical sketches of specimen members of the anthropological community, arranged by year of birth, see Appendix 2.

Conclusions

What relationships obtained between careers and theories? Anthropologists
born in the second and third quarters of the nineteenth century experienced normative inconsistency and dramatic change. The older of these
groups saw considerable confusion in their society's judgment of individuals; in a time of economic prosperity it permitted hardworking dissenters
to grow wealthy and yet set limits on their upward mobility – denying them
full participation in the scholarly life of the elite universities, for example.
Their work, evolutionist anthropology, stressed the uncoordinated course
of social change: the disparity between the progress that might be made by
specific classes or in certain spheres of material culture versus the irrational
attitudes and institutions that nevertheless persisted as "vestiges" of less
advanced culture. The second group witnessed the development of distinctive class identities, each with its specified occupational and behavioral
characteristics, each class defining its peculiar character in opposition to
the others. With their views reinforced by their observation of Britain's
participation in international conflicts, its actions as a colonial power and
party to World War I, they explained social change as the product of
conflicts between peoples of different cultures.

The divergent class relationships experienced by the two generations
explained their different views of race – which both confounded with class.
For evolutionist anthropologists, those physical differences that distinguished peoples and subpopulations could be altered through behavior,
just as class position could. Their successors were certainly able to point
to scientific evidence that corroborated their view that racial traits were
unaffected by environmental factors. But the hardening of class lines that
they witnessed seemed to substantiate their hereditarianism.[80] Their argument that race was unaffected by culture could be turned to both conservative and liberal purposes, as we shall see in time.

Anthropologists born at the turn of the century produced functionalist
accounts that described stable social orders in which an individual's character was formed by general cultural patterns. Their vision was shaped by
both the national experience and the structure middle-class careers had
assumed during their lifetimes. Their view of the individual reflected then-
current notions of the state's responsibilities toward its citizens. Living in
an era of considerable domestic and international strife, they imputed to
their subjects less troublesome existences than they themselves enjoyed –
wishful projections that anthropologists and general readers alike found

---

[80] For an argument similar to this one, see Douglas Lorimer, *Class, Colour and the
Victorians* (New York, 1978).

appealing. But their description of the life cycle of individuals in any given society surely derived from their own professional experiences, for they were negotiating a career course with specified sequential steps toward success – a course structurally similar to that of other middle-class careers. The very uncertainty of their career prospects during the interwar years must have intensified their concern to perform their occupational roles properly. By virtue of their own histories, the emigré scholars who figured so prominently in the functionalist cohort were probably especially prone to project a vision of stable order on whatever society they contemplated; attempting to adapt to British society, they looked for formulaic behavioral rules which they could easily learn. Nevertheless, they were right to judge British middle-class norms to be highly conventionalized.

The functionalists generalized their observations to all cultures. As Malinowski argued, the Trobriand Islanders were no different from the population of an "Eastern European ghetto, an Oxford College, or a Fundamentalist Middle West community."[81] In each of these societies, individuals gained the rights accorded full adult members as they learned to conform to cultural expectations. Whatever these expectations were, individuals were not free to choose not to internalize them – just as they were not responsible for their inherited physical traits. British society in the mid-twentieth century had eliminated many of the normative inconsistencies that had troubled the evolutionists, at the apparent cost of eliminating the creative eccentricities in individual adaptive behavior evolutionists considered essential to progress.

Thus, the reforms introduced in the nineteenth century in the cause of meritocratic ideals had paradoxical results in the twentieth century. The upwardly mobile fitted themselves into a social order that seemed to be extraordinarily stable, although it was in fact only of recent creation. And when they did so, they saw no special virtue in advertising the social distance they had traveled. The contradiction between meritocratic reality and self-presentation was notable in anthropology, not the least because as a growing field after World War I anthropology offered unusual opportunities for upward mobility to some of its practitioners. While their analyses of exotic cultures implied that none would have survived the processes of natural selection without the adaptive trait of meritocratic norms, they themselves were prone to affect upper-class airs. Malinowski boasted of his aristocratic Polish ancestry – although his paternal grandfather had lost the family lands and his childhood was spent in impoverished circumstances.[82]

[81] Malinowski, *Crime and Custom in Savage Society* (London, 1926), 52.
[82] For Malinowski's family history, see Crystyn Cech, "Malinowski: Edgar, Duke of Nevermore," *Journal of the Anthropological Society of Oxford* 12 (1981): 179; and

And Mr. Smith and Mr. Brown became Elliot Smith and Radcliffe-Brown.
That they chose to do so was indicative of the character of their milieu.
Theirs was not the style of their nineteenth-century intellectual forebears,
who observed that men of great distinction had emerged from "every social
grade, from the highest order in the peerage down to the factory hand and
simple peasant."[83] Evolutionist anthropologists certainly shared their
society's obsession with establishing orderly relations of dominance and
submission, but they insisted that what deference they were paid should be
granted in recognition of their achievements, not their lineage.

Grazyna Kubica, "Bronislaw Malinowski's Years in Poland," *Journal of the
Anthropological Society of Oxford* 17 (1986): 141.
[83] Galton, *English Men of Science* (see chap. 1, n. 28), 21.

Chapter 3

Civilization and its satisfactions

Before World War I, anthropologists assumed that explanations of human behavior were necessarily historical: current human characteristics had to be understood as products of the physical evolution of the human species and the development of social institutions. Both the evolutionists and the diffusionists, whom I treat in this chapter and the next, respectively, expected their research to yield laws of historical change. Evolutionists and diffusionists measured the repetitive rhythms of history differently, however, deriving generalizations about the pace of human evolution from the experiences of change provided in their particular eras.

The evolutionists described steady and gradual development, the expression of an inexorable progressive direction in history that was impeded only by irrational resistance to the inevitable. The diffusionists and their intellectual kin were to chart an episodic past – periods of stasis intermittently punctuated by moments of drastic change. The evolutionists' account rested on a premise diffusionists were to repudiate: the premise that human beings were naturally creative. Hence, evolutionists reasoned, progress was the sum product of innovations that were made every day by ordinary people, and were so slight as to be nearly imperceptible. "Nature is not full of incoherent episodes, like a bad tragedy," Tylor asserted, echoing Darwin; "nature never acts by leaps."[1] Because they saw a consistent pattern in history, evolutionists expected future developments to sustain established trends. And because their experience disposed them to evaluate historical trends positively, they were prepared to advocate social policies that would accelerate the pace of evolution.

It was axiomatic to their theory that all of nature was governed by the same inexorable laws, and that evolution was recognizable from specific developments. As Francis Galton wrote in 1883, "The whole of the living world moves steadily and continuously towards the evolution of races that are progressively more and more adapted to their complicated mutual needs and to their external circumstances."[2] All of nature exhibited the same

---

[1] E. B. Tylor, *Primitive Culture* (New York, 1889 [orig. London, 1871]), Vol. I, 2.
[2] Francis Galton, *Inquiries into Human Faculty* (London, 1883), 303.

adaptive mechanisms, whether exercised consciously or unconsciously. But conscious calculation played a greater role in adaptation the greater the distance an organism had traveled from the conditions of primeval slime, and, within human societies, the greater had been the progress from the earliest state of human existence. Evolutionary adaptation led to increasingly efficient use of resources.

For individual organisms and whole societies alike, efficiency entailed the development of functionally specialized parts that were smoothly coordinated: interlocking mechanisms within a single organism, interdependence between coevolved species, and cooperation between individuals in a society. Human beings were the most physically evolved of creatures because their diverse physiological needs were met by anatomically differentiated systems, which worked together harmoniously. Human social evolution was marked by the progressive division of labor. A highly refined division of labor elicited from individuals both their greatest talents and their capacity to act as moral beings: they performed for society the services they were as individuals best suited to provide; and, because they were incapable of doing very much for themselves, they were obliged to engage in mutual aid if they were to survive. Moreover, efficiency in social organization led to even higher levels of efficiency: as rationally purposive behavior assumed a greater role in human affairs, the pace of evolution accelerated.

Evolutionists saw the same historical processes in evidence in Britain as they found elsewhere. The personal histories and objectives of the founders of the Anthropological Institute indicated the sorts of changes evolutionists regarded as signs of a general pattern of progress: one, the application of scientific principles to the solution of diverse problems, effecting improved living conditions; two, the determination of individuals' social rank on the basis of their achievements, leading to an enlarged role for the most productive individuals in the direction of societal affairs; three, the differentation of specialized professional careers, and the recognition that trained experts should be given jurisdiction in specific social spheres. Evolutionists were critical of many features of late-Victorian culture, but so many of its constituent elements apparently attested to the imminent realization of their middle-class ideal that their analyses might seem to have confounded the actual with the possible. Nevertheless, they wrote as much to direct their society as to celebrate it.

Much of evolutionist theory can be read as justification for the reforms so important to the professionalizing classes in the late nineteenth century. And when anthropologists during this period prosecuted the cause of their discipline – campaigning for university positions and the mooted imperial bureau, and constituting the Anthropological Institute in a form conducive to both free intellectual competition and gradual change – they acted on the precepts they derived from observations framed in evolutionist terms. But evolutionists' observational sphere and practical ambitions extended far beyond the social world of their class, evidently comprehending all forms of life. While many of the trends anthropologists identified were linked to their occupational interests, the linkages between the general and the particular were often indirect. In this chapter, then, I explicate both the reasons why evolutionists' descriptions seemed realistic to their readers and evolutionists' purposes – the general cultural patterns their model seemed to explain and some practical issues anthropologists addressed.

I describe evolutionists' model in schematic fashion, defining a general line of reasoning and ignoring the eccentric deviations from it entertained by individual practitioners. Evolutionist theory admitted of baroque variation, and a reader of nineteenth-century anthropological argument may be tempted to assess it so intellectually muddled as to defy outline – rendered schematic only by those such as W. H. R. Rivers, who caricatured it in 1911 when he announced to the British Association for the Advancement of Science that he could no longer accept it.[3] But evolutionist research was guided by recognizable principles. While late-nineteenth-century thinkers were apt to articulate evolutionist theory most clearly when they described the methodological difficulties of its application to data analysis, they still affirmed its explanatory power.[4]

Evolutionist theory derived from an ancient tradition. Nevertheless, when nineteenth-century thinkers took up this tradition, they reshaped it to fit their circumstances. Some attention must be paid to the modifications they made in order to understand their purposes. Nevertheless, the intellectual lineage of the evolutionist model is practically irrelevant to an explanation of its appeal for anthropologists. I argue that they found it believable for three reasons. First, the anthropological community's division of labor – the allocation of different research tasks within the population – fostered acceptance of evolutionist assumptions. Second, all manner of social trends apparently confirmed evolutionist hypotheses. Third, anthropologists advocated particular policies, and found mandates for them in the natural laws evolutionist theory defined. I discuss some of the anthropologists' most important causes here. Because evolutionist

---

[3] See, for example, W. H. R. Rivers, "The Ethnological Analysis of Culture," 1911 Presidential Address, Section H of the British Association for the Advancement of Science, *Nature* 87 (1911): 356–60.

[4] See, for example, G. Lawrence Gomme, "On the Method of Determining the Value of Folk-Lore as Ethnological Data," Appendix to the *Fourth Report of the British Association for the Advancement of Science Committee on the Ethnographical Survey of the United Kingdom* (London, 1896), 626–56.

notions suffused Victorian culture, full documentation of the relationship between anthropological ideas and social practices in nineteenth-century Britain would require many volumes.

The evolutionists' creed

Some essential features of the anthropological model employed by late nineteenth- and early twentieth-century anthropologists were outlined by Aristotle and elaborated by Christian theologians. In sum, these thinkers believed that all of the world's societies could be arrayed on an ascending scale of civilization. The stage along this scale that any given society had reached could be determined by assessing both the character of its political structure and the quality of its citizens' conduct: the more advanced a society, the greater the degree to which it assigned power to the occupants of formal political offices and the more elaborated and orderly was the hierarchy in which these offices were arrayed; the more advanced a society, the greater the degree to which individuals' behavior was the product of reason rather than emotion. That a polity had attained a high level of development was revealed by its citizens' obedience to an articulated legal code, which could not have been promulgated in the absence of a language nuanced to express fine moral distinctions. The higher the moral standards of a population, the more readily it would recognize the truths of Christian doctrine when it happened to be exposed to them, since it had already apprehended a close approximation of Christian truth. Questions about the precise character of a society could be determined by use of what was to be termed the "comparative method": missing information about any given population could be supplied from knowledge about other societies judged in the same stage of development.[5]

From ancient times to the Victorian era, then, questions about the course of natural history and the perfectibility of humankind had been couched in theological terms, and evolutionists were obsessed with theological issues. George Stocking has calculated that Victorian anthropologists devoted a substantial proportion of their attention to analysis of the

---

[5] As John Burrow points out, the intellectual lineage of this framework can be traced back almost indefinitely. See his *Evolution and Society* (Cambridge, 1966), 11. On the precursors to evolutionist theory in the early modern period, see Anthony Pagden, *The Fall of Natural Man: The American Indian and the Origins of Comparative Ethnology* (Cambridge, 1982). For a summary account of the entire tradition of evolutionist thought, see Kenneth Bock, "Theories of Progress, Development, Evolution," in Tom Bottomore and Robert Nisbet, eds., *A History of Sociological Analysis* (New York, 1978), 39–79.

social-psychological foundations of religious belief (only questions about the development of marriage customs engaged them to an equal degree).[6] In the aggregate, however, their attitude to religion was hostile. Anthropologists intended to repudiate Christianity, "theologians all to expose," as E. B. Tylor and Andrew Lang (1844–1912) jointly declared.[7] "The resemblance of many of the savage customs and ideas to the fundamental doctrines of Christianity is striking," J. G. Frazer observed, implying that modern peoples should reject these doctrines as irrational.[8] Many prominent Victorian anthropologists were of dissenting origins, their families having rejected the ritual and beliefs of the established church, and they may well have judged uncompromising opposition to religion to be the continuation of a progressive trend. In their day, "to be an anthropologist was generally considered equivalent to being an agnostic and a free-thinker," as the writers of a memorial tribute to A. C. Haddon observed.[9]

Evolutionists agreed with Frazer that the legal and moral precepts fundamental to civilization – "the rights of property and the sanctity of the marriage tie" – had their origins in religious sentiments, but argued that in the modern world such sentiments represented "the sour crabs and empty husks of popular superstition on which the swine of modern society are still content to feed."[10] To be sure, not all anthropologists were equally vehement. Francis Galton and John Lubbock, for example, were reluctant to dismiss Christian doctrine altogether.[11] But they were not proponents of traditional religiosity. Lubbock proclaimed that "the love of God is best shown by the love of man," and Galton was certain that whatever deity might exist was unsusceptible to human entreaties, documenting his belief with a statistical survey that demonstrated the inefficacy of prayer in curing the sick and dying.[12]

Yet, vestiges of Christian doctrine remained in the evolutionists' account of human development. Certainly, they repudiated the theologically derived assumption that the social behavior of backward peoples preserved the base

---

[6] George W. Stocking, Jr., *Victorian Anthropology* (New York, 1987), 188.

[7] Quoted in Ibid., 190–1.

[8] J. G. Frazer in a letter to his publisher, George MacMillan, November 8, 1889, Macmillan Collection, Frazer Correspondence, British Museum.

[9] A. M. Quiggin and E. S. Fegan, "Alfred Cort Haddon, 1855–1940," *Man* 40 (1940): 97. For an analysis of this anthropological generation's concern to expose many, if not all, religious practices as foolish by the standards of scientific reasoning, see Paul L. F. Heelas, "Intellectualism and the Anthropology of Religion," D.Phil. dissertation, Oxford University, 1974.

[10] Quoted in Ackerman (see chap. 1, n. 14), *J. G. Frazer*, 71.

[11] Galton's views are quoted in Pearson, *Galton* (see chap. 1, n. 26), Vol. II, 425. On Lubbock see Stocking, *Victorian Anthropology*, 151.

[12] John Lubbock, *The Use of Life* (London, 1894), 301; and see Daniel J. Kevles, *In the Name of Eugenics* (New York, 1985), 11.

condition into which mankind was plunged by the original Fall from God's grace. And by insisting that all natural change was gradual, they rejected "catastrophism" – the explanation of change as the product of occasional intervention in worldly affairs by a capricious deity. Nevertheless, because they described human evolution as some function of environmental factors, and assumed natural resources to be bounded, they advanced an argument in which nature replaced original sin as the limiting constraint on human perfectibility.

This argument had been formulated at the end of the eighteenth century by the clergyman Thomas Malthus as a refutation of Enlightenment assertions that there were no limits to the possibilities of human improvement through the exercise of reason. In the middle of the nineteenth century, Malthusianism was transmuted into the principle of natural selection by Charles Darwin and Alfred Russel Wallace.[13] But theirs were exercises hardly outside the long established province of natural theologians, who saw in nature revelation of the wisdom of God's plan. Indeed, many evolutionists resembled Malthus's theological opponents, seeing more benevolence than cruelty in the design of nature.[14] Moreover, natural theologians had seen the act of nature study as the ideal vehicle for developing moral sensibility, and the worship of beauty in nature was one of the few aesthetic pleasures sober reformers such as the intellectual aristocracy permitted themselves.[15]

Furthermore, when the evolutionists postulated the "psychic unity" of all mankind, they promulgated a secularized version of a creed once framed in religious terms. That is, they insisted that human beings everywhere shared the same biologically grounded intellectual and psychological characteristics. "The savage is possessed of human reason and speech," they observed, indicating that his "brain-power . . . enables him to receive more or less of the education which transforms him into a civilized man." In the second third of the nineteenth century, the anthropological community had been sharply divided between those who argued that the races of mankind were separate species and those who maintained that all races were variants of a single species; evolutionists took the latter position, while factoring out the appeal to the biblical story of creation that had been essential to its original construction.[16]

---

[13] Robert M. Young, *Darwin's Metaphor* (Cambridge, 1985), 23–55.

[14] See David Elliston Allen, *The Naturalist in Britain* (London, 1976). For a nearly Panglossian description of the wisdom of nature, see John Lubbock, *British Wild Flowers Considered in Relation to Insects* (London, 1882).

[15] Annan, "Intellectual Aristocracy" (see chap. 1, n. 29), 251.

[16] The quotation is from E.B. Tylor, *Anthropology* (London, 1892, revised [orig. 1881]), 54; and see Stocking, "What's in a Name?" (see chap. 2, n. 39).

Evidently, what distinguished evolutionist theory from its theological precursors was its substitution of biological explanations for judgments of individual and cultural variation that had been previously rendered in moral terms. Describing social progress as a product of the efforts of biologically driven human beings to cope with their natural environment, evolutionists' scheme enjoyed wide currency subsequent to the publication of Darwin's theory, which anthropologists were wont to invoke. Nevertheless, social evolutionists relied on a model of humankind's biological nature that owed as much to Lamarck and Spencer as to Darwin – or, at least, to Darwin as he came to be understood. That is, they charted a teleological, not unpredictable course of evolution, and they made little use of the concept of natural selection.

Moreover, they believed in the inheritance of acquired characteristics, calculating that the more frequently individuals performed learned habits the more deeply these habits were ingrained in their biological natures, to be transmitted to their children. Of course, Darwin himself employed use-inheritance to explain evolution, particularly when he analyzed the development of human mental and moral qualities, and the publication of the *Origin of Species* in 1859 did not immediately effect a theoretical revolution. For at least a half a century thereafter, prominent biological scientists as well as anthropologists continued to describe the inheritance of acquired characteristics, and, indeed, some naturalists counted Darwin's accounts of the operation of this transformist mechanism among his more important contributions.[17]

Opinion about the mechanism of inheritance varied somewhat within the anthropological community. The average anthropologist's view was closer to Spencer's than to Galton's. Spencer maintained in 1887 that the extraordinarily rapid progress society was making demonstrated that acquired characteristics were inherited.[18] The same evidence suggested opposite conclusions to Galton: "Sudden eras of great intellectual progress cannot be due to any alteration in the natual faculties of the race," he wrote in 1883, "because there has not been time for that"; rather, altered circumstances elicited productive application of inherited aptitudes that had not previously been exploited.[19] The popularizer of the distinction between nature and nurture, Galton regarded inherent human traits as practically unaffected by environmental factors, as other figures who were

---

[17] My identification of Lamarckist tendencies in British anthropology owes much to George W. Stocking, Jr., "Lamarckianism in American Social Science, 1890–1915," in his *Race, Culture and Evolution* (New York, 1968), 234–69, although in this essay Stocking treats a scholarly population different from mine.

[18] Quoted in Young, *Darwin's Metaphor*, 51.

[19] Galton, *Human Faculty*, 179.

also concerned primarily with physical anthropology rather than with cultural analysis were likewise inclined to do.

Perhaps seeking to reconcile Lamarckists and Darwinians, Tylor conjured up a historicist formulation in which both of their explanations of heredity had some justification: susceptibility to modification by environmental influences was a trait the human species lost through civilization, and observed changes in populations of given areas were best explained as consequences of breeding between people of different stocks, brought together by migrations. But Tylor himself was incapable of sustaining this line of reasoning, pointing to such recent environmentally induced changes in physical type as had been witnessed among the children of British migrants from rural to urban areas, and among the descendants of Africans and Europeans found in the United States.[20] No evolutionist anthropologist entirely dispensed with Lamarckist explanations, however. Galton himself resorted to them when accounting for the development of humankind's higher moral qualities (as did his cousin Darwin), describing "inherited conscience" as "the organized result of social experiences of many generations."[21] It was only thus that he could account for the direction of human history. And Galton's disagreement with Spencer did not extend to a dispute over the end product of evolution. Like other members of the anthropological community, they agreed that the evolutionary process transformed human beings into moral creatures; originally selfish, they eventually became naturally altruistic.[22]

Psychic unity was the common denominator of evolutionists' arguments. Though evolutionists granted – indeed, insisted – that all of the world's peoples could be graded according to their propensity to reason soundly, they argued that people's mental capacities differed by degrees rather than kind. In all ages and places, social institutions had been developed by persons acting purposively on the basis of rational judgments, although their reasoned decisions might have rested on false premises. If all persons were endowed with the innate abilities that had enabled some peoples to develop civilized institutions, given the stimulation to do so, it followed that when diverse peoples gradually acquired the habits of civilization they were likely to do so through the process of "independent invention"; civilized practices were the natural choices of human beings functioning as adaptive creatures. This was not to suggest that every one of the world's cultures was necessarily in the process of evolution, for in the absence of novel

---

[20] Tylor, *Anthropology*, 73–86.
[21] Galton, *Human Faculty*, 212.
[22] Ibid., 300.

stimuli a people who had achieved perfect adaptation to their environment would not modify their way of life.[23]

Environmental factors constrained evolution by affecting its pace but not its direction. In the process of adapting to their environment, individuals acquired characteristics that were transmitted to their descendants, but ecological peculiarities did not lead peoples to develop idiosyncratic behavioral and biological characteristics without parallel in other cultures. The course of human evolution was teleological. The necessity of environmental adaptation was the stimulus to the realization of humankind's innate potential, which was naturally expressed in an ordered sequence of stages of maturation. From the axiom that "like causes produce like effects," it followed that the course of evolutionary advance was everywhere the same. Because peoples who had attained equivalent levels of social development reasoned in equivalent fashion, they would effect evolutionary advance in equivalent manner. To be sure, peoples might acquire new cultural elements by "diffusion," through contact with other peoples. Nonetheless the pace of evolutionary advance was hardly quickened when peoples learned from one another. That is, no matter how a people came to adopt new practices, they did not do so until they were ready for them; their adoption of specific customs indicated that their culture was animated by the mental outlook characteristic of the phase of evolution in which these customs appeared.

Evidently, a model of individual psychology was at the core of evolutionists' explanation of social change. They understood the culture of a group as the psychology of its individual members writ large. The dynamics of individual psychological development showed that maturation was a process of socialization into group habits. Because all peoples progressed along the same course of development of civilization, the maturation process of all individuals recapitulated the evolutionary history of the groups to which they belonged. Therefore, whatever distinctions obtained between individuals and societies were differences of degree. Individuals and societies could be ranked relative to one another according to the stage of development they had reached, which was a consequence of the rate at which they had evolved.[24]

---

[23] See, for example, John Lubbock, *The Origin of Civilisation and the Primitive Condition of Man* (Chicago, 1978 [orig. 1870]), 325–62; E. B. Tylor, "On the Tasmanians as Representatives of Paleolithic Man," *Journal of the Anthropological Institute* 23 (1893): 150.

[24] See, for example, E. W. Brabrook, "Presidential Address to Section H of the British Association, 1898," *Nature* 58 (1898): 527–32; A. E. Crawley, "Totemism Unveiled," *Nature* 84 (1910): 31–2; A. C. Haddon, "The Ethnography of the Western Tribes of the Torres Straits," *Journal of the Anthropological Institute* 19 (1888–9): 297–444; A. W. Howitt, "Further Notes on Australian Class Systems," *Journal of the Anthropological*

Each stage of evolution was represented as an integrated culture complex, an amalgam of interdependent habits, beliefs, and social structures. However irrational or cruel given features of early phases of evolution appeared to modern observers, these features were necessary elements of "primitive" cultures, and the maturation process of societies (as well as of individuals) required ordered passage through each of its developmental stages. Hence, anthropologists relying on the comparative method could use information available about any society classified in a given stage of evolution to supplement knowledge of other societies judged to have reached an equivalent level of development. Apparently incongruous elements in a people's culture did not threaten the evolutionists' historicist scheme, for they could be identified as yet-uneradicated "survivals" of earlier phases of the society's developmental history, portents of future trends, or isolated culture traits somehow acquired from other peoples.[25]

Evolutionists equated rationality and morality, assuming that societies' capacity to effect material advance through scientific management of human and natural resources increased in conjunction with their progressive repression (or thorough eradication) of their populations' base animal instincts. Hence, evolutionists collapsed all of the dimensions of human variation onto a single axis. By their unitary standard, it was possible to rank all of the members of a single population and all of the societies that had ever existed. By their standard, it was possible to equate contemporary primitives, the ancestors of modern Europeans, the Classical Ancients, European peasants, and the residents of Britain whose behavior was somehow pathological – criminals, the

---

Institute 18 (1888): 40, 66; W. H. R. Rivers, The Todas (London, 1906), 4; Tylor, Anthropology, 432–4. E. B. Tylor, "Presidential Address to Section H of the British Association for the Advancement of Science, 1884," Nature 30 (1884): 451. For a historian's account of the place of diffusionist explanations in evolutionists' schemes see George W. Stocking, Jr., "Matthew Arnold, E. B. Tylor, and the Uses of Invention," American Anthropologist [n.s.] 65 (1963): 788–9.

[25] The comparative method was not peculiar to anthropologists, but was characteristic of all varieties of nineteenth-century social science. See, for one discussion, Stefan Collini, Donald Winch, and John Burrow, That Noble Science of Politics (Cambridge, 1983), esp. 209–46. For some anthropological statements of faith in the method's utility, see R. R. Marett, ed., Anthropology and the Classics (Oxford, 1908), esp. Gilbert Murray, "Anthropology and the Greek Epic Traditions Outside Homer," 68–91; E. B. Tylor, "Anniversary Address," Presidential Address to the Anthropological Institute, Journal of the Anthropological Institute 21 (1891–2): 400; James George Frazer, Folk-Lore in the Old Testament (London, 1919), vii–xi. For one illustration of the intellectual sleights of hand that could be performed to explain incongruous elements in cultures supposed to be at a given stage of development, see E. B. Tylor, "On a Method of Investigating the Development of Institutions Applied to Laws of Marriage and Descent," Journal of the Anthropological Institute 18 (1888): 245–72.

The physical homogeneity of populations of backward peoples: the Caribs as represented in E. B. Tylor's *Anthropology* (1892). He remarks on the facing page, "The people whom it is easiest to represent by single portraits are uncivilized tribes, in whose food and way of life there is little to cause difference between one man and another."

insane, and the chronically unemployed "residuum."

The primitives of other cultures, and within Britain, were all represented as examples of incomplete realization of human potential. All of these relationships were analogous: primitives to Europeans; children to adults; women to men; the poor to the elite. When children grew to maturity, their development recapitulated both the moral and material history of the race; while negotiating the moral stages of past ages, they played with the tools of their ancestors – the bow and arrow used by the hunter, and the rattle of the witchdoctor. Evolution was still proceeding in modern society, led by its accomplished and virtuous elite. In sum, humans in a state of nature participated in a "Hobbesian war of each against all"; and the "history of civilization [was] the record of attempts which the human race has made to escape from this position." Among relatively primitive peoples, the growth of a sense of obligation to act to protect the poor and helpless in their midst heralded the emergence of the altruistic sensibility that distinguished advanced societies.[26]

Analogies among primitives, children, the underclass, women were accurate because physical and cultural evolution were interdependent. Racial characteristics were not only determinants of culture but also were themselves determined by all aspects of individuals' and peoples' cultures: willful behavior, traditional practices, material possessions, and natural surroundings. Because physical and behavioral development were correlated, parallel distinctions could be made among groups of people and among individuals within societies. The social class of an individual was a function of his or her level of achieved maturity. Thus, viewed in the aggregate, non-Western peoples were like the children of European societies, but their societies were differentiated; their ruling classes were closer to British gentlemen in manners and attitudes than were their subordinate folk. A similar pattern of individual variation obtained within modern societies. Children of advanced societies resembled primitive peoples, with flat noses, forward-opening nostrils, wide-set eyes, large mouths, and undeveloped frontal sinuses. And the lower orders in Britain displayed physical capabilities of strength and endurance that their social superiors had lost during the course of their maturation into rational beings.[27]

How did modern man emerge, Tylor asked, replacing the "wildman of the forest, forgetful of yesterday and careless of tomorrow ... so wanting in

---

[26] The quotation is from Thomas H. Huxley, *Social Diseases and Worse Remedies* (London, 1891), 21–2, 34.

[27] For some examples see John Beddoe, "Anniversary Address," Presidential Address to the Anthropological Institute, *Journal of the Anthropological Institute* 20 (1890–1): 348–59; George Harley, "Comparison Between the Recuperative Bodily Power of Man in a Rude and in a Highly Civilized State Illustrative of the Probably Recuperative Capacity of Men of the Stone Age in Europe, *Journal of the Anthropological Institute* 17 (1887–8): 108–18; C. Hose, "The Natives of Borneo," *Journal of the Anthropological Institute* 23 (1894): 171; H. Ling Roth, "On the Signification of Couvade," *Journal of the Anthropological Institute* 22 (1892–3): 204–6; John Venn, "Cambridge Anthropometry," *Journal of the Anthropological Institute* 18 (1888): 140–54; Galton, *Human Faculty*, 245. For Spencer's account of the physical maturation of the child, see the description in Bruce Haley, *The Healthy Body and Victorian Culture* (Cambridge, Mass., 1978), 92.

foresight to resist passion and temptation, that the moral balance of a tribe easily goes wrong?"[28] Differences of opinion among anthropologists over the details of evolution rarely led to disputes about its significant features – the cultivation of habits of mind that made modern man accept high moral and rational standards; and the overall pattern in which clusters of social institutions developed in turn, each cluster both reflecting and shaping emergent mental advance. Anthropologists agreed that the development of humankind's intellectual capabilities was fundamental to evolution. Primitives' understanding of the forces that shaped their environment was imperfect. Their world was animated by the spirits of the dead and by nature powers – whimsical forces that could be influenced through magic. However they had achieved this end state, modern peoples appreciated that the natural world was subject to invariant laws. They recognized that they could control their environment only if they could determine natural laws through scientific observation, and thus learn to predict the effects of their actions. Hence, when modern peoples worshipped they acknowledged a single, unmovable god, and their worship was purged of magical ritual.

Changes in family structure were basic to the evolution of social institutions, and these changes exemplified humankind's growing moral sense and rational understanding. Primitive peoples had loose morals and no comprehension of biological relationships. Whatever the primordial form of the family (a much debated issue), it was different from the monogamous union found in modern society. Descent was reckoned through the mother, both because the mechanics of reproduction were not understood and because loose behavioral norms resulted in uncertainty about childrens' parentage. Kinship relations were vague, denoted by "classificatory" kin terminology that identified groups of people who played the social roles that in modern societies were restricted to individuals with specified biological relationships; for example, all coresident women of one generation might be addressed and treated as "mother" by all members of the next generation. The monogamous family developed as understanding of reproductive biology grew. Modern marital unions were sanctioned by religious and not civil law, denoting recognition that family members were bound together by moral obligations and not merely practical purposes. Moreover, once the biological role of the father was understood, his responsibilities became clear; he was obliged to exercise benevolent authority over his family and to satisfy women's special needs for protection.

Concomitant with changes in family structure were changes in economic and political organization. Primitive peoples were unsettled in habitation and undisciplined in labor, living by hunting, fishing, and gathering wild

---

[28] Tylor, *Anthropology*, 407–8.

plants. Becoming pastoralists and settled agriculturalists, they developed notions of private property and became more productive through the division of labor, their efforts yielding a surplus. This surplus supported the development of material culture and the elaboration of social stratification – the growth of significant individual differences of wealth and power within populations. As social changes engendered the institution of private property, persons recognized the obligations of individual responsibility. The division of labor encouraged the growth of individuality per se – the opportunity for individuals to exploit their particular talents and develop refined skills.

Among the delimited roles characteristic of modernizing societies was that of political leader, whose function was to coordinate the specialized activities of the members of a differentiated society. The political leader's importance grew with the rise of the state. The state was a natural accretion, the product of fusion of families into clans, clans into tribes, and tribes into nations. With evolution, the office of political leader became hereditary. Yet, paradoxically, as succession to kingship became routinized, the occupant of the office lost real power. Hereditary kings presided over burgeoning state bureaucracies, which articulated the popular will and in various ways constrained the kings' freedom of action.[29]

The theoretical structure and methodological strictures of evolutionist anthropology represented a clear research program. Using the comparative method to extract maximum value from their data, anthropologists worked to specify the details of the developmental process they had outlined – the characteristics of each of the stages of evolution and the mechanics of societal transition from one stage to another. Indeed, although various factors conspired to discredit the evolutionist paradigm in the second decade of the twentieth century, its demise was at least in part a consequence of directed research. Accumulated evidence was sufficient to

---

[29] The general model presented here is so general as to defy specific attribution. On the family in particular, see Tylor, "On a Method of Investigating the Development of Institutions Applied to Laws of Marriage and Descent." On the development of occupational specialization, see Herbert Spencer, "Professional Institutions," *Popular Science Monthly* 47 (1895): 34–8, 164–75, 364–74, 433–45, 594–602, 739–48. On the emergence of the state, see Andrew Lang, "The Primitive and Advanced in Totemism," *Journal of the Anthropological Institute* 15 (1905): 315–36; Andrew Lang, "Tribe and Family," *Fortnightly Review* 80 (1903): 782–91; N. W. Thomas, *Kinship Organization and Group Marriage in Australia* (Cambridge, 1906), 111–2, 127–37. On the development of the institution of the monarchy, see J. G. Frazer, *The Golden Bough* (2nd ed., London, 1894), Vol. I, 208–10 and passim; Herbert Spencer, "Political Forms and Forces and 'Political Heads–Chiefs, Kings, Etc.'," *Fortnightly Review* 35 (1881): 271–84, 521–33, 650–61; Tylor, *Anthropology*, 429–38.

resolve many of the problems raised by the evolutionist model, confirming some hypotheses and disconfirming others, and new anthropological schemes satisfactorily addressed those problems that could not be resolved within the evolutionist framework.[30]

The social structure of evolutionist research

The ties that linked members of the anthropological community were informal in the nineteenth century. Today, it might seem surprising that anthropologists then were capable of collective pursuit of specific research objectives, given that they did not have the experiences that now mold scholars into members of self-conscious, professional groups – groups within which practitioners may differ over specific issues but still are in fundamental agreement about the nature of their fields' research problems

[30] Despite anthropology's lack of institutionalization in the nineteenth century, its practitioners were engaged in puzzle solving. Indeed, the propositions of evolutionist anthropologists may have been more susceptible to refutation than those of their successors. Judgments of the degree to which this community of scholars – or any other group – are working in concert to solve collectively-identified puzzles are bound to differ. For views contrary to mine, see Ian Langham, *The Building of British Social Anthropology* (Boston, 1981), 19; Stocking, *Victorian Anthropology*, 257–62. I would argue that a study such as Hobhouse, Wheeler, and Ginsburg's (1915; see chap. 1, n. 33) could not have been produced without decades of concerted effort to document evolutionist generalizations – and that this study could not have been framed as a refutation of many evolutionist assumptions unless it was clear what these assumptions were. Nor was this the only study of its type, although it was the most systematic one. Using Australian data, N. W. Thomas revealed inconsistencies in evolutionist argument, and Bronislaw Malinowski constructed a new functionalist synthesis – before he had set forth in the field. See Thomas, *Kinship Organization and Group Marriage in Australia*; Bronislaw Malinowski, *The Family Among the Australian Aborigines* (London, 1913).

Some intractable evolutionist puzzles remained unsolved by such a summary of accumulated ethnographic evidence; to these, the new anthropological schools addressed solutions. One such puzzle was the existence of kinship systems that mixed matriarchal and patriarchal principles, defying the evolutionist prediction that patriarchy would displace matriarchy. One solution to this puzzle was presented by the diffusionists, who argued that different methods of reckoning kinship relationships within a given society represented legacies of migrations of peoples with different social systems to a given area; see Rivers, "The Ethnological Analysis of Culture." Another solution was proposed by the functionalists, who argued that different kinship relationships served different societal needs for the maintenance of orderly relationships among individuals, whose positions in the social structure might otherwise lead to conflict; see A. R. Radcliffe-Brown, "The Mother's Brother in South Africa," in *Structure and Function in Primitive Society* (New York, 1965 [essay orig. 1924]), 15–31.

and about the criteria used to judge whether problems' solutions are
satisfactory. In the nineteenth century, individuals joined the disciplinary
community without first undergoing a common course of intellectual
socialization. And the community had no exclusionary mechanisms save
public disapproval – no screening procedures that limited access to membership in learned societies; no significant punitive sanctions (such as
loss of livelihood) that might be imposed on those whose opinions fell
outside the range of diversity tolerated by the majority. Nevertheless,
late-nineteenth-century anthropologists did manage to define and resolve
research problems. That they did demonstrates as well as anything can that
their identity as a group derived from their common historical experience,
which gave them a sense of shared purpose. And that they did surely
indicated to evolutionist anthropologists themselves that their vision of
social order effected through voluntary cooperation was realizable.

The constitution of the anthropological community shaped the character
of its work, however. It fostered an epistemological outlook and a division
of disciplinary labor – Baconianism and distinct roles for foot soldiers who
collected data and the scholars who interpreted them. The recognized elite
members of the anthropological community were armchair scholars, who
analyzed data that had been collected by others. Scholars' understanding of
human physical variation depended in large part on interpretation of bones
– and occasional live specimens – brought to Britain from exotic parts.[31]
Their descriptions of human social variation made use of every possible
source of information about human behavior, past and present. Scholars
also undertook to elicit the sort of evidence they wanted. Sometimes they
circulated privately printed questionnaires. Sometimes, under the auspices
of their learned societies, they conspired to direct their potential field
agents. For example, at irregular intervals, the Anthropological Institute
and the British Association together issued *Notes and Queries on Anthropology for the Use of Travellers and Residents in Uncivilized Lands*. This book-
length questionnaire, the first version of which appeared in 1874, was in
each instance produced as a collaborative effort by the leading anthropological lights of the day.

To be sure, prominent members of the anthropological community such
as Galton, Huxley, and Tylor had as young men undertaken journeys on
which they encountered exotic peoples, but an episode of field exploration
was not a necessary stage in an anthropologist's career. Frazer achieved
his considerable reputation without ever leaving Europe, although he did

---

[31] See, for example, the report of the Anthropological Institute's meeting of April 26,
1887, including "Exhibition of Natives of Queensland, by Mr. R. A. Cunningham,"
Journal of the Anthropological Institute 17 (1887): 83–4.

venture as far from home as Greece (which, given his interests, might be counted as fieldwork). None of these men, however, had qualms about using data collected by others on the customs of places they had never visited. Frazer, for example, made use of all manner of information he acquired from extensive reading, as well as responses to questionnaires he circulated among missionaries, colonial administrators, travelers, and others.[32]

Setting tasks for their unknown collaborators, elite anthropologists of necessity presumed that it was possible to collect facts that were in no way contaminated by theories. Theirs was a position characteristic of practitioners of all varieties of natural history in the nineteenth century, although anthropologists clung to it rather longer than others. Geologists and biologists – Charles Darwin the most distinguished among them – who undertook theoretical synthesis of information also relied in large part on material they solicited or found. Frazer clearly articulated their methodological assumptions. Although he could speak eloquently of the value of analysis based on the researcher's own fieldwork, he defended his own methods by arguing that the separation of the roles of data gatherer and synthesizer served the goal of truly scientific analysis: devoid of theoretical bias, the person in the field would not be tempted to report only such evidence as supported his or her hypotheses; having not gathered their data themselves, scholars could consider impartially the material available to them.[33]

Dependent as they were on an unseen army of amateur collectors, scholars were practically obliged to assume that observers could confront the natural world without intellectual biases – indeed, that significant information would present itself to naive observers. Most important, their research organization conformed to the social pattern they saw as the basis of all progress, not just scientific advance. To wit, anyone who wished to participate in their enterprise could make a contribution to knowledge, however small, and the accumulated product of the efforts of many would eventually yield meaning to the experienced analyst. The structure of their research represented in microcosm the meritocratic order they wished to

---

[32] See J. G. Frazer, "Questions on the Manners, Customs, Religious Superstitions, &C of Uncivilized and Semi-Civilized Peoples," *Journal of the Anthropological Institute* 18 (1888): 431–9. For one discussion of the general structure of natural history research, see, for example, Roy Porter, "Gentlemen and Geology: The Emergence of a Scientific Career, 1660–1920," *The Historical Journal* 21 (1978): 809–36.

[33] J. G. Frazer, "Obituary: Canon John Roscoe," *Nature* 130 (1932): 918. And, for a general exposition of this argument, see Richard Yeo, "An Idol of the Marketplace: Baconianism in Nineteenth-Century Britain," *History of Science* 23 (1985): esp. 284–5.

effect in their society, an order in which individuals played roles commensurate with their abilities and training.

The theories – and some specialized methods – of evolutionist anthropologists were suited to their discipline's organization. Their comprehensive theoretical framework permitted extraordinarily economical use of evidence accumulated without systematic coordination of research efforts: there were no data that could not be somehow slotted into descriptions of staged societal evolution. And the statistical techniques developed by men such as Galton were appropriate to the research structure of the anthropological community. As E. W. (Sir Edward) Brabrook (1839–1930) observed, if anthropologists sought help with their inquiries from "every direction," they need not trouble themselves about the accuracy of any given individual's judgments, but could trust "rather to the general laws of numbers than to the skill of individuals to eliminate errors."[34]

The evolutionist model I have described enjoyed currency so long as the roles of amateur data collector and scholarly interpreter remained separate. Of course, later scientists continued to investigate the course of change in the natural world, but prosecuted rather different arguments. The division between different forms of scientific labor dissolved when the university system expanded, creating new employment possibilities for scholars; the "new school of professors" embraced the research ideal, elevating the prestige of scholarship based on empirical investigation relative to that derived from formal principles. Hence, academically employed practitioners of various forms of natural history came to see fieldwork as essential at roughly the same time. The expectation that scientists were necessarily fieldworkers became commonplace in disciplines of natural history around the era of the First World War.[35] And, like their anthropologist contemporaries, in this period British field naturalists turned to community studies, to detailed investigations of the relationships of plant and animal species in particular ecological settings.[36]

Finally, the assumptions of evolutionist anthropology served the objectives of the men of affairs who constituted so large a portion of the anthropological community in its preprofessional era. Eager to apply the lessons of anthropology to practical matters, they wanted to believe that the import of evidence was obvious. Their attempts to derive prescriptive implications from the evidence at their disposal would have been thwarted

---

[34] E. W. Brabrook, "On the Organization of Local Anthropological Research," *Journal of the Anthropological Institute* 22 (1892): 271.
[35] Allen, *Naturalist*, 238.
[36] See A. G. Tansley, "The Early History of Modern Plant Ecology in Britain," *Journal of Ecology* 35 (1947): 130–7.

by the suggestion that their data were in some systematic way shaped by observers' biases. Similarly, their historicism was essential to their objectives. If they were merely projecting inevitable trends into the future, their recommendations were scientific judgments, not political choices. They were not proposing to alter the course of history but to accelerate the pace of evolution – a goal to be achieved in part through eradication of the survivals of barbarism that persisted incongruously in even the most advanced of societies, and in part by deliberate engineering of the social changes that would inevitably be effected spontaneously in the fullness of time.[37] Tylor's "reformer's science" thus purported to be expertise of the sort claimed as the basis of their occupational status by all varieties of professionals in the nineteenth century – a synthesis of natural laws from which derived practical skills, which could be impartially applied in the appropriate situations.

Evolutionist argument could thus justify social intervention in Britain's colonies as well as in Britain. Indeed, when Britain's colonial rulers presented themselves as agents of improvement in the lives of subject peoples, they were wont to do so by arguing that they were negotiating their charges' smooth passage through the stages of evolution anthropologists described.[38] Hence, a highly schematized variant of nineteenth-century anthropology served the purposes of imperial administrators until the end of the colonial era, long after evolutionist anthropology had ceased to be respectable in British academic circles; as later anthropological schemes did not, the evolutionist model could both justify colonial rule and provide administrators with specific objectives.

Nevertheless, one must treat the domestic and colonial applications of the evolutionist model separately, since the model was modified in the colonial context. Britain's armchair anthropologists were pessimistic that social engineering could accelerate the evolution of subject peoples. They reasoned that the more backward a society was, the less likely it was to respond positively to calculated efforts to reform it, not the least because its people were unaccustomed to making rational choices of any sort. Primitive social systems were extremely fragile – the products of instinctive reactions and unconscious adaptations. Britain's colonial rulers explained the strategies they developed for dealing with different sorts of subject peoples

---

[37] For one discussion of these issues, see George W. Stocking, Jr., "Ideas and Institutions in American Anthropology: Thoughts Toward a History of the Interwar Years," in Stocking, ed., *Selected Papers from the American Anthropologist* (Washington, D.C., 1976), 31–6.

[38] See, for example, Sir Everard im Thurn, "A Study of Primitive Character: Presidential Address, 1914, Section H of the British Association," *Nature* 94 (1914): 68–74.

in evolutionist terms, but they could not accept the full implications of the evolutionist scheme. Had they done so, they would have questioned the very legitimacy of colonial authority, particularly when it was exercised over very primitive peoples whose precarious social order might be utterly destroyed by the unexpected intrusion of colonial agents. Instead, imperial officials argued that they were simulating the natural course of evolution by proceeding cautiously and transforming traditional societies very gradually. In this chapter, then, I describe only those habits of mind and behavior that were transported virtually unmodified to the colonies. In Chapters 5 and 6, I treat, respectively, the peculiar character of evolutionist anthropology as it was practiced in the colonies as a policy science, and scholarly evolutionists' contribution to Britain's sustained debate over the legitimacy of colonial rule.

The Victorian social order

To a degree, questions about anthropologists' peculiar views of British culture, and the influence of such views on the conduct of national life are nonsensical. Evolutionist anthropology was premised on a model of natural development that was widely believed, and the social trends that it plotted were expressed in many national institutions. The organizing principle of much of Victorian thought was as evident in literature and in other sciences as it was in anthropology: the inhabitants of the natural and social realms were infinitely variable and hyperfecund, all continuously manifesting the processes of transformation, differentiation, and proliferation, and yet all were somehow interdependent. The task of the observer was to elucidate the hidden order underlying the profusion of the material world, to discern the relationships among its various parts, to recognize the process of growth and decay governing all life forms, and to describe all natural processes in historical terms.[39]

Moreover, Victorians were highly self-conscious about their tendencies to explain all phenomena historically, seeing their intellectual sensibilities as themselves engendered by historical changes. As Mill observed in 1831, the very notion of a "spirit of the age," the dominant concept of the time, was a new one.[40] It is no wonder that Victorian anthropologists advanced a highly qualified form of cultural relativism – describing the beliefs and practices of primitive peoples as appropriate to their stages of development, if not rational by absolute standards – since they regarded themselves as creatures of their own particular moment.

[39] See Gillian Beer, *Darwin's Plots* (London, 1983), 8, 16, 47, 110, and passim.
[40] Quoted in Haley, *Healthy Body*, 47.

Historical interpretations of all natural processes admitted of pessimistic as well as optimistic forecasts. As Gillian Beer has observed, in the 1870s and 1880s many feared that "decadence may be an energy as strong as development, and extinction a factor far more probable than progress."[41] Evidently, evolutionists were among the optimistic interpreters of their age, because they were, as members of the middle class, major beneficiaries of recent social trends. Perhaps the most fundamental change in their society – the altered constitution of the state – had enlarged their power. Simultaneous trends portended the realization of a meritocratic political order, indicating the direction of evolutionary advance. The civil service had been reformed to their advantage – and was itself gaining real power as the state became more centralized. Just as the achieving middle class gained opportunities to secure power and influence, the activities of the monarch were transformed into splendidly inconsequential ceremonials for the diversion of the simple-minded masses.

Significantly, colonial officials acted to transform the indigenous polities in their domains in a fashion that paralleled the changes being effected in the British monarchy at the same time. Colonial officials proclaimed themselves concerned to "bolster" the authority of the traditional rulers of subject peoples, but instead acted to transform them into constitutional monarchs. Officials took great pains to compile detailed records of the ceremonial forms and regal trappings of the indigenous nobility, in order that British agents might act to uphold tradition. Indeed, many of the inquiries colonial rulers considered anthropological were undertaken for this purpose. But officials' actions often served to transform indigenous rituals into empty show, instead of strengthening royal authority. Though colonial rulers professed some regret about this outcome, they represented themselves as the nearly involuntary agents of natural historical forces.

That is, the conduct of colonial administration was predicated on the theory of inexorable historical change fundamental to the legitimation of constitutional monarchy in Britain: if the emotionally compelling traditional forms of government were sustained, the masses would willingly follow their rulers' instructions. Implicit in this theory was the assumption that the British masses and the majority of colonial subjects were fundamentally alike; both were creatures of habit, unaccustomed to examination of their conditioned responses. Furthermore, constitutional monarchies in Britain and in the colonies were predicated on the assumption that traditional rulers themselves appreciated the historical forces that led to the diminution of their powers, since traditional rulers were more evolved members of the human species than were their subjects, and thus were capable

---

[41] Beer, *Darwin's Plots*, 145.

of rational understanding of their historically shaped roles. Progressive monarchs recognized that they were obliged to transfer power to those more capable of responding to the general needs of society than they were. Decisions might be made in monarchs' names, with monarchs' consent, but they would be based on judgments made by those best suited to render them – in Britain, elected officials; and in the Empire, colonial civil servants, who were charged with protecting subject peoples from the selfish partisans of particular interests, who were found both among the indigenous populations and among European agents.[42]

Evolutionists' equation of progress with the increasing differentiation and specialization of labor also represented a calculation of natural law on the basis of trends that had improved the lot of the British middle classes. What could have been more self-congratulatory than their account of the benefits individuals and society received from the organization of self-regulating, knowledge-based professional groups? As organized groups, the professions supposedly worked to realize simultaneously higher standards of rational action and cooperative behavior. And individuals working as professionals were obliged to submit to the collective judgment of their peers, hence becoming both more capable practitioners and better persons. Moreover, the professions' meritocratic standards – which allowed members of the middle classes willing and able to work hard to achieve social eminence as professionals – also served the interests of society as a whole. Huxley summarized the positive consequences of professional reforms in 1884: the person who sought the care of the physician, and the state that employed the civil servant or military man, now had guarantees of competence beyond the personal character of the practitioner.[43]

But evolutionists did not see the new professions as unique occupations. Professions merely exemplified a trend observed throughout the nation's workforce. And evolutionists observed that whenever the tasks of a given occupation were refined and rationalized, its practitioners were able to provide their employers – and by extension, the general public – with services of high quality. When Spencer traced the emergence of differentiated roles, he pointed to a range of careers, including those of poet,

---

[42] David Cannadine, "The Context, Performance and Meaning of Ritual: The British Monarchy and the 'Invention of Tradition,'" c. 1820–1977," in Eric Hobsbawm and Terence Ranger, *The Invention of Tradition* (Cambridge, 1983), esp. 120–32. And for one illustration of the translation of the British model of constitutional monarchy to the colonies, see the essay that follows Cannadine's in this collection: Bernard S. Cohn, "Representing Authority in Victorian India," esp. 184–8. And see my *The Imperial Bureaucrat* (see chap. 2, n. 14), 44–5.

[43] T. H. Huxley, "The State and the Medical Profession," *The Nineteenth Century* 15 (1884): 228–38.

musician, and journalist.[44] Lubbock remarked upon the life of the urban working man employed in commerce or industry: "Confined to one process, or perhaps, even one part of a process ... he acquires ... a skill little short of miraculous."[45]

Moreover, when evolutionists linked the refinement of a society's division of labor with the elaboration of status distinctions, they were revealing an obsession with social position that was hardly peculiar to the middle classes to which they belonged. To be sure, their concern to establish a meritocratic order in which each individual would deservedly enjoy a precisely gauged measure of respect expressed a peculiarly middle-class ideal, but their attention to the refinements of status hierarchies was found in every quarter of Britain during the period spanning the last decades of the nineteenth century and the first of the twentieth. That it was so prevalent indicated the class structure of this time, which one historian has identified as the "zenith of class society," in which the "distribution of income was skew and the economic distance between the classes was greater than ever before."[46]

Indeed, so strongly impressed were they by their culture's emphasis on status distinctions that colonial officials projected it onto the societies they governed. They undertook to define social hierarchies within their domains comparable to those of Britain. For example, the differentiated class system that was given official formulation in Britain in the 1911 census, in which the threefold classification of workers into skilled, semiskilled, and unskilled first appeared, was translated into colonial terms. Thus, in India, "the census definition of caste reached its height of elaboration with the censuses of 1901 and 1911."[47]

But perhaps the best indicator that concern with class distinctions was a truly general phenomenon – characteristic of the culture as a whole rather than merely of some segments of society – was its manifestation among the working class. Among laboring men, the gross distinction between the skilled and the unskilled was inadequate to explain the subtleties of occupationally structured social relationships. Even among unskilled workers, there were gradations of prestige. As Stedman Jones notes, on "the docks, ship workers looked down upon shore workers and permanent laborers despised casuals. A bricklayer's labourer looked down upon the navvy. English coasters despised Irish coasters, and all unskilled labourers ... felt entitled to look down upon the sweep."[48]

[44] Herbert Spencer, "Professional Institutions."
[45] Lord Avebury [John Lubbock], *Essays and Addresses, 1900–1903* (London, 1903), 104.
[46] Perkin, *The Rise of Professional Society* (see chap. 2, n. 8), 27f.
[47] Hesterman, *The Inner Conflict of Tradition* (see chap. 2, n. 14), 202.
[48] Stedman Jones, *Outcast London* (see chap. 1, n. 32), 338.

The proliferation of specialized niches among the domestic servant class alone illustrates the general trend. In the 1830s, advertisements solicited applicants for positions in domestic service that fell into seven categories; by the 1870s, thirty-three distinct positions of household servants had emerged. Of course, the differentiation of this class was a function of the elaborating distinctions that obtained among the segment of the population who employed them as servants, whose status could be calibrated from the character of their households; by the end of the century, the minimal qualification for membership in the middle class was employment of a nurserymaid to look after the children.[49] The elaboration of the household hierarchy was also a function of the sheer size of the servant class, itself a testament to the character of the class system as a whole; the population of the work force employed in domestic service was never higher than at this time, roughly one in six.[50]

When the servant-employing classes sought education for their male children, they looked to the public schools, which were, apart from the ancient foundations, creations of the latter part of the nineteenth century. (The ancient institutions were also restructured at this time.) Viewed as a whole, the public school system may be the most telling illustration of the increasing elaboration and specification of middle-class status in the Victorian era. And because the schools were managed by pedagogical principles consistent with evolutionist theories, it is fair to judge that these theories formalized the middle-class outlook. The creators of the public schools intended their institutions to be socially integrated communities, preparing their charges to play their proper roles in society. Reasoning in terms that also justified the management strategies developed by the rulers of Britain's colonial empire, they judged that if each school were socially homogeneous, the population of each school would develop feelings of community loyalty and solidarity – that is, that each student would learn habits of altruistic regard for the welfare of his fellows.

The public schools together constituted a highly differentiated system. Each school was intended to serve a particular segment of the middle and upper classes, and its fees were set appropriate to the means of the parents of its intended clientele. All of the participants in the public school system understood the hierarchical order it constituted, although individual schools' positions in the hierarchy were bound to shift somewhat, particularly if they came under the authority of ambitious headmasters. Thus, although its fees were to rise and its clientele to become children of

---

[49] Jonathan Gathorne-Hardy, *The Rise and Fall of the British Nanny* (Newton Abbot, Devon, 1972), 678.
[50] Perkin, *The Rise of Professional Society* (see chap. 2, n. 8), 79.

more privileged backgrounds, Lancing was originally intended to serve the upper portion of the middle classes – the children of "gentlemen with small incomes, solicitors and surgeons with limited practices, unbeneficed clergymen, naval and military officers and the like – whereas a school such as Hurstpierpoint was designed for a lower portion of the middle classes – sons of "tradesmen, farmers, clerks."[51] And the schools prepared students for particular occupations. Haileybury, for example, was associated with the Indian Civil Service, whereas Cheltenham and Clifton were among the schools that were thought appropriate for boys destined for careers in the army.

Furthermore, the structure of school governance considered essential to the public school as an institution was developed in the last third of the nineteenth century. From the most recent recruit to the student body to the headmaster, every member of the school had his allocated measure of responsibility, prestige, and prerogative. When boys secured positions of power in the school social system, their rank was denoted by formal insignia and special privileges of no significance outside the closed world of the school – license to wear colored waistcoats and snow boots, to walk arm-in-arm with other boys, for example – signs of rank that, whatever their intrinsic significance, impressed upon the students the importance of hierarchy.[52]

Most significantly, the reorganization of the school was seen as a civilizing mission, designed to control the savage impulses natural to the child. To the reforming headmaster of Marlborough, for example, school reorganization destroyed the informally arrogated power of the "tribes" that had previously run the school, whereas to the headmaster of Haileybury the reform of the schools had eliminated "open barbarism."[53] The constitution of the public school, then, was premised on the evolutionist assumption that the socialization of the child recapitulated the process of civilization of the human race.

Given that colonial subjects were thought to be in various stages of childhood, it is not surprising that it was a cliché of the colonial service that the administrative structure of colonial rule translated the organization of the public school into local terms. Traditional rulers were equated with school prefects. Indigenous political structures were shaped into the fundamental units of colonial administration, the Native Authorities that mediated between the colonial regime and colonial subjects, which were

[51] J. deS. Honey, *Tom Brown's Universe* (New York, 1977), 49, 53.

[52] See, for example, Anthony Powell, "The Wat'ry Glade," in Graham Greene, ed., *The Old School* (London, 1934), 156–7.

[53] Quoted in Honey, *Tom Brown's Universe*, 105, 108.

frequently analogized to school houses; these were exhorted to display team spirit in performing such assigned tasks as tax collection and road building. Furthermore, in order that those members of the indigenous population entrusted with responsibility should have proper regard for the precise measure of status accorded them, they were given rules of etiquette for official situations – the right to sit or stand, for example, and to wear certain articles of clothing.[54]

The equation of the British child with the exotic primitive was a staple of the middle-class culture purveyed in novels and journalism, as were other elements of evolutionist argument – for example, the interaction between nature and nurture; and the parallel between the characteristics of different orders in the British class hierarchy and the cultures of societies at different stages of evolution. Explaining children's passionate involvement in their games, for example, Robert Louis Stevenson concluded that "they dwell in a mythological epoch, and are not the contemporaries of their parents."[55] In *The Way We Live Now*, Anthony Trollope ponders the differences between a fictional sister and brother: was the daughter as virtuous as the son was reprehensible because they had inherited different traits, or had their parents raised them differently?[56] And to Thomas Hardy the behavior of rural peasants was like that of savages.[57]

In particular, the equation between the urban underclass and primitive peoples was assumed by journalists who undertook investigations of the life-styles of the poor, writers who worked in the tradition of social exploration that links figures such as Henry Mayhew and George Orwell. Writing at midcentury, for example, Mayhew described the urban poor as "wandering tribes in civilized society," characterizing them in racial and cultural terms no different from those applied to exotic primitives; they were "distinguished for their high cheekbones and protruding jaws – for their use of slang language – for their lax ideas of property – for their general improvidence – for their repugnance to continuous labour – for their disregard of female honor – their love of cruelty – their pugnacity – and their utter want of religion."[58] In *How the Poor Live* (1883), George

---

[54] See, for example, my *Imperial Bureaucrat* (chap. 2, n. 14), 22–3; Cohn, "Representing Authority in Colonial India."

[55] Quoted in Ed Block, Jr., "Evolutionist Psychology and Aesthetics: The Cornhill Magazine, 1875–80," *Journal of the History of Ideas* 45 (1984): 471.

[56] Anthony Trollope, *The Way We Live Now* (New York, 1982 [orig. London, 1875]), 17–18.

[57] See Beer, *Darwin's Plots*, 237–9.

[58] Quoted in Eileen Yeo, "Mayhew as a Social Investigator," in E. P. Thompson and E. Yeo, eds., *The Unknown Mayhew* (London, 1971), 86–7.

Sims reports the existence of "a dark continent that is within easy walking distance of the General Post Office."[59]

Indeed, reasoning in the Lamarckist terms that guided evolutionist anthropology and popular culture alike, C. F. G. Masterman argued in 1901 that the urban underclass were a "new city race." Brought into the city by steadily worsening agricultural economy, the urban underclass represented people who had degenerated to a truly barbarous condition – "stunted, narrow-chested, easily wearied; yet voluble, excitable, with little ballast, stamina, or endurance."[60] Furthermore, observations made by persons ranging from members of the laboring classes themselves to members of the British Association's Anthropometric Committee gave such assertions plausibility. Measurements of school children indicated that their height was directly proportional to their place on the social scale. Among adult males, members of the professional class were the tallest, while the highest stratum of the laboring class was significantly stronger and taller than the lowest.[61]

The assumptions that guided the observations of journalists and social survey researchers also inspired many efforts to uplift the unemployed urban poor. These efforts represented attempts to lead the poor to the stage of social development they had not reached independently – to oblige them to accept the discipline of steady habitation and labor. For example, schemes were advanced to create labor colonies in which the poor would be taught either agricultural or industrial skills; after their training experiences, the poor were expected to emigrate to the vast, uncultivated lands of the colonies to take up agricultural labor, to find industrial employment, or to work on the land in Britain – that is, to return to the healthy conditions from which they or their progenitors had emigrated earlier, with supposedly disastrous consequences. Few of these projects were realized, but one of those that was, that proposed by the Salvation Army's General Booth in his *In Darkest England and the Way Out* (1890), was recognizably akin to the so-called industrial missions then operating in Africa. Booth's "nomads of civilization" were also intended to embrace both Christianity and the habits of regular work. Echoes of his approach to the reform of the poor were to be heard as late as 1909, when both the majority and minority

---

[59] Quoted in Peter Keating, "Introduction" to Keating, ed., *Into Unknown England* (Manchester, 1976), 14.

[60] C. F. G. Masterman, "Realities at Home," in Masterman, ed., *The Heart of the Empire* (New York, 1973 [orig. London, 1901]), 8.

[61] Hobsbawm, *Workers* (see chap. 1, n. 23), 227–8. Francis Galton et al., *Final Report of the Anthropometric Committee of the British Association for the Advancement of Science* (London, 1883), 17, 29.

The frontispiece to William Booth's *In Darkest England and the Way Out* (1890).

signatories to the report of the Royal Commission on the Poor Laws agreed that the incorrigible poor – the "residuum" who resisted all efforts to make them responsible members of society – should be incarcerated in work camps.[62]

The Victorian identification of the lower orders as savages may explain one peculiar feature of legal history: the nearly complete tolerance of a custom fabled in the song and story of the sea, the practice termed "survival cannibalism" habitual among shipwrecked sailors bereft of food supplies. According to one internal memorandum circulated within the Board of Trade, sailors were by nature "stupid, superstitious, barbarous, depraved and degenerate." Given the equation between cannibalism and the basest savagery in the popular mind, sailors' habits served to confirm this characterization. (Unlike their larger audience, however, anthropologists did not use cannibalism as an index to evolutionary development. Tylor observed that the practice disappeared "with the rise of civilization [and was] more and more kept down by the growing sense of the dignity of man"; not all primitive peoples were cannibals, however, and those who were took up the practice for various reasons, among them the desperate need for food – such as shipwrecked sailors felt – which in primitives' case was a consequence of "reckless improvidence.") British courts may have been long inhibited by the exclusion of the sea per se from their territorial jurisdiction. Nevertheless, it seems significant that the only sailors ever tried for murder because they had indulged in cannibalism were the survivors of the wreck of the yacht *Mignonette*, who had preyed upon the lowly cabin boy. They were tried and convicted in 1884 – but were obliged to serve less than a year in prison.[63]

The Victorian concern to delimit hierarchies of status and specialized functions was not confined to distinctions of class and behavior, but was also translated into spatial terms that formalized social relationships. The very notion of a city altogether distinct from the country was a recent one, explained G. L. (Sir Lawrence) Gomme (1853–1916), one of the organizers of the Folk-Lore Society, founded in 1878 to advance the arguments of evolutionist anthropology in the study of folklore – which

[62] William Booth, *In Darkest England and the Way Out* (London, 1890). One "industrial mission" is described in G. Shepperson and T. Price, *Independent African* (Edinburgh, 1958). And see A. W. Vincent, "The Poor Law Reports of 1909 and the Social Theory of the Charity Organization Society," *Victorian Studies* 27 (1984): 347; and A. M. McBriar, *An Edwardian Mixed Doubles: The Bosanquets Versus the Webbs* (Oxford, 1987), 51, 303.

[63] E. B. Tylor, "Cannibalism," in *Encyclopaedia Britannica*, 9th ed. Vol. 4 (New York, 1877), 714, 713; A. W. Brian Simpson, *Cannibalism and the Common Law* (Chicago, 1984), 109, 111, 161, 232, 288, and passim.

Gomme defined as "the anthropology of the civilized races."[64] From the second third of the nineteenth century, he observed in 1898, London gradually assumed its modern form. At the beginning of Victoria's reign, the area that was to be unified under a single government structure in 1888 was a loose conglomerate of small villages, some of them quite rural in character, each largely governed by local acts. The consolidation of city government represented a case in which social processes that operated on a large scale were replicated in microcosm – illustrating a fundamental precept of evolutionist theory. That is, the city grew by accretion and developed a structure for functional integration just as the nation did.

The area within London's future government unit came to function as an integrated whole as its diverse activities became spatially segregated. Thus, London's growth exemplified the processes of development realized in the evolution of every form of life. Workplaces were differentiated from residential areas, and the neighborhoods of the living were removed from the burial grounds of the dead. Residential neighborhoods were themselves differentiated by class. Among the newly defined areas of the city were contained tracts of recreational parkland. The progressive interdependence of the citizens of London was the product of their increasing occupational differentiation and the concomitant delimitation of the diverse spheres of their lives – work, home, and leisure.[65]

The architecture of Victorian Britain paralleled the morphology of the city in microcosm. Those who could afford to build grand houses constructed them with elaborately differentiated spaces designed to accommodate highly specific activities. The greater the means of the owner, the more likely it was that his house would be built with rooms set aside for the domains of males, females, children, guests, and upper and lower servants. In the homes of the wealthy, for example, eating places were built for each meal of the day and for every class in the household: main meals were served in the dining room, the schoolroom, the nursery, the upper servants' hall and the lower servants' hall; for the adult owners of the house and their guests, breakfast and tea would each be served in separate rooms.[66]

Other forms of Victorian architecture realized the same sense of the relationship between social status and segregated place manifested in the grand country house. The asylum, for example, organized inmates' society in spatial terms that correlated with disease, class, and sex. And the asylum

[64] On the definition of folklore, see Gomme, "The Value of Folk-Lore as Ethnological Data," 627. For a general characterization of the approach of Gomme's generation, see Richard M. Dorson, *The British Folklorists: A History* (Chicago, 1968), 205.
[65] G. Lawrence Gomme, *London in the Reign of Victoria* (London, 1898), 1–29.
[66] Mark Girouard, *The Victorian Country House* (New Haven, 1977), 27–9.

of this period was optimally situated in a park that provided a natural illustration of moral order. The inmates' "field of vision embrac[ed] hill and valley, wood and water, in their most agreeable combinations," according to a Victorian observer. Evidently, the architects of the asylum, like the British naturalists, assumed that nature itself constituted a special realm – the moral one.[67]

Women constituted a substantial proportion of the population of the Victorian asylum. Their vulnerability to mental illness was evidence of the special needs of women for protection – needs that justified the development of the patriarchal, monogamous, nuclear family, which anthropologists identified as one of the most important achievements of evolutionary advance. Like other types of primitive beings, woman was irrational. Her irrationality was a direct function of her sexuality. Indeed, the more protracted her childhood, the more likely she was to develop those characteristics crucial to civilization; late onset of menstruation was associated with high moral standards and the capacity to reason soundly. Alas, the perpetuation of the human species required women to mature sexually. And it was their sexual impulses that led women to the most extreme form of irrational behavior – certifiable lunacy – which was conceptualized as regression to a lower stage of evolution. To be sure, for both men and women of this era, disease of any sort was conceived as a degenerative process, compounded of physical and moral elements. But women collapsed into illness from a condition supposedly initially lower than men's. More susceptible than men to physical and mental illness, they were subjected to more extreme medical therapies.[68]

The structure of the middle-class Victorian family, and its household, represented an environment in which it was easy to see women as children and savages. Typically, husbands were considerably older than their wives, and wives' behavior toward their husbands was surely affected by the age discrepancy between them, as well as by their legally subordinate status. "It was not unknown," Lenore Davidoff observes, "for an upper-middle-class man to raise a ward or poor relation with the intention of making her his wife when she reached her middle or late teens." And because during the last third of the century the servant class in even upper-middle-class households was composed largely of women (men from the strata that had previously provided servants being by then able to find alternative forms of employment), the bearers of lower-class culture with whom middle-class

---

[67] Elaine Showalter, *The Female Malady, Woman, Madness and English Culture 1830–1980* (New York, 1985), 35.

[68] Beer, *Darwin's Plots*, 214–15; Showalter, *Female Malady*, esp. 51–164; and see Haley, *Healthy Body*, 47.

Victorians had the most regular contact were generally female; household demographics encouraged conflation of categories.[69]

Anthropologists in action

Evolutionists did not suffer the paralysis of will that often afflicts modern academics – the fear that because their research findings are (inevitably) incomplete they cannot move from information to action. Having rejected traditional piety, they transmuted their religious impulses into a new imperative. This Francis Galton explicitly identified as "the religious significance of the doctrine of evolution," the obligation to "endeavor to further evolution, especially that of the human race."[70] Assigning more weight to heredity than to environment in the production of human virtue, Galton saw the future improvements of the race as a consequence of enlightened breeding, but recoiled at the prospect of state intervention in human reproduction until the very end of his life, when he decided that some individuals were so recognizably degenerate that it was dangerous to permit them to propagate.[71] Galton himself did not recommend, or foresee, the abominations that would be committed in the name of eugenics, however. And in practical terms, his recommendations were indistinguishable from those of his Lamarckist fellows. In the aggregate, evolutionists worked to realize a specific goal: a society rationally managed, populated by a citizenry imbued with altruistic motives, a society that expressed the forces of history they identified.

But the secular trends anthropologists – and others – observed in their society were not all equally clear. The progressive elaboration of the division of labor was a straightforward process, for example. The direction evolution portended for womankind, by contrast, was not entirely certain. Evolutionist thinkers construed the natural basis of sexual variation differently. To Darwin, man was a fully evolved woman. "With women the powers of intuition, of rapid perception, and perhaps of imitation, are more strongly marked than in man," he wrote in *The Descent of Man*. He judged that these traits indicated that women's "faculties are characteristic of the lower races, and therefore of a past and lower state of civilization." To Spencer, woman was like man in an arrested state of development.[72] Such

---

[69] Lenore Davidoff, "Class and Gender in Victorian England," *Feminist Studies* 5 (1979): 93–4.

[70] Galton, *Human Faculty*, 337.

[71] Ibid., 332, 336; and see Kevles, *Eugenics*, 91.

[72] Quoted and analyzed in Flavia Alaya, "Victorian Science and the 'Genius' of Women," *Journal of the History of Ideas* 38 (1977): 264–5.

a formulation suggested the possibility that woman's inferior status was not permanent. From such ambiguities in evolutionist reasoning derived different projections of – and prescriptions for – the future social order. Evolutionists' vision of an advanced society featured an enlarged role for persons like themselves, and required meritocratic reforms such as I have discussed already. But their vision also involved improvement of those segments of the population who were deficient by their standards. Here I describe some of the policies they advocated in pursuit of that end.

Writing about the laboring classes in 1848, John Stuart Mill had asserted that "prospect of the future depends on the degree in which they can be made rational beings."[73] Evolutionist thinkers sustained his expectation, relying in large part on the spread of education for its fulfillment. They differed somewhat in their estimation of the function education was to play in the life of society and individuals, however. Few took the extreme position of Spencer, to whom education was valuable only insofar as it taught skills essential to self-preservation, and education devoted to the cultivation of "tastes and feelings" was a waste of time.[74] Lubbock's views were more representative. Lubbock identified attitudes such as Spencer's as vestiges of an earlier stage of social development. "Now we advocate Education," he wrote in 1894, "not merely to make the man the better workman, but the workman the better man."[75]

Lubbock was well placed to affect national policy. Among the roles he performed in the cause of advancing education were service on three royal commissions charged with evaluating educational institutions, and representation of the University of London in Parliament for decades. To be sure, he advocated educational change for the utilitarian reasons characteristically advanced by reformers in his day: Britain could not compete with other world powers (and especially with Germany) in commerce and industry unless its workforce was trained in science and modern languages.[76] But he evidently judged the spiritual benefits of education as important as the practical ones.

Lubbock argued that the progressive specialization of the labor created a spiritual vacuum in the lives of modern workers, at the same time as it effected a higher material standard of living. This vacuum would be filled somehow, and for both society's and individuals' sakes it was vital that it be filled with spiritually sustaining pursuits. A modern worker's life without

---

[73] Mill, *Principles* (see chap. 1, n. 7), Vol. II, 333.
[74] Quoted in Richard Jenkyns, *The Victorians and Ancient Greece* (Cambridge, Mass., 1980), 277.
[75] Lubbock, *Use*, 97.
[76] Avebury, *Essays*, 243–8.

such pursuits was in fact less varied and therefore less gratifying than that of the savage or the peasant. And workers seeking to relieve the monotony of their existence would turn to drink or crime less "from irresistible temptation or deliberate wickedness" than out of boredom – unless they were educated to use productively the free time that was one of the un-doubted benefits they gained as their society evolved by becoming more efficient – a benefit Lubbock had a hand in increasing, promoting legisla-tion for secular holidays and shorter working hours.[77] Lubbock worked to bring education to the working class, serving as president of the University of London's extension services, which were, in fact, very successful; in 1897, Gomme noted, more than fourteen thousand students attended evening classes offered in roughly seventy centers.[78] Moreover, Lubbock argued that social statistics demonstrated the benefits of education; con-sequent to the passage of the 1870 Education Act, crime and pauperism were decreasing at a remarkable rate.[79]

Among the recreations the laboring classes might enjoy in their leisure time was museum visiting, and the museums anthropologists established at the end of the century exemplified their educational objectives. Anthro-pological museums were intended to provide experiences especially illumi-nating to the newly leisured and newly enfranchised artisan and lower-middle classes. Anthropologists believed that these classes reasoned in the concrete terms characteristic of the more primitive members of the human species. Hence, museum builders assumed that these classes could under-stand the message conveyed in an ordered display of material objects more easily than they could judge the merits of a written argument presented in a political tract. Museums were designed to represent spatial correlates of hierarchical social order and to document the process of evolution. Architectural plans structured museum visitors' experiences.

Moving among the exhibits in intended fashion, visitors were expected to be impressed by the ordered progress of humankind's development from a savage to a superior state. They would observe that examples of each type of artifact, arrayed in a developmental sequence, had been modified very slowly over time. Thus, the act of viewing museum displays would impart a clear political lesson: responsible citizens did not press for precipitous change, but recognized that social evolution was necessarily gradual.[80] On this point, anthropologists of diverse political views were agreed. General

[77] Ibid., 103, 98.

[78] Gomme, *London*, 175.

[79] Lubbock, *Use*, 98–100.

[80] David K. van Keuren, "Augustus Pitt-Rivers, Anthropological Museums and Social Change in Later Victorian Britain," *Victorian Studies* 28 (1984): 171–89.

Augustus Pitt-Rivers (1827–1900), a leading museum figure and an active member of the Conservative party, and the Liberal Lubbock (Pitt-Rivers's son-in-law) alike equated progress with gradualism.

On the question of the appropriate means for realization of the cooperative society toward which evolution was directed, however, anthropological argument rationalized different answers. How were the lower strata to become functional members of society? Nineteenth-century liberal opinion was prepared to extend the franchise to the "higher working class" – for example, to those who had demonstrated their independent capacity to organize for mutual aid, the trade unionists and cooperators.[81] To traditional liberals – anthropologists and others – voluntarism animated social progress, and state regulation of any sphere of human activity constituted an impediment to the expression of progressive impulses. They envisioned the incorporation of the lower orders into the body politic as a consequence of a freely entered tacit contract: charity recipients would become morally upright, self-sustaining citizens if the prosperous voluntarily extended aid to them.

During the period effectively bounded by the passage of the New Poor Law of 1834 and the passage of an act granting noncontributory old-age pensions in 1908, this informal contract governed the national provision of social welfare services, for official agencies depended on myriad private charities. Particularly notable were the self-help organizations that proliferated among the working classes in the decades before World War I: societies collecting funds that members could use when the disasters of sickness and death occurred; the cooperative movement that provided discounted commodities.[82] As A. M. McBriar has observed, "The range, variety, and multiplication of voluntary charitable institutions and of individual donations for worthy causes in Victorian England was a matter of comment by foreigners and self-congratulation by the British."[83] Self-help among the working classes and voluntary giving by the more prosperous apparently militated against class conflict. Lubbock, for example, argued that "it is greatly owing to the numerous charitable agencies, the greater sympathy between rich and poor . . . that there is no such feeling in favor of Socialism and Anarchy as exists in some other countries."[84]

So completely has Herbert Spencer been identified with the rationalization of voluntarism and minimal government in Britain (and the

---

[81] Hobsbawm, *Workers*, 227.
[82] Perkin, *The Rise of Professional Society*, 110.
[83] McBriar, *Mixed Doubles*, 41. See also Greta Jones, *Social Hygiene in Twentieth Century Britain* (London, 1986), 12–13.
[84] Lubbock, *Use*, 179.

United States) during the late nineteenth century that we tend to overlook the influence of figures with similar views. One such figure was E. W. Brabrook, a leader of ánthropological activity and an important civil servant. Sometime president of the Anthropological Institute, the Folk-Lore Society, Section H, Section F (Economic Science and Statistics), and the Sociological Society, as well as one of the organizers of the BAAS's Ethnographical Survey of the United Kingdom, Brabrook embodied the state's dependence on voluntary organizations in his occupational persona: he was the assistant and later chief registrar of Friendly Societies between 1869 and 1903, and received a knighthood in recognition of his work. As men such as Galton were also prepared to do in this era, Brabrook wished to apply different normative standards to those he considered beyond redemption for some reason; in 1910, for example, he was a member of a delegation to the home secretary agitating in support of the Mental Deficiency Act passed in 1913, which provided for the institution-alization of mental defectives.[85]

But Brabrook espoused voluntary cooperation for the prosecution of virtually every activity conducted by responsible citizens, including the collection of vital statistics with policy relevance.[86] He regarded such innovations as state old-age pensions with alarm, fearing that they might discourage self-reliance. This virtue was the object of the societies he supervised in his official capacity. Such groups as trade unions, building societies, and cooperative societies were products of "the free and sponta-neous efforts of the industrial population to better their condition." But these societies did more than encourage thrift and keep their members independent of the poor law. They served as vehicles for moral evolution. Members who did not need to draw upon their societies' funds because they had not suffered destitution or illness did not resent having paid insurance money without benefit to themselves, but regarded their financial participation as "an altruistic and charitable act." Moreover, the develop-ment of these societies testified to the operation of evolutionary laws in every quarter of society, among the working classes as well as the wealthy. They pointed to the emergence of "the productive form of society" based on "the ideal of co-operation."[87]

Brabrook, who was sixty-one in 1900, was of a generation of liberals determined to resist state regulation of practically any form. He even

---

[85] Jones, *Social Hygiene*, 54.

[86] Brabrook, "Organisation," 262–74.

[87] E. W. Brabrook, Presidential Address to the Economic Science and Statistics Section of the British Association for the Advancement of Science, 1903, *Journal of the Royal Statistical Society* [ser. A] 66 (1903): 615, 607, 611.

argued against legislation intended to enlarge his occupational domain by compelling all friendly societies to register with the state, maintaining that regulation could not save ill-managed societies from "inevitable" collapse and would unfairly penalize those societies that managed quite well on their own.[88] But even before his retirement Brabrook was regarded as old-fashioned in government circles. A man such as G. Lawrence Gomme, forty-seven in 1900 and clerk to the London County Council, embodied the new fashion in liberal thought – and a variant of evolutionist argument advanced with increasing frequency by the turn of the century. Gomme, too, was knighted in recognition of his work in the civil service, and in his occupational role he was an advocate of government centralization, effected through the consolidation of London government.

For Gomme, government actions were not inimical but essential to the creation of the sense of community that was the goal of evolutionists of every stripe. And the centralization of authority served to elevate the level of rationality of government services, permitting the substitution of admin-istration for partisan politics. What local jurisdictions remained were sur-vivals of an antecedent stage of development.[89] His approval of the scheme to provide old age pensions was far less qualified than Brabrook's. It was not perfect, but it was desirable in its object. And at least as important as the end served by the old age pension act was the innovative, cen-tralized administrative mechanism developed for its administration, which marked a qualitative leap forward toward the rationalization of government structure.[90]

Whether by fortune or intention, then, Gomme was in a position to effect social changes of the sort envisioned by the self-proclaimed "New Liberals" of the early twentieth century. Nineteenth-century anthropol-ogists had been traditional liberals, envisioning society as a voluntary compact of atomistic individuals. New Liberals described their position in historicist terms – as an adaptation to the social order as it had evolved since the nineteenth century. They argued that the state had to assume paternalistic powers because in modern society ordinary persons were powerless to protect themselves against all manner of threats to their welfare. Their collectivism retained the stamp of traditional liberalism, however, for it did not entail subordination of individual interests to the needs of the state. New Liberals saw their variety of collectivism as a step advancing progressive evolution, which resulted in the development of

---

[88] Ibid., 606. And see Brabrook's obituary in *The Times*, March 21, 1930, p. 19.

[89] Gomme, *London*, esp. 201–3.

[90] Lawrence Gomme, "Introduction," to H. J. Hoare, *Old Age Pensions* (London, 1915), v–viii.

individuals imbued with altruism. As the evolutionist sociologist – and professed New Liberal – L. T. Hobhouse wrote in 1911, an advanced society was an harmoniously integrated one, in which "an individual right ... cannot conflict with the common good."[91] This was not an altogether novel argument. In the nineteenth century, socialists had described their goals as the natural result of evolutionary trends.[92] But what had been radical political opinion in the nineteenth century had by the early twentieth become nearly conventional.

The evolutionist account of the changing role of women in developing society also admitted of creative interpretation. In 1883, for example, the anthropologists who comprised the British Association Anthropometric Committee forecast nothing less than the extinction of human species if the position of women continued to improve. The committee reported that changes in habits were producing permanent changes in the physical character of the race, and, in particular, were resulting in the gestation of infants with such large heads that they (and/or their mothers) could not survive the process of birth.

> The degenerating influence of town life and sedentary occupations ... together with the new movement for the education of women, favor the production of large heads and imperfectly developed bodies of women in this and other civilised countries, and a corresponding disproportion between the size of the head and the circumference of the pelvis.[93]

But the logic of evolutionist argument did not dictate antifeminist conclusions. If it suggested to some that women were condemned by their biological role to remain forever in a subordinate position, at best paternalistically protected, it suggested to others that women were evolving toward full equality with men. In particular, feminists agitating for greater civil rights in British society were able to legitimate their cause by pointing to the evolutionist trends toward increasing opportunity for individualist expression and increasing specificity of property rights. The passage of the 1882 Married Women's Property Act indicates that such arguments proved persuasive.

---

[91] Quoted in Stefan Collini, *Liberalism and Sociology* (London, 1979), 126. For analysis of the New Liberalism, see Collini, passim, as well as Peter Clarke, *Liberals and Social Democrats* (Cambridge, 1978).

[92] For one discussion of socialist evolutionary theory, see John Laurent, "Science, Society and Politics in Late Nineteenth-Century England: A further Look at Mechanics' Institutes," *Social Studies of Science* 14 (1984): 595–608.

[93] Quoted in *Report of the Papers and Discussion of the Cambridge Meeting of the British Association, 1904, on the Alleged Physical Deterioration of the People and the Utility of an Anthropometric Survey* (London, 1905), 11.

National deliberations about the legal status of married women were premised on the same assumption that informed evolutionist anthropologists' model of the social order: the family was the basic unit of society, and its organizational principles should be consistent with those that governed society as a whole. Prior to the passage of the act, unmarried women had almost the same rights associated with the possession of property as men. (Women who held property of sufficient magnitude to entitle men to the franchise could not vote, however.) But if a propertied woman married, her possessions became legally those of her husband, signaling state sanction of the notion that the family unit on which social order rested was necessarily a hierarchical, patriarchal one.

Feminists argued that the course of evolution was leading toward the development of a more egalitarian family structure. The new family order served the needs of a state that was becoming more democratic, socializing children to behave in a fashion appropriate to their duties as citizens. And feminists could enlist members of the anthropological community such as Sir Henry Maine in their cause. With his permission, feminists included among the tracts they distributed during the course of their campaign for legal reform an address given in 1873 by Maine entitled "The Early History of the Property of Married Women." In it, he cast the history of the legal rights of women in the terms of the movement from personal relations based on "status" to those based on "contract," thus associating enlarged women's rights with progress from barbarism to civilization.[94]

Furthermore, men of more radical temper who were prominent in anthropological circles, such as Karl Pearson, forecast even greater advances for women if past evolutionary trends were sustained. A man active in diverse efforts to change social policy, eugenics prominent among them, Pearson agreed with feminists that the changing status of women was linked to evolving notions of property and individuality. He pointed to societies in earlier stages of development ranging from those of "the most primitive Aryan civilisation as evidenced in the fossils of philosophy and folklore, to the Greeks of the Periclean age, to the Germans of Tacitus, to the feudal civilization, to the medieval town in 1500." The age of ruthless individualism was about to come to an end, he declared, and with its end would come ever-growing opportunities for self-realization for women. As other evolutionist thinkers had done, Pearson prophesied a future superior society distinguished by its sense of collective responsibility. In it, women would be able both to fulfill their individual impulses for self-expression and to serve the needs of society by producing its future citizens. The value

[94] Lee Holcombe, *Wives and Property* (Toronto, 1983), 4–7, 186.

of all of women's contributions (including the propagation of the race) would be properly recognized and rewarded.[95]

Finally, we can see concrete evidence of the importance of anthropological argument in practical action in several late-nineteenth-century debates over the perennial "Irish Question." Ireland was England's oldest colony, and debates over policies for Ireland had always been framed in the terms used for other colonies. Britain's policy toward Ireland differed from that realized in its other colonies, however, for it admitted the possibility of full assimilation, not the least because Ireland's geographical proximity permitted political annexation. The fundamental Irish Question was whether the Irish were capable of assimilating English culture and behaving responsibly as full citizens of a parliamentary regime. In the late nineteenth century, debates over the practicability of assimilation focused on two issues: Irish land reform and Irish Home Rule. In both instances, assimilationists prevailed, and in both instances anthropological arguments figured in the decisions.

The 1881 Irish Land Act and subsequent reforms designed to make the Irish a "race of freeholders" were premised on evolutionist arguments: the reform of the Irish land system was essential to move the country along "the paths of industry and progress"; and when Irish tenant farmers were granted fair rents, free sale, and fixity of tenure, they would gain legal rights approximating those of Englishmen, ceasing to be "serfs" in a feudal society.[96] Sir Henry Maine may have been horrified that his views were adduced in support of Irish land reform, believing that the Irish were insufficiently socially advanced to enjoy economic rights based on contract rather than status, but the liberal view of Irish capacities clearly prevailed in this instance.[97] The view that the Irish could be assimilated was expressed by prominent members of the anthropological community such as John Lubbock and T. H. Huxley, and it justified their opposition to Irish Home Rule.

Their opinions were supported by evidence collected by two committees organized and supported by the British Association for the Advancement of Science – the committee appointed to conduct "Systematic Examination of the Heights, Weights, and Other Physical Characters of the Inhabitants of the British Isles," which operated between 1875 and 1883; and the "Ethnographical Survey of the United Kingdom," which functioned

[95] Karl Pearson, "Women and Labour," *Fortnightly Review* 61 (1984): 561–77.
[96] For example, T. W. Russell, MP (Unionist), "Ireland and Irish Land Once More," *Fortnightly Review* 75 (1901): 19, esp. 2, 3, 12.
[97] Clive Dewey, "Images of the Village Community: A Study in Anglo-Indian Ideology," *Modern Asian Studies* 6 (1972): 318.

between 1892 and 1910. The chairmen of these committees at different times included Francis Galton and E. W. Brabrook, and their members represented the anthropological elite, including, among others, General Pitt-Rivers, John Beddoe (1826–1911), A. C. Haddon, Sidney Hartland, and Arthur Evans. Their research found the British people to be a mixture of different stocks, and identified populations living in isolated areas in the British Isles that had distinctive racial and cultural characteristics. But the most important national patterns of variation the committees found were associated with class rather than with region. The urban poor, in particular, were conspicuously stunted. And there were no gross distinctions to be made among the populations of England, Ireland, Scotland, and Wales.[98]

The most telling evidence of the liberalism of evolutionist anthropologists may be their position on the Irish Question, paradoxical though this conclusion seems in the light of the sorry subsequent history of Ireland. The secession of the Unionists from the Liberal party in the debate over Gladstone's Irish Home Rule Bill has been frequently identified as a manifestation of conservative reaction, evidence that the Unionists were disenchanted with the liberal reforms that had brought a larger fraction of the population into the nation's political life. Many historians have judged the debate over Home Rule as to have been proximate cause of the flight from liberalism by the Victorian intelligentsia, who considered that the quality of the nation's political life had declined as the electorate had been enlarged – proof positive that working men could not, in fact, be transformed into rational beings.[99] It has often been assumed that support of Irish Home Rule denoted a liberal outlook – a belief that the Irish were equal to Englishmen, capable of self-government and entitled to choose independence; certainly, this was Gladstone's official view. (He also thought that Irish radicals would be less dangerous sitting in Dublin than in Westminster.) And many opposed Home Rule with racist arguments framed in conventional evolutionist terms: the Irish were a feminine race, more like savages than Englishmen, and incompetent to govern themselves.

But the proponents and opponents of Irish Home Rule did not divide neatly into liberals and conservatives, respectively. There were some, such as Sidney and Beatrice Webb, who justified Home Rule in racist terms. Visiting Ireland in 1892, they wrote to their friend Graham Wallas that "Home rule [sic] is an absolute necessity in *order to depopulate the country*

---

[98] See van Keuren, "Human Science in Victorian Britain: Anthropology in Institutional and Disciplinary Formation, 1863–1908," (see chap. 2, n. 43), 119–27.

[99] The classic argument of this position is that of John Roach, "Liberalism and the Victorian Intelligentsia," *Cambridge Historical Journal* 13 (1957): 58–81.

of this detestable race.[100] Justified in such terms, Home Rule would not necessarily render Ireland an independent nation, but would reduce the political status of Ireland to one of an Empire Dominion. Granted separate status, Ireland would not be an integral part of Britain. It would no longer send representatives to Parliament, but would assume the federal relationship that had already been defined for other parts of the Empire that defied assimilation – such as India.[101]

When anthropologists opposed Irish Home Rule on the grounds that the Irish were not racially distinguishable from other British citizens, then, they were articulating a clearly liberal political position. Indeed, their forecast of the future of the Irish on racial grounds was a particularly optimistic one. Such men as the historian E. A. Freeman also judged the Irish to be of the same stock as the English, and reasoned that the Irish were therefore capable of assimilation – eventually; given sufficient time, the Irish could become productive members of British society, but their historical experiences had made them so resentful of the English that they would long remain a destructive element within the nation, and should therefore be granted Home Rule.[102] With the benefit of hindsight, we might judge anthropologists' policy recommendation unfortunate. But their argument was admirable.

Conclusions

The historian attempting to comprehend the social changes of Victorian Britain becomes herself something of an evolutionist anthropologist, both in her method and in her explanatory framework. She finds in every aspect of Victorian culture evidence to support evolutionist hypotheses. From their development of a cult of athletics to their organization of the zoological garden, Victorians acted to structure their lives in the fashion anthropologists pronounced natural.[103] And however natural in fact were

[100] On Gladstone's motives, see W. C. Lubenow, "Irish Rule and the Great Separation in the Liberal Party in 1886: The Dimensions of Parliamentary Liberalism," *Victorian Studies* 26 (1983): 175. For a general discussion of Irish Home Rule and ethnic stereotyping, see L. P. Curtis, Jr., *Anglo-Saxons and Celts* (Bridgeport, Conn., 1968), esp. 61–73, 100; the Webbses' view is quoted on p. 63, and the italics are theirs. It is of some interest that Sidney Webb was, as Lord Passfield, to serve as colonial secretary between 1929 and 1931 in the Labour Government of Ramsay MacDonald.

[101] E. A. Freeman, "Parallels to Irish Home Rule," *Fortnightly Review* 52 (1889): 293–8. And see Christopher Harvie, "Ideology and Home Rule: James Bryce, A. V. Dicey and Ireland, 1880–1887," *The English Historical Review* 91 (1976): 298–314.

[102] C. J. W. Parker, "The Failure of Liberal Racialism" (see chap. 2, n. 34), 827, 839.

[103] See, for example, Haley, *Healthy Body*; Harriet Ritvo, *The Animal Estate* (Cambridge, Mass. 1987).

the processes anthropologists described, the character of their world gave their observations undeniable plausibility. Whichever phenomenon anthropologists chose to contemplate – children's games, city dwellers' physical traits, civil service reform, clinical psychopathology, constitutional monarchy – seemed to manifest the workings of evolutionary processes.

Moreover, evolutionist reasoning proved remarkably durable because it was incorporated in conventional wisdom. Survivals of unilinear, teleological developmental notions persist today in observations made everyday in ordinary situations. British culture is not peculiar in this regard. The folk anthropology of other parts of the industrialized West is much the same. I invite my readers to lend a sensitized ear to opinions voiced regularly on the street and in the living room to satisfy themselves of the persistence of social evolutionist ideas. In particular, conventional, white male-dominated middle-class culture has continued to draw comfort and inspiration from the assumptions that peoples of underdeveloped countries are closer to the lower primates than are those of the West, that the child is a natural savage whose instinctive impulses must be suppressed, that adult women retain some of the inherent irrationality of the child, and that the underclass and the deranged are primitive peoples in our midst.

Just as telling an indication of the commonsensical status of evolutionist argument today is its expression in various forms of countercultural protest, which reject conventional values and institutions. The persistent belief that the biological constitution of the human species preserves the memory of the history of evolution as it was once charted by anthropologists is expressed in the expectation that individuals will be restored to their primordial selves if they participate in contrived rites that are imagined primitive ceremonials or remove themselves to unimproved land. This assumption informs all manner of contemporary cultural phenomena, from feminist performance art to all-male retreats to the wild. To be sure, participants in these activities invert the evolutionist hierarchy of savage and civilized, but, in staging deliberate attempts to effect the process evolutionists would have described as "degeneration," they presume the accuracy of the evolutionists' recapitulation hypothesis.

Neither belief in a natural hierarchy of human beings nor the assumption that a reconstruction of the circumstances of primitive peoples will elicit primitive emotions does a traditional evolutionist anthropologist make, however. Critical to the nineteenth-century scheme of things was belief in the inevitability of progress, and in the potential for improvement that every living creature possessed. Every individual and group had the capacity to advance along the evolutionary scale. And because developmental advance was natural, it could be easily accomplished; or, at least, to the late twentieth-century observer, it seems that a century ago individual and collective change was regarded as a nearly effortless process – in contrast to the view that came to prevail around World War I. Their optimistic forecasts of relatively rapid progressive change testified to the experiences of social mobility that nineteenth-century anthropologists had enjoyed. Moreover, they were not merely passive beneficiaries of social change. Some of anthropology's leading figures were able to play active roles in effecting the changes their discipline justified. No wonder they were so confident that they had discovered the natural laws that governed human behavior.

Chapter 4

The savage within

"When the anthropology of anthropologists comes to be written," A. M. Hocart (1883–1939) pronounced, "future generations will have to explain why the first quarter of the twentieth century was so fascinated by fear, why that emotion was made to account for everything, for weddings, for funerals, for religion itself." Hocart oversimplified matters, but his judgment pointed to a fundamental intellectual change: in the era of World War I, anthropologists no longer charted the course of human history as the progressive triumph of the forces of reason over those of original instinctive emotion. They now believed that "savage impulses" always remained "dormant in the heart of civilised man," ready to "spring to life again," as R. R. Marett wrote in 1917. This insight was a lesson taught most forcefully by the war. As W. H. R. Rivers observed, the behavior of soldiers in the stressful conditions of battle demonstrated that "suppressed instinctive tendencies" could be released even in the most restrained of men.[1]

Even before the war, however, anthropologists of every theoretical persuasion were reappraising the role of emotions in social life. Finding evidence of an ineradicable irrational element in human conduct, they judged that emotionally charged behavior was not necessarily socially destructive. Indeed, reversing his earlier position, J. G. Frazer had by 1909 determined that modern peoples upheld the norms of their society for utterly irrational reasons, no less than savages. Similarly, Bronislaw Malinowski argued in 1922 that individuals' conformity to societal norms was prompted by feelings of collective solidarity, not by sensible calculations of the benefits to be gained from social order. Hocart observed that emotional commitments were essential even to scientific inquiry – the most rational of human activities. Indeed, the greatest error promulgated by

---

[1] A. M. Hocart, "Fear and the Anthropologists," *Nature* 134 (1934): 475; R. R. Marett, "The Psychology of Culture Contact, Presidential Address to the Folklore Society," *Folk-Lore* 28 (1917): 14; W. H. R. Rivers, "Inaugural Address to the Medical Section of the British Psychological Society," *The Lancet* 1919 (1): 891.

anthropological studies, said Rivers, was the belief that primitives were distinguished from modern peoples by the prelogical, irrational character of their thought and behavior; close investigation of simple societies "leads us into no mystical dawn of the human mind, but introduces us to concepts and beliefs of the same order as those which direct our own activities."[2]

How then were anthropologists to explain systematically the relationship between the personality structure of the individual and the constitution of society? Nineteenth-century anthropologists had assumed that a society was the sum of its individual parts, and to a characterization of the human mind and a contingent model of individual learning they joined a developmental scheme of social evolution. This scheme became incoherent if its Lamarckist premises no longer seemed tenable. One possible solution to the anthropologists' intellectual quandary was suggested at the turn of the century by Durkheim and his followers, whose work was widely read in Britain – by anthropologists of every theoretical persuasion, folklorists, sociologists, and others. The British functionalists, who dominated anthropology by the 1930s, declared Durkheim peculiarly their own, however, and produced an Anglicized version of his scheme that described individual responses as simple products of cultural conditioning, rendering the individual as such epiphenomenal. To be sure, social determinism figured in evolutionist and diffusionist theories, each of which described the effect of culture on the expression of human potential. But functionalists took social determinism to extremes – perhaps because their major theorists, Malinowski and Radcliffe-Brown, spent most of their working lives outside their native societies, and knew from experience that the behavioral skills specific to each alien culture in which they found themselves were not natural but learned.

Functionalists postulated that individuals' modes of thinking and feeling were "collective representations," imposed on them by their society. And collective representations were rational by relative rather than by absolute standards – appropriate insofar as they served to motivate individuals to play their proper social roles. Malinowski taught his students to repudiate the excessive Durkheimianism of Radcliffe-Brown – "a sociological determinism of culture which is just as dangerous and one-sided as the point of

---

[2] J. G. Frazer, *Psyche's Task* (London, 1909); Bronislaw Malinowski, *Argonauts of the Western Pacific* (London, 1922), 90–1; A. M. Hocart, "Ritual and Emotion," in Lord Raglan, ed., *The Life-Giving Myth and Other Essays* (London, 1952 [essay orig. 1939]), 53; W. H. R. Rivers, "Medicine, Magic, and Religion," The Fitzpatrick Lectures to the Royal College of Physicians Lecture I, *The Lancet* 1916 (1); 65. Malinowski noted the change of heart of Frazer, his sometime mentor, with considerable approval; see his "Memorandum for the Rockefeller Foundation Written for Mr. Embree in March 1926," preserved in the Oldham Papers, Box 1 OUODP.

view of the environmentalist or the materialist." Students were obliged to recognize that the subject of their inquiries was not "so completely dominated by the group ... that he obeys the commands of his community, its traditions, its public opinion, its decrees, with a slavish, fascinated, passive obedience."[3] But Malinowski insisted that individuals' choices were framed by their cultures, and pronounced his theoretical dicta accordingly: "As sociologists, we are not interested in what A or B may feel *qua* individuals ... only in what they feel *qua* members of a given community."[4]

Functionalists allowed that general human biological characteristics limited the variability of cultural forms to a degree; to survive in its environment, every society had to develop institutions that served the basic biological requirements of self-preservation. For example, every society had to contrive means of regulating individuals' sexual drives. And every kinship structure had to cope with the needs women had during pregnancy and childbirth. But functionalists reasoned that the biological characteristics of the individual members of a society were not as such critical to the group's capacity to adapt to its environment. Successful adaptation was a product of social organization, and could be achieved in many ways. And social organization rigorously shaped the expression of humankind's innate endowments.[5]

The group of anthropologists who chronologically and intellectually stood between the evolutionists and the functionalists were the diffu-

---

[3] See, for example, Gunter Wagner's paper for Malinowski's seminar, "Theory of Culture," 26 October, 1933, preserved in the Perham Papers, Box 10, OUODP; in this paper, Wagner dutifully criticized not only Radcliffe-Brown but also the evolutionists and the diffusionists – the anthropological factions the functionalists had to defeat to achieve paramountcy in the discipline. Wagner is evidently restating Malinowski's argument here. See, for example, Malinowski, *Crime and Custom in Savage Society* (see chap. 2, n. 81), 3–4.

[4] Malinowski, *Argonauts*, 23.

[5] See, for example, Malinowski, "Parenthood – the Basis of Social Structure" (see chap. 1, n. 9), esp. 117–19, 132–3, 154; Bronislaw Malinowski, "Psychoanalysis and Anthropology," *Nature* 112 (1923): 650–1; A. R. Radcliffe-Brown, "The Methods of Ethnology and Social Anthropology," in M. N. Srinivas, ed., *Method in Social Anthropology* (Chicago, 1958 [essay orig. 1923]), 3–38; A. R. Radcliffe-Brown, "The Social Organization of Australian Tribes," *Oceania* 1 (1930): 30. One is bound to observe that the British functionalists were blind to the biological basis of Durkheim's formulations, and also chose to ignore the evolutionist character of his theory. See Robert A. Nye, "Heredity, Pathology and Psychoneurosis in Durkheim's Early Work," *Knowledge and Society* 4 (1983): 103–42. On Malinowski's efforts to integrate psychological and social analysis, in particular, see George W. Stocking, Jr., "Anthropology and the Science of the Irrational: Malinowski's Encounter with Freudian Psychoanalysis," in Stocking, ed., *Malinowski, Rivers, Benedict and Others* (Madison, Wis., 1986), 13–49.

sionists, who explicitly rejected uncompromising social determinism. They fought their theoretical battles on two fronts – against their predecessors and successors. Diffusionists fairly represented the functionalist position that "social facts are of a special order, just as objective and independent as any other facts of nature, and require their own special mode of explanation" (an axiom from which no functionalist, however interested in psychology, would have dissented); and diffusionists agreed that a people's social organization was important to its environmental adaptation. But diffusionists insisted that any adequate account of social processes required attention to "motives derived from the psychology of the individual state."[6] The dynamics of individual personality structure were to a degree independent of social facts, derived from human biology and explicable in Mendelian terms.

The diffusionists' research program retained all of the elements that had figured in evolutionist anthropology, linking explanation of humankind's biological evolution with a model of individual psychology at once physiological and cultural, and mandating investigation of the course of human history as some function of individual psychology. The comprehensiveness of their scheme reflected their training, for, more than any other group of figures treated in this study, the diffusionists commanded knowledge of the diverse fields the evolutionists had intended to synthesize. The diffusionists came from the first generation of anthropologists to be thoroughly dominated by academics. But in their generation the professionals who framed anthropological argument were in large part employed in fields other than anthropology. Engaged in the effort to relate their specialized areas of expertise to one another, diffusionists produced analyses far more complex – and esoteric – than did evolutionists.

Diffusionists also addressed a general audience, and the appeal of diffusionism in the World War I era must be explained as the product of general cultural factors, at least in part, for its model expressed widely held sentiments. It explained human adaptation and cultural change in pessimistic fashion, stressing the unconscious and irrational features of human motivation. Obviously, the diffusionists had been affected by the horrors of World War I and by the social turmoil of the years before the war. But the mode of expression of general attitudes through anthropology was shaped by the peculiar constitution of the discipline at the time. The leading exponents of diffusionism brought to their analysis of social phenomena the training they had received as physicians. Their argument was defined in the context of medical research and practice, and sheer force of numbers alone made physicians especially prominent in the

---

[6] See W. H. R. Rivers, "The Primitive Conception of Death," in G. Elliot Smith, ed., *Psychology and Ethnology* (London, 1926), 36–7.

anthropological community during the first two decades of the twentieth century. The internal constitution of the discipline shaped its focus, making its central concerns those that had consistently occupied anthropologists who studied the physical features of human evolution. The physicians in the anthropological community were predisposed to accept central tenets of diffusionist argument, not the least because they had been among its first members to endorse the Mendelian model of heredity.

Moreover, when diffusionists prescribed a historical approach to cultural analysis, arguing against the functionalists, they were reasoning as medical diagnosticians. Functionalists insisted that however customs had originated and been modified over time, they were sustained in the present only because they fulfilled some current needs; indeed, in the past they might have served very different purposes. Rivers, who was the diffusionists' most eminent spokesman, countered that a people's beliefs and habits could no more be understood without a knowledge of their history than a patient's symptoms could be interpreted and treated without knowledge of his or her personal history.[7] Because physician-anthropologists were concerned to treat social pathologies, they also considered the relativist assumptions of functionalist method to be nonsensical. Functionalists were prepared to label individual responses as defective only if they represented a failure of individual adjustment to collective norms, suspending judgment of cultural norms themselves. By contrast, physicians brought to cross-cultural analysis their professional diagnostic categories, and could judge a social structure pathological if it produced many individual cases of the psychopathologies they had been trained to recognize. By comparing cultures across time and place, paying particular attention to societies' responses to the stresses of historical change, they would work "toward construction of a science of social psychology," as Rivers stated.[8]

The most controversial feature of the diffusionists' work was their historical account of cultural evolution, articulated by Elliot Smith and Perry before the First World War, when they were at Manchester University, the former as professor of anatomy and the latter as reader in comparative religion. After the war, the two moved to University College, London, where, as professor of anatomy and reader in cultural anthropology, they established a graduate training program designed to realize their vision of

[7] W. H. R. Rivers, *Dreams and Primitive Culture* (Manchester, 1918), 16.

[8] W. H. R. Rivers, *History of Melanesian Society* (Cambridge, 1914), Vol. II, 596. This was the position Rivers maintained to the end of his life. See his "Psychology and Politics," in *Psychology and Politics and Other Essays* (London, 1922 [essay orig. 1922]), 8. The psychological focus of diffusionism was also apparent in the work of those of its adherents who were not medically trained. See, for example, W. J. Perry, "The Isles of The Blest," *Folk-Lore* 32 (1921): 150–80.

anthropology as "Human Studies," a discipline integrating every form of
biological and cultural analysis of humankind past and present. Only a
small group of persons joined them to constitute the diffusionist school
proper, endorsing their entire research program, including its socio-
historical component – a fantastic account of the invention of culture.[9]
  The conspicuously bizarre aspects of diffusionism, and the disrepute
into which it fell in the 1930s, should not blind us to the school's earlier
importance, however. The history of anthropology told from the standpoint
of the discipline's present practitioners tends to emphasize the school's
sectarian character – to explain that because the diffusionists' work was
inherently flawed the school attracted few fervent adherents even at the
height of its reputation in the era of World War I, and deservedly lost
whatever influence it had after the functionalists became paramount in the
discipline. But the diffusionists did not begin as cranks. Their scheme
incorporated a general theoretical framework that appealed to an audience
far larger than avowed diffusionists – an audience that included other
members of the anthropological community as well as persons outside it. I
pay special attention to two features of their scheme: a psychological model
that explained both social change and individual pathology, which figured
in the applied psychology developed around the time of World War I; and a
normative political theory, which could be abstracted from the particulars
of their account of human social history. I treat these two aspects of the
diffusionists' work separately, since they appealed to somewhat different
intellectual constituencies. Those who focused on diffusionism's psychological aspects were concerned primarily to explain the impact of social
forces on individuals qua individuals, whereas the greater anthropological
community appreciated diffusionist analysis as a contribution to the understanding of group behavior; the respective emphases of these overlapping
populations gave their work rather different prescriptive political implications. I consider the elaboration of diffusionist argument into social
psychology in this chapter; diffusionist political theory is discussed in
Chapter 6.
  As social psychologists, diffusionists had a practical objective much like
that of the evolutionists. That is, they were concerned to foster social
harmony, and assumed that the irrational behavior of the laboring classes
constituted a major cause of social pathology. Believing the physicocultural
characteristics of members of these classes to be susceptible to modification, evolutionists had expected them to develop into rational, cooper-

[9] An outline of diffusionists' history can be gleaned from any number of diffusionist
tracts. See, for example, W. J. Perry, *The Children of the Sun* (London, 1923); G. Elliot
Smith, *The Evolution of the Dragon* (Manchester, 1919); and G. Elliot Smith, *Ancient
Egyptians* (London, 1911).

ative beings through behavioral change – to be effected in large part through moral persuasion, the instrument of much nineteenth-century British social welfare policy. Diffusionist research disconfirmed evolutionist prophesy by demonstrating the nearly immutable physical character of the human species. Diffusionists reasoned that what cultural variation obtained among peoples was a function of their social organization, not their natural endowments – which were far less variable among populations judged in the aggregate than they were among individual members of a population. Various forms of social organization elicited different elements of inherited human potential. The logical implication of this argument was that the cure for social pathology was social structural reform.

Largely inspired as it was by the search for the origins of pathological behavior in the workplace (including the battlefield), the social psychology rooted in diffusionist research served to advance a new view of the British worker, and by extension a reformulation of British social welfare policy: workers would not be affected by moral exhortations, for their behavior – however irrational – was an involuntary response to the realities of their situations, and amiable relations between workers and employers required improved working conditions; the organization of society as a whole placed many individuals in positions in which they could not care for themselves or others, whatever their strengths of character might be. To be sure, in the post–World War I era various factors conspired to provoke British industry to adopt new management strategies and to compel the state to provide more social services. But the new social psychology that had its origins in anthropological inquiry both rationalized and inspired change in this period.

Orthodox diffusionism and its denominations

According to the diffusionists, the evolutionists had been wrong to explain similarities in the cultures of peoples all over the world as the result of independent invention. The psychic unity of humankind had not led peoples everywhere to evolve independently in parallel fashion. Rather, what cultural similarities obtained among peoples were the result of diffusion. The beliefs and practices of so-called primitives were not indicators of arrested development, for the cultures of primitives, like those of advanced peoples, were products of complex histories. Nevertheless, judged by absolute standards, the developments of Western civilization constituted progress. And the basis of all innovations associated with progress was a culture complex the diffusionists termed the "Archaic Civilization." It had been invented only once, in ancient Egypt, and, spreading throughout the

world, had been variously elaborated by its recipients. The Archaic Civilization was a cultural sport, but it survived because it appealed to the instinct
common to people everywhere – the instinct of self-preservation, or the
fear of death.

Elliot Smith and Perry described the details of the development of the
Archaic Civilization in a fashion akin to sensationalist tabloids' accounts of
the contributions to world history made by extraterrestrials. Yet, it was
paradoxically the absurdity of their narrative of the origin of the Archaic
Civilization that made it seem plausible to them. Seeking to formulate laws
of human social development, they believed that their generalizations had
to be consistent with the then-current scientific explanation of biological
evolution – a Darwinian interpretation tempered by Mendelism. Therefore,
they reasoned, the origin of a new civilization was an unpredictable, chance
variation, just as the origin of a new species was. Originating in a single
place, a new species of culture became dispersed through migration to
various locations, there to undergo adaptation to local conditions.[10]

Virtually all of the features of the Archaic Civilization were determined
by the peculiar environment of Egypt, and none of them was the product of
human design. Critical to the Archaic Civilization, for example, was the use
of metal tools. The invention of metal tools was accidental: crude copper
ore, easily obtained in Egypt and used by its women (and possibly its men)
as a cosmetic, somehow dropped into a fire and turned to metal. The utility
of metal was then recognized, and it was fashioned into implements, which
were put to both peaceful and military purposes – the building of stone
monoliths, and the consolidation and defense of the Egyptian kingdom.
Settled agriculture was developed because the fertile lands of the Nile
Valley yielded "a natural crop of barley." When the consumers of this yield
realized that they could enlarge it by deliberate cultivation, they generated
an agricultural surplus, which was differentially distributed among the
population. Thus, for the first time in human history there emerged a
hierarchy of social classes, dominated by the occupants of offices in the
new state.

The religious elements of the Archaic Civilization also developed fortu-
itously, although they survived because they served fundamental human
needs. Elaborate rituals for the dead were inspired by the instinctive drive
for self-preservation; these rituals included mummification and building
monuments. Nevertheless, the impetus to develop mummification techniques was unintended: the dry climate of Egypt preserved corpses, and the

---

[10] The discontinuous element in this narrative is, of course, the Mendelian modification.
Otherwise, the diffusionists' model is Darwin's. See Charles Darwin, *The Origin of
Species* (London, 1872, 6th ed., Vol. I: 10; II: 135; II: 140.

Egyptians worked to improve upon the effects of nature because they believed that preservation of the body conferred immortality. The techniques used in mummification were inherently distasteful. That mummification practices nevertheless proved attractive to peoples all over the globe demonstrated the strength of the instinct of self-preservation. Historical accident made the people of the Archaic Civilization sun worshippers. Their religion was brought to them by a racially distinct people of Asiatic (Armenoid) origin, who came to Egypt during the early dynastic period.

After absorbing the Archaic Civilization in Egypt, the migratory Armenoids became the agents of its diffusion abroad, the "Children of the Sun." They wandered in search of precious substances such as gold, pearls, turquoise, copper, tin, and flint, which they imagined to be "Givers of Life." Peoples everywhere found their culture appealing, and, not the least because they were equipped with metal weapons, the Children of the Sun became the rulers of whatever areas they colonized. Peoples touched by the Archaic Civilization themselves carried it to new locations. The culture the migrants carried was not everywhere identical, for diffused culture was modified to suit local circumstances. Adaptation of diffused culture usually constituted degeneration, but the racially superior peoples of Europe had modified the Archaic Civilization for the better, creating modern culture. The Archaic Civilization was an arbitrary amalgam of practices: there was no natural connection between the building of megalithic monuments, sun worship, and mummification. Therefore, diffusionists reasoned that wherever in the world two of these three practices were found together they must have been transmitted by the Children of the Sun, rather than independently invented.

Critical to this explanatory scheme was the assumption that degeneration was a recurring element in human history. At all times and places, societies had experienced cultural decline because the individual personality was vulnerable to regression. The diffusionists argued that the evolutionists had underestimated the importance of diffusion in cultural innovation because they had refused to believe that even very early humans possessed the skills necessary for traveling great distances over land and water. To believe this, it was necessary to accept that the descendants of the ancient wanderers of the world had lost skills their ancestors possessed, and evolutionists were reluctant to do so. Evolutionists identified any form of degeneration as pathology of a severe order, assuming that the natural course of human history was progressive, and that whenever useful skills were learned, they would figure in future progress.[11]

[11] See, for example, W. H. R. Rivers, "Medicine, Magic and Religion," Lecture I of 1917, *The Lancet* 1917 (2): 919–23. For an earlier example of Rivers's thinking along these

Although wholly committed diffusionists represented a small anthropological sect, they nevertheless included a range of figures of major and
minor importance to the history of anthropology. The most distinguished
diffusionist convert was Rivers, who befriended Elliot Smith in 1896, when
the latter came from his native Australia to do graduate work at Cambridge, shortly becoming a Fellow of St. John's, Rivers's college. Indeed,
Smith credited Rivers for directing him to anthropology; in the winter of
1900–1, Rivers, who had himself only recently taken up anthropology,
came to Egypt, where Smith was professor of anatomy at the Government
Medical School, to avail himself of the opportunity to study the workmen
employed in an archaeological dig by David Randall MacIver and Rivers's
former student Anthony Wilkin, and urged his friend to undertake new
research.[12] Lately, new attention has been paid to the diffusionist writings
of A. M. Hocart, whom Rivers called "a disciple after his own heart" after
working with him on the Percy Sladen Trust Expedition to the Solomons
in 1908–9. But Hocart's work attracted relatively little notice during his
lifetime, not the least because his formal ties to the anthropological community were weak. The only successful application Hocart made for an
academic appointment was for the chair of sociology at the Egyptian
University at Cairo (which he took up in 1934, following Evans-Pritchard),
and he had few institutional connections with the discipline in Britain
beyond his brief tenure as an honorary lecturer at University College and
service on the Royal Anthropological Institute Council.[13]

The disrepute into which diffusionism fell in British anthropological
circles – indicated by the failure of any of Smith and Perry's students

lines, see his "The Disappearance of Useful Arts," originally published in 1912,
reprinted in *Psychology and Ethnology*, 190–210.

[12] We are bound to observe that the range of interests Elliot Smith came to embrace was
very like that of his Cambridge mentor, Alexander Macalister; see Appendix 2 for
biographical sketches of both. Nevertheless, Elliot Smith evidently considered Rivers a
more desirable intellectual ancestor. Rivers urged Smith to undertake study of the
preserved brains of predynastic Egyptians, and these remains suggested to Elliot Smith
(although they do not to us) problems in social anthropological analysis. See Elliot
Smith's "Introduction" to *Psychology and Ethnology*, xiii–xiv.

[13] Hocart was seriously considered for at least two major appointments, however – the
chairs at Cambridge and Sydney. For a reappraisal of Hocart see Rodney Needham's
"Editor's Introduction" to a reprint of Hocart's *Kings and Councillors* (Chicago, 1970
[orig. Cairo, 1936]), xiii–xcix. Needham's essay both reviews recent appraisals of Hocart
and permits us to recognize Hocart's intellectual identity as a diffusionist. The Rivers
quotation comes from this essay (p. xviii). Hocart himself thought that the diffusionists'
methodology was valuable, but had some doubts about their account of evolution. He did
not wish to be thought one of the "sun cranks," as he wrote to A. C. Haddon from
Ceylon on September 9, 1927, HP, CU, Env. 4. But the diffusionists embraced him as
one of their own because they recognized affinities between his work and theirs.

to find employment teaching anthropology in Britain – did not extend throughout British university circles. The two men worked with figures who became prominent in religious studies in Britain, and in this field a modified version of the diffusionist historical saga compelled academic respect.[14] Elliot Smith worked with persons who became eminent practitioners of paleoanthropology – the specialized area in which Elliot Smith's expertise was acknowledged by anthropologists of every persuasion – and one of these, Raymond Dart, was employed by the only university that tolerated unreconstructed diffusionists, the University of the Witwatersrand in Johannesburg.[15] There was one man prominent in post–World War II social anthropology who flirted briefly with diffusionism: it was C. Daryll Forde (1902–73), who took his Ph.D. at UCL in prehistoric archaeology.[16] No trace of Forde's sometime enthusiasm remained in his work, however, after he trained in social anthropology as a postdoctoral fellow at Berkeley. But his institutional ties doubtless figured in his selection to preside over the reorganization of anthropology teaching at UCL after World War II as the college's first professor of anthropology.

I must stress that the diffusionists' eclipse could not have been predicted in the era of World War I. During this period diffusionists enjoyed considerable respect in scientific circles. In particular, Rivers and Elliot Smith

[14] J. R. Porter, "Two Presidents of the Folklore Society: S. H. Hooke and E. O. James," *Folklore* 88 (1977): 131–45.

[15] Dart joined the faculty of the University of the Witwatersrand in 1923 as professor of anatomy, achieving international recognition for the work he did indicating that the human species originated in Africa, but dabbled in historical speculations of the diffusionist sort. In 1946, Wits appointed a recently retired member of the Nigerian Colonial Service, M. D. W. Jeffreys, who had done a Ph.D. at UCL in 1934. Jeffreys taught social anthropology, and seems to have been the only convinced diffusionist who was able to secure an academic appointment to do so. On Dart's paleoanthropological career, see Roger Lewin, *Bones of Contention* (New York, 1987), 50–60. For some specimens of Dart's diffusionist effusions, see his "The Historical Succession of Cultural Impacts upon South Africa," *Nature* 115 (1925): 425–9; idem, "Foreign Influences of the Zimbabwe and Pre-Zimbabwe Eras," *NADA (The Native Affairs Department Annual, Southern Rhodesia)* 32 (1955): 19–30; idem, "The Earlier Stages of the Indian Transoceanic Traffic," *NADA* 34 (1957): 95–115; idem, "Death Ships in South West Africa and South-East Asia," *South African Archaeological Bulletin* 17 (1962): 231–4. For some articles indicating that Jeffreys kept the diffusionist faith, see his "Zimbabwe and Galla Culture," *South African Archaeological Bulletin* 9 (1954): 152; and his "Manga-Mecca," *NADA* 9 (1967): 21–4.

[16] See, for example, Forde's conventional diffusionist effort, *Ancient Mariners: The Story of Ships and Sea Routes* (London, 1927). This was one of a series of books written for popular consumption which were edited by Elliot Smith and published by Gerald Howe, Ltd. Titled "In the Beginning of Things," this series itself was an indicator of the public enthusiasm for diffusionism.

were elected to numerous offices in British learned societies, and Rivers saw fit to make his 1911 Presidential Address to Section H of the British Association the occasion of his announcement of his conversion from evolutionism to diffusionism.[17] Figures such as A. C. Haddon and Bronislaw Malinowski, pillars of past and future anthropological orthodoxy, described the initial broadcasts of the diffusionist school with cautious respect, although they both came to oppose the school vigorously.[18] Indeed, Haddon produced work in which he explained cultural change as the product of contact between migrating peoples, citing diffusionist research results as evidence for his own conclusions.[19] Significantly, the *Encyclopaedia Britannica* commissioned Elliot Smith to write the article on anthropology for its 1922 volumes; the author of this entry in the 1910 edition had been E. B. Tylor, and Bronislaw Malinowski would be selected in 1926.

The conclusion of the diffusionist saga varies with the narrator. Anthropologists' version of the story tells us less about the intrinsic bankruptcy of diffusionist ideas than about the divorce of anthropology from psychology that occurred in Britain after World War I. Diffusionist ideas were not thoroughly discredited in academic circles, but were elaborated after the war, primarily by those students and colleagues of Rivers who became psychologists rather than anthropologists. British social psychologists developed a model of human learning consistent with the theory of social change embedded in diffusionist research. This model relied both on evidence Rivers's students accumulated through psychological experimentation and on ethnographic data, some of which they themselves gathered in the field and some of which they gleaned from others' work. Indeed, Rivers's psychological followers were recognized as "the modern British school of academic psychology" at the same time as their views were being repudiated by their contemporaries among academic anthropologists.[20] The pattern of disciplinary differentiation evident in the split between the previously overlapping fields of anthropology and psychology – the definition of intel-

[17] Rivers and Elliot Smith were both fellows of the Royal Society, presidents of Section H of the British Association, and fellows of the Royal College of Physicians. For further biographical data, see Appendix 2,

[18] For early respectful reviews see A. C. Haddon, "The Ethnological Nature of Shells," *Nature* 100 (1918): 482; A. C. Haddon, "Ethnographic Studies in Melanesia," *Nature* 95 (1915): 319–21; B. Malinowski, "New and Old in Anthropology," *Nature* 113 (1924): 299–301. C. G. Seligman, for one, thought that Malinowski's praise of the diffusionists' ideas as "brilliant" had been rather too extravagant. See Seligman to Malinowski, January 28, 1924, MP, YU.

[19] A. C. Haddon, *The Wanderings of Peoples* (Cambridge, 1911), 56.

[20] A. G. Tansley, "The Relations of Complex and Sentiment," *British Journal of Psychology* 8 (1922): 120.

lectual communities on the basis of practically incompatible theories – is common enough in the history of science.[21]

Moreover, given Rivers's institutional positions, it is not surprising that a larger portion of his intellectual legacy should have been left to psychologists than to anthropologists. Rivers figured in many learned circles, including those of sociology, physiology, psychiatry, and folklore, as well as anthropology and psychology. But the teaching appointments he held at Cambridge from 1893 until shortly before his death in 1922 were in physiological and experimental psychology. He offered lectures in social anthropology, but he did so gratis. After Rivers's death, Cambridge appointed his (and Haddon's) student W. E. Armstrong to lecture on social anthropology in a temporary capacity between 1922 and 1926, during which time Armstrong taught Gregory Bateson (among others) Riversian psychological anthropology. But when Haddon retired in 1926, to be replaced as reader by T. C. Hodson, Armstrong lost his chance for a permanent appointment; Cambridge had evidently taken seriously Haddon's argument that anthropology was the intellectual basis of colonial administration, for Hodson was a retired Indian Civil Servant.[22] Moreover, Rivers was an arbiter of scholarship in psychology more than in any other field, since, along with Frazer's friend James Ward, he founded the *British Journal of Psychology* in 1904. Finally, after Rivers's death in 1922, the most prominent scientist among the diffusionists was Elliot Smith. Rivers's students could not construct a diffusionist coalition in anthropology without Smith, who was a notoriously difficult person, countenancing no deviation from his (sometimes inconsistent) personal doctrine.[23]

It was possible to extract a viable research program from diffusionism, however. The diffusionist model was coherent, although it was extremely complex, requiring demonstration that individuals' behavior was the product of their neuroanatomy, their innate psychological responses, their personal histories, and their cultural conditioning. To be sure, the diffusionists' historical narrative was far from sensible in its details. In gross outline, however, it had a rationale: it fit the general pattern that human history had to have taken if human nature was accurately described by

---

[21] In the United States after World War I, for example, anthropology and psychology also became mutually exclusive, although their division of intellectual spheres did not mirror the British one. See, for example, Clark Wissler, "Opportunities for Coordination in Anthropological and Psychological Research," *American Anthropologist* [n.s.] 22 (1920): 1–12.

[22] James Urry, "W. E. Armstrong and Social Anthropology at Cambridge, 1922–26," *Man* [n.s.] 20 (1985): 412–33.

[23] On the hazards of dealing with Elliot Smith, see C. G. Seligman (whose relations with him were quite cordial) to Bronislaw Malinowski, May 12, 1923, in MP, LSE.

diffusionist psychologists and their allies in the biomedical sciences. We can elicit the logic of the diffusionist argument if we pay particular attention to three scientific episodes: one, the 1898 Cambridge Anthropological Expedition to Torres Straits; two, the conduct of a series of paleontological investigations – one of which involved the fraudulent "Piltdown Man" remains – all of them yielding consistent results, which attracted national

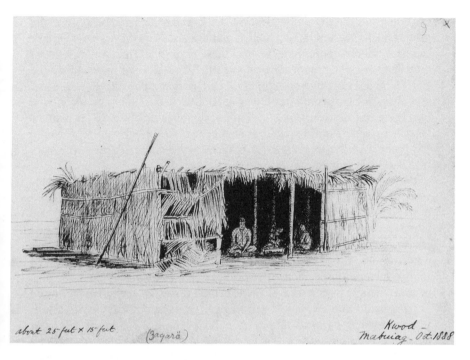

about 25 feet × 15 feet.   (Bagarä)   Kwod –
Matuiag – Oct. 1888

A. C. Haddon turning to anthropological matters: two of the drawings he
did on his first trip to Torres Straits. Reproduced by permission of the
Syndics of Cambridge University Library (Haddon Papers).

attention when they figured in the deliberations of the Inter-Departmental
Committee on Physical Deterioration convened by the government after
the South African War to assess the physical condition of the British
population; three, the experiments on nerve regeneration performed between 1903 and 1908 by Rivers and (Sir) Henry Head (1861–1940). The
conclusions drawn from these episodes, together with those derived from
related projects, informed the work diffusionists did as military psychiatrists
during World War I. This was the most important work they did as a
group, and it had a lasting impact.

The origin of intellectual lineages in the Torres Straits

The intellectual pedigree of modern British social anthropologists conventionally – and with considerable justification – begins with the members of

the 1898 Cambridge Anthropological Expedition to Torres Straits. In the discipline's received family history, the expedition's members were the professional ancestors of the later functionalists. Nonetheless, it is equally (perhaps more) appropriate to see these figures as the progenitors of diffusionism and its psychological variant. The evidence provided by the expedition disconfirmed evolutionist generalizations. The diffusionist model served to explain the findings the evolutionist scheme could not, identifying the Torres Straits islanders as adaptive creatures no different in psychological character from any other human beings, whose behavior represented the product of the interaction of fundamental biological nature with particular circumstances.

Between April and November of 1898, the expedition went to do fieldwork among the Melanesian peoples resident in a cluster of some twenty-eight islands in the waters between Australia and New Guinea. The islanders were hardly untouched by European culture. From the seventeenth century, Dutch, Spanish, and British ships had sailed through their waters. From 1863, they had been subjected to formal Anglo-Australian rule of increasing specificity. From 1871, they had suffered the attentions of missionaries. By the time of the expedition, most of them had converted to Christianity and learned Pidgin English, facilitating communication with the anthropologists. And they were participants in the colonial economy, largely as suppliers of pearl-shell and pearls (although trade had declined around the time of the expedition, because the local waters had been overfished). By the anthropological standards of the day, they were especially important subjects for analysis, for if they were not studied soon, their disappearing culture would no longer be available for inspection. And the islands were an ideal venue for anthropological work, because they had been touched by colonialism in very different degrees, making them good subjects for comparative analysis.

The expedition was organized by A. C. Haddon, who had paid his first visit to Torres Straits in 1888 in his earlier incarnation as a zoologist, intending to study the coral reefs and marine biology there. Before he departed for the islands, however, his friend J. G. Frazer asked Haddon to collect anthropological information for him. Perhaps provoked by Frazer's request, Haddon found himself in the islands increasingly drawn to anthropological matters. The Cambridge expedition was the product of his resolve to return to Torres Straits with a scientific team capable of conducting a thorough anthropological investigation, and it was so named because the university made the largest single contribution to its support (and provided additional funds when the expedition ran over budget). Funds also came from the Royal Society (prompted by Frazer and Galton), the British

Association, and the Royal Geographical Society, supplemented by a small sum from the territorial government of Queensland.[24]

Haddon was accompanied by W. H. R. Rivers and Rivers's former students C. S. Myers (1873–1946) and William McDougall (1871–1938); Myers's friend C. G. Seligman; Sidney Ray (1858–1939); and Anthony Wilkin (1878–1901), a promising Cambridge undergraduate. All but Rivers and Wilkin went on to Borneo from the Torres Straits for further work, but this phase of their research, which was part of the original expedition plan, yielded relatively inconsequential results.[25] Significantly, all but Ray and Wilkin had come to anthropology from the biomedical sciences. Rivers, Myers, McDougall, and Seligman had all been trained as physicians, and for all of them the Torres Straits Expedition was their initiation into anthropology. Their medical training not only shaped their research but also facilitated it, since many islanders came to them in the first instance to get medical attention in the dispensary they set up immediately.[26]

Not all of the members of the expedition left professional descendants. Ray, an expert on the languages of Oceania, spent his entire career as a primary school teacher. Wilkin, who served as the expedition's photographer and did some of its ethnographic research, had before his premature death produced some exotic travel literature and undertaken archaeological excavation. But he is best remembered because a Cambridge fellowship to support field research was established in his memory (it was first awarded in 1906 to Radcliffe-Brown). Haddon and Rivers spawned a distinguished anthropological lineage at Cambridge, however, including Radcliffe-Brown and W. J. Perry; Gregory Bateson, also a recipient of the Anthony Wilkin Studentship, was the last notable Haddon student to work in the anthropological mode the Torres Straits Expedition was intended to promote. As the first professor of ethnology at the London School of Economics, Seligman was one of Malinowski's teachers, and Malinowski himself supervised most of the future leaders of the discipline at the LSE during the interwar period. But some of the LSE students worked closely with Seligman, most notably Evans-Pritchard, whose early research reflected Seligman's influence.[27]

[24] See Haddon's account books; the letter written on behalf of the Royal Society to Haddon by J. Keltie, 14 October, 1897; and the proceedings of the Cambridge University Senate Meeting of 9 November, 1899, in HP, CU, Envs. 1021 and 1049.

[25] The most significant product of this research was a collaborative effort between William McDougall and a colonial civil servant in Borneo, Charles Hose, *The Pagan Tribes of Borneo* (London, 1912).

[26] A. C. Haddon, *Headhunters Black, White, and Brown* (London, 1901), vii–viii, 22.

[27] The relationship between Seligman and Evans-Pritchard was not based simply on personal affinity (although Evans-Pritchard's famous antipathy toward Malinowski may

Members of the Cambridge expedition to Torres Straits also figure prominently in the academic genealogy of British psychology.[28] At Cambridge, Rivers and Myers taught F. C. (Sir Frederick) Bartlett (1886–1969). A line of academic succession was established from Rivers to Myers to Bartlett. Myers followed Rivers as director of the Cambridge Psychological Laboratory in 1907, and was succeeded by Bartlett after he founded (with H. J. Welch) the National Institute of Industrial Psychology in 1921 and left Cambridge. Myers replaced Ward as Rivers's coeditor of the *British Journal of Psychology* in 1911, becoming its sole editor in 1913; and Bartlett replaced Myers in 1924, retaining the editorship until 1948. Bartlett became the first professor of experimental psychology at Cambridge, and until his retirement in 1952 worked to expand the department at Cambridge and to extend its influence in British psychology; in 1960, most of the occupants of chairs of psychology in British universities had been Bartlett's students. McDougall did not fulfill his earlier promise after he left Britain in 1920 for the United States, where he was employed first at Harvard and then at Duke. But prior to his military service in World War I, McDougall had been from 1904 Oxford's Wilde reader in mental philosophy, and had worked with a number of graduate students who later achieved some eminence in British psychology.

Prominent among McDougall's students was the man generally termed Britain's "first professional psychologist," the immensely influential and posthumously notorious (Sir) Cyril Burt (1883–1971), who was also linked to the Cambridge network through Myers, serving briefly as Myers's assistant in the Cambridge Psychological Laboratory from 1912 to 1913 and later working for the National Institute of Industrial Psychology. The statistical psychological research of Francis Galton, Karl Pearson, and Charles Spearman provided the principal intellectual inspiration for Burt's work, and his career as a public figure realized their practical ambitions. But the Torres Straits researchers also did work that prefigured Burt's – the tests he constructed to measure individual aptitudes, and the statistical analyses

---

have reinforced it) but rather had a recognizable intellectual dimension. Evans-Pritchard's approach to analysis of traditional magic and medicine taken in his monograph *Witchcraft, Magic and Oracles Among the Azande* (Oxford, 1937) is very like that outlined by Seligman, and also followed Rivers. The latter acknowledged Seligman's influence in his Fitzpatrick Lectures to the Royal College of Physicians, delivered in 1916 and 1917, which were in part based on research he had done with Hocart in Eddystone Island. See especially lecture two of the series by W. H. R. Rivers titled "Medicine, Magic and Religion," *The Lancet* 1916 (1): 117–23. For Seligman's efforts to make peace between Evans-Pritchard and Malinowski, see his letter to the latter, 13 November, 1930, MP,YU.

[28] See, for example, Hearnshaw, *A Short History of British Psychology* (chap, 2, n. 70), 172–3.

he performed to weigh the relative importance of inheritance and environmental stimulation on intelligence – although Rivers and his colleagues would certainly not have approved Burt's manufacture of fraudulent data to support his hereditarian claims. Furthermore, Burt sustained his mentors' interest in the psychology of primitive peoples, and in specific problems that had been investigated in the Torres Straits Expedition.[29]

Haddon saw the development of anthropology as a field science as "merely one phase of an attitude of mind that is influencing many departments of thought"; in his original field of zoology, in psychology, in sociology, in all manner of disciplines, "arm-chair philosophers" were recognizing the necessity of "a combination of the observational with the comparative method."[30] The Torres Straits Expedition was intended to realize this new scientific attitude by fulfilling Haddon's "long felt" expectation "that psychological investigations must be undertaken before any real advance could be made in ethnology."[31] If exotic peoples were studied with the methods of the psychological laboratory, generalizations about their modes of thought would at last have a scientific basis; and psychological evidence about such peoples would provide common ground for the disciplines of psychology and anthropology, drawing them closer together and enlarging the comparative dimension of each. Haddon set about realizing his project by assembling a team of men skilled in psychological investigation – Rivers, Myers, and McDougall – entrusting the management of its research to Rivers. Seligman, engaged as the expedition's medical specialist, also assisted Rivers in psychological work.

Haddon could scarcely have acted earlier to formulate his interdisciplinary goal, however. At the time that he organized the expedition, experi-

[29] On Burt's career see, for example, ibid., 201–7. Burt's interest in "primitive psychology" led to his employment to train recruits to the Colonial Education Service, discussed in the next chapter. On Burt's concern to investigate one problem Rivers studied in the Torres Straits, the relation of color perception to eye pigmentation, see, for example, his request for information, "Colour Blindness and Pigmentation," *Man* 44 (1944): 79–80.

[30] A. C. Haddon, "Presidential Address to Section H of the British Association for the Advancement of Science," *Reports of the British Association for the Advancement of Science* 75 (1905): 512.

[31] C. Haddon, "Introduction," *Reports of the Cambridge Anthropological Expedition to Torres Straits*, Vol. I (Cambridge, 1935), xii. This is a position that Haddon maintained consistently. It is of some interest that when he praised Bronislaw Malinowski's first major work, *Argonauts of the Western Pacific*, he did so because it "provides unusual documentary evidence of exceptional value for the elucidation of native psychology"; see Haddon's "Ceremonial Exchange," *Nature* 110 (1922): 473. Malinowski would not have quarreled with Haddon's reading of his work, but he would have seen its emphasis as misplaced.

mental psychology was a very recent development in Britain. Galton's anthropometric laboratory, set up in 1884, was Britain's first psychological laboratory, and in it Galton measured individual differences of physical energy, sensory discrimination, and reaction time – phenomena that interested the Torres Straits investigators. Before returning to Torres Straits in his anthropological incarnation, Haddon himself undertook investigations like Galton's in Ireland, helped by Galton's "greatest encouragement and ... fullest assistance." Experimental psychology had been installed in British universities only in 1897: with the aid of financial support from patrons who included Galton and Lubbock, University College, London had purchased laboratory equipment previously the property of Hugo Münsterberg (who was moving from Freiburg to Harvard); and Michael Foster had persuaded Cambridge to provide a room for experimental psychology. Rivers was in charge of both of these laboratories. In securing Rivers's services, Haddon succeeded in enrolling the preeminent experimentalist of his day, the man British psychologists have continued to acknowledge as their first scientific experimentalist.[32]

The research ideal that had prompted the expedition continued to appeal to its members. They inspired a number of their graduate students to undertake interdisciplinary research: Bartlett did fieldwork in Swaziland; as a graduate student at Oxford, Hocart not only did fieldwork in the Pacific but also did psychological laboratory experiments with McDougall, odd though this seems in the light of his later scholarship.[33] And Rivers and his associates continued to argue that anthropology must avail itself of the methods and findings of psychology. This thesis was but a part of a sermon on the intellectually dysfunctional consequences of overspecialization that Rivers preached to every one of his audiences, from the Royal College of Physicians to the Royal Anthropological Institute. To Rivers's protégés, such as Seligman, Bartlett, and McDougall, psychology and anthropology had special affinity, as can be seen from their programmatic public addresses.[34]

---

[32] Hearnshaw, *A Short History of British Psychology*, 134–5; D. J. Cunningham and A. C. Haddon, "The Anthropometric Laboratory of Ireland," *Journal of the Anthropological Institute* 21 (1891): 35.

[33] A. M. Hocart and William McDougall, "Some Data for a Theory of Auditory Perception and Direction," *British Journal of Psychology* 2 (1908): 386–405.

[34] See, for examples, W. H. R. Rivers, "The Unity of Anthropology," Presidential Address, *Journal of the Royal Anthropological Institute* 52 (1922): 12–25; C. G. Seligman, "Anthropology and Psychology: A Study of Some Points of Contact," Presidential Address, *Journal of the Royal Anthropological Institute* 54 (1924): 13–46; William McDougall, *Anthropology and History*, The Robert Boyle Lecture (London, 1920); F. C. Bartlett, "Anthropology in Reconstruction," The Huxley Memorial Lecture, *Journal of the Royal Anthropological Institute* 73 (1943): 9–16.

Rivers's associates won considerable professional recognition, but it was discipline-specific, as can be judged from their careers in learned societies. Myers, for example, claimed responsibility for the acceptance of anthropology as a subject suitable for examination in a Cambridge tripos in 1913 and, had he made his career in an earlier era, would probably have been recognized as a leader of both anthropology and psychology. But though Myers served on the RAI Council (as did McDougall before he left Britain for the United States), he never presided over an anthropological association. Myers was, however, the first president of the British Psychological Society and twice president of the Psychological Section of the British Association for the Advancement of Science – Section J. Bartlett's organizational activities were restricted to psychology, and he served as president of both Section J and the British Psychological Society. And though he bore the banner of psychology in anthropological circles, Seligman became president only of Section H and of the RAI.

The Torres Straits Expedition was a watershed in the histories of both anthropology and psychology. For anthropology, it served to inspire at least one of the changes Haddon wanted: the fusion of the previously separable tasks of theorist and data collector. Yet, the younger generation who followed Haddon into the field created an anthropology very different from his. Research in the field came to be equated with the methodology of functionalist anthropology – characteristically analysis of a small society at a moment in time, resulting from participant observation by an anthropologist who for a year or so lived alone among an exotic people (sometimes accompanied by a spouse – and usually with European missionaries, traders, or colonial officials not very far away).

When anthropologists became fieldworkers, they did not necessarily become functionalists, however. Field research did not have to be ahistorical. And functionalists were obviously not the only anthropologists to see fieldwork as crucial to the explication of their theses. Rivers, for example, argued that fieldwork was essential to diffusionist research: direct observation was required to distinguish the fundamental social structure of a people from the superficial trappings of material culture, for a people might have acquired many of the accouterments of advanced society without modifying their ancient social organization; and field research permitted the anthropologist to disaggregate those features of a culture that reflected fundamental psychological drives from those that reflected a people's social structure.[35]

---

[35] W. H. R. Rivers, "The Ethnological Analysis of Culture," Presidential Address to Section H of the British Association in 1911, reprinted in *Psychology and Ethnology*, 133–7.

Indeed, it is just as appropriate to describe the Torres Straits Expedition as the culmination of a tradition of research as it is to see it as a revolutionary break. As J. L. Myres pointed out, it marked the end of an era for natural history: there were to be no more large-scale ventures mounted by naturalists of any variety, expeditions on which each member was expected to contribute a specialized skill to a complex research project.[36] And the organization of the expedition preserved one element of the structure of evolutionist anthropology, for old-style evolutionists also practiced team research, albeit of an uncoordinated sort. Furthermore, the six volumes that eventually resulted from the expedition's work were for the most part devoted to the sort of material armchair anthropologists found useful – that is, straightforward descriptions of diverse customs. In them, various features of social life were generally treated in isolation from one another. And the reports did not present the culture of the Torres Straits as a phenomenon sui generis, as the functionalists' detailed studies of particular areas were to do. Instead, they were predicated on the evolutionist assumption that the significance of the Torres Straits findings could be elucidated only by comparing data on the islanders' beliefs, behavior, and physical characteristics with data available for other peoples, European as well as non-Western.

The expedition's research featured two notable innovations, however, each of them conceived by Rivers. These were the use of the "genealogical method" and the conduct of psychological experiments of the sort usually performed in European laboratories. As developed by Rivers, the genealogical method was an instrument of survey research, useful to investigators spending only a brief time in the field.[37] Consisting of the compilation of informants' family histories, the method permitted rapid accumulation of social and vital statistics – patterns of marriage alliances; differential birth and death rates; and the incidence of aptitudes, disease, and congenital deformities among the population. Indeed, it may be appropriate to see both the organization of the Cambridge Expedition and the results obtained by the genealogical method as akin to those of a series of surveys of the British poor, the first of them mounted by Charles Booth and Seebohm Rowntree in the 1880s, which took the family or household as the basic unit of analysis, surveys with which anthropologists were certainly familiar.[38]

---

[36] Myres, "The Science of Man in the Service of the State," (see chap. 2, n. 43), 50.

[37] Rivers's anthropological methods were generally designed to facilitate speedy research, and were admired by the anthropological community for this reason. See, for example, A. M. Hocart's review of Rivers's *The History of Melanesian Society* (*Man* 15 [1915]: 89–93), which praises its factual accuracy while questioning some of its conclusions.

[38] See, for example, Francis Galton's 1902 Huxley Memorial Lecture to the Anthro-

This comparison probably would not have seemed odd to Rivers, who, like so many of his contemporaries, viewed primitives as akin to the British underclass.[39] Furthermore, the social surveys were expected to guide action to aid the poor to improve their lives, and were, as such, designed to elicit causal relationships, just as were Rivers's genealogical inquiries. Survey researchers also investigated the degree to which the pattern of behavior displayed by their subjects was a function of the habitual conditioning they received as members of a particular social group, and to the degree to which their behavior reflected their individual constitutions.[40]

More important, Rivers's genealogical method bears an intellectual family resemblance to the investigatory approach followed by Francis Galton, who compiled pedigrees to support his hereditarian views. Because he was a member of the sociointellectual community in which Galton figured prominently, Rivers was certainly familiar with Galton's genealogical research, although he did not cite it in descriptions of his method; and he developed his techniques to serve some purposes quite different from Galton's. Nevertheless, Rivers also intended his method to resolve issues that concerned Galton, for investigators who used the genealogical method as Rivers intended would take care to distinguish biological from adopted children. Thus, they could weigh the relative importance of heredity and environment in the determination of individual characteristics, and identify hereditary influences on fertility and pathology.

The precise nature of Rivers's relationship to Galton is practically irrelevant, however, for the intellectual habits of both men had a common antecedent – their medical training. When anthropologists took up the genealogical method, they were appropriating the medical practice of taking patients' histories. The immediate precursor of Rivers's method lay in the medical research on color vision which he had done prior to his trip to Torres Straits: the family histories he had compiled while analyzing individuals who were unable to identify colors accurately. Indeed, given that Rivers represented the analysis of culture as a task analogous to that of medical diagnosis, it seems that he himself believed that he had transferred his medical skills to anthropology.[41]

pological Institute, "The Possible Improvement of the Human Breed," reprinted in his *Essays in Eugenics* (London, 1909), 9–11.

[39] For one account of the British social survey, see Raymond Kent, "The Emergence of the Sociological Survey, 1887–1939," in Martin Bulmer, ed., *Essays on the History of British Sociological Research* (Cambridge, 1985), 52–69. And see Rivers, *Dreams and Primitive Culture*, 16–21.

[40] See, for example, McBriar, *Mixed Doubles* (chap. 3, n. 62), 268–74, 342.

[41] For some discussion of the genesis of the "genealogical method" and the possible influence of Galton on Rivers, see Ian Langham, *The Building of British Social Anthropology* (Boston, 1981), 67–71. In the published reports of the Cambridge Expedition to

In sum, the innovations of the Torres Straits Expedition figured in the modification of future anthropology, but research of the sort done in Torres Straits was not to be replicated precisely. Perhaps Rivers's formulation of the "genealogical method" served to intensify later social anthropologists' already considerable concern with kinship. Future social anthropologists would not conduct genealogical research in order to elucidate patterns of biological inheritance, however. And they were more concerned to translate into formal terms the social rules for contracting kinship alliances than they were to follow Rivers's injunction to use his method to specify the degree to which actual practices departed from professed rules. Nor was the research done in Torres Straits much imitated by future psychologists, as Bartlett was to point out.[42]

The laboratory in the field

With the equipment they had brought to Torres Straits, Rivers and his associates created a psychological laboratory there.[43] For four months, Rivers, Myers, and McDougall lived and worked on one of the Eastern Islands in Torres Straits, Mer, chosen as the site of intense study because it was so difficult of access that it was relatively unaffected by European influence (although Rivers was later to argue that a people such as the island's residents, Christianized and English-speaking, could not be expected to give authentic primitive responses).[44] With Seligman's assistance, Rivers supplemented the results of the Mer research with some comparative data. The two men spent five weeks on Mabauig, one of the Western

Torres Straits, Rivers does not describe the method as he applied it on the expedition, but refers the reader to his "A Genealogical Method of Collecting Social and Vital Statistics," *Journal of the Anthropological Institute* 30 (1900): 74–82, which contains no acknowledgments. For the sort of (rather disparaging) references Rivers made to Galton, see W. H. R. Rivers, "Introduction," *Reports of the Cambridge Expedition to Torres Straits*, Vol. II (Cambridge, 1901), 5.

[42] F. C. Bartlett, "Psychological Methods and Anthropological Problems," *Africa* 10 (1937): 403.

[43] Haddon's account book for the expedition includes the following psychological apparatus: light tests, spring balance, chronometer, sphygmomanometer, time marker, color tests, eye tester, diagrams, brass box, wools and types, Galton's whistle, obach cells, ohrmesser, whistle and mounting, scents, syren whistle, handgrasp dynamometer, induction coil and wire, marbles, dynamograph, pseudoptics, diapason, musical instruments, as well as some other bits of equipment and materials necessary for running and repairing them.

[44] W. H. R. Rivers, "A General Account of Method," in Barbara Friere-Marreco, ed., *Notes and Queries on Anthropology*, 4th ed. (London, 1912), 124.

Islands in Torres Straits, which was an area integrated into the colonial economy, as well as a week on the island of Kiwai, part of British New Guinea.[45]

Generating quantifiable data that could be compared with the results of experiments done in European laboratories, the expedition's psychological tests measured the "special senses" of sight, hearing, smell, and touch, using introspective and objective procedures. In large part, these were aptitude tests, comparable to those later used by Myers's industrial psychology organization for purposes of vocational guidance and selection.[46] The researchers' methods permitted disaggregation of aptitudes and achievements, between individuals' sensory capacities and the level to which they had developed their natural talents.

Rivers and his associate did not simply replicate European experiments in novel settings, however. Because they were able to observe their subjects both under experimental conditions and in everyday life, they were able to specify the various factors that affected the islanders' performances in psychological tests. In some respects, individuals' performances varied from day to day, modified by transitory conditions such as fatigue. In other respects, individuals' performances were consistent. Subjects consistently varied from one another because of their individual differences of maturity, personality, and innate capacity – visual and auditory acuity, age, temperamental characteristics, and ethnic backgrounds (which the researchers classified as biological factors). And the test results displayed general patterns – products of cultural factors that had shaped both subjects' trained perceptions and their interest in attending to any given task they were set by the psychologists.

By the standards employed in the Torres Straits experiments, then, the research done in European laboratories was inadequately controlled, for European psychologists were usually ignorant of the array of personal and cultural factors that affected test responses. Thus, the experiments conveyed lessons as much methodological as substantive, and had implications for future research in both anthropology and psychology. To anthropologists, the experiments disconfirmed conventional evolutionist wisdom about primitives' sensibilities. To psychologists, they demonstrated the unreliability of laboratory research conducted in ignorance of subjects' social situations; when researchers evaluated and reported their results,

---

[45] Unless otherwise noted, the description of the Torres Straits work that follows summarizes A. C. Haddon, ed., *Reports of the Cambridge Anthropological Expedition to Torres Straits*, Vol. II (Cambridge, 1901, 1903), See esp. 1–6, 25–6, 40–8, 64, 70, 83, 95, 127, 130–1, 137, 148, 177–82, 192–5; and Part II, 120–85.

[46] See, for example, "Vocational Guidance and Selection," a report on a lecture given by Myers, *The Lancet* 1920 (2): 1014–15.

they were obliged to specify the different situations in which they performed their experiments. For example, Rivers himself subsequently did
this when he described his studies of the effects of ingesting noxious
substances on individuals' experiences of potentially fatiguing tasks, which
he conducted with the assistance of McDougall and others.[47]

Observations of behavior seemed to provide partial confirmation of the
travelers' reports of primitives' extraordinary sensory skills. The islanders
were capable of identifying both faint sounds and distant objects that
were imperceptible to Europeans and seemed more tolerant of pain than
Europeans were, although their sense of smell did not appear to be highly
developed. Perhaps evolutionist argument was correct: peoples who possessed only primitive cultural institutions were also in a primitive stage of
physical development – closer to the lower animals than were Europeans.
Yet, the islanders' performances on psychological tests were not very
different from those of Europeans. How were the islanders' test results to
be reconciled with observations of their behavior? The researchers postulated that if tests of the islanders failed to find consistent differences
between their natural endowments and those of Europeans, whatever variations obtained between the sensory skills of primitives and Europeans had
to be products of cultural conditioning rather than biological propensities.

Particularly compelling evidence of the importance of cultural conditioning to sensory skills was provided by tests of the islanders' vision and
hearing. By objective measures, the islanders' vision was generally superior
to Europeans': few of them were deceived by the psychologists' optical
illusions, which usually fooled Europeans; and few of them suffered from
myopia, astigmatism, or color blindness. The islanders were somewhat
more sensitive to red and less sensitive to blue than Europeans were,
however. Rivers explained that their slight insensitivity to blue was congenital, a consequence of the intense pigmentation of the macula lutea in
the retina, but that this localized region of perceptual deficiency was
practically insignificant; the islanders readily recognized blue on the per-
ipheral retina. In contrast to their vision, the islanders' hearing was not as
acute as Europeans' – or, at least, it was inferior to that of the researchers.
Their defective hearing was quite possibly the result of their habits – a
consequence of repeated pearl diving. Nevertheless, the islanders were
highly responsive to auditory as well as visual stimuli; this finding demonstrated that their sensory skills were learned, and not simple functions of
their physical capacities.

In sum, by virtue of their established habits of close attention to minute

[47] W. H. R. Rivers, *The Influence of Alcohol and Other Drugs on Fatigue*, The Croonian
Lectures delivered at the Royal College of Physicians in 1906 (London, 1908).

stimuli, habits sustained in an environment with which they were very familiar, the islanders developed skills necessary to survival in their particular habitat. If they were transported to another environment, they would certainly be no more capable of observational feats than Europeans would be if they found themselves in equally novel circumstances. The conclusions of the Torres Straits researchers thus resolved a debate that had raged in anthropological circles – and in other quarters of the scientific community – during the 1880s, confirming a judgment that Galton had reached on the basis of impressionistic evidence.[48]

Among the studies conducted in Torres Straits, those of color vision are of special interest: their results addressed questions of the greatest importance to the scientific community, and the procedures used by Rivers and his associates illustrate their efforts to combine anthropological and psychological methods. Had the anthropologists not performed psychological tests, they might have taken the islanders' crude color nomenclature as an index to their capacities, and assumed that the islanders were congenitally incapable of refined perceptual distinctions. Instead, the researchers concluded that the islanders had developed color terms appropriate to their practical daily tasks, since experimental evidence indicated that the islanders could discriminate between colors just as Europeans did. Had the researchers not been able to observe the islanders' behavior, they might have disregarded some of their results, for the aesthetic preferences the islanders expressed during testing seemed unlikely, and suggested that the experimenters had given inadequate pretest instructions to their subjects. Yet, when the islanders were observed dressed in the finery they chose to wear to church, they were seen to express the same color preferences they had articulated under questioning. Finally, the islanders' relative insensitivity to blue could be interpreted only with reference to comparative data on the color sensibilities of other peoples, primitive as well as civilized. Primitives everywhere were insensitive to blue, and this finding was symptomatic of a general phenomenon: unlike Europeans, primitives had little aesthetic interest in nature, which was indicative of their lack of higher mental development overall.

In the study of vision, Rivers was a recognized master. Indeed, nearly

---

[48] See, for example, the notes and letters in *Nature* 31 (1985) headed "Civilisation and Eyesight": 12 February, 340; 19 February, 359–60; 26 February, 386–8; 5 March, 407–8; 12 March, 433–4; 19 March, 457–8; 2 April, 503–4; 16 April, 552–3. See also R. Brudenell Carter, "The Influence of Civilisation Upon Eyesight," *Journal of the Society of Arts* 33 (1885): 239–50; Minutes of the meeting of the Anthropological Institute on March 25, 1885, Francis Galton, president, in the chair, *Journal of the Anthropological Institute* 15 (1885): 113–31; Galton, *Inquiries Into Human Faculty* (see chap 3, n. 2), 132.

half a century after Rivers contributed an essay on vision to E. A. Schäffer's
Textbook of Physiology (1900), Erwin Ackernecht observed that his article
was "still regarded as one of the most accurate and careful accounts of the
whole subject in the English language."[49] Rivers's work in the Torres
Straits enabled him to consolidate his position of authority in this field, and
it was in his day a very important field indeed. Answers to vital questions
posed by diverse scholars and policymakers turned on elucidation of the
mechanisms of color vision.

The classicists who figured prominently in the anthropological community, concerned to establish parallels between the peoples of the ancient
world and contemporary primitives, asked the question first posed by the
future Prime Minister W. E. Gladstone in 1858: Did the vagueness of
color terminology used by the ancient Greeks indicate that they were at a
lower stage of evolution than modern Europeans and congenitally incapable
of refined color discriminations? To them, Rivers responded that although
the color terms used by Homer were equivalent to those of the least
advanced of the peoples studied by the Torres Straits researchers, the very
slight deficiency in the islanders' innate color sensitivity was insufficient to
account for their crude color nomenclature – and that ancient peoples
such as the Egyptians evidently had possessed a fully developed color
sense, although the fact that they did was not directly relevant to the case
of the Greeks. Though there were obvious cultural parallels between
peoples of the ancient world and contemporary primitives, and color terminology was associated with cultural development, there was no causal
link between sensitivity to color and the physical evolution of the human
species per se.[50]

Far more important to both policymakers and a congeries of scientists
were the studies of color vision prompted by concerns about the safe
conduct of vital occupations. The last quarter of the nineteenth century
witnessed a veritable explosion in studies of the variability of color perception among individuals. These were conducted by practicing physicians, physiologists, experimental psychologists, and anthropologists all over Europe.
Research on color vision had a recognizable impetus: in April 1876, a
catastrophic railroad accident occurred in Sweden because a color-blind
railway employee misperceived a signal, and the investigations that followed
the accident showed that the culpable employee was by no means the only
railway worker to suffer from color blindness.[51]

---

[49] Erwin H. Ackerknecht, "In Memory of William H. R. Rivers, 1864–1922," *Bulletin of
the History of Medicine* 11 (1942): 478–9.

[50] W. H. R. Rivers, "Primitive Color Vision," *Popular Science Monthly* 59 (1901): 44–58.

[51] R. Steven Turner, "Paradigms and Productivity: The Case of Physiological Optics,
1840–94," *Social Studies of Science* 17 (1987): 52–3.

In Britain, concern over the occupational hazards posed by color blindness prompted the Royal Society to appoint a Committee on Colour-Vision in 1890. Men who had earlier led the scientific debate on the etiology of visual acuity among primitive peoples were included on the committee: its chairman, Lord Rayleigh, a future Nobel Prize winner in physics whose various accomplishments included the solution of a perennial problem in optics, the explanation of the blue color of the sky; Francis Galton, and R. Brudenell Carter, an ophthalmic surgeon. Also on the committee was Michael Foster, Rivers's Cambridge ally. Taking extensive testimony from men involved in railway traffic and navigation, clinicians, and other interested parties, the committee was in the first instance concerned to establish the very existence of color blindness, which many employers refused to recognize. In particular, officials of the mercantile marine and the navy expected youths unhappy at sea to feign disorder to gain release from service, and chose to deny the reality of color blindness in order to prevent any unwanted loss of personnel.

The committee's conclusions were unambiguous: the testimony they had heard, as well as the ample available scientific literature, indicated that color blindness was a genuine disorder that was fairly widespread. They recommended mandatory testing for all workers whose responsibilities required accurate color discrimination. They judged that of the available tests for color blindness, Holmgren's colored wool test was superior, since it tested perceptual skills per se, rather than knowledge of color names – which was often rudimentary among persons of the lower classes, and nonexistent among foreign workers. This was the test the Torres Straits researchers adopted. But the Torres Straits Expedition was linked to the committee by more than procedural agreement.

In the light of the research subsequently done in Torres Straits, it is especially significant that the Royal Society committee's findings indicated that color blindness could be temporary as well as congenital. Temporary perceptual disability could be caused by disease, fatigue, mental shock, psychological depression, or excessive consumption of tobacco – which was particularly injurious if coupled with heavy alcohol use. When witnesses testified to the existence of temporary color blindness, they were sympathetically questioned by Michael Foster. The committee as a whole endorsed his view that defective color vision could result from situational factors.[52] The Torres Straits researchers were able to confirm this view

[52] Royal Society Committee on Colour-Vision (Lord Rayleigh, Lord Kelvin, R. Brudenell Carter, A. H. Church, J. Evans, R. Farquharson, M. Foster, F. Galton, W. Pole, G. G. Stokes, W. de Abney), "Report of the Committee on Colour-Vision," *Proceedings of the Royal Society of London* 51 (March–May 1892): esp. 290, 293, 296, 298, 311, 328–35, 339, 343.

with a different sort of evidence, finding persistent social factors that affected perception. Their work with disturbed soldiers during World War I was to build both on the findings considered by the Royal Society committee and on their field research.

In the model of individual adaptation embraced by Rivers and his colleagues, each person constituted a bounded economy with limited resources, which could be expended to develop only some of his physical or mental talents; and his social situation determined how his resources would be allocated. Rivers explained that the residents of simple societies possessed innate capacities little different from those of Europeans, but because they devoted so much of their attention to developing their powers of acute sensory observation they cultivated their sensory capacities at the expense of their intellectual skills. Exclusive concentration on the concrete particulars of their lives was necessarily "a distinct hindrance to higher mental development," he wrote, allowing that this might seem paradoxical, since "the growth of intellect depends on material which is furnished by the senses, and it therefore at first sight may appear strange that elaboration of the sensory side of mental life should be a hindrance to intellectual development." But individuals could not develop every one of their potential skills, since they did not have infinite personal energies, and "if too much energy is expended on the sensory foundations, it is natural that the intellectual superstructure should suffer."[53]

The findings of the Torres Straits Expedition could not be reconciled with the Lamarckist theory on which evolutionist anthropology had been premised. Clearly, the Torres Straits islanders exercised their sensory capacities to an extraordinary degree, but there was no evidence that their long-established habits had altered their natural endowments. Nor did environment affect physical characteristics, for if it had done so, physical variation would have been greater between groups than within them. Instead, when a given human endowment, such as vision, was studied in different populations, such as Englishmen and Papuans, the range of variation in each population was virtually identical, although the frequency distribution of degrees of visual acuity possessed by members of each

---

[53] Rivers, in *Torres Straits Reports*, Vol. II, 44–5. For later work of this sort see W. H. R. Rivers, "The Colour Vision of the Natives of Upper Egypt," *Journal of the Anthropological Institute* 31 (1901): 229–47; W. H. R. Rivers, "Observations on the Senses of the Todas," *British Journal of Psychology* 1 (1905): 117–26. It is of interest that during Malinowski's intellectually formative years, when he was especially interested in psychoanalysis and spoke explicitly of social evolution, he rendered near-Riversian analyses of primitive culture as distinguished by excessive attention to the sensory side of life – which Malinowski, unlike Rivers, was prepared to equate with sexuality. See Stocking, "Anthropology and the Science of the Irrational," 36.

population could be very different. Certainly, there were some truths in evolutionist argument. The innate capacities of individuals that social structures selectively developed were legacies of the phases of the biological evolution of the human species, and represented stratified layers of individual personality. Children could not distinguish colors until they were nearly two, for example, and learned to recognize red before blue, indicating that the sociobiological development of the child recapitulated the history of the race.[54] Moreover, evolutionists had correctly arrayed various sorts of social structures on a hierarchical developmental scale. But the correlations anthropologists had been accustomed to make among race, environment, and culture were spurious.

Do these bones live?

Conclusions compatible with those reached by the Torres Straits researchers were justified by work done around the same time in a different area of anthropology – human paleontology, the excavation and analysis of ancient remains. Elliot Smith figured prominently in the discovery and interpretation of key pieces of paleontological evidence: the remains of some six thousand individuals who lived in Egypt from approximately 4000 B.C. through the end of the Middle Empire over two thousand years later, which were excavated during 1907 and 1908; and the improbable collection of assorted bones found in Sussex in 1912, the so-called Piltdown Man which was seen as proof of the considerable antiquity of the human species (whether interpreted as an early ancestor or as an offshoot of the stock that gave rise to humankind and that was itself extinguished). The Piltdown findings seemed suspicious to some as soon as they were found, and they were exposed as a forgery in 1953. But, however intriguing is the question of the perpetrators of this infamous hoax, it is most significant that the Piltdown remains were understood no differently from unexceptionable paleontological evidence.

In believing the Piltdown findings to be important, Elliot Smith was in distinguished scientific company. His fellow analysts of the remains included such figures as (Sir) Arthur Smith Woodward (1864–1944), the British Museum's leading paleontologist, and (Sir) Arthur Keith (1866–1955), curator of the Hunterian Museum of the Royal College of Surgeons and a respected spokesman for the scientific community on the national scene. Patriotism certainly figured in the credence given to the Piltdown findings, heralded as the first major paleontological discovery made in

---

[54] Rivers, "Primitive Color Vision," 55.

England. Moreover, British scientists also claimed that their judgments of
paleontological evidence were particularly perceptive; they alone in the
international scientific community recognized the significance of all accumulated information.

To British researchers, paleontological evidence demonstrated that
neither ecological nor cultural factors altered humankind's biological
characteristics: for millennia, the physical characteristics of the human
species had remained remarkably stable. What changes had occurred in the
characteristics of populations resident in given areas did not indicate evolution but the migration of peoples with different hereditary traits into the
areas. When different stocks mixed, their offspring were as likely to be
inferior to the parent stocks as superior, for there was no inherent direction
to the developmental history of humankind. And in remains dating from
remote antiquity could be recognized the distinct patterns of assortment of
hereditary traits that represented the various racial types contemporary
observers identified.

Evidence to support these conclusions came from paleontologists working all over the world. But the most extensive documentation for them had
been unearthed in Egypt. The preserved remains of ancient Egyptians had
the same racial characteristics as the population Elliot Smith observed
during his nine years of residence in Egypt. And Elliot Smith was by no
means the first to note the extraordinary stability of Egyptian racial character. For some considerable time, the renowned Egyptologist W. M. F. (Sir
Flinders) Petrie (1853–1940) had been excavating, analyzing, and shipping
home vast quantities of ancient Egyptian remains, aided by the apprentices
he put to work in the field (who briefly included Anthony Wilkin). And
Karl Pearson and his students had used their biometrical techniques to
analyze Petrie's evidence. To be sure, Egyptologists and biometricians
rendered opinions that differed in matters of detail. So did Elliot Smith's,
Smith Woodward's, and Keith's interpretations of the Piltdown findings,
which were contingent on their constructions of other pieces of paleontological evidence. But all of these researchers were intent on proving a
fundamental point: the antiquity of the present character of the human
species. Their disputes concerned the ways ancient remains should be
interpreted to substantiate their judgment.[55]

---

[55] For evidence that paleontologists were themselves aware that their differences of
opinion over the Piltdown remains were associated with the ways that they wished
to interpret other findings, see the letter from G. Elliot Smith to Arthur Keith,
September 27, 1913, in the archives of the John Rylands Library, University of
Manchester. And see "The Ancient Inhabitants of the Nile Valley," unsigned review
of G. Elliott Smith and F. Wood Jones, *The Archaeological Survey of Nubia, Report for
1907–8*, Vol. 2 (Cairo, 1911), *Nature* 85 (1911): 310–12; unsigned news report on a

Like the members of the Torres Straits Expedition, the British pale-ontologists joined in the repudiation of Lamarckist theory voiced by a spectrum of biological scientists at the turn of the century. The new model of heredity was supported by new explanations of biological mechanisms such as August Weismann's hypothesis of immutable "germ plasm," as well as by the rediscovery of Gregor Mendel's formulation of laws of inheritance. Some hereditarians, however, such as the anti-Mendelian biometricians, based their views on observed variations alone. And some members of the anthropological community made extravagant hereditarian claims, explaining every sort of physical and behavioral variation as the product of heredity.

To wit, the biometrician Karl Pearson argued in his 1903 Huxley Memorial Lecture to the Anthropological Institute that biological laws governed not only the inheritance of physical characteristics but also inter-generational transmission of qualities of temperament and aptitude: in families, strong correlations were found for the distribution of traits be-tween the generations, and they were equally strong for diverse characters – head shape, height, intelligence, and such traits as vivacity, assertiveness, introspective tendencies, popularity, conscientiousness, quick temper, good nature, and sullenness. Others prosecuted this line of argument further. In his 1905 Huxley lecture, John Beddoe asserted that modern research confirmed ancient popular wisdom; temperamental and physical characters were themselves correlated: very nervous people were usually either very dark or very fair; institutionalized maniacs typically had ruddy complexions; and violent criminals invariably had brown eyes. The key to these associ-ations, C. G. Seligman was to suggest later, might lie in the ontogeny of the individual, for the fetus developed skin, hair, and the central nervous system from the same embryonic tissue.[56]

discussion at the International Congress of Medicine, 1913, *Nature* 91 (1913): 640–1; unsigned, "Paleolithic Man," *Nature* 90 (1912): 438; Elliot Smith, *Ancient Egyptians*, 116–17, 104–5, 122–4; Arthur Keith, "Modern Problems Relating to the Antiquity of Man," *Nature* 90 (1912): 268–71. David MacIver, "Recent Anthropometrical Work in Egypt," *Journal of the Anthropological Institute* 30 (1900): 95–103; Charles S. Myers, "The Future of Anthropometry," *Journal of the Anthropological Institute* 33 (1903): 36–40; Charles S. Myers, "Craniometry," *Man* 3 (1903): 28–32; Karl Pearson, "Egypt: Craniology," *Man* 5 (1905): 116–19; W. Flinders Petrie, "On Our Present Knowledge of the Early Egyptians," *Journal of the Anthropological Institute* 28 (1899): 202–3. The extreme antiquity of man, said Arthur Keith, did not mean that his physical evolution had ended; it was still proceeding, albeit very gradually. See his "Concerning the Rate of Man's Evolution," *Nature* 116 (1915): 317–20.

[56] Karl Pearson, "On the Inheritance of the Mental and Physical Characters in Man and Its Comparison with the Inheritance of the Physical Characters," *Journal of the Anthropological Institute* 33 (1903): esp. 185–205; John Beddoe, "Colour and Race,"

These views gained the widest possible audience when they figured in the 1904 Report of the Inter-Departmental Committee on Physical Deterioration, convened in 1903 by the government to consider the possibility that the low physical standard exhibited by many of the men who presented themselves for service in the South African War attested to the degeneration of the British race. The committee heard testimony from two men prominent in the anthropological community, both of them associates of Haddon: John Gray (1854–1912), a civil servant on the technical staff of the Patent Office, who was a member of the council of the Anthropological Institute and had served as secretary of the Anthropometric Committee of the British Association; and D. J. Cunningham (1850–1909), professor of anatomy at the University of Edinburgh, who both held office and received honors from the Anthropological Institute, served as chairman of the Anthropometric Committee of the British Association, and was tied to the Torres Straits researchers' network. Cunningham had worked with Haddon in Ireland collecting anthropometric data for the British Association, and he collaborated with him in an effort to set up an anthropometric laboratory there that replicated Galton's London establishment.

In preparation for questioning these men, the members of the Inter-Departmental Committee evidently familiarized themselves not only with the British Association Anthropometric reports but also with the studies of Karl Pearson. They were prepared to entertain the theory the British population was degenerating over time as the characteristics acquired in unhealthy urban conditions were inherited by offspring and, in particular, as the effects of liberation were rendering British women incapable of motherhood. And they taxed the anthropologists they questioned with extracts from the reports of the British Association Anthropometric Committee, which suggested support for a Lamarckist theory of degeneration.[57] The Inter-Departmental Committee members also entertained Karl Pearson's altogether different explanation of the degeneration of the population – that what characteristics British adults were transmitting to their children were entirely unaffected by habit and environment, but that in the aggregate the nation's physical quality was declining because the better class of people were not reproducing while inferior people were doing so out of proportion to their numbers.

The anthropologists spoke against both of these theories of degeneration. They argued that the available evidence on the physical condition of

---

Journal of the Anthropological Institute 35 (1905): 237; Seligman, "Anthropology and Psychology," 24–5.

[57] In particular, the Inter-Departmental Committee remarked upon the passage from the British Association report that I have quoted on page 112.

the British population was itself inconclusive; although it had been ac-
cumulating for decades, it had not been gathered in any sort of systematic
fashion. The data that most convincingly demonstrated that acquired
characteristics were not inherited, indicating that racial degeneration could
not have occurred as alarmists imagined, were the findings of paleontologists – students of ancient Egyptian remains, as well as researchers who
compared the Neolithic and modern populations of Sweden. Cunningham
allowed that alcoholic and syphilitic parents did produce defective children,
but denied any other sort of acquired degenerative influences. He was
particularly concerned to deny that the changing role of women was harmful to the race, arguing that liberation had, if anything, positive (nontrans-
missable) effects – freeing women from restrictive corsets and encouraging
them to take healthy exercise. Cunningham also expressed astonishment
that Pearson's eugenic notions could be taken seriously, arguing that "it is
stocks and not classes that breed men of intellect . . . stocks [that] are found
in all classes, high and low." The qualities of the British race represented
"a mean physical standard which is the inheritance of the people as a
whole," and "the tendency of the race as a whole will always be to maintain
the inherited mean."

To both Gray and Cunningham it was clear that the mixture of stocks
that comprised the British population was a fortuitous one, and that the
British racial inheritance was superior to that of other nations. Gray was an
admirer of Pearson, and in his testimony he discussed the possible ill
consequences of unfortunate breeding patterns, stressing that the population might degenerate through admixture with undesirable immigrants. In
his testimony, however, Cunningham indicated repugnance at the thought
that the government might undertake to regulate reproduction. Given his
Galtonian emphasis on the racial inheritance of the nation as a whole, he
stressed that the observed characteristics of the British population represented the effects of environmental stimuli on the expression of inherited
traits. Whatever physical reverses the British population might have sustained, these could be undone with proper diet, housing, and exercise.
Cunningham's view prevailed in the report of the committee, which endorsed his suggestions for social welfare measures – many of which soon
passed into law.[58]

The hereditarian conclusions supported by paleontological evidence

---

[58] See the testimony of D. J. Cunningham and John Gray in the *Report of the Inter-
Departmental Committee on Physical Deterioration* (London, 1904), Vol. II, 95–107,
140–50. The Cunningham quotations are on pp. 102 and 91. For one assessment of
the significance of the committee report, see Perkin, *The Rise of Professional Society*,
(chap. 2, n. 8), 58–9.

could be reconciled with the explanations of the Torres Straits researchers, but could also be used to justify a conception of the relation of nature and nurture Rivers and his colleagues would not accept. That is, they did not see the culture of a society as the sum product of the inherited traits of its population, a simple function unaffected by any factors save those that altered the population's health. To be sure, Rivers and Haddon, their colleagues, and their students judged peoples' cultures to be at least partially determined by their particular inherited qualities. Thus, the Torres Straits islanders, for example, were typically of a "demonstrative nature"; as a people, the Todas were more intelligent than the Torres Straits islanders; Australian aborigines were as a group of very low intelligence, but were nevertheless notable for their extraordinary memory capacity.[59] If the composite inheritance of a people predisposed them toward certain types of behavior, it did not determine their culture, however. At different times in the history of every people, peculiar circumstances would encourage selective expression of some of their traits. And because the differences among populations of human beings were in absolute terms quite small, it was possible for all peoples to be socialized into the cultural habits of any of the societies of the world.[60]

Charting social evolution: brains, nerves, and memory

Understanding the biological, psychological, and cultural determinants of human behavior as interactive systems that were to a degree qualitatively distinct, Rivers's students and colleagues considered innate drives to have no proximate relationship to some social phenomena. For example, when Melanesians behaved in culturally prescribed fashion, their actions resulted in unintended social changes that were explicable only as derivatives of

---

[59] These specific characterizations are from Rivers, *Reports of the Cambridge Anthropological Expedition*, Vol. II, 4; Rivers, "The Senses of the Todas," 322–3; C. G. Seligman, "Psychology and Racial Differences," in Morris Ginsberg et al., *Psychology and Modern Problems* (New York, 1936), 65. See also A. C. Haddon, "Social Constructiveness," *British Journal of Psychology* 18 (1928): 400–5; and Gregory Bateson, *Naven* (Stanford, 1958 [orig. Cambridge, 1936]), 65. It is notable that when Bateson's book came out, its anthropologist readers were capable of ignoring his appeals to hereditary temperamental characteristics among its subjects and representing it as a strictly functionalist account. See, for example, S. F. Nadel's review of it, *Man* 38 (1938), esp. 45.

[60] See, for example, A. M. Hocart, "The Divinity of the Quest," in Raglan, *The Life-Giving Myth and Other Essays*, 95; Seligman, "Psychology and Racial Differences," 85–7; McDougall, *Anthropology and History*, esp. 8–22; Bateson, *Naven*; G. Elliot Smith, "Race, Nationality, and Culture," unpublished lecture, n.d., archives of the John Rylands Library, University of Manchester.

their social system, as social facts sui generis; and Melanesians had distinctive psychological characteristics that were consequences rather than causes of their cultural organization. But Riversians argued that in order to understand human biology, psychology, and culture, it was necessary to analyze their interaction; nothing could be learned by focusing on one element in human behavior, and bracketing consideration of the others. Because the culture of a people was the cumulative product of their peculiar historical experiences, it followed that the anthropologist could most readily distinguish between the factors of innate nature and cultural nurture in their behavior by attending to their responses to novel conditions.[61]

What, then, was the relationship between the characteristics common to all human beings and the peculiar character of each individual, between the character of the individual and that of the group to which he belonged? Rivers and the other Torres Straits researchers described these relationships in terms that young anthropologists rejected after World War I; the notable exception to this generalization was Gregory Bateson, who in the 1930s was an intellectual deviant in his generation of anthropologists. Social psychologists such as Bartlett and his students continued to cast their analyses in Riversian terms, however. They argued that every "individual possesse[d] in common with all other human beings" a "group of instinctive tendencies" that had "their unique arrangement in every person."[62] Then, each individual was distinguished by "differences of temperament or constitution."[63] Though persons of every quality of intellect and personality were found everywhere, the frequency distribution of individual types varied from population to population, and the character of each group was derived from the individuals comprising it. The quality of culture of any given people was the product of their natural inclinations and their mode of social organization.

When established social habits were somehow abruptly disturbed, individual pathology would result. Individual pathology represented the release of instinctive impulses necessarily controlled in orderly society. And the psychological mechanisms of repression, activated in every individual during childhood, were features of the primeval biological program of the human species, fundamental to any sort of cooperative human endeavor. It is from the diffusionists' identification of the range of conditions that

---

[61] Rivers, "The Primitive Conception of Death," in *Psychology and Ethnology*, 36–50; and see also his "Medicine, Magic, and Religion," *The Lancet* 1917 (2): 918–23, 959–64.

[62] See F. C. Bartlett, "The Psychology of Culture Contact," *Encyclopaedia Britannica*, 13th ed. (London, 1926), Vol. I, 770.

[63] For example, Rivers, *The Influence of Alcohol*, 121.

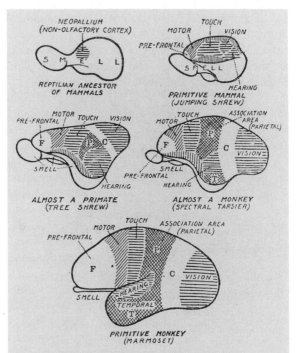

FIG. 1. A series of diagrams to suggest the origin of the neopallium in the ancestor of mammals ; the rapid development of this cortical area in mammals, as touch, vision, hearing, as well as control of skilled movements, attain an increasing significance, the growing cultivation of vision which leads to the emergence of the Primates, the increased reliance on vision brings about an enhancement of skill in movement (and a marked expansion of the motor territory) and of tactile and auditory discrimination. (Based in part on the work of Profs. W. E. Le Gros Clark and H. H. Woollard.) From "Human History" (1930).

The physical evolution of the mind according to G. Elliot Smith, from his "Evolution of the Mind," *Nature*, February 17, 1934. Ltd.

induced pathological states that we can recognize the premises that informed their analyses of both ancient migrations and contemporary social disorder. That is, they represented as functionally equivalent the responses elicited from primitives confronted by migrants bearing an alien culture and those of modern peoples dealing with situations for which they were totally unprepared, such as the stresses of modern warfare. It is worth quoting Rivers at length, since he articulated clearly the basic outline of the diffusionist explanation of social stability and change, relating social dynamics to the unconscious features of human personality.

The frequency of psycho-neuroses in the great communities of the modern world is the direct consequence of the fluid and unorganised character of their civilization. In savage communities where long ages of freedom from external influence have allowed culture to become organised and stable, the psycho-neuroses are absent or hardly to be detected. . . . In such communities there has come about a stable adjustment between instinctive tendencies and social ideals, leaving no room for the conflict which forms the essence of the psycho-neuroses. Similarly, I believe that a comparative study of the frequency and severity of neuroses among the great civilisations of the modern world will show that this frequency and severity are definitely correlated with the fluidity or instability of the culture and with the extent to which national ideals call for repression of instinctive tendencies. The perfect social organisation is one in which instinctive tendencies, out of harmony with social ideals, have so come under control that they no longer form the grounds of conflict or give occasion for it only in the presence of exceptional stress and strain.[64]

The diffusionists' description of the relationship of social factors to the expression of instinctive tendencies was derived from their understanding of the evolution of the brain and the nervous system – the anatomical loci of human thought and feeling. The crucial step in the evolution of the modern human species was the development of the brain as an organ of conscious calculation, rather than merely a receptor of sensory data. Memory, and the ability to act on the basis of it, was the distinguishing feature of the evolved human being. In the evolved human brain each neopallial area had a special mechanism – the nature of which would be specified by future scientific research – which enabled it to act as a "recording apparatus," so that every new stimulus would "awaken memories of foregoing states of consciousness, by means of which the latest impression can be tested and compared with others which have impinged upon this neopallial mechanism on previous occasions," to quote Elliot Smith.[65]

A model of the brain's function isomorphic with Elliot Smith's description of its structure was articulated by Henry Head. A distinguished neurologist and comparative physiologist and the editor of the neurological

---

[64] W. H. R. Rivers, "Inaugural Address." See also W. J. Perry, *The Children of the Sun*, 495–7; William McDougall, *The Group Mind* (London, 1920), 241–2; Charles S. Myers, *Mind and Work* (London, 1920), 163; C. G. Seligman, "Temperament, Conflict and Psychosis in a Stone-Age Population," *British Journal of Medical Psychology* 9 (1929): 187–202.

[65] G. Elliot Smith, "Some Problems Relating to the Evolution of the Brain," The Arris and Gale Lectures of the Royal College of Physicians, *The Lancet* 1910 (1): 223.

journal *Brain* from 1905 to 1922, Head had strong personal and intellectual ties to Elliot Smith, Rivers, Myers, and Bartlett.[66] Head explained that individuals were able to sustain a constant course of adaptation to ever changing environments because they monitored their behavior with reference to an internalized picture of themselves, their "schemas" (differentiated within each individual into specific "schemata"). Schemas themselves were continually modified, as changes in individuals' behavior were incorporated into their inner pictures of their postures and actions. Without the mental functions represented by the schema, human beings could not have evolved into tool-using creatures, for individuals' mental images of themselves were comprised of their bodies plus their material appendages – their clothing and tools of every type, from cutlery to automobiles. The operation of the schema also explained the general process of learning: skills acquired consciously became skills exercised unconsciously by being incorporated into the individual's schema.

The schema functioned efficiently to maintain the individual's adaptive capacity, however, only so long as the individual did not suffer a diminution of "vigilance" – a general receptivity to stimuli that operated on both conscious and unconscious levels – which could be impaired by factors ranging from social situations, to the temporary effects of disease or drugs, to permanent injury. Head's notion of vigilance also informed his account of the operation of nervous sensibility, since he argued that "consciousness stands in the same relation to the vigilance of the higher centres as adapted and purposive reflexes to that of lower rank in the neural hierarchy."[67] And he conceptualized this hierarchy in evolutionary terms, following the example of the Spencerian neurologist Hughlings Jackson, whose ideas Head revived, elaborated, and popularized.[68]

The process by which the nervous system developed in the human species was elucidated by a series of experiments planned and evaluated by

[66] For one articulation of these ties, see the letter from G. Elliot Smith to George G. Campion, October 14, 1921, archives of the John Rylands Library, University of Manchester.

[67] Henry Head, "The Conception of Nervous and Mental Energy," *British Journal of Psychology* 14 (1923): 143.

[68] For a summary of Head's career, see Charles S. Myers, "Obituary Notice: Sir Henry Head, 1861–1940," *British Journal of Psychology* 32 (1941): 5–14. On the concepts of the schema and of vigilance, see Head, "The Conception of Nervous and Mental Energy," 126–47. And see R. C. Oldfield and O. L. Zangwill, "Head's Concept of the Schema and Its Application in Contemporary British Psychology," *British Journal of Psychology* 32 (1942): 267–86; 33 (1942–3): 58–64, 113–29, 143–9. For a critique of the notion of vigilance, see F. C. Bartlett, "A Critical Review of *Aphasia and Kindred Disorders of Speech* by Henry Head," *Brain* 49 (1926): 581–7. And see Hearnshaw, *A Short History of British Psychology*, 70–3.

Rivers and Head, performed by Rivers on Head between 1903 and 1908. These experiments are invariably described in disciplinary histories of psychology as "classic," although they do not have for psychologists the mythic status that the Torres Straits Expedition has for anthropologists. Neurologists have also continued to find the results of these experiments intriguing, although they were quick to suspect Rivers's and Head's explanation of their findings. The experiments began when Head, then full physician at the London Hospital, underwent an operation in which the radial and external cutaneous nerves of his left forearm were severed in the region of his elbow, small portions of the nerves were excised, and the ends were reattached with silk sutures. For the next four and half years, Head traveled every weekend to Cambridge, where, sitting blindfolded in Rivers's rooms, he endured tests of cutaneous sensibility on the affected regions of his arm, tests that determined the course of the regeneration of his nerves.

To Rivers and Head, the regeneration of Head's nerves recapitulated the evolution of nervous sensibility: first he regained "protopathic" sensibility; subsequently, he regained "epicritic" sensibility. When his sensibility was of a protopathic character, his responses to stimuli were classified as being of the "all-or-none" variety: he was sometimes insensible to touch, but when he experienced sensation, he could not identify which part of his arm was being stimulated; and he could not distinguish degrees of heat, cold, or pressure in the stimulation applied. When he regained epicritic sensibility, he could differentiate among qualities of stimulation and could specify the affected region of his arm.

Clearly, protopathic and epicritic sensibilities were of qualitatively distinct orders. Therefore, the experimenters concluded that the regeneration of Head's nerves recapitulated a history of human evolution effected in disjunctive leaps, assuming that the two types of sensation were produced within two separate systems of nerve fibers. Types of sensibility could be related to the structure of the brain: the inner layer of the cerebral cortex, the first of its parts to develop in the human species, governed individuals' protopathic responses, whereas the outer layer governed higher functions. And the factors that weakened the individual's vigilance occasioned a degeneration of sensibility, as Head's own experience showed; a weakened human organism would regress toward the protopathic level.[69]

[69] For one fairly extensive summary of the experiments, see Langham, *The Building of British Social Anthropology*, 57–60. For an evaluation of the experiments in a standard history of psychology, see Edwin G. Boring, *A History of Experimental Psychology* (New York, 1950), 491. On the neurologists' view of the experiments, see D. Denny-Brown, "The Release of Deep Pain by Nerve Injury," *Brain* 88 (1965): 725–38. On the relation between protopathic sensibility and brain structure, see Seligman, "Psychology and Racial Differences," 61–3.

The diffuse character of the notions of vigilance and of types of sensibility permitted explanation of a range of physical and cultural phenomena in terms of evolution and degeneration. For example, the temporary color blindness occasioned by physical disability, mental stress, or substance abuse which the Royal Society Committee on Colour-Vision had identified could be represented as an illustration of the causes and consequences of diminished vigilance. Experimenting on himself, Rivers demonstrated in a different way the correlation he had found between the highly developed physical skills and the inferior intellectual ones of the Torres Straits islanders. Under the influence of alcohol, Rivers lost the capacity to perform intellectual labors, but managed greater feats of muscular strength than he had ever accomplished before. Alcohol had weakened his vigilance, depressing "the activity of some higher nervous mechanism which serves to control and keep in check muscular activity, and ... when this control is weakened, increased amounts of work can be executed."[70] His vigilance diminished, Rivers had become less of an epicritic and more of a protopathic being.

But Rivers and his associates argued that no socialized being, however primitive, existed in a wholly protopathic condition, for protopathic urges were literally anti- or presocial, representing those features of human nature that could not be affected by any sort of environmental stimulation. Indeed, Riversians judged that primitive societies were notable for their capacity to act cooperatively, and thus their assessment of these societies was quite different from that of the evolutionists and rather more like that of the functionalists.[71] Truly protopathic conditions were pathological, resembling but not identical to primitive states of consciousness and behavior. For example, cerebral injury might lead to a nearly total loss of aesthetic sensibilities. When a person lost his musical sense through injury, he or she might lose the capacity to distinguish between tones; or he or she might retain the ability to distinguish differences of loudness, pitch, duration, and quality of sounds, but be unable to appreciate the relationship among sounds that together constitute a musical tune. Yet, as Charles Myers observed, however rudimentary primitive music was, it denoted a sensibility far more refined than that of afflicted persons.[72]

The only normal human beings who operated on a protopathic level were infants. But the affective states that came naturally to the child

---

[70] Rivers, *The Influence of Alcohol*, 105.
[71] W. H. R. Rivers, *Instinct and the Unconscious* (Cambridge, 1922), 95–9, See also Seligman, "Psychology and Racial Differences," 63.
[72] C. S. Myers, "The Beginnings of Music," in E. C. Quiggin, ed., *Essays and Studies Presented to William Ridgeway* (Cambridge, 1913), esp. 576–80.

figured only in the unconscious of the adult, since the modes of response appropriate to childhood were thoroughly inappropriate to adulthood. One of the characteristics of the vigilance of the mature adult, then, was the repression of protopathic affective impulses. To quote Rivers:

> The special character of the reactions of the human infant is that they consist largely of explicit expressions of affective states and of immediate responses to external stimuli. If the modes of consciousness connected with these forms of reaction persisted without modification in later life, they could only interfere with the very different and far more complex reactions of the adult. There is a definite reason why the conscious states connected with infantile reactions should become unconscious. Even in an animal whose life history is as uniform as that of Man the different phases are sufficiently distinct to provide an ample reason why experience should become unconscious. This reason is to be found in the diversity of the different phases of the life-history and incompatibility of the reactions of one phase with those of another.[73]

In primitive societies, however, individuals were not required to thwart their impulses so severely as were the highly civilized. Thus, in the rituals and everyday routine practices of primitive peoples could be observed those features of fundamental human nature that civilized peoples expressed only in encoded form in dreams – symbolic representations of desired results and expressions of conflicts.[74] In the civilized adult, then, mental disorder constituted degeneration; neurosis and psychosis expressed "a process of regression to primitive and infantile states."[75] The assumption that the primitive, the infantile, and the pathological were alike was also, of course, fundamental to evolutionist anthropology. Diffusionists differed from their predecessors in arguing that the transition from lower to higher states of consciousness and self-control (or vice versa) was abrupt rather than continuous.

In particular, the diffusionists' equation of primitive ritual and civilized dream preserved a tenet of evolutionist anthropology: the Frazerian interpretation of primitive ritual as an exercise in wish fulfillment. Such an interpretation of dreams was also Freudian, and Frazerian anthropology had been useful to Freud in the elaboration of his argument. Not surpris-

---

[73] W. H. R. Rivers, "Why Is the 'Unconscious' Unconscious?" *British Journal of Psychology* 8 (1918): 241–2.

[74] Rivers, *Dreams and Primitive Culture*. See also G. Elliot Smith and T. H. Pear, *Shell-Shock and Its Lessons* (Manchester, 1917), 61–3, 97. C. G. Seligman, "The Unconscious in Relation to Anthropology," *British Journal of Psychology* 18 (1928): 375–6.

[75] Rivers, "Inaugural Address," 891.

ingly, given their concern to explain unconscious motives and apparently irrational behavior, the diffusionists were as a group the anthropologists most approving of Freudian theory and psychoanalytic method. As individuals, the diffusionists assumed positions on Freudianism that were various, and sometimes confused.

Rivers was the most enthusiastic Freudian among them, although he argued that Freud exaggerated the importance of sexual urges in human motivation; the sexual urge appeared to be the primary human drive only because society laid such stress upon its repression, whereas urges such as the instinct of self-preservation were probably more significant. Elliot Smith defended the psychoanalytic method for the treatment of mental disorder, explaining the etiology of mental illness in terms of the particular experiences of the individual, and arguing that the cure required revelation of repressed memories of traumatic experiences – memories that were expressed in symbolic form in dreams. But Smith insisted that the only universal human drive was fear, dismissing Freudian personality theory as a superficially disguised variant of the evolutionist doctrine of the psychic unity of humankind. Nevertheless, his formal assessment of Freudian theory illustrates his propensity to overstate his case when debating his enemies (real and imagined), a characteristic that certainly did his cause no good. In fact, Elliot Smith's explanation of the appeal of certain cultural practices to peoples all over the world was evidently Freudian in content if not in name, depending as it did on the premise that peoples everywhere found compelling such natural symbols as the cowrie shell, suggestive of female genitalia. Obviously, no different from the evolutionists, the diffusionists identified general patterns of social change that were functions of individual psychology.[76]

Finally, the diffusionists described the results of contact between peoples as products of biopsychological mechanisms. Even when no deliberate efforts were made to exterminate a people, their population was likely to decline after they had been brought under the influence of bearers of a superior culture, and among the causes of this decline was psychological demoralization, evident in a failure to reproduce. Certainly, there were nonpsychological reasons that birth and death rates were affected by cul-

[76] The British psychoanalyst Ernest Jones provided Freud with an anthropological bibliography, so it is not surprising that his anthropological evidence had British origins. The work Freud found useful was evolutionist anthropology, and it is of minor interest that he cited some work of Rivers's that was reported by Frazer. See Edwin R. Wallace, IV, *Freud and Anthropology* (New York, 1983), 173–5, 232. See, for example, W. H. R. Rivers, "Freud's Psychology of the Unconscious," *The Lancet* 1916 (1): 912–14; Smith and Pear, *Shell Shock*, 91; G. Elliot Smith, "Shell Shock and the Soldier," *The Lancet* 1916 (1): 816.

ture contact. Migrants (such as colonialists) were frequently responsible for introducing indigenous populations to noxious substances such as opiates and strong alcohol; lacking social traditions inhibiting substance abuse, the indigenous populations would become debilitated through excessive consumption of intoxicants. New weapons, such as firearms, would make traditional feuds far more hazardous for combatants. And population movements spread disease as well as culture; ailments that were minor among migrants could prove fatal to those previously unexposed to them.[77]

The most powerful cause of population decline among a population suffering contact with migrants, however, was their loss of interest in life. This resulted from the assault on traditional values by the bearers of different ones. Only if an afflicted people were provided with a new set of life-affirming values would they again consider it worthwhile to bring children into the world. The diffusionists' argument suggested – although it never explicitly stated – that the introduction of new culture could at once provoke a people's degeneration and inspire their recovery. In ancient times, the peoples invaded by the Children of the Sun undoubtedly recognized that the migrants possessed superior material culture, but the host population were drawn to the Archaic Civilization because of its spiritual message. The recipients of the Archaic Civilization were like the demoralized primitives who embraced Buddhism and Christianity in the historically documented and the (then) present. They gained from adopting a new religious creed a reanimation of that most protopathic of instincts, the will to live.[78]

It was not until the post–World War I period that a younger Rivers student, the social psychologist F. C. Bartlett, succeeded in integrating the general arguments made by Haddon, Rivers, Elliot Smith, Head, and their disciples. Bartlett was not interested in neuroanatomy per se, but, citing the diffusionists' work, he suggested that natural human patterns of processing information explained why social change usually occurred as a result of contact between peoples. Experimental evidence substantiated Rivers's generalization that the greater was the disparity between the cultures of two peoples in contact, the more likely it was that the novel culture of migrants would impress its recipients, showing that the human imagination was

[77] C. G. Seligman, "On the Occurrence of New Growths Among the Natives of British New Guinea," *Imperial Cancer Research Fund Scientific Reports* 3 (1908): 26–40; W. H. R. Rivers, "The Dying-Out of Native Races," *The Lancet* 1920 (1): 43–4.

[78] Rivers, "The Dying-Out of Native Races," 109–10; Perry, *Children of the Sun*, 480–1; A. M. Hocart, "The Life-Giving Myth," in Lord Raglan, ed., *The Life-Giving Myth and Other Essays* (London, 1952) [essay orig. 1935]), 18; W. H. R. Rivers, "The Contact of Peoples," in G. Elliot Smith, ed., *Psychology and Ethnology* (London, 1926 [essay orig. 1913]), 299–317.

captured by "the novel, the extraordinary, the unlikely." Bartlett's research on memory used an elaborated model of Head's notion of the schema, which incorporated learned cultural habits as well as physical ones, demonstrating that selective learning and defective memory were natural mechanisms of human adaptation. Individuals invariably assimilated novel information in distorted form because they needed to reconcile it with their previous experiences. And individuals could never replicate past behavior exactly. These traits enabled human beings to adapt to an ever-changing environment, modifying their ideas and behavior to suit the exigencies of the moment. Moreover, Bartlett explicated the relationship between the protopathic and epicritic instincts and the schematically selective fashion in which groups incorporated new cultural elements. The group acting to protect itself from danger (to both its members as individuals and to the group as a whole) was prompted by protopathic instincts, and was as such especially prone to adopt new ritual skills. When the group adapted new culture to suit its established practices, it was acting to preserve the cohesion of the group, and thus obeying epicritic impulses.[79]

The only element of diffusionist argument that Bartlett discarded was Head's notion of vigilance, which Bartlett dismissed as too vague to be useful. In so doing, however, Bartlett cast the scheme of his predecessors in more optimistic form: whereas the model of the human being whose vigilance was variable was of a creature highly susceptible to degeneration as well as capable of evolution, Bartlett's ideal-typical natural humans, in contrast, were beings constantly making functional adaptations to their situations. And through Bartlett, the Riversian approach persisted in British psychology. Indeed, one might argue that the anthropological antecedents of British social psychology gave it a distinctive character. The crude stimulus–response models of Bartlett's American behaviorist contemporaries, for example, could not appeal to those trained by him to recognize the selective and constructive character of both perception and memory, and the importance of individuals' experience and their cultural conditioning to their behavior.[80] Bartlett shared with his American contemporaries, however, a faith that the postwar world could be remade (although his hopes for change rested on a model of the human being as an adaptive creature that was quite different from theirs). But in the World War I era,

[79] F. C. Bartlett, *Psychology and Primitive Culture* (New York, 1923), 40–3, 193; Bartlett, "Critical Review," 585–6; F. C. Bartlett, *Remembering* (Cambridge, 1932), 16, 160, 201, 273, and passim.

[80] Bartlett, "Critical Review," 585–6; Sir Frederic Bartlett, "The Bearing of Experimental Psychology upon Human Skilled Performance," *British Journal of Industrial Medicine* 8 (1951): 209–17. And see also D. B. Broadbent, "Frederick Charles Bartlett," *Biographical Memoirs of Fellows of the Royal Society* 16 (1970): 1–13.

Riversian psychology had a distinctly pessimistic tenor. Its pessimism then accounted for its general appeal – and acknowledged practical utility. And it is to this era that we now return.

Shell shock

Rivers, Elliot Smith, Head, and their associates explained to clinicians and laymen alike the vulnerability of individuals to degeneration. Their expertise was quite relevant to the social phenomena of World War I, for on the battlefields of the war soldiers succumbed in large numbers to psychological disorders that had no physiological basis – in psychological parlance, "functional disorders." All the physicians who figured in Rivers's intellectual circle served in the military medical service, and all but Seligman published reports of their diagnoses and treatments of battle-induced mental disorders. These disorders came to be categorized collectively as "shell shock" – a term coined by Myers that gained general circulation.

Shell shock afflicted so many soldiers that it posed a serious problem for the military. According to the official responsible for military pensions, approximately 200,000 men were discharged from duty because they were mentally incapable of active service. Soldiers pensioned for psychological reasons were a substantial fraction of the total number of 1.3 million military pensioners; save for those disabled by wounds and amputations, men severely afflicted by functional nervous disorders constituted the largest single category of pension recipients in 1922. Furthermore, in all probability there were additional seriously disturbed veterans whom the state did not support (or supported under rubrics that carried no social stigma). And there were certainly many soldiers whose psychological afflictions were not sufficiently severe as to be incapacitating – shell-shock victims who were never medically diagnosed.[81]

To Riversian psychiatrists, soldiers' behavior constituted degeneration to primitive states. They identified shell shock as an extreme form of psychological pathology that differed from other sorts of disorders in degree rather than kind. All manner of psychological disturbances manifested the degeneration to which every individual was vulnerable, and constituted evidence that individual personality structure was a stratified system embodying stages of evolution. In its most severe form, shell shock constituted regression to protopathic states. The therapy that was appropriate for shell shock, then, necessarily engaged the unconscious features of human per-

---

[81] Martin Stone, "Shellshock and the Psychologists," in W. F. Bynum, Roy Porter, and Michael Shepherd, eds., *The Anatomy of Madness*, Vol. II (London, 1985), 243–52.

sonality, primitive features repressed by the maturing individual, and was largely Freudian.

The shell-shock victim could present physical symptoms, but his disorder had no physical cause. Rather, the soldier succumbed to mental collapse in order to escape an intolerable situation: he was unable to cope with the conflict between his instinctive drives for self-preservation and the lesson impressed upon him during his military training – that he was obliged to behave as if he had no fears in situations that were in reality fraught with peril.[82] And the soldier's breakdown had a systematic character, shaped by his habituated patterns of response. His hallucinations and delusions were products of the operation of his schema, for his pathological mental states represented his efforts to "rationalise and schematise his new sensations" – the awful experiences of war – in terms consistent with his previous modes of interpreting his observations and acting upon them.[83] Likewise, mental pathology was the result of the operation of repressive mechanisms usually appropriate in everyday life, but dysfunctional in the novel military situation in which the soldier found himself; it was "not repression in itself which is harmful, but repression under conditions in which it fails to adapt the individual to his environment."[84]

The military mind found repugnant this diagnosis of the significance and treatment suitable for shell shock. The military were inclined to treat shell shock cases as disciplinary problems, reasoning that the only genuine psychological disorders were those with identifiable organic causes: if examination of disturbed soldiers showed them to be afflicted with organic disease, they were lunatics who ought to be confined to asylums; otherwise, shell-shock victims were cowards who deliberately feigned illness in order to escape from active duty, and ought to be shot.[85] A survey of the case histories of the soldiers executed during World War I suggests that many might well have been diagnosed as shell-shock victims, rather than punished as rebels, had they had the good fortune to be examined by sympathetic physicians. And a number of those executed for violations of military discipline had in fact been treated for shell shock at earlier stages in their military careers.[86]

The punitive attitudes of the military were exacerbated by their class biases. The shell-shocked officer had a good chance of receiving some sort of therapy, whereas the ordinary soldier was likely to be punished. Indeed,

---

[82] W. H. R. Rivers, "Inaugural Address", 891.

[83] G. Elliot Smith, "Shell Shock and the Soldier," *The Lancet* 1915 (1): 815.

[84] Rivers, "The Repression of War Experience," *The Lancet* 1918 (1): 173.

[85] Martin Stone, "Shellshock," 247–50.

[86] Anthony Babington, *For the Sake of Example* (New York, 1983), 28–9, 71, 82–3, 91–2, 136–43, and passim.

one of the most celebrated cases of identified shell-shock victims – that of Siegfried Sassoon – indicates that disturbed men of the officer class could have the diagnosis of shell shock thrust upon them, particularly if they had been decorated and if punishing them would cause the military public embarrassment. While he was on leave in England for medical reasons, Sassoon was influenced by Bertrand Russell to make a public announcement of his disapproval of the war and refusal to return to it, whereupon his friend Robert Graves arranged to have his case reviewed by a medical board. Diagnosed as neurasthenic, he was sent to be treated by Rivers in a military hospital in Scotland. Rivers agreed with Sassoon that he was not suffering from shell shock, and humorously proposed a (clearly unclinical) diagnosis of "antiwar complex." Thus protected from the consequences of his political views, Sassoon was free to spend some months occupying himself in improving his golf game and having soothing conversations with Rivers (whom he admired enormously), until he himself determined to return to the front.[87]

From the official statistics on shell-shock victims released at an early stage of the war and at its end, however, one can judge that the treatment of mentally disturbed ordinary soldiers grew progressively less punitive during the course of the war, although officers and men were never treated with equal sympathy. Initially, the percentage of officers who succumbed to shell shock was estimated to be four times that of other ranks, but ultimately it was concluded that officers were only two times as prone to mental collapse as ordinary soldiers. Nevertheless, we can assume that throughout the war the military sustained its reluctance to excuse shell-shocked ordinary soldiers.[88]

The military view of psychological disturbance was not very different from the approach to mental illness that had prevailed in British psychiatric circles before the war: mental illness could not be genuine unless it had some organic cause. Extrapolated to the military context, this assumption led to the original conjecture that shell shock must have been caused by the vibrations of exploding shells, which somehow damaged the central nervous system. Military habits of diagnosis also led to therapeutic preferences. From the start of the war, the shell-shock therapies of military choice were physical, ranging from a rest cure involving isolation, massage, and a milk diet, to the administration of a course of electric shocks. The rest cure, a traditional procedure favored by the regular army, proved an inefficient

---

[87] One of Sassoon's accounts of his experience is in *Sherston's Progress* (New York, 1937), Part I, "Rivers," 3–72.

[88] Thomas W. Salmon, *The Care and Treatment of Mental Diseases and War Neuroses ("Shell-Shock") in the British Army* (New York, 1917), 13.

method of restoring soldiers to battle readiness. But shock therapy seemed to work, and became quite popular. There was little concern to explain its effectiveness, however. (In truth, this diagnostic indifference was emblematic of military medicine. "Soldier's heart," another widespread military affliction that elicited suspicion of malingering, was also diagnosed and treated without regard to its underlying causes – defined functionally as "exaggerated manifestations of healthy responses to effort" and treated with a course of exercises adopted because they somehow rehabilitated soldiers.)[89]

The successful operation of shock therapy, insofar as it was explained at all, was described as an illustration of the power of "suggestion." A soldier who had lost his voice, for example, would be told that he would be cured after electric shocks were applied to his larynx – and he would be – and soldiers awaiting their turn with the doctor outside the treatment room would hear the patient respond, and would be in a state of exaggerated readiness to recover. The psychological therapy of suggestion was far from the analytic method the Riversian psychiatrists favored, however. There is presumptive evidence that the ordinary shell-shocked soldier was more likely than the officer to be given such summary treatment. It is impossible to compile definitive statistics because official records are still closed; however, it is possible to infer that the two classes of soldiers received different therapies both from the existence of some special hospitals established for the exclusive care of officers and from participants' statements. Nevertheless, during the course of the war, the military grew more tolerant of analytic treatments. By the end of the war the military was running short courses to train large numbers of physicians in dream analysis and other analytic techniques appropriate to treating shell shock as a functional disorder.[90]

In sum, the anthropologically informed model of battle-induced mental disorder had four parts: First, although individual differences of heredity and experience were not entirely irrelevant to the responses of soldiers to their war experiences, these individual characteristics were far less important determinants of a soldier's behavior than were the features of human nature common to all military men (and others). Second, the pathological degeneration to which fighting men were subject could be caused by either physical insult or psychic distress. Third, the pattern of onset of degener-

---

[89] Joel D. Howell, "'Soldier's Heart': The Redefinition of Heart Disease and Speciality Formation in Early Twentieth-Century Great Britain," *Medical History* 29 (1985), Suppl. No. 5: 41–44.

[90] For summaries of fashions in treatment see Stone, "Shellshock"; H. Crighton Miller, "Preface" to Miller, ed., *Functional Nerve Disease: An Epitome of War Experience for the Practitioner* (London, 1920), vi–vii.

ation was the same for all casualties of the war, whether the pathology was of a functional nature or the result of a wound. Fourth, though the symptoms of functional and physical disorders might be indistinguishable, treatment of the disorder required determination of its etiology.

First, the war demonstrated that "a psychoneurosis may be produced in almost anyone if only his environment be made 'difficult' enough for him." The stresses of the war were quantitatively, not qualitatively, distinct from the strains of everyday life. Before the war, it had been conventional to assume that those symptoms characteristic of shell shock – whether diagnosed as "neurasthenia" or "hysteria" – would be presented only by persons somehow congenitally deficient – men diagnosed as "neuropaths," or women. If no organic cause could be identified for mental disorder, it was usually dismissed as imaginary. As Elliot Smith wrote, in collaboration with Myers's former student T. H. Pear, the experiences of the war showed that

> the pessimistic, helpless appeal to heredity, so common in the case of insanity, must go the same way as its lugubrious homologue which formerly did duty in the case of tuberculosis. In the causation of the psychoneuroses, heredity undoubtedly counts, but social and material environment count infinitely more.... In the military hospitals there have been hundreds of patients suffering from psychoneuroses who are demonstrably neither women or neuropaths.[91]

Moreover, the Riversian psychiatrists insisted that the shock of immersion in the social situation of the war could be sufficiently brutal to obliterate whatever psychic reserves individuals possessed by virtue of their prewar experiences. They believed that the proportion of soldiers who suffered from shell shock was about the same in all ranks. Perhaps officers were more likely to succumb to psychological ailments of the neurasthenic type, and enlisted men to disorders of the hysteric or dissociative type, but conventional distinctions between types of mental illness were practically specious (for civilians in peacetime as well as soldiers). Neither the virtues of character nor the habits inculcated by experience protected the soldier, for "officers of the highest intelligence, education, and morale were by no means immune," and shell shock also affected "the seasoned veterans of the Regular Army, a particularly fine class of men."[92]

[91] Smith and Pear, *Shell Shock*, 87–8, 94. See also Henry Head, "Observation on the Elements of the Psychoneuroses," *British Medical Journal* 1920 (10): 389; William McDougall, "The Nature of Functional Disease," *American Journal of Psychiatry* [n.s.] 1 (1922): 339; William McDougall, "Summary," in Miller, ed., *Functional Nerve Disease*, 184.

[92] William McDougall, *Outline of Abnormal Psychology* (New York, 1926), 2–3; see also

That so many individuals succumbed to shell shock demonstrated the point that Rivers and his associates had been making since the days of the Torres Straits Expedition: those features of human nature that were expressed at any given moment were functions of the social situation in which individuals found themselves. Indeed, Riversians argued that the comparative frequency of shell shock among the various fighting forces in the war was particularly telling evidence of the relationship between general human nature and cultural peculiarities. To wit, soldiers in every nation's army succumbed to shell shock, but there was a greater proportional frequency of psychological casualties among the British soldiers than among the French; the norms of their culture required British soldiers to suppress their fears during their waking hours, rendering them more susceptible to collapse than the French. There might be no factual basis to the widespread belief that within the British forces officers were more prone to shell shock than other ranks, but if shell-shock rates did indeed vary by rank, this variation was to be interpreted as the product of cultural differences within Britain. As veterans of the public school system, the officer class had been inculcated with British values in their purest form, and had thus learned to repress all types of emotion. The diffusion of the public school ideals to other educational institutions in the years before the war had undoubtedly narrowed the cultural gap between Btitain's elite and masses, however, and the average citizens who served as ordinary soldiers had evidently learned the behavioral habits that rendered individuals vulnerable to shell shock.[93]

Second, the array of symptoms displayed by a soldier whose disorder was of a purely functional origin might be the same as that displayed by one who had sustained a wound. Shell-shock victims presented many symptoms, ranging from dramatically decreased or increased affective response to sensory diffuseness of the sort surgically induced in Head and characterized by loss of sensitivity to pain, inability to identify the locus of stimulation, inability to specify degrees of heat and cold, and so on. But all of the forms of shell shock "unleashed primitive sensibility" of a protopathic sort to some degree.[94] Soldiers who succumbed to such disorders as blindness, paralysis, amnesia, or mutism displayed not merely some protopathic traits but wholly protopathic states, for their conditions were of the all-or-none variety, and their bodies were performing only

G. Elliot Smith, "Shell Shock and the Soldier," *The Lancet* 1916 (1): 853; Charles S. Myers, "Contributions to the Study of Shell Shock," *The Lancet* 1916 (1): 467; Head, "Elements of the Psychoneuroses," 391; McDougall, "The Nature of Functional Disease," 340.

[93] Rivers, *Instinct and the Unconscious*, 209; McDougall, *Abnormal Psychology*, 139–40.
[94] Myers, "Contributions to the Study of Shell Shock," 609.

those functions essential to sustain life.[95] An injured soldier might also degenerate into a primitive condition. A man whose wound affected his cerebral cortex, for example, retained only those language skills characteristic of primitives. It was significant that

> though he had lost the power of naming colours, [he] should still be able to say that an object is the same colour as the lapel of his tunic or the band on his arm, having been reduced by neural injury to the state of the many peoples who denote colours by their resemblance to natural objects, and have only two or three names by which they can name colours in independence of the objects of which the colours are attributes.[96]

That the same symptoms could result from organic or psychological causes demonstrated the reality of functional disorders.

Furthermore, the onset of shell shock was sudden, no different from the onset of physical injury. True, there might be intimations that the soldier was suffering from excessive stress. As he found himself increasingly incapable of dealing with his fears, his dreams would reveal his emotional turmoil. But the soldier's daily behavior would be unaffected by his inner state until, finally, his accumulated fears reached a critical level. At this juncture in his psychological career, a stressful event of even the most trivial sort would be sufficient to precipitate an emotional collapse. This pattern of the onset of shell shock, if not necessarily the symptoms presented by its victim, fit the all-or-none pattern characteristic of protopathic responses, for it was not the intensity of the precipitating stimulus that affected the soldier but its mere affliction.[97]

Finally, to the diffusionist anthropologist-psychologists, the history of a patient's illness was critical to determining the proper treatment for it. Clearly, physical and mental afflictions were on some level undifferentiated: physical wounds could cause the loss of mental functions, whereas psychological distress could produce physical symptoms. Why not then treat the symptoms of shell shock with physical therapies? Rivers and his colleagues argued that treatment could not be effective unless it addressed the causes of disease. A wound required medical attention. Functional disorder required psychological therapy. The physician had to elicit from the shell-shocked soldier a report of the fears that he had repressed, perhaps by

---

[95] Rivers, *Instinct and the Unconscious*, 53–5, 208; Myers, "Contributions to the Study of Shell Shock," 464.

[96] Rivers, "The Unity of Anthropology" 21.

[97] For example, W. H. R. Rivers, "Appendix on 'Wind-Up,'" in *The Medical Problems of Flying*, Medical Research Council Special Report, No. 53 (London, 1920), 261–4; McDougall, *Abnormal Psychology*, 138.

questioning the soldier directly or perhaps breaking through his defenses with the aid of light hypnosis or mild drugs. The soldier could be restored to health only if he learned to manage his fears on some conscious level. He might do so simply by learning to articulate his fears with his physician's assistance, or he might require specific suggestions from his therapist.[98]

Evidently, this approach to shell shock had met with considerable resistance from the military, particularly in the early stage of the war. C. S. Myers was but one of the therapeutically minded physicians who reported opposition to their methods in army hospitals. Indeed, Myers became so frustrated that at the end of 1917 he resigned his position as supervisor of all psychological treatment available to the British Armies in France. Why did the analytic treatment of shell shock gain increasing acceptance during the course of the war? Evidently, the sheer volume of shell-shock cases encouraged trials of all sorts of therapies, in the hope that some might prove successful. More important, the military inclination to treat shell shock as a disciplinary problem did not suit public opinion, and public opinion was reflected in the official government view of battle-induced psychological disorder. Newspapers expressed sympathy for shell-shock victims, private charities were established to help them, and concern for their welfare was expressed in Parliament.

From the start of the war, the government view of shell shock was the same as that of Rivers and his associates: shell shock was both a genuine disorder and a temporary one, which could be induced in anyone by the stresses of battle; soldiers were not to be stigmatized by being treated as ordinary lunatics, but had to be treated in special military hospitals. Perhaps the official view of the deficiencies of an earlier war's soldiers – the recruits for the South African War – affected the government's attitude in this one; only a decade before World War I, after all, a government commission had determined that soldiers' physical inadequacies reflected their unfortunate circumstances, not their defective constitutions, and this conclusion could with little difficulty be extended to cover mental as well as physical disorders. Government spokesmen stressed the situational and involuntary nature of shell shock; soldiers did not choose to collapse under the strain of battle, but succumbed unwillingly while doing their patriotic duty. Indeed, the first shell-shock victims were all brave volunteers, since Britain did not introduce conscription until 1916. Therefore, their aberrations were presumed to be temporary (a presumption eventually belied by the vast number of soldiers pensioned for permanent mental disability

---

[98] C. S. Myers, "Autobiography," in *Occupational Psychology* 44 (1970 [orig. printed 1936]): 10.

and/or removed to conventional asylums after the war). As William Brace, Under Secretary in the Home Department, said in Parliament on June 17, 1915:

> If the soldiers who lost their reason in consequence of the hardships of the war were put in the ordinary asylums of the country it would in the judgment of those who have a right to speak on this matter be one of those experiences for which the soldiers after their recovery would not thank the nation.[99]

The disparity between the military and government views of shell shock is indicated by Myers's wartime career; after resigning his position working for the Army Medical Service in France, he found satisfaction working for the War Office, inspecting the hospitals for shell-shock victims that had been established throughout Britain.[100] Clearly, the government (as well as popular) interpretation of battle-induced mental disorder was congruent with that of Rivers, Elliot Smith, and their colleagues. And in any conflict between the military and the government, the latter was bound to hold the balance of power.

Riversian psychologists insisted that the stressful conditions that occasioned soldiers' mental breakdowns were only quantitatively different from the sorts of conditions common in peacetime. And among the lasting effects of the war were the recognition of the reality of functional disorder and an increased respect for psychoanalysis both within and without medical circles. Moreover, the analytic approach favored by British psychiatrists and laymen alike was Riversian – one which held that Freud had overemphasized the importance of the sexual drive in human motivation but acknowledged the value of his theory of the unconscious and his psychoanalytic method.[101] And the proven utility of anthropologized psychology in one specific social situation – that of the military in combat – suggested that the psychocultural dynamics of other clearly delimited social spheres might be analyzed and altered by the methods used in the war. In particular, the workplace seemed an especially appropriate venue for the practice of wartime techniques, not the least because the postwar period promised to bring a return of the extraordinarily hostile relations between management and labor that had marked the years immediately preceding

---

[99] "Treatment of Mental Strain in Soldiers," News item, *The Lancet* 1915 (1): 1377. See also *The Lancet* 1915 (1): 352, 412, 1059. And see Stone, "Shellshock," 253–4.
[100] Myers, "Autobiography."
[101] See, for example, Dean Rapp, "The Reception of Freud by the British Press: General Interest and Literary Magazines, 1920–1925," *Journal of the History of the Behavioral Sciences* 24 (1988): 191–201; Stocking, "Anthropology and the Science of the Irrational," 29.

the war, but had been halted for the duration by labor co-optation and government conciliation.[102] Furthermore, industrial reorganizations after the war created conditions in which a new specialized craft of industrial psychology could develop.

The savage in the workplace

In view of the developmental history of the diagnosis of traumatic neurosis, it is hardly surprising that the lessons of the war were applied to industrial management. The first traumatic neurosis so described was a consequence of industrial accidents, the nervous disorder that frequently afflicted casualties of railroad disasters. First identified in 1864 by (Sir) John Eric Erichsen, called in turn "railway spine" and "railway brain," it was initially explained as the product of traumatic lesions. The etiology of this affliction became the subject of considerable debate in Britain and on the Continent (where Charcot pronounced it a variant of male hysteria), and by 1910 younger British physicians had dismissed all appeals to microlesions of the nervous system or physiological disturbances of the brain caused by jarring; they were convinced that railway accident victims suffered from a functional disorder that combined the symptoms of hysteria and neurasthenia. Established as a genuine complaint despite its lack of organic basis, this disorder entitled victims to legal redress for injury; they were not greedy malingerers, but ought to receive just compensation for their sufferings – from which they were expected to recover.[103] We have already seen how concern over rail and sea safety led to investigations of color blindness, and that investigations indicated that this deficiency could be the temporary result of physical or mental trauma. The experiences of the war confirmed the reality of functional disorders. But they did more than build on prewar industrial medicine: they showed that functional disorders were not simply the responses to stress that individuals had qua individuals, but were engendered in social situations. It was this insight that distinguished postwar industrial psychology, and it was an insight that derived from the Torres Straits Expedition as well as wartime experience.

---

[102] Perkin, *The Rise of Professional Society*, 174, 184–5, 202.
[103] See Peter John Lynch, "The Exploitation of Courage: Psychiatric Care in the British Army, 1914–1918," Unpublished M. A. thesis, University College, London, 1977, 64–9; also Edward M. Brown, "Between Cowardice and Insanity: Shell Shock and the Legitimation of the Neuroses in Great Britain," in Everett Mendelsohn, Merritt Roe Smith, and Peter Weingart, eds., *Science, Technology and the Military: Sociology of the Sciences Yearbook* 12, Pt. II (1988): 323–45.

The practical social scientific specialty of industrial psychology was largely created by Charles Myers, who traced the inspiration for his post-war work to a suggestion made to him during the war by T. H. Pear. Myers's consulting firm, the National Institute of Industrial Psychology (NIIP), operated virtually without commercial competitors in Britain until the 1950s, often working with the government-sponsored Industrial Fatigue Research Board (after 1929, the Industrial Health Research Board), a subsidiary of the Medical Research Council. The NIIP received some philanthropic support, but it depended largely on contracts from government, commerce, and industry (and a few contracts from unions). Its success can be measured in both commercial and academic terms. It suffered some lean years, but it was a thriving concern for much of its existence between 1921 and 1973. And sometime NIIP workers found employment not only in government and the private sector but also in universities. Moreover, by formal measures of recognition, it is apparent that the workers of the NIIP had the intellectual respect of the profession, for at least five members of the interwar NIIP staff became presidents of the British Psychological Society.[104]

Myers interpreted industrial unrest as a phenomenon akin to shell shock: it was compounded of stressful social conditions and individual pathological responses. Psychologically disturbed workers had hardly regressed to the protopathic level, since the stresses to which they were subject were not of the utmost severity, but they had lost their sense of collective solidarity. Alienated laborers exhibited symptoms of physical disorder and behaved antisocially because "overstrain must produce a loss of 'higher' control, leading to the short-circuiting of 'lower' nervous processes, whereby their energy is wastefully dissipated." Disturbed individuals would cope with their problems by projecting their own deficiencies onto others; if the stresses to which they were subject were inflicted on them as members of a group, they and their fellows would likely band together in collective protest. The social situation in which workers and management found themselves would become "pathological" when both groups felt they could not trust the other one, leading each to behave in a manner that in fact justified distrust: laborers would restrict output, and management would act punitively, creating a "vicious circle" of progressively antagonistic acts by both parties. The task of the industrial psychologist, then, was to reconstitute the social community of management and workers. The psychologist could recognize the restoration of collective sentiments in the workplace from practical achievements: when management made decisions,

---

[104] For various reminiscences about the early days of the NIIP, see the pieces of the Jubilee Volume of its journal: *Occupational Psychology*, 44 (1970).

they would take account of workers' views; workers would be protected from arbitrary dismissal; and management and labor would work together productively.[105]

How were these happy conditions to be engineered? Psychologists would administer aptitude tests to identify the individuals temperamentally and intellectually suitable for various occupations, would undertake time and motion studies of industrial tasks to determine the most efficient way to perform them, and would study the physical conditions of the workplace in order to determine the ideal environment for the performance of any given task. But these procedures alone would not accomplish industrial reform. The worker could not be understood by means of a "superficial analogy with a piece of engineering mechanism," not the least because "the mental and bodily differences between workers are such that it is impossible to train, or to expect, each worker to perform the same operations in identically the same way." Furthermore, all aspects of each industrial situation had to be understood in toto, for each was unique. In essence, each workplace had its own culture. Hence, the conclusions of a study of production difficulties in one factory could not be generalized to another, even when the problems of both seemed comparable. The improvement of the physical conditions of labor and the provision of sufficient financial incentives to hard work alone would not suffice to create the efficient worker. At least as important were

> the mental atmosphere of the works, the character of which is largely dependent on management and leadership on the one side, on loyalty and comradeship on the other, and on the satisfaction of each worker's instincts and interests, which are by no means confined to what money will buy him outside the factory.[106]

In order to realize their developmental potential, individuals needed to feel themselves members of a community of mutually caring persons, and to feel the identity of their interests with those of society – as Rivers would also have observed. The individuals' need for belonging explained why workers who were joined in collective solidarity with their fellow laborers would find their lives entirely changed for the better; they would become not merely contented workers but well-adjusted persons. When workers felt themselves the objects of benevolent concern, they would apply themselves vigorously to their tasks; hence the mere presence of industrial psychologists in the factory would often serve to improve productivity even before any organizational changes were made in the workplace. Industrial

---

[105] Myers, *Mind and Work*, 163, 167, 190.
[106] Ibid., 28, 27, 30; see also 22.

psychologists served a therapeutic function for the workers, not the least because psychologists were acting as surrogates for management when they expressed concern for workers' welfare.[107]

When Myers observed that workers who believed themselves objects of concern would immediately become happier and more productive, he was describing the same phenomenon that would be labeled the "Hawthorne Effect" by the American practitioners of the anthropologically glossed "Human Relations" school of industrial psychologists, who were, like him, opposed to the engineering approach to factory management identified with Frederick Winslow Taylor. It is customary to represent the appeal to the Hawthorne Effect as an exercise in wishful thinking, an argument that appealed to employers who wished to make no structural changes in their workplaces and no concessions to unions' demands for increased compensation. With the psychologists' endorsement, employers could with very slight financial investments undertake to make their workers feel better – and solve their labor problems. There is much merit in this argument.[108] Nevertheless, it is important to note that Myers and his like-minded colleagues were imputing to workers the aspirations that they themselves felt as professionals. That is, like other professionals old and new, industrial psychologists believed that their identity both as workers and as citizens derived from their membership in a group with a strong sense of corporate solidarity.

A good deal of the work done by Myers and his associates bore little (if any) relation to their goal of restructuring the workplace environment. Many of the tasks they performed had very limited objectives. The NIIP provided vocational guidance to young people who came to the institute as clients, accepted commissions to administer vocational aptitude tests to candidates for specific jobs, conducted time and motion studies to determine how workers could minimize fatigue, and during the impoverished times of the 1930s deigned to undertake product marketing studies. Nevertheless, the NIIP staff refused to become the compromised agents of management interests. They would not take on clients concerned only to maximize output and profits. They insisted that job design had to be sufficiently flexible to permit workers to accomplish their tasks in the manner best suited to their natural capacities, rather than engineered to mandate the "one best way" to perform any given task. And the NIIP sought to improve communication among different strata within organizations, undertaking attitude surveys among workers, for example, in order

---

[107] Ibid., 28.
[108] The ideas of the Human Relations school bear considerable resemblance to Myers's. See, for example, Richard P. Gillespie, *Manufacturing Knowledge* (New York, 1991).

to reveal the sources of their dissatisfaction that were unknown to management.[109]

The NIIP flourished because at the moment of its creation it suited the needs of industry. In the postwar period of industrial unrest, highlighted by the General Strike of 1926, the institute's claims to expertise in engineering social harmony had evident appeal. Perhaps more important, the institute's first decade of existence coincided with a period of unprecedented industrial concentration. The giant firms created in postwar mergers had highly elaborated bureaucratic structures, and their hierarchical orders included a new occupational niche – one filled by the managerial class, whose expertise was not the business of the firm per se but the coordination of its activities. The managerial role required just those skills the industrial psychologists commanded. Serving the management sector of some of the firms consolidated in the postwar era, the NIIP helped smooth the transition into a new industrial order, developing new recruitment procedures, job definitions, and structured relationships between management and laborers.[110]

It is important to stress, however, that the coincident emergence of the NIIP and large-scale industry was more than fortuitous. The same general attitude shaped both the postwar industrial reorganization and the new applied psychology – the belief that the sum total of a nation's, a social group's, or an individual's resources did not determine accomplishments as much as did rational resource management. This was an appealing idea in an era in which Britain no longer believed its potential resources to be practically limitless, and it was an idea articulated most forcefully from the second half of the nineteenth century by the new class of brain workers who wished to rationalize all activities through the application of the scientific method.

But the experiences of the war years demonstrated conclusively the importance of social structural conditions to the expression of individuals' potential – and not just through the breakdown of men of fine character, intelligence, and skill on the battlefield. On the home front, the expanded wartime economy depended on many persons previously thought to be

---

[109] For example, Eric Farmer, "Early Days in Industrial Psychology: An Autobiographical Note," *Occupational Psychology* 44 (1970): 32; C. R. Frisby, "The Development of Industrial Psychology at the N.I.I.P.," ibid., 37–9; Winifred Raphael, "The N.I.I.P. and Its Staff 1921–1961," ibid., 68.

[110] See, for example, D. C. Doyle, "Aspects of the Institutionalization of British Psychology: The National Institute of Industrial Psychology, 1921–1939," unpublished Ph.D. thesis, University of Manchester, 1979, 5 and passim. American industrial reorganization also figured in the appeal of the Human Relations school. See Gillespie, *Manufacturing Knowledge*.

congenitally incapable of functioning as productive members of society, who proved competent to hold jobs when the opportunity to secure them was presented. Individuals' responses to diverse wartime conditions served to justify the expansion of British social services and the creation of the welfare state.[111] Indeed, Rivers took the lessons of the war to heart. Having determined that social conditions could engender psychopathology, he evidently concluded that he should take an active part in shaping society. At the time of his premature death in 1922, he was standing as the Labour candidate for the parliamentary seat of the University of London – the previous occupants of which included John Lubbock and Michael Foster. Concerned above all to develop clinical applications for his theories, Rivers was not making a decisive break with his past in embarking on a political career, but was taking a step consistent with the conclusions to be drawn from his investigations and experiences.[112]

Conclusions

The figures described in this chapter, and especially Rivers, had a considerable impact on British intellectual life in the World War I era. In large measure, this was a consequence of the personal ties they had to members of the intelligentsia. Before the war, Rivers had come to know Bertrand Russell, and his acquaintanceship with H. G. Wells and G. B. Shaw quite possibly also dated from before the war. His social horizons expanded when he treated Siegfried Sassoon for shell shock, though, for his new

[111] See, for example, McBriar, *Mixed Doubles* (chap. 3, n. 62), 358.

[112] Richard Slobodin points out that when Rivers turned to politics, he professed commitment to socialism, and that as Labour's candidate he ran on a platform that included increased taxation of the wealthy, empowerment of the League of Nations, nationalization of mines and railways, and considerable transfer of power to colonized peoples – independence for Egypt, acceptance of the Irish Free State Constitution, and self-government for India. Upon Rivers's death, H. G. Wells became the candidate for the University of London seat – and did so badly in the election that he lost his deposit.

My account of Rivers's life and work is in substantial agreement with Slobodin's, with one important exception: unlike him, and unlike virtually every other chronicler of Rivers's career, I see intellectual continuity in the various aspects of Rivers's scholarship and political activity. I suspect that the scholarly habit of seeing Rivers's diverse activities – and particularly his enthusiasm for diffusionism – as discrete phases in his personal development springs from the desire to dismiss as aberrations those aspects of Rivers's work that have fallen out of scholarly regard, and hence preserve the reputation of a man who was held in extraordinarily high scientific esteem. See Slobodin, *W. H. R. Rivers* (New York, 1978), 80–1 and passim.

friend introduced him to a range of literary figures, including Robert Graves and Arnold Bennett. Furthermore, in describing Rivers in his memoirs, Sassoon made Rivers a hero of the literature inspired by the war. Graves undertook to understand the morbid tendencies he observed in himself and society, discussing psychoanalytic concepts with Rivers, and with Head as well, and used his new knowledge in his writing. Head explained the physiopsychological economy of the person to Roger Fry, whose explanation of the character of prehistoric and primitive art – that it attests to the mental habits of people whose way of life develops their sensory skills at the expense of their intellectual ones – is recognizably derived from the same scheme that informed Rivers's account of the culture of the Torres Straits islanders. T. S. Eliot applied Rivers's interpretation of Melanesian society to his own, arguing that in Britain as well as Melanesia an assault on traditional values was leading to extinction of the will to live.[113]

Links to the intelligentsia were not peculiar to the anthropologists of this era, however. Anthropologists had had such ties in the past, and they would have them in the future. Anthropologists of this period were distinguished by the influence they had on national policies in their professional capacities. Men such as John Lubbock and John Evans clearly had had a greater impact on British life than did the likes of Rivers, Head, D. J. Cunningham, and Karl Pearson. But members of the older generation were more persuasive because inherited fortune and personal industry had placed them in powerful positions, from which they were able to speak in anthropologically informed tones. When Cunningham prescribed the expansion of social welfare services, however, and Rivers and his colleagues acted to make the treatment of shell-shocked soldiers humane rather than punitive, they were effective because they were recognized as trained experts. No sweeping policy changes were to be implemented at anthropologists' prompting in the future.

How can one account for the influence of these anthropologists? Perhaps their opinions carried weight because they spoke to a population lately convinced of the value of scientific expertise, yet still thoroughly conditioned to respond to authority. Perhaps the anthropologists were persuasive because so many of them were physicians, and could rely on the deference habitually accorded to members of their professional species, whereas the earlier and later generations of anthropologists could not. Perhaps the very

---

[113] Slobodin, *Rivers*, 68. See also Martin Seymour-Smith, *Robert Graves. His Life and Work* (New York, 1984), 90–7; Roger Fry, "The Art of the Bushmen," in his *Vision and Design* (New York, 1957 [essay orig. 1910]), 94–5; T. S. Eliot, "Marie Lloyd," in his *Selected Essays* (New York, 1950 [essay orig. 1923]), 405–8.

breadth of their knowledge was compelling; they could dazzle those they advised about such mundane issues as the causes of industrial accidents or the nutrition of the British worker with references to arcana about ancient Egyptians. But the most important reason for the appeal of their message was surely its accessibility: they were addressing a people who knew from personal experience how individuals' fortunes could be altered by the circumstances in which they were placed in their capacities as members of social groups – whether these were the recent creations of individuals voluntarily banding together for common advancement, such as professional associations and trade unions, or organizations to which individuals submitted, such as the military or the recently restructured industrial workplace – and were prepared to acknowledge the importance of social structure in individual lives.

Chapter 5
The colonial exchange

All of the varieties of anthropologists described in this study – evolutionists, diffusionists, functionalists – sought support for their work on the grounds that it would be useful to colonial administrators. As dominance of the discipline shifted from one school to another, colonial administrators confronted new problems, and each school couched its appeals to its putative patrons in terms of their current needs. Nevertheless, the most remarkable characteristic of British colonial adminstration may well be its extraordinary consistency: prominent features of its structure and ideology were sustained not only from one territory to another but also from the nineteenth century through the era of deliberate decolonization. Absent an alliance of specific actors in the peculiar circumstances of the 1920s, anthropologists might not have secured the official sponsorship they had long sought. But the functionalists were then able to strike a responsive chord in official hearts because they echoed ideological refrains long dear to colonial rulers.

Officials in the Colonial Office and persons who worked closely with them; the leaders of missionary societies; and the agents of wealthy philanthropists, concerned both to do good and to create a stable world order in which international trade could flourish – all became patrons of functionalist anthropology. Without the support of such figures, the functionalist school would almost certainly still have become the dominant one in British anthropology during the interwar period, but its victory might well have been neither so swift nor so complete. Functionalists' successful appeals for patronage changed anthropology as an academic discipline.

Nevertheless, functionalists were not wholly beholden to their new supporters, and did not become their creatures. To be sure, because anthropologists' patrons agreed that Africa's colonial rulers needed expert guidance, and were prepared to finance field research in Africa, the functionalist generation trained in the interwar years – the first sizable cohort of professional anthropologists – was composed largely of Africanists. But their analyses were not simply functions of their patrons' directions – as, indeed, scientific ideas rarely are. Rather, unlikely alliances were formed among anthropologists, colonial policy makers, and philanthropists. But close contact among the parties to these alliances did not dispel the illusions each had about the others, and many of the outcomes of the parties' negotiations were unanticipated.

In fact, the intended recipients of functionalists' expert advice, the field staff of Britain's African territories, did not take to viewing their tasks in functionalist terms. Constrained by the organizational structure and official objectives of imperial rule, they developed a distinctive variant of evolutionist anthropology to rationalize and guide their consistent managerial practices. Only as the colonial era was drawing to a close did some officials abandon the pretext that they were merely the agents of inexorable historical forces, whose decisions constituted obedience to scientific laws of social evolution. Their evolutionary theory had obvious ties of filiation to the parent model in Britain, but its speciation occurred in the isolated circumstances of the colonies. Colonial anthropology was a congeries of formulae developed to meet the practical needs of a specific client, less like academic anthropology than like other technical enterprises sponsored by particular government agencies or industries.[1]

If the history of colonial anthropology shows us little about the development of anthropology as a discipline, it illuminates colonial social history – a matter of considerable significance in the general scheme of things. Colonial anthropology rationalized systematic policies of colonial officials that had long lasting consequences. In the postcolonial era, new nations have faced various problems fostered by colonialism. Of course, the most important of these has been that their new nation status has little altered their subordinate position in the world economy. But new nations have also had difficulties creating political orders for themselves. Their political problems were in no small part engendered during the colonial era by officials who believed that their decisions were dictated by evolutionist social science.

---

[1] Such technical enterprises come in both social and natural scientific varieties. For one example of the social scientific type, see the highly stylized variant of ecological sociology used by U.S. Government bureaucrats in managing federal support of home mortgages; see my "Sociological Theory as Occupational Ideology: Chicago Sociology and Urban Planning Policy," *Theory and Society* 9 (1980): 201–19. One example of the natural scientific type is the field of toxicology, which assesses the health and environmental hazards posed by various substances, a research specialty especially useful in protecting industry against legal action. For one discussion of the differences between toxicologists and academic scientists who evaluate the same phenomena, see Brendan Gillespie, Dave Eva, and Ron Johnston, "Carcinogenic Risk Assessment in the United States and Great Britain: The Case of Aldrin/Dieldrin," *Social Studies of Science* 9 (1979): 265–301.

Anthropology as the science of colonial administration

Before World War I, anthropologists addressed colonial officials concerned with the problems of pacifying and controlling reluctant subjects.
As the strategists of the unsuccessful campaign to create an imperial
bureau of ethnology did, anthropologists in this era stressed that unless
colonial officials were trained to appreciate the cultures of subject peoples
they were bound to make decisions that would cause offense – and inspire
rebellion. Furthermore, before World War I, both evolutionist and diffusionist anthropologists were wont to prophesy the disintegration (even
extinction) of recently pacified societies unless traditional custom was
accorded proper respect. To be sure, evolutionist and functionalist explanations of peoples' vulnerability to degeneration were different: evolutionists
maintained that the social bonds of primitive societies were particularly
fragile, since they rested on unconscious accommodations rather than the
rational calculations of advanced peoples; diffusionists reasoned that primitives were no different from other peoples and thus were susceptible to
psychological breakdown if confronted with catastrophic change. But
the conclusion of evolutionist and diffusionist arguments was the same:
colonial regimes might find themselves with no peoples to govern if they
did not avail themselves of anthropological expertise.[2]

Recall that in the late nineteenth and early twentieth centuries, Britain
was vastly expanding its colonial holdings. At this time, anthropologists
were still striving to establish the legitimacy of their discipline. The character of anthropologists' rhetoric in this period was a function both of the
precarious authority of British rule in much of the Empire and of the
institutional insecurity of the discipline. By arguing that the protection of
subject peoples served Britain's interests, anthropologists reconciled their
liberal principles with the reality of imperial expansion undertaken for
geopolitical and economic purposes. Anthropologists' self-advertisements
were congruent with the views of the liberal wing of the pro-imperialist
bloc in Britain: self-interest required Britain to act to preserve traditional
cultures, for in those tropical areas that were unsuitable for European
settlement, areas that constituted a considerable portion of the Empire and
housed those backward societies particularly vulnerable to disintegration,
peoples could not serve as laborers in the economic enterprises of Empire
unless their cultures remained viable.[3] Furthermore, anthropologists seek-

---

[2] See, for example, W. H. R. Rivers, "The Government of Subject Peoples," in A. C.
Seward, ed., *Science and the Nation* (Cambridge, 1917), 302–28.

[3] For a specimen statement of the imperialist position that the indigenous societies
of colonial possessions had to be preserved so that their peoples could produce the
goods Britain required, see Mary Kingsley, *West African Studies* (London, 1899),

ing to promote their discipline saw imperialists as their natural patrons. A figure such as J. G. Frazer might express some reservations about anthropology's utility in guiding Britain's future development, but he argued that colonial officials could not control their subjects without anthropological training.[4]

By the interwar period, however, the authority of Britain over its colonial subjects had become much more secure, and seemed likely to persist far into the foreseeable future. The threats to social stability in the colonies that then presented themselves were those engendered by colonialism itself: in white settler territories, the propensity of the settlers to encroach on indigenous peoples' rights and lands; in areas in which European enterprises depended on local workers, the difficulties of making tribesmen into wage laborers; in places remote from European economic activity, resistance to administrators' efforts to effect changes they saw as progressive reforms in pacified and stabilized traditional societies; in every regime, the demands of colonial subjects (particularly the Western-educated) for a greater voice in their own government. Anthropologists claimed no expertise in the management of colonial nationalism, but represented themselves as exceptionally qualified to analyze and prescribe solutions for every other problem confronting colonial governments in the postwar era.[5]

Whatever the changes in the colonial situation, however, anthropologists' relations with their potential patrons had changed because their professional authority was greater. They were not so desperate for support that they felt compelled to present a united front to colonial officials. Their discipline had been recognized in academe, their major learned society had been granted a Royal Charter, and officials had taken some tentative steps toward recognition of anthropology's administrative value. Rival anthropol-

367–8. Other proponents of imperialism were quite prepared to sacrifice the welfare of subject peoples for Britain's economic gain. Their views are discussed in H. G. C. Matthew, *The Liberal Imperialists* (London, 1973), 154, 158; Bernard Semmel, *Imperialism and Social Reform* (Cambridge, Mass., 1960), 65, 98, 131–3. One of these was F. D. Lugard; see his entry of 19 May, 1891, in *The Diaries of Lord Lugard*, ed. Margery Perham with Mary Bull (Evanston, Ill., 1963), 179. Lugard argued, however, that Indirect Rule could serve the interests of the British and subject peoples alike; doing so was its "dual mandate."

[4] For Frazer's doubts about the utility of anthropology as futurology, see his *The Scope of Social Anthropology* (London, 1908), 5. For his argument that colonial officials be trained in anthropology, see his statement quoted in a news report, "The Teaching of Anthropology at the Universities," *Nature* 93 (1914): 725. It is of some parenthetical interest that A. C. Haddon saved a clipping of this article, in HP,CV, Env. 4072.

[5] See, for example, B. Malinowski, "Memorandum on Colonial Research," *Colonial Research*, December 1927, in Oldham Papers, Box 2, OUODP.

ogical schools now competed for the greater official support they were certain was forthcoming, each claiming that its approach was particularly useful.

For example, Bronislaw Malinowski argued that functionalist theories and findings were more serviceable in the colonial context than those of the evolutionists and the diffusionists, since the historical interests of both of these schools led them to esoteric investigations of the "quaint" and "fantastic" aspects of tribal life, rather than "the actual way in which primitive politics are worked." Malinowski's defense of functionalism was invariant, whether he was addressing government officials or private philanthropists, conducting private correspondence, or writing for publication.[6] His diffusionist rival, Elliot Smith, countered that a larger number of colonial administrators and candidates for colonial posts were drawn to his program at University College, London than were attracted to Malinowski's and Seligman's courses at the London School of Economics; his students were able to recognize that UCL was imparting useful knowledge. And in fact, UCL successfully competed for students with colonial interests in the 1920s, as Seligman noted with alarm in a letter to Malinowski.[7]

There were, of course, some anthropologists who could not appeal for patronage in the conventional terms of the day. As the archaeologist-classicist William Ridgeway observed ruefully to A. C. Haddon, benefactors of anthropology such as the Rockefeller Foundation would support only that research which promised to be useful in "the alleviation of the sufferings of humanity"; archaeologists could not defend their work in these terms.[8] Because physical anthropologists had not demonstrated a link between race and culture – indeed, had indicated that no such link existed – philanthropists likewise could be persuaded that their work was not worthy of support.[9] And the odd eccentric, such as A. M. Hocart,

[6] See, for examples, Malinowski's articles: "Practical Anthropology," *Africa* 2 (1929): 22–38; "The Rationalisation of Anthropology and Administration," *Africa* 3 (1930): 405–30; "The Present State of Studies in Culture Contact," *Africa* 12 (1939): 27–48; and his Colonial Office Memorandum: "The Teaching of Anthropology to the Political Officers of the Gold Coast Service," 17 October, 1929, in CO 96.668.6441, PRO. For his negotiations with the Rockefeller Foundation see, for example, "Memorandum for the Rockefeller Foundation written for Mr. Embree in March 1926," in Oldham Papers, Box 2, OUODP; and the 1929 memorandum on his conversation with John Van Sickle of the foundation, in RF.
[7] See, for example, G. Elliot Smith to E. Embree of the Rockefeller Foundation, letter of 18 December, 1926, in RF; C. G. Seligman to B. Malinowski, letter of 24 September, 1926. in MP,LSE. Seligman thought, however, that the diffusionists and the functionalists ought to be able to work together; see his letter to Malinowski, 5 December, 1923, in MP,LSE.
[8] Sir William Ridgeway to A. C. Haddon, 3 October, 1926, in HP, Env. 4.
[9] Malinowski, "Memorandum for Mr. Embree."

debunked his contemporaries' grantsmanship. Anthropologists could never understand an alien culture as well as they did their own, he said, and urged those who wished to undertake social reform to do so at home.[10]

Nevertheless, there was one constant theme in the pleas for support made by anthropologists of every persuasion before World War II: there was little conflict between research pursued for purely scientific ends and that which might be put to practical purposes. As Haddon told an audience of missionaries in 1903, anthropological research was useful only because it had yielded scientifically valid laws.[11] Certainly, anthropologists were constrained to represent themselves as impartial scientists. Working in politically volatile situations, they could not permit themselves to be perceived as agents of particular parties, as Radcliffe-Brown wrote to Haddon from South Africa in 1921.[12] Charged with running practical courses at the universities of Cape Town and Sydney, Radcliffe-Brown avoided possible controversies by determining that the most useful training he could give missionaries and colonial officials was in general anthropological principles.[13] Malinowski allowed that the emphasis of anthropological investigation might be somewhat different if research were intended to solve practical problems rather than resolve theoretical disputes. But he insisted that only as anthropology became scientific could it "play the same part in constructive policy as physics and geology have played in engineering."[14]

Certainly, when we consider the range of arguments used to justify the definition of anthropology as a practical science before the Second World War, we observe differences between the scientific principles successive schools of anthropologists claimed to have discovered. At the turn of the century, anthropologists reasoning in the evolutionist mode argued that their work was useful because it enabled colonial administrators to recognize the characteristics shared by primitive peoples everywhere. After World War I, anthropologists of various persuasions suggested that colonial officers could use the general principles they had discovered to help "the

[10] A. M. Hocart, "Applied Anthropology," *Man* 31 (1931): 259.

[11] Haddon's opinions are reported in "The Teaching of Ethnology at Cambridge: Lectures to Missionaries," *Manchester Guardian*, 15 January, 1903, in HP,CU, Env. 4072.

[12] See A. R. Radcliffe-Brown to A. C. Haddon, letter of 12 November, 1921, in HP,CU, Env. 4.

[13] See A. R. Radcliffe-Brown to A. C. Haddon, letter of December 18, 1922, HP,CU, Env. 4; letter of 13 November, 1925, in HP,CU, Env. 5; letter of 15 November, 1926, HP,CU, Env. 5.

[14] See Bronislaw Malinowski to E. Day of the Rockefeller Foundation, letter of 20 May, 1930, in RF. Malinowski's analogy of anthropology and the natural sciences was recurrent (see the refs. in n. 6).

native ... develop along his own lines."[15] Nevertheless, at both times there was a consensus that scientific and practical purposes were naturally related.

No advertisement for anthropology seemed more likely to appeal to colonial officials than the one made also in pleas for influence within Britain: that anthropology was value-neutral, technical expertise, grounded in scientific method, enabling practitioners to identify causes of social conflict and formulate solutions equitable to all parties, thus transforming political issues into administrative ones. Indeed, anthropologists' competence in conflict resolution was especially important in the colonies. As Malinowski proclaimed, the colonial situation was founded on antagonism. Colonial administrators, European settlers, colonial investors, missionaries, and every class of the subject population, from the most Europeanized to the people in the bush – all racial groups and economic classes engaged in colonial relationships had "deeply rooted personal interests at stake" that created "irreconcilable differences." Malinowksi debunked descriptions of colonial societies as stable, integrated cultures, even when they were written by his students. And he argued that anthropologists' objective understanding of the colonial situation compelled them to use their knowledge on behalf of subject peoples – those residents of the Empire most likely to be exploited by colonialists.[16] Malinowski's recommendation that colonial regimes avail themselves of anthropological expertise was thus very like that Haddon had made decades earlier: social unrest was inevitable unless colonialists were taught to respect the values and rights of subject peoples.

Malinowski was the functionalists' chief negotiator with anthropology's colonial patrons. Since his claims were so like his predecessors', why were his efforts far more successful than theirs? Recall that earlier anthropologists also had good reason to assume that colonial regimes would be receptive to their entreaties, accurately assessing the strong technocratic element in the ideology and conduct of colonial rule. Colonial officials might have argued that one of their missions was to spread the British ideal of parliamentary democracy, but they frequently declared that their subjects were not yet ready for democratic institutions. Colonial regimes were autocratic, their policies made by civil servants who were supposedly above politics. The very few nonofficials who occupied government offices

---

[15] For the turn of the century view, see Haddon, "The Teaching of Ethnology"; for the post–World War I view, see C. G. Seligman to William Beveridge, Director of the London School of Economics, 13 March, 1924, copy in RF.

[16] Malinowski, "The Rationalisation of Anthropology and Administration," 422. And see "The Anthropology of Changing African Cultures," Malinowski's introduction to Lucy Mair, ed., *Methods of Study of Culture Contact in Africa* (London, 1938), xiii.

were expected to act as consultants to officials, rather than to serve as representatives of groups who might legitimately oppose government policy. The objectives of colonial rule seemed ideally realized through the application of scientific principles. Indeed, as was already remarked, many British social reformers considered colonial regimes exemplary, both because they had replaced politics with administration and because they selected and rewarded their staffs according to meritocratic standards – the values dear to the new middle class from which so many anthropologists and colonial officials were drawn.

The obstacles to colonial regimes' acceptance of any sort of scientific advice were various – as was also noted earlier. Required to operate on small budgets, colonial governments employed few technical advisors. Furthermore, in the hierarchy of colonial offices, members of the technical services were subordinate to generalist political officers, who arrogated to themselves the prestige of the "educated amateur" gentlemanly class – although few of them came from it. Most important, political officers reveled in the mystique of practical experience. They described themselves as "practical men." Though they saw themselves as impartial experts, they represented their expertise as knowledge derived from experience of peculiar colonial conditions. Political officers believed that members of the colonial technical services were prone to do more harm than good: Scientifically trained experts formulated their policies on the basis of general principles, rather than recognizing that the reforms they wished to effect – however meritorious in the abstract – might be unsuited to the sociopolitical conditions of particular places.

However high the office the practical man of colonial political administration eventually attained, his career almost always began in a rural area, where he worked with very few other (and often no other) colonial officials. The rural officer's work was the basis of colonial rule, and colonial regimes were able to represent their relations with their subjects in benevolent terms because they believed in the reality of a highly romanticized view of the rural officer's accomplishments. No matter what were the actualities of colonial administration, political officers' idealized image of themselves affected colonial policy making at every level. And this image figured in the triumph of functionalist anthropology: functionalists' descriptions of their research methods were very like political officers' accounts of their administrative procedures. Earlier anthropologists had defended their methods in rather different terms, and colonial administrators did not see them as kindred spirits.

The rural colonial official was supposed to travel frequently among his subjects with no European companions, making personal contact with as many of his charges as possible. In truth, he toured with a retinue of local people – bearers, guides, servants, and interpreters – but these were nearly invisible in his official reports and memoirs. The rural officer was directed to immerse himself in the life of his district, and for this purpose spent his free time in such pursuits as nature study, big game hunting, and amateur anthropological investigation. He believed that a thorough understanding of his subjects was as much intuitive as intellectual, and that it allowed him to recognize their special character. He often proclaimed (erroneously) that his administrative decisions had no analogues elsewhere, that they were formulated to suit the unique needs of his people. The functionalist anthropologist also claimed to reach understanding of his or her research subjects through a process of nearly mystical communion with them, a process that also depended on sustained personal contact with them with (at least supposedly) none of the distractions that other Europeans might provide. And like the colonial official, the functionalist anthropologist emphasized that each people were at least to some degree unique, and could be understood only on their own terms.

Speaking the language of heroic colonial administration, functionalists secured colonial patronage. Anthropologists then undertook to sabotage their patrons' plans, using the resources they were guaranteed to pursue esoteric research rather than practical inquiries. Intimations of changed anthropological opinion were recognizable immediately prior to World War II, but it was not until after the war that many of the rising generation denounced their professional fathers, declaring that scientific and applied anthropology were qualitatively distinct enterprises. S. F. Nadel articulated the opinion shared by figures such as Monica Wilson, Audrey Richards, and Max Gluckman: "purely objective, 'a political' social science is nothing but a fiction."[17] When anthropologists worked for colonial regimes, declared Isaac Schapera and E. E. Evans-Pritchard, they served two masters: the scientific community; and the government, whose specific needs were bound to compromise the conduct of their research.[18]

---

[17] For an early expression of such views, see Godfrey Wilson, "Anthropology as a Public Service," *Africa* 13 (1940): 46–7. See the attack on applied anthropology by E. E. Evans-Pritchard, "Applied Anthropology," *Africa* 16 (1946): 94–5. So disturbing did E. W. Smith, the editor of *Africa*, find Evans-Pritchard's manifesto that on 3 April, 1948, he circulated a questionnaire to anthropologists, including Monica Wilson, Audrey Richards, Max Gluckman, and S. F. Nadel. Nadel's response, representative of the group, is quoted here. The responses to the questionnaire are in Lord Hailey's Papers, OUODP.

[18] See, for example, Evans-Pritchard, "Applied Anthropology"; Max Gluckman, "Malinowski's 'Functional Analysis' of Social Change," *Africa* 18 (1947): 121; I. Schapera, *Some Problems of Anthropological Research in Kenya Colony*, International African Institute Memorandum No. 23 (London, 1949), 3.

Anthropologists enjoyed the luxury of their new moral stance because they had been guaranteed research support under the 1940 Colonial Development and Welfare Act and through the Colonial Social Science Research Council (CSSRC), established in 1944 as a component of the Colonial Research Council. The Committee on Anthropology and Sociology of the CSSRC dispensed government funds that were intended to finance utilitarian projects, but because the committee was composed of academics the funds could be and were consciously turned to anthropologists' own purposes.[19] Although the committee evaluated and supported applications for applied anthropological studies, it rarely saw them as intellectually significant. Nor were those who undertook them expected to make distinguished careers. The academics who rendered judgment as members of the committee, as well as those who wrote applicants' recommendations, considered that those persons who were suited to conduct investigations of practical problems were those who lacked the talent to make theoretical contributions to the discipline.[20]

Certainly, post–World War II anthropologists were not voicing dangerous opinions when they effectively denounced colonial regimes, since they were addressing officials engaged in a process of colonial divestiture. Nevertheless, we can judge that the rhetoric of postwar anthropologists bespoke the relative freedom from patrons' control their discipline had achieved as much as a political orientation. Anthropologists' arguments were, after all, inconsistent. They described their enterprise as scientific when it treated issues they found academically interesting. Anthropology was declared incapable of rendering impartial scientific judgment – of providing technical information that could be used by anyone – when it was asked to serve nonacademic masters. Provided with control over the allocation of monies for their research, anthropologists behaved as have other scientists in patronage systems managed by peer review, setting their own research priorities and giving lip service to their patrons' desires.

The CSSRC Committee on Anthropology and Sociology cast its procedures in strictly bureaucratic form. It commissioned surveys that evaluated the state of knowledge of various regions.[21] The committee drew up

---

[19] See, for example, E. E. Evans-Pritchard's remarks at the June 21, 1955 meeting of the Committee on Anthropology and Sociology, of which he was chairman; in CRC.

[20] E. R. Leach, for example, in endorsing the grant application of Glyn Jones in his letter of 12 January, 1949 to the Colonial Research Council, makes it clear that he would not wish his truly talented students to do applied research; in CRC.

[21] Between 1945 and 1950, the CSSRC commissioned reports included those by Raymond Firth on Malaya and West Africa, Isaac Schapera on Kenya, Daryll Forde

a "short list" of "urgent projects," completion of which would both fill the gaps in knowledge indicated in its surveys and satisfy the research needs of colonial governments.[22] It invariably described the projects it funded as those given "high priority" in the regional surveys.[23] To be sure, anthropologists could not afford to disregard their patrons' desires entirely. When colonial governments broadcast their interest in specific research projects, investigators were found to do them and CSSRC support was granted. Governments were wont to complain that research results were unsatisfactory, though, for the goal of providing advice that would help make development schemes successful was essentially irrelevant to the committee's deliberations. As the Secretary to the CSSRC noted, the Committee on Anthropology and Sociology perceived its obligation to be the support of research of academic importance rather than the satisfaction of government needs.[24] Certainly, there were anthropologists who benefited both intellectually and professionally from the opportunities to work in the colonies, and there was some research that proved useful in development administration. But these were unintended consequences of the committee's actions.

This is not to say that the maintenance of colonial rule per se became irrelevant to the practice of anthropology. Beginning in the 1960s, British anthropologists developed considerable anxiety over their intellectual identify, in no small part as a consequence of political change. In whatever way anthropologists wished their research subjects to perceive them, in the colonial era they were recognized as members of the ruling class – and their inquiries were likely to be answered. In the postcolonial era, anthro-

on the Gambia, W. E. S. Stanner on Uganda and Tanganyika, and E. R. Leach on Sarawak.

[22] Colonial Research Council, "Control and Administration of Research in the Colonies," Appendix E: "Note on the Scientific Direction of Colonial Social Sciences Research," June 21, 1950, in CRC.

[23] See, for example, Colonial Research Council, "Reports on Progress Made in Various Fields of Colonial Research," 19 October, 1949; CSSRC Report for 1951/52; CSSRC, "Proposed Combined Investigations of Luo and Iragi Customary Law and Land Tenure by Gordon Wilson," Note by the Secretaries, E. C. Willis and E. M. Chilver, 30 December, 1952; CSSRC, "Tenth Annual Report," in the Colonial Research Council Report for 1953–4, 47–84. All in CRC.

[24] See E. M. Chilver's notes for the chairman of the CSSRC for its meeting of June 21, 1955, in CRC. Colonial governments did indeed complain that the anthropological research being done under their auspices was irrelevant to their purposes. See, for example, Note by the Secretaries of the CSSRC on the "Socio-economic Survey of the Rural Areas of the Colony Peninsula of Sierra Leone," by G. R. Collins and E. M. Richardson, 17 April, 1953, in CRC; and E. M. Chilver's notes for the CSSRC chairman for the meeting of 22 March, 1955, commenting on the general dissatisfaction with Philip Mayer's work in Kenya, in CRC.

pologists from the industrialized world have considerable difficulty doing research among non-Western peoples, not the least because independent nations resent the implicit identification of anthropologists' subjects as primitives. When anthropologists are permitted to work in new nations, they are likely to be required to consent to formal restraints on their conduct, and to find their potential informants resistant to their attentions.[25]

Moreover, the end of the colonial era eliminated a major source of British anthropologists' financial support. There were to be no more research funds supplied by the CSSRC. Grant recipients were told that they must be in the "writing up" stage by 1960. Evans-Pritchard, the chairman of the Committee on Anthropology and Sociology, warned of the disasters to come when a large cohort of previously funded researchers were "thrown on the [academic job] market" around 1960.[26] In fact, just as the era of imperial rule ended, the British university system expanded, providing new employment opportunities for anthropologists. When the university boom years ended, however, anthropologists found themselves competing for considerably diminished resources, and took to quarreling fiercely with one another. Partisans of any given theoretical view disputed the rights of all others to exist within the discipline. A more tolerant atmosphere had prevailed in more prosperous times. From the vantage point of the 1970s, it seemed that anthropology had never been more financially secure than it was before colonialism ended. Many anthropologists concluded that the viability of the discipline depended on colonial rule, and that therefore the very legitimacy of anthropology was questionable.

Indeed, anthropological investigations were profoundly influenced by colonialism in two important ways: first, anthropologists' relationships with their subjects were shaped by political conditions; second, colonial rule altered the shape of traditional society, and thereby determined anthropologists' findings. These points will be elaborated in this and later chapters. Suffice it to say here that by winning the endorsement of colonial officials, the functionalists created for a time happy working conditions for anthropologists. No matter what the political message of functionalist anthropology was, it was little affected by direct pressure from outsiders. And the anthropological community believed itself united in the pursuit of collective intellectual goals – although it fragmented soon enough when research funds became scarce.

---

[25] See, for example, June Nash, "Nationalism and Fieldwork," *Annual Review of Anthropology* 4 (1975): 225–45.

[26] See C. E. Lambert, Secretary to the CRC, "Progress Report," March 1, 1956; Minutes of the Committee on Anthropology and Sociology, meeting of 22 June, 1954, in CRC.

The savage within

Scientific anthropologists versus colonial "practical men"

In principle, colonial rulers were committed to use anthropological data, no matter by whom collected. For British policy was everywhere predicated on the assumption that the best guarantee of assent to colonial rule was the preservation of subject peoples' traditional institutions, except in those rare instances in which indigenous practices were, in the stock phrase, "repugnant to natural justice and morality." In fact, customs judged repugnant would not be suppressed unless colonial rulers were relatively confident of their authority; thus, for example, the British in India banned *sati*, the self-immolation of Hindu widows on their husbands' funeral pyres, in the 1820s, but in the Sudan tolerated restitutive rather than repressive punishments for murder until the 1950s.[27] In establishing their authority, British colonialists co-opted traditional leaders, enrolling them as stewards of British rule, a strategy born of necessity. At the beginning of the colonial occupation, indigenous leaders were hardly subordinate. Colonial officers then had to be certain that they had correctly identified these leaders, lest the real rulers of indigenous polities organize resistance. And officials had to follow local custom in negotiating alliances with traditional leaders. Later, even if colonial rulers managed to transform indigenous chiefs and princes into constitutional monarchs, officials had to manage their stewards diplomatically, for the occupants of traditional offices could still serve as symbolic rallying points for discontent. A determination of the use made of anthropological evidence by the managers of British colonial rule is thus fundamental to understanding the character of British imperial order.

Political officers acted to make indigenous leaders effective stewards of their rule by zealously preserving the appearance of chiefs' previous power. Colonial bureaucrats were instructed to be alert defenders of the authority of traditional leaders. They were to resist whatever threats were presented to customary habits of deference and obedience, since subject peoples would be good citizens of the Empire only if they were good citizens of their traditional polities. Officials justified colonial rule by seeing it as a force for progressive change, and thus they did not intend to rigidify the constitutions of traditional polities. They believed that they could secure their subjects' cooperation if they introduced changes very gradually, reconciling reforms with local custom. Theirs was the ideology of administration according to the precepts of Indirect Rule. Its bible was *The Dual Mandate in British Tropical Africa*, written by F. D. (later Lord) Lugard (1858–1945) and first published in 1922.

---

[27] See Douglas H. Johnson, "Judicial Regulation and Administrative Control: Customary Law and the Nuer, 1898–1954," *Journal of African History* 27 (1986): 64, 73.

Lugard did not invent Indirect Rule, however, but explicated principles long implicit in the practice of imperial administration. To wit, when British authority over much of the Indian subcontinent was secured by the East India Company, by the beginning of the nineteenth century, the company determined to preserve the semblance of political continuity by maintaining the offices and pageantry of the Mughal emperor and the semi-independent kingdoms known as the "princely states."[28] By the middle of the nineteenth century, the constitutional theory of imperial rule was becoming fully articulated. In the Gold Coast (now Ghana), for example, chiefs were recognized as the proper representatives of the peoples under British protection, and were employed as intermediaries.[29] In India, the 1857 rebellion occasioned the imposition of formal British rule (and the deposition of the figurehead emperor) and a shift in administrative opinion away from the view that Indians could ever be expected to behave according to the tenets of classical British political economy to the position that a stable order could be guaranteed only by the preservation of traditional modes of social integration (although peculiarities of local political ecology gave the official approach various forms). Indian administrators from this period looked for inspiration (if not literal imitation) to the "Punjab system," developed in an area quiescent during the rebellion by Sir John Lawrence, chief commissioner of the Punjab from 1856 to 1859 and viceroy of India from 1864 to 1869, in collaboration with his brother, Sir Henry Lawrence. Their system was heavily authoritarian, but it was marked by its insistence on respect for indigenous custom.[30] By the end of the nineteenth century, as a contemporary observer remarked, the British in Africa were prompted by the spirit of enlightened self-interest to adopt "the general policy of ruling on African principles through native rulers."[31]

By the twentieth century, colonial officials had developed a highly schematized constitutional model of Indirect Rule. The political officer was supposed to deal with a properly constituted Native Authority, which, in the ideal scheme of things, willingly followed his advice, although it might be compelled to obey his orders. The Native Authority consisted of a head of state, acting alone or in consultation with lesser dignitaries, performing both executive and legislative functions; a Native Treasury, responsible for collecting taxes, which (less a percentage paid to the colonial government)

---

[28] See, for example, Cohn, "Representing Authority in Victorian India" (chap. 3, n. 42), 170–1.
[29] David Kimble, *A Political History of Ghana* (Oxford, 1963), 172.
[30] Eric Stokes, *The English Utilitarians and India* (Oxford, 1959), 268–7.
[31] Sir George Goldie, quoted in Kingsley, *West African Studies*, 401–2.

financed Native Authority operations and projects; and Native Courts, dispensing justice according to indigenous principles. Unfortunately, not all traditional polities could be readily transformed into properly constituted Native Authorities, and the ideal-typical model of Indirect Rule was rarely realized. Because the goal of Indirect Rule represented as much a general orientation as a blueprint for action, political officers construed their charge creatively – an issue to which we shall return.

Members of the Indian Civil Service were never obliged to take formal instruction in anthropology. They were expected to become fairly knowledgeable about Indian custom, however.[32] The first official pleas for the anthropological training of colonial officers were made by members of the ICS, the earliest probably being that made in 1876 by D. C. J. Ibbetson, a Punjab officer of considerable influence who was concerned to preserve (or, if necessary, restore) traditional communal land ownership in order to secure for the British the political loyalty of the masses.[33] And ICS men were conspicuous among the colonial officials who became prominent members of the anthropological community before World War I. For example, H. H. (Sir Herbert) Risley (1851–1911), appointed India's first census commissioner in 1901, was elected president of the Royal Anthropological Institute in 1910. He used his presidential address to describe the ineffectiveness of the colonial officer ignorant of traditional custom, who might foment revolt through misunderstanding.[34] Another ICS man, Sir Richard Carnac Temple (1850–1931), toured Britain after his retirement as chief commissioner of the Andaman and Nicobar Islands in 1904, delivering pleas for the establishment of a university curriculum in anthropology designed to train colonial officers; one of these speeches was his 1913 Presidential Address to Section H of the British Association.[35]

Temple's inherited and achieved position in colonial circles made him an ideal advocate for practical anthropology. He was the son of Sir Richard Temple, first baronet, who had worked with John Lawrence in the Punjab. And he was the half brother of C. L. Temple (1871–1929) who, as

---

[32] Too avid an interest in ethnography might negatively affect the career of an ICS officer, however. See, for example, H. A. Rose, "Obituary: William Crooke 1848–1923," *Folk-Lore* 34 (1923): 382–5.

[33] On Ibbetson's anthropological views see Charles Morrison, "Three Styles of Imperial Ethnography: British Officials as Anthropologists in India," *Knowledge and Society* 5 (1984): 145. On his administrative work, see P. H. M. van den Dungen, *The Punjab Tradition* (London, 1972), 125, 130, 147–8, 169, 217–19, 243.

[34] Sir Herbert Risley, "The Methods of Ethnography," Presidential Address, *Journal of the Royal Anthropological Institute* 41 (1911): 10–11.

[35] These speeches are collected in Sir Richard C. Temple, *Anthropology as a Practical Science* (London, 1914).

Lugard's chief secretary and lieutenant-governor, was charged with realizing the ideal of Indirect Rule in Northern Nigeria. Nigeria was the jewel in the crown of the African empire, by far the most populous and potentially prosperous of Britain's African territories, and the Northern Nigerian system became the model emulated by British administrators elsewhere in Africa. Richard C. Temple was a notorious egotist, whose claims to influence may be suspect. Nevertheless, during the course of his campaign, the first courses including instruction in anthropology were developed to train political officers bound for the Sudan. And in the 1913–14 academic year, Radcliffe-Brown, who had done his field research in Temple's former official preserve, was appointed to give a course of lectures in social anthropology at the university in Birmingham, the site of the British Association meeting at which Temple gave his Presidential Address to Section H.[36]

When men such as Risley and Temple urged that administrators be given anthropological training, however, they were not arguing that the professional anthropologist was necessarily better equipped to understand traditional societies than was the colonial administrator of long years' service. C. G. Seligman tried to persuade Temple that anthropological inquiries could be conducted far more efficiently by a trained professional than by a well-meaning amateur, arguing that "a stranger capable of thinking along anthropological lines can generally discover more in a few weeks than the most sympathetic administrator has been able to find out, perhaps in the course of years."[37] Temple and his kind allowed that professionals might be useful in training colonial officials, but judged academics' knowledge inferior to that of men who had long experience of life in the colonies. Moreover, they suspected that an academic anthropologist commissioned to do research for them would be unprepared to recognize the sort of information they required.

Men such as Risley and Temple regarded with evident disdain the work of renowned armchair scholars. Risley observed that if such figures as Herbert Spencer or John Lubbock had had some personal knowledge of "even a single tribe of savage men," they would have been forced to realize

---

[36] Morrison notes that the "blandly egotistical tone of his autobiography was deplored even by his [Temple's] relatives"; see his "Three Styles of Imperial Ethnography," 162–3. For Temple's descriptions of his victories see his *Anthropology as a Practical Science*, 3, 42. Radcliffe-Brown's selection of his fieldwork site may well have been prompted by Temple, who urged Haddon to send one of his students there; see Temple to Haddon, 16 March, 1906, quoted in David Tomas, "Tools of the Trade: On the Production of Ethnographic Observation on the Andaman Islands 1858–1922," *Colonial Situations*, ed. George W. Stocking, Jr. (Madison, Wis., 1991).

[37] Quoted in Temple, *Anthropology as a Practical Science*, 44.

"the extreme difficulty of entering into savage modes of thought, of the imperfection and untrustworthiness of testimony, and of the extraordinary fluidity and mutability of custom itself"; field experience would give them "profound distrust of the statements made in books of travel" and give them that indescribable "sense of the place" without which understanding of another culture was impossible.[38] Reviewing Radcliffe-Brown's *The Andaman Islanders*, Temple wrote approvingly of Radcliffe-Brown's use of fieldwork method, which made his knowledge of subject peoples more like that of the colonial official than that of the armchair anthropologist. But Temple took Radcliffe-Brown to task for his presumption that because he had been academically trained, his research was superior to that of the colonial official than that of the armchair anthropologist. the Andamanese (and whose work was in fact a valuable resource for Radcliffe-Brown).[39]

Because men such as Risley and Temple were representative colonial types, it is important to understand how they viewed anthropology. Both of them were "practical men." As amateur anthropologists, they were old-fashioned field naturalists, disdaining theory as an aid to accurate judgment. To such men, the pursuit of all varieties of natural history was a physical exercise, and it was, as such, an activity that developed character rather than mind. To Temple, anthropology represented "cultured sympathy," and in the government of subject peoples, he wrote, "intellect is all very well, but sympathy counts for very much more."[40] No different from other conventional colonial rulers, he exhibited the attitudes inculcated by the public schools, which encouraged contempt for "the 'bounder', the 'prig', and the 'bookworm'" – types who were in theory (if not in practice) excluded from the colonial services.[41]

Thus, for men such as Temple the colonial officer who attended to anthropological phenomena was behaving in a fashion appropriate to his official obligations. From the early nineteenth century, the ideal colonial administrator was portrayed as a man of action, akin to the field naturalist. He was conventionally described as the "father and mother" of his people.[42] His rapport with his subjects was developed during the course

---

[38] H. H. Risley, "The Study of Ethnology in India," *Journal of the Anthropological Institute* 20 (1890–1): 238.

[39] Temple wrote a number of reviews of *The Andaman Islanders*. Perhaps the most critical was "A New Book on the Andamans," *Nature* 110 (1922): 106–8.

[40] Temple, *Anthropology as a Practical Science*, 40.

[41] The quote is from F. D. Lugard, *The Dual Mandate in British Tropical Africa* (Hamden, Conn., 1965 [orig. London, 1922]), 139. For a representative analysis of the public school ideology, see Rupert Wilkinson, *The Prefects* (London, 1964).

[42] For some discussion of the colonial administrative ideal that informed British rule

of constant touring, and was termed "tact" in colonial parlance. When Temple spoke of the "sympathy" necessary to good colonial administration, he was giving another name to "tact." Of necessity, academic anthropologists had to describe themselves as scholars, thus appearing to men such as Temple to be suspect "bookworms" – hardly the sorts of men colonial officers expected to understand the practical realities of administrative life.

The opinions of men such as Temple about academic anthropologists seemed amply justified by the employment history of Northcote W. Thomas, the only person who might be described as a professional anthropologist who was formally attached to the staff of any British colonial regime (not just commissioned to do a specific project) until the very end of the interwar period. A Cambridge graduate, trained in classics and history, Thomas was a competent, even original, armchair scholar prior to his appointment as a government anthropologist in 1908. The Colonial Office engaged him after consultation with recognized leaders of anthropology – E. B. Tylor, C. H. Read, and J. G. Frazer. Moreover, after his appointment, Thomas himself used the offices of the RAI to find himself an advisory committee of distinguished scholars – Read, Henry Balfour, William Ridgeway, A. C. Haddon, and C. G. Seligman (of whom only the last two were familiar with field research).

Thomas was employed in response to a petition from the acting commissioner of Northern Nigeria: a professional was needed to make sense of the unwieldy data accumulated by the chief magistrate of the Gambia, who had circulated an ethnographic questionnaire to political officers all over British West Africa in 1906. The colonial secretary, Lord Crewe, objected that "a single person, however high his scientific attainments, could not possibly accumulate materials as extensive or as valuable as could be gathered by a whole body of district officers," but the Colonial Office was then prepared to give greater credence to distinguished scholars' opinion than to his.[43] Thomas was put on official notice, however, that "purely scientific research ... must not interfere with his main work," as Alex

everywhere, see Hugh Tinker, "Structure of the British Imperial Tradition," in Ralph Braibanti, ed., *Asian Systems Emergent from the British Imperial Tradition* (Durham, N.C., 1966), 37–9; I. F. Nicholson, *The Administration of Nigeria, 1900–1960* (Oxford, 1969), 233.

[43] The distribution of the questionnaire by A. W. Russell, Chief Magistrate of the Gambia, and the petition by the Acting Commissioner of Northern Nigeria, Sir William Wallace, are documented in the Colonial Office Memorandum of 6 November, 1908, in CO 520.76, PRO. At least some of the responses to the original questionnaire are in the files of the RAI, Manuscript Collections 189, 202.

Fiddian, a permanent member of the Colonial Office staff, noted in his file.[44]

Arriving in the then-separate colony of Southern Nigeria to take up his first colonial post, Thomas immediately began behaving in a fashion that seemed calculated to cause offense. He had utterly unsatisfactory dealings with local officials, whom he believed himself entitled to order about because he had been appointed by the Colonial Office.[45] He discarded the questionnaire results he had been hired to synthesize. But his research style was not in itself unusual. He replicated the original project in his own fashion. For the most part, his conclusions rested on evidence provided him by political officers, to whom he distributed his own questionnaire and the then-current edition of *Notes and Queries on Anthropology*. This was the style of research that a man such as Risley practiced in his capacity as the census commissioner for India.[46]

The government of Southern Nigeria declared itself pleased with the results of one of Thomas's projects, his investigation of the causes of theft, since his analysis justified repressive policies. The imposition of a criminal code in Nigeria similar to that of Britain was not suitable for the local inhabitants, said Thomas; in traditional society, harsh punishments were imposed for crimes, and Africans would not be deterred from criminal behavior unless they feared severe reprisals.[47] Thomas's investigation of the consequences of liquor consumption by Africans failed to show deleterious effects, however, and his employers did not welcome his findings.[48] And he spent much of his time conducting the very sort of impractical research he was instructed not to do – in particular, analyzing linguistic data.[49] When Lugard became the first governor of united Nigeria in 1912, he decreed that "the trained man from outside should go."[50]

Thomas had alienated his employers as much by his personal style as by his findings. He was clearly eccentric. A man who proposed to "ingratiate

---

[44] N. W. Thomas to the Colonial Office, 30 June, 1909, in CO 520.90, PRO. Alex Fiddian, the member of the Colonial Office staff with the greatest interest in anthropology, wrote of Thomas's mandate in his minute of 21 July, 1910, in CO 520.100, PRO.

[45] See the letter from Acting Governor F. S. James of Northern Nigeria to the Colonial Secretary Lewis Harcourt, 19 June, 1912, in CO 520.115.6486, PRO.

[46] Morrison, "Three Styles of Imperial Ethnography," 154.

[47] See Thomas's memorandum and officials' comments, written in 1912, in CO 520.121 and CO 520.113, PRO.

[48] N. W. Thomas to the Colonial Office, 30 June, 1909, in CO 520.90, PRO.

[49] N. W. Thomas to the Colonial Office, 8 January, 1912; Alex Fiddian, Minutes of 1 April, 1912, both in CO 520.121, PRO.

[50] Described in Alex Fiddian, Minutes of 1 Januray, 1931, in CO 583.176.X1005 (30), PRO.

[him]self with [his] subjects" by donning false teeth filed in African fashion was not likely to be regarded by colonial officials as a person who would raise the "prestige" of the British among the Africans.[51] As one of the civil servants in the Colonial Office, J. W. Flood, wrote:

> Mr. Northcote Thomas was a recognized maniac in many ways. He wore sandals, even in this country, lived on vegetables, and was generally a rum person. I can quite understand that the people of Nigeria did not want to have an object like that going about and poking into the private affairs of the native communities.[52]

Thomas was not dismissed from colonial service, however. He was sent to Sierra Leone, where the government wished an investigation conducted of the "Human Leopard Society," a supposedly cannibalistic secret order. This investigation was typical of the inquiries political officers routinely pursued, inquiries about indigenous customs to determine whether they were so harmful to the local inhabitants that the government was obliged to suppress them. Reasoning somewhat inconsistently, the government believed that the practices of the Human Leopard Society had become more savage in the colonial period both because Africans, disoriented by the stresses of social change, had regressed to a more primitive stage of social development and because Africans calculated that European rule had freed them from their obligations to uphold customary law.

Thomas's report on the society hinted that his employers' suspicions were correct. But Thomas refused to divulge the identities of the murderers he had interviewed, arguing that the anthropologist's code of professional ethics required him to maintain the confidentiality of the relationship he had with his informants.[53] Furthermore, in Sierra Leone as in Nigeria, Thomas violated the conditions of his employment, using time that ought to have been spent on official business to pursue his linguistic research. After one tour of duty in Sierra Leone, he was sent home, his dismissal charitably euphemized as part of the general wartime retrenchment.[54]

The history of Thomas's colonial employment served as a cautionary tale in official circles for decades after his removal from the service of Sierra Leone. His case proved to colonial officials that the practical man could not employ the professional anthropologist for routine administrative purposes. They decided that professionals might be useful in training political

---

[51] N. W. Thomas to Alex Fiddian, 24 October, 1908, in CO 520.76, PRO.
[52] J. E. W. Flood, Minutes of 19 December, 1930, in CO 583.176.X1005 (30), PRO.
[53] See Colonial Office, Minutes of 14 November, 1915, in CO 267.563, PRO.
[54] See Alex Fiddian, Minutes of 4 November, 1915, in CO 267.569, PRO.

Northcote Thomas diverted by the esoteric, impractical aspects of anthropological research: one of a series of children's drawings, annotated by Thomas, which he collected in Nigeria. Reproduced by permission of the Syndics of Cambridge University Library (Haddon Papers).

officers, however. And, after 1924, men selected to serve as administrators in tropical Africa were obliged to take a year-long course at Oxford or Cambridge that included instruction by the universities' anthropologists – a burden never imposed on probationers of the services of the British Empire outside Africa. But the course was not rigorous. The postwar Gold Coast government, at least, took anthropology more seriously; it required its probationary officers to write original anthropological essays and to take examinations in "native custom" – although they did not have to pass them.[55]

[55] These practices began in the Eastern Province of the Colony Region in 1922 and subsequently became general in the Gold Coast. See C. E. Skene, Acting

After World War I, the governments of the Gold Coast and Nigeria began the practice of employing official government anthropologists. The first of these was R. S. Rattray, appointed by the Gold Coast in 1920. Later, Margaret Field served in this capacity in the Gold Coast. And, during the interwar period, Nigeria appointed as government anthropologists C. K. Meek, H. F. Matthews, and R. C. Abraham. All of these save Field had been colonial administrators. Field developed an interest in anthropology after coming to the Gold Coast to teach secondary school chemistry, taking a Ph.D. at UCL. In addition, a number of political officers were relieved of their regular duties for brief periods to do anthropological research, among them the Gold Coast's A. W. Cardinall and Nigeria's P. A. Talbot, Ward Price, H. W. Hunt, and M. D. W. Jeffreys – who also earned a Ph.D. from UCL. What anthropological training these figures received was, for the most part, acquired during short leaves from government service.[56] Colonial government anthropologists did research that differed little from that done by ordinary officers of the political service in regard to theoretical approach, content, and practical application.

Moreover, colonial governments disdained the services of professional anthropologists, even when they were offered these services at no cost to themselves. To wit, between 1925 and 1927, the Colonial Office and the governors of the East African territories considered a proposal to create a research agency in East Africa to be dedicated to scientific investigation of every aspect of African welfare, producing knowledge useful to the colonial governments. The Rockefeller Foundation, apparently convinced that the social problems of multiracial areas in East Africa offered instructive parallels to the uneasy relations between races in the United States, expressed willingness to finance this agency, which would have been headed by an anthropologist in at least one of its putative incarnations. The governor of Kenya, Sir Edward Grigg, was enthusiastic about this proposal, but his fellow governors were not. Sir Donald Cameron, governor of Tanganyika (now part of Tanzania) and future governor of Nigeria, one of

Commissioner of the Central Province of the Colony, "Unofficial Diary," 22 January, 1932, in NAG; A. F. E. Fieldgate, Deputy Provincial Commissioner, Eastern Province of the Colony, "Unofficial Diary," 20 February, 1932, in NAG.

[56] The government anthropologist within our purview who won the greatest respect in British anthropological circles was R. S. Rattray. For his biography, see Appendix 2. C. K. Meek, like several other government anthropologists, was awarded an Oxford D.Sc. in recognition of his achievements, and was a lecturer in anthropology at Oxford for a brief period after World War II. Significantly, when Field tried to behave as a professional anthropologist in Britain, and applied to the CSSRC for funds, she was denied support because she "did not have adequate anthropological qualifications," although she had a Ph.D. from UCL. See G. I. Jones's comment on her application for a grant, Minutes of the Committee on Anthropology and Sociology for the meeting of 4 October, 1955, CRC.

the most influential colonial figures of the interwar period, stated the view that prevailed: "scientific study" was unnecessary to the creation of a "sound system of native government"; the advice professionals gave colonial governments in East Africa might be offered gratis, but it would be worthless. Because Grigg alone had to deal with a substantial population of European settlers, who saw every measure designed to protect the Africans and Indians in Kenya as a violation of their rights, and who had between 1922 and 1925 threatened to enlist the aid of South Africa in outright resistance, he alone welcomed the prospective research institute, anticipating that its reports would be helpful to him in his battles with the settlers.[57]

Political officers characteristically voiced sentiments like Cameron's. Debating Malinowski on the pages of the journal *Africa* in 1930, for example, P. E. (later Sir Philip) Mitchell, then a provincial commissioner in Tanganyika and later governor of Uganda, declared the work of the professional anthropologist useless to the practical man. The professional insisted on conducting research according to his own scientific standards, a process that took considerable time. The political officer was obliged to act long before the professional's investigations were complete. Moreover, the professional's study was replete with esoteric details, which obscured the information the administrator needed – if, indeed, the information the administrator required could even be found in the anthropologist's report.[58]

When professional anthropologists went to the colonies to do their own research, they were regarded with considerable suspicion by colonial officials. From the field, Malinowski's students wrote to him about the lack of sympathy in administrative quarters for the anthropological viewpoint, which obliged them to take stands against those official policies they judged harmful to the peoples they were studying. To make matters worse, the anthropologists feared that their research subjects assumed them to be government spies.[59] In order for anthropologists to do fieldwork, they had

---

[57] See especially Donald Cameron to L. C. M. S. Amery, Secretary of State for the Colonies, 4 December, 1926; and Edward Grigg's testimony to the Colonial Office's "Committee of Civil Research," on 25 March, 1927; as well as other papers in the file on the Committee of Civil Research, in RAI, Ms. 168. See also J. H. Oldham to L. C. M. S. Amery, 24 November, 1925; Despatch from Sir Edward Grigg to the Colonial Office, 11 June, 1926; Sir F. D. Lugard, Confidential Memorandum, "Notes on the Kenya Question," 15 May, 1927; all in Oldham Papers, Boxes 2, 2, and 1, respectively, OUODP. And see John Cell, "Lord Hailey and the Making of the African Survey," *African Affairs* 88 (1989): 483.

[58] P. E. Mitchell, "The Anthropologist and the Practical Man," *Africa* 3 (1930): 217–23.

[59] See, for example, Audrey Richards to Malinowski, 10 May, 1933; Margaret Read to Malinowski, 6 July, 1935; Sir Hubert Young, Governor of Northern Rhodesia, to Audrey Richards, 23 July, 1935, all in MP,YU.

to secure permission both from the Colonial Office and from the regime of the territory in which they wished to work, and these negotiations were conducted in an atmosphere of mutual distrust; officials at every level of the colonial hierarchy feared that anthropologists doing research would act as unsettling influences on indigenous communities.[60]

Given the strong objections by the practical men of the political service to scientific anthropologists, it is not surprising that anthropologists first moved into powerful circles on the basis of their appeal to the technocrats of the colonial services. Significantly, the unprecedented government anthropology department in the Gold Coast was inaugurated during the regime of Sir Gordon Guggisberg, governor from 1919 to 1927. Guggisberg's colonial career was most unusual: he entered colonial service as a surveyor, a technician, rather than as a member of the political service, from whose ranks colonial governors were usually drawn. Scientific anthropology gained advocates within the Colonial Office when it seemed applicable to a task of one of the colonies' technical services – the provision of education to colonial subjects.

Educational concerns were addressed by a committee appointed by the Colonial Secretary in 1923 – the Advisory Committee on Education in the Colonies (originally the Advisory Committee on Native Education for the British Tropical African Dependencies). Among the members of this committee were Lord Lugard, J. H. Oldham (1874–1960), secretary of the Church Missionary Society from 1921 to 1938, and Hanns (later Sir Hanns) Vischer (1876–1945), the committee's paid secretary, who had been Lugard's minister of education in Northern Nigeria. The committee had to include missionary representatives, since, as one of its memoranda noted,

---

[60] These were matters of some concern to the Rockefeller Foundation, whose fellowships were supporting anthropological fieldwork. See an interoffice memorandum by Tracy Kittredge describing a conversation he had with J. H. Oldham, Director of the International African Institute, 17 October, 1932, in RF; and see T. O. Ranger, "From Humanism to the Science of Man: Colonialism in Africa and the Understanding of Alien Societies," *Royal Historical Society Transactions* [5th ser.] 26 (1976): 418.

During the period I am describing, the Rockefeller Foundation was reorganized, so that support for anthropology fell under various rubrics. I have not attended to changing foundation structure in the account that follows, however, not the least because its grantees dealt with a number of foundation officers whose charge was not restricted to the social sciences. Those interested in foundation structure might wish to consult Martin Bulmer and Joan Bulmer, "Philanthropy and Social Science in the 1920s: Beardsley Ruml and the Laura Spelman Rockefeller Memorial, 1922–1929," *Minerva* 19 1981): 347–407. My description of the relationship between Rockefeller patronage and anthropological development is in substantial agreement with George W. Stocking, Jr., "Philanthropoids and Vanishing Cultures," in Stocking, ed., *Objects and Others* (Madison, Wis., 1985), 112–45.

missionaries educated more than 90 percent of the students in British colonial territories.[61] Therefore, official efforts to reform the education of subject peoples could not succeed unless missionary bodies cooperated with the Colonial Education Service.[62]

Colonial rulers' demands for educational reform were straight forward: Africans must be taught to be good Africans, willing to play their proper roles in society, not permitted to become imperfect copies of Europeans. This goal implied, as Lugard had argued in 1912, that Africans should not be taught dangerous ideas, which might inspire them to demand self-government before they were capable of exercising it. Perhaps, for example, they should not learn English history, since if they were to do so, they would learn of Cromwell's revolutionary methods and of "the events that led to Parliamentary (and Party) government," and might imagine that their own societies were ready for the constitutional changes that had been effected in Britain.[63] In Nigeria, as elsewhere, the missionaries had been responsible for giving Africans ideas above their station. "In their anxiety to establish the belief in the equality of all followers of the same creed," missionaries had encouraged the convert "to discard his manners and change his mode of living for one followed by his pastor." Furthermore, Lugard observed, misguided mission efforts encouraged nationalism; "when the Governor of Lagos was stoned in the streets of the town, the rabble was encouraged to do so by well educated Natives, English trained and clothed."[64]

The committee, with Oldham as its most active member, was determined to develop educational programs suited to the "mentality, aptitudes, occupations and traditions" of subject peoples. They wished education to be "an agent of natural growth and evolution. Its aim should be to render the individual more efficient in his or her condition of life... and to promote the advancement of the community as a whole." Africans should not be educated to become poor imitations of Europeans, provided with skills suitable only for clerks working in the towns. Instead, African men should be trained to be skillful and contented farmers, and African women

[61] "Educational Policy in Africa," 13 April, 1923, in IMC/CBMS, Box 219.
[62] See S. M. Grier, Director of Education, Southern Provinces of Nigeria, to J. H. Oldham, March 1926, in IMC/CBMS, Box 274.
[63] F. D. Lugard to the Secretary, Church Mission Society, 2 August, 1912, in IMC/CBMS, Box 273.
[64] "Notes on Education," Southern Nigeria Report, May 1909, in IMC/CBMS, Box 273. For another illustration of the conventional argument that the African must be made a good African, not a poor imitation of a European, see Donald Cameron's memorandum on "Native Administration in Tanganyika," 16 July, 1925, quoted in John Iliffe, *A Modern History of Tanganyika* (Cambridge, 1979), 321.

to be sensible housewives and mothers. The vernacular, not English, was the proper medium for practical education. This scheme was objectionable to African nationalists, who observed that it was intended to dampen colonial subjects' aspiration. And colonial governors argued that the scheme was impracticable because there were so many vernaculars: extraordinary resources would be required to provide textbooks in every one of them, and to train teachers competent in every one of them. Nevertheless, the committee's plan was partially implemented.[65] And with the encouragement of the committee, a training program was established for entrants to the Colonial Education Service, which was also open to missionaries; its faculty included Cyril Burt, who held forth on primitive psychology.[66]

Seeking imitable models for the education of Africans, the committee investigated educational policies of other colonial regimes and the schools established for black Americans. These investigations led them to discussions with representatives of philanthropies in the United States: the Phelps–Stokes Fund, the Carnegie Corporation, and the Rockefeller Foundation. These philanthropies had invested in educational institutions for black Americans, in which students were both taught practical skills and trained to assume leadership roles in their own communities.[67] In 1924, the committee decided to appeal to these foundations for assistance in establishing an international research body. In this instance, the negotiations between colonial reformers and philanthropic patrons were to prove successful, unlike those over the mooted East African research agency, in which Oldham also played a prominent role.[68]

Oldham and Vischer wrote a "Memorandum on the Place of the Vernacular in African Education and on the Establishment of a Bureau

---

[65] The quotation is from the Advisory Committee White Paper of 13 March, 1925. See also J. H. Oldham to Sir Herbert Read of the Colonial Office, 30 May, 1924; Hanns Vischer to W. Ormsby-Gore, Secretary of State for the Colonies, 24 March, 1924; J. H. Oldham to Hanns Vischer, 24 April, 1924; J. H. Oldham to Hanns Vischer, 1 May, 1924; J. H. Oldham to Hanns Vischer, 6 October, 1924; Hanns Vischer to J. H. Oldham, 25 March, 1926; all in IMC/CBMS, all Box 219.

[66] Letter from J. H. Oldham to a large number of officials of missionary societies, 21 March, 1927, IMC/CBMS, Box 220.

[67] Vischer was particularly interested in inspecting the Hampton Institute. See J. H. Oldham to Dr. Thomas Jesse Jones of the Phelps-Stokes Fund, 15 November, 1923, in IMC/CBMS, Box 219. For one discussion of the intentions of U.S. philanthropists which makes it clear that their notions on black education and the general organization of black communities were very similar to those held by members of the Advisory Committee, see Paul Jefferson, "Working Notes on the Prehistory of Black Sociology: The Tuskegee Negro Conference," *Knowledge and Society* 6 (1986): 133–8.

[68] Oldham apparently at one point considered becoming head of the mooted research group himself. See Cell, "Lord Hailey," 484.

of African Languages," arguing that language study was vital because language was "the gateway to the soul of a people and the expression of what is distinctive in their national character and traditions."[69] In 1925, a formal proposal for the creation of the International Bureau of African Languages and Cultures was drafted by Edwin W. Smith (1876–1957), who had been a missionary in southeastern Africa and became a prominent figure in anthropological circles. The institute's proponents considered that anthropological expertise was essential to their enterprise, and they enlisted anthropologists in their campaign. In particular, they came to depend on Malinowski, who apparently did not point out to them that his methodological emphasis on the mastery of indigenous languages did not imply their view. (Malinowski insisted that anthropologists learn to speak the language of their subjects, neither relying on interpreters nor resorting to such means of communication as Pidgin English; but although he was wont to declare that language offered a clue to "native mentality," he and his followers were not concerned with sociolinguistic analysis as such.)[70]

The institute organizers' enthusiasm for anthropology, and for Malinowski's version of it in particular, was in no small part a consequence of Oldham's recent change of heart on the subject. In mid-1925, he had been of the opinion that anthropologists were useless to his causes, being "more interested in theoretic aspects of the subject than its practical application." Chastised for this view by Sir Walter Fletcher, who ran the Medical Research Council, Oldham demanded that Fletcher lead him to useful anthropologists. In fact, Fletcher was able to say only that the most suitable men were unavailable: Rivers, "our most fertile anthropologist," had suffered an untimely death; Haddon was too old to undertake new projects; and Elliot Smith and Myers were "both chiefly interested in other things." But Oldham had been inspired to undertake the search for anthropologists himself, and arranged to meet with people at the London School of Economics, the site of work Rockefeller Foundation officials assured him was good. There he found Malinowski, whom he was to describe as "the most creative and original mind in the field and in his own way a great man."[71]

[69] "Memorandum on the Use of Vernacular in Education and the Establishment of a Bureau of African Languages," 1924, in IMC/CBMS, Box 221.
[70] See, for example, Hilary Henson, *British Social Anthropologists and Language: A History of Separate Development* (Oxford, 1974), esp. 47, 91–105; Malinowski, "Memorandum on Colonial Research," December 1927.
[71] J. H. Oldham to Walter Fletcher, 8 September, 1925; Fletcher to Oldham, 22 September, 1925; Oldham to C. M. Lloyd of the *New Statesman*, 18 September, 1925; Lloyd to Oldham, 21 September, 1925; Oldman's memorandum on his conversation with Dr. Abraham Flexner of the Rockefeller Foundation, 25 October, 1925; Oldham

For his part, Malinowski happily recognized the value of official supporters; the advertised utility of his work in the Trobriands had, after all, secured him funds from Australia's Department of External Affairs.[72] It did not matter that he had never done research in Africa. He not only established cordial relations with Oldham but also managed to impress Lugard, whose ideas he persuaded himself were very much like his own.[73] In alliance with colonial policymakers he elicited patronage for the International African Institute, which became a mechanism for the dispersal of funds to functionalist anthropologists – who were thereby assured dominance of their discipline. But functionalists' views were to have little impact on the conduct of administration in the colonies, for changes of opinion at the center of colonial power did not result in a thoroughly restructured colonial order.

Monopolizing patronage: functionalism triumphant

In 1926, the International Institute for African Languages and Cultures – now simply the International African Institute – was founded, with Lugard as the first head of its executive council (serving until 1945, shortly before his death) and Vischer as its organizing secretary. Oldham was to serve as its administrative director from 1931 to 1938, resigning from its executive council in 1945. Its organizational structure made the IAI an international body, but it was dominated by British figures and interests. Its constitution forbade the IAI to undertake political action. Formal disavowal of political motive was essential to secure the support of patrons such as the Rockefeller Foundation, concerned to avoid becoming "entangled in any matter that might involve controversy," which would impede "the whole future usefulness of the Rockefeller Boards."[74] In practice, avoidance of controversy meant alliance with colonial regimes. The IAI charter required that sponsored projects secure official approval, and recommended that research workers undertake projects colonial governments themselves proposed.[75] The institute was formally dedicated to fostering productive

to Sir Malcolm Hailey, 30 May, 1935. All are in the Oldham Papers, OUODP, and all but the letter to Hailey are in Box 2; it is in Box 1.

[72] See Mulvaney and Calaby, 'So Much That Is New' (chap. 1, n. 27), 322.

[73] For evidence of this relationship, see Lugard's letters to Malinowski, 14 November, 1928 and 11 January, 1933, in MP,YU.

[74] J. H. Oldham, notes on his conversation with Dr. Wycliffe Rose of the Rockefeller Foundation, 27 October, 1925, in Oldham Papers, Box, 1, OUODP.

[75] International African Institute, "A Five-Year Plan of Research," *Africa* 5 (1932): 10–13. Malinowski's presence is conspicuous in this document.

interchanges among all those engaged in the African field: anthropologists, colonial officials, missionaries, merchants, and Africans themselves. Its journal, *Africa*, became a forum for all of its constituents.

The founders of the IAI courted diverse patrons, reasoning that the institute should be beholden to no one in particular if it were to be an independent, impartial agency. There were twenty-odd initial supporters of the IAI, and they were a diverse lot: various British colonial governments; the French, Italian, and German governments; a range of financial and trading companies with African interests; and the Carnegie Corporation and the Rockefeller Foundation. Together, the Rockefeller and Carnegie philanthropies contributed almost half the initial institute budget – and Rockefeller money was to constitute an increasingly large percentage – so philanthropists came to play an extremely powerful role in institute affairs.[76] This is not to suggest that the Rockefeller Foundation intended to act at cross-purposes with colonial regimes, for it wanted the IAI to become "more and more closely connected in various unofficial ways with the various colonial services."[77]

Once Malinowski joined the IAI inner circle, he used his Rockefeller Foundation connections to both strengthen the institute as an organization and turn its offices to his own purposes. It was he who persuaded the Rockefeller Foundation to make its initial five-year grant of £5,000 to the institute. Malinowski assured the foundation that its funds would be put to constructive use, supporting the application of anthropology as "social engineering" in areas "into which western capitalism is pressing." If knowledgeable experts intervened in areas in which Europeans and primitive peoples were in contact, he said, they could "prevent untold waste and suffering."[78] The relationship Malinowski enjoyed with the foundation ensured its continued support of the IAI. And he was able to use the IAI as a vehicle for acquiring even greater foundation support. Because Rockefeller monies were available to finance the field research of Malinowski's students, almost all of them became Africanists.

When the Rockefeller Foundation began to distribute funds to British anthropology, it dispensed them to every faction. It gave Elliot Smith's department at UCL a series of grants for a variety of projects. The largest of these was the 1920 grant for the Department of Anatomy building.

---

[76] Detailed records of every step of the organizing process of the IAI are in Boxes 204 and 205 of the joint archive of the International Missionary Council and the Conference of British Missionary Societies.

[77] E. E. Day to S. M. Gunn, 21 August, 1930, in RF.

[78] Interview between Malinowski and John Van Sickle of the Rockefeller Foundation in 1926, reported in the "Memorandum re the International Institute of African Languages and Cultures," in RF.

Housing anatomists, histologists, physiologists, biochemists, pharmacologists, psychologists, and anthropologists, the building gave physical form to Elliot Smith's broadly synthetic vision of academic research. Until he and his colleagues joined to "correlate the biological and cultural aspects of anthropological inquiry" in the "serious study of human evolution," Elliot Smith told the foundation, anthropology had lacked "the strict discipline of science," and was plagued by "the two evils of scholasticism and stereotyped formalism."[79] Evidently, the foundation initially found his project attractive, and at least as late as 1925 foundation representatives were commending Elliot Smith as a "first-rate man" in their discussions about anthropology.[80]

In 1927, the year after the IAI was organized, the Rockefeller Foundation "torpedoed" Elliot Smith's plans, to use his verb. The foundation observed that it appreciated Elliot Smith's considerable skills as an anatomist, but that it would not give him additional funds for anthropological research.[81] It had come to believe that the only truly scientific anthropology was the fieldwork-based functionalism of Malinowski's school. In vain, Elliot Smith protested that the functionalists held no monopoly over fieldwork. Indeed, he said, no scientific skills were required "to sit on a Melanesian Island for a couple of years and listen to the gossip of villagers."[82] His students usually came to UCL after they had already spent some time living among primitive peoples, whom they had easily understood without benefit of specialized training.[83] Certainly, the foundation was not unique among anthropology's supporters and practitioners in equating scientific anthropology with field research. It is significant that in order to ensure his election to the readership in cultural anthropology at UCL in 1924, Perry had to promise to do fieldwork (a promise he kept, although he spent only a brief period studying the Pondo of South Africa because of ill health).[84] Nonetheless, the foundation view reinforced prevailing anthropological opinion in the 1920s.

The Rockefeller Foundation was generous also in its support of the RAI from 1924 until 1930. The foundation evidently hoped that anthropology's diverse factions would be able to resolve their considerable differences

[79] G. Elliot Smith to E. Embree of the Rockefeller Foundation, 1 December, 1926, and 10 February, 1927; both in RF.
[80] J. H. Oldham, notes on conversation with Dr. Abraham Flexner of the Rockefeller Foundation, 4 February, 1925; in Oldham Papers, Box 1, OUODP.
[81] G. Elliot Smith to R. M. Pearce of the Rockefeller Foundation, 30 October, 1929, in RF.
[82] G. Elliot Smith to E. Embree, 18 December, 1926, in RF.
[83] G. Elliot Smith to Herrick of the Rockefeller Foundation, 13 February, 1927, in RF.
[84] C. G. Seligman to B. Malinowski, n.d., in MP,LSE.

under the auspices of the RAI. Because the institute persisted in tolerating every disciplinary sect, the foundation determined in 1929 that the purposes it "had in mind in making its grant ... seem not to have been fulfilled." The RAI had not settled the disputes that "still seriously impede the progress of work among the British anthropologists," and so its Rockefeller support was sharply cut."[85] Malinowski had urged the foundation to make this decision, as C. G. Seligman, the RAI's negotiator with the foundation, suspected – although Malinowski assured his teacher and colleague that he had not.[86]

Not without significance for the Rockefeller Foundation was Malinowski's affiliation with the London School of Economics (LSE), to which the foundation was heavily committed. Institutional loyalty per se figured in such foundation decisions as its determination not to support the anthropology program at University College.[87] Embodying the "fundamentally conservative character of English radicalism," the LSE commended itself to the foundation because it was one of the few academic institutions in which "the academic and the actual come together," as, regrettably, they did not in any American institution.[88] Malinowski's research seemed to exemplify the foundation ideal. As Rockefeller employee Edmund Day wrote: "He represesents a type of thinking and research which is of unusual value in the promotion of our general social science program."[89]

The triumph of functionalism in British anthropology, then, was in no small part a consequence of the support its practitioners received from the Rockefeller Foundation's donations to the LSE and the IAI. Malinowski's famous seminars at the LSE were run according to the IAI ideal, attended not only by anthropologists but also by visiting missionaries, colonial officials, merchants, and Africans.[90] The fellowships distributed through the IAI were allocated to those whose work promised to prove useful to colonial governments, and nearly all of the recipients of these fellowships attended

[85] See the letter from James G. Shotwell of the Carnegie Endowment for International Peace to Beardsley Ruml of the foundation, 6 May, 1924; John Van Sickle's Diary, meeting with C. G. Seligman, 6 October, 1930; the quotation is from an interoffice memorandum by E. E. Day, 27 February, 1929; all in RF. See also B. Malinowski to J. H. Oldham, 11 June, 1929, in Oldham Papers, Box 1, OUODP.

[86] Malinowski to E. Day, 3 August, 1929, in RF; B. Malinowski to C. G. Seligman, 26 November, 1936, in MP,YU; B. Malinowski to J. H. Oldham, 11 June, 1929, in Oldham Papers, Box 1, OUODP.

[87] J. Van Sickle interoffice memorandum, 22 January, 1930, in RF.

[88] Memorandum written for Beardsley Ruml, 12 November, 1923, in RF.

[89] E. Day to J. Van Sickle, 6 November, 1929, in RF.

[90] See, for example, B. Malinowski to Leonard Barnes, 3 May, 1934, in MP,YU. It is of some parenthetical interest that the participants in Malinowski's seminar included Jomo Kenyatta, future nationalist leader of Kenya.

Malinowski's seminars.[91] The IAI journal, *Africa*, published work by Malinowski and his students, and IAI funds subsidized their monographs. The Rockefeller Foundation was not the only source of support for field research for pre–World War II anthropologists, but it was the most important one, and the foundation changed its policy on those of its fellowships that it allocated directly so that Malinowski's students could take advantage of them.[92]

A list of the recipients of Rockefeller grants administered by the IAI is a roll of distinguished anthropologists, including Meyer Fortes, Hilda Beemer Kuper, Lucy Mair, S. F. Nadel, Kalervo Oberg, Margaret Read, Audrey Richards, Isaac Schapera, Gunter Wagner, and Monica Hunter Wilson. Whatever the protests that they might have made after World War II, recipients of Rockefeller largesse were quite willing before the war to assure representatives of the foundation that they were eager to implement "the more practical results which were the object of their work."[93] In the reports that they sent from the field to the IAI describing the progress of their sponsored research, they almost invariably wrote of the help they had received from local colonial officials and missionaries, and often specified the social problems their work addressed.[94] They understood, as Malinowski wrote to the foundation when he asked for an extension of its initial five-year grant to the IAI, that the foundation was not interested in "the production of useless and merely ornamental research workers, however valuable their research might be academically."[95]

Because the IAI brought anthropologists into contact with colonial officials, it changed the audience for anthropologists' work. Its organization both reflected and affected changing opinion at the highest level of colonial rule – among the stable population of civil servants in the Colonial Office who exercised considerable influence on the short-tenured colonial secretaries, as well as among some of the most prominent policy makers. It is

[91] See the "International African Institute, 'Five Year Plan'"; Rockefeller Foundation interoffice memorandum, July 1940, in RF.
[92] B. Malinowski to J. Van Sickle, 9 December, 1929; and E. E. Day to J. Van Sickle, 10 December, 1929, in RF.
[93] See T. B. Kittredge's report on his interview with IAI fellows M. Fortes, S. F. Nadel, and S. Hofstra at the LSE, 7 June, 1935, in RF.
[94] See the progress reports by IAI fellowship recipients, all in the Perham Papers, Box 10, OUODP: I. Schapera, 8 August, 1932; T. J. A. Yates, 12 June, 1933; N. de Cleene, 22 March, 1933; K. Oberg, December 1934; G. Wagner, September–December 1934; H. Beemer, 30 January, 1935; M. Hunter Wilson, March–June 1935; G. Wagner, April–June 1935; H. Beemer, July 1935; K. Oberg, August 1935; E. K. Matthews, December 1935–February 1936; G. Wagner, January–May 1937; H. Kuper, May 1937; M. Fortes, May 1936–May 1937.
[95] B. Malinowski to J. Van Sickle, 21 March, 1934, in RF.

frequently argued that colonial administrators turned to anthropologists only in desperation, when their policies failed because they did not understand indigenous societies.[96] The Aba Riots, which occurred in Nigeria in December of 1929, are often cited in particular; these were protests against the colonial government's dismantling of the Native Court system and its imposition of so-called warrant chiefs with no traditional credentials.[97] Yet before the riots Lugard had been enrolled in the cause of scientific research; Malinowski had been consulted about the training of future political officers, and colonial governments had been instructed that they must adopt a functionalist approach in the anthropological inquiries they sponsored, since only functionalism lent itself to practical application.[98] In fact, the greatest impetus to changed official opinion was probably the threat of civil war in Kenya, which in 1923 elicited the British Government declaration that in Kenya African interests must be treated as paramount, followed in 1924 by a government report proclaiming that economic development in East Africa must be centered on indigenous peoples; a similar report on West Africa in 1926 indicated that this was Britian's policy for all of its tropical African territories.

The Aba Riots did serve to consolidate opinion among the permanent staff of the Colonial Office, however. Before the riots, Alex Fiddian had often been the only civil servant prepared to sponsor administrative anthropology. After the riots, many of his colleagues altered their views about anthropology. They attributed their conversion to changes in the discipline itself; functionalist anthropology seemed to them uniquely appropriate for administrative use. As G. J. F. (Sir George) Tomlinson observed, anthropological research must be directed to problems "which are of immediate and practical importance to the Administrative Officer. What I mean is that they [colonial anthropologists] should be followers of the school of which such men as Professor Malinowski are the chief exponents." As Fiddian said, "It is no use arguing; anthropology is a science and must be treated as such."[99] The staff of the Colonial Office were now prepared to accept the

---

[96] See, for example, George Foster, *Applied Anthropology* (Boston, 1969), 187.

[97] Whatever the impact of the riots on general colonial policy, they were followed in Nigeria by appointments of political officers to undertake anthropological inquiries – after officials there consulted academics. See Alex Fiddian, "Anthropological Investigations in Nigeria," 16 December 1930, CO 583.176/1003.6652, PRO.

[98] B. Malinowski, "The Teaching of Anthropology to the Political Officers of the Gold Coast Service," Memorandum for the Colonial Office, 17 October, 1929; Colonial Office file on "Anthropological Research Work, Proposals for Carrying Out," minutes and correspondence between May and October, 1929, all in CO 96.688.6441.1929, PRO.

[99] G. J. F. Tomlinson, minutes of 7 January, 1931; Alex Fiddian, minutes of 1 January, 1931. Some members of the Colonial Office staff were not converted: J. E. W. Flood,

argument anthropologists had been making since the nineteenth century: it was because anthropology was scientific that it was useful. It seems unlikely, however, that any event in the colonies would have occasioned their conversion, absent the support given anthropology by the powerful figures in the IAI.

Before turning to consideration of the actual influence of anthropology on African colonial administration, we must consider the impact on anthropology of another American foundation, the Carnegie Corporation. Carnegie provided substantial funds to the IAI during its early years: £1,000 toward publications and £1,000 for a study of East African tribal conditions. More important, it subsidized Lord Hailey's influential *An African Survey*, a massive project first published in 1938 that had its ultimate antecedents in the unsuccessful efforts to create an East African research agency. Like the Rockefeller Foundation, the Carnegie Corporation saw its role as assisting the British colonial regimes to govern more efficiently.[100] Hailey, a former member of the Indian Civil Service, was as influential in his day as Lugard had been in his. Indeed, Hailey fittingly succeeded Lugard as the chairman of the IAI's Executive Council, and he consistently argued that anthropology could be useful to colonial administrators, provided that it was functionalist anthropology.[101]

Following Hailey's recommendations in *An African Survey*, the Colonial Development and Welfare Act of 1940 allocated funds for research useful in the prosecution of a newly agressive development policy throughout the colonial Empire.[102] Hailey believed that without the aid of anthropologists it was impossible to implement the development schemes mandated by the act. "Anthropologists are difficult folk to deal with," he wrote in 1940 to Malcolm MacDonald, then colonial secretary, but they had to be suffered

for example, persisted in his belief that academic anthropologists would inevitably do research too arcane and too thorough to be put to practical use by the political officer who required information to deal with pressing problems; see his minutes of 19 December, 1930. All of these are in CO 583.176.X1005 (1930), PRO.

[100] See, for example, Whitney Shepardson of the Carnegie Corporation to Lord Hailey, 23 January, 1947, Hailey Papers, OUODP. It is of some interest that when the Carnegie Corporation was looking for a man to supervise a comprehensive survey of race relations in the United States – the project that became Gunnar Myrdal's *An American Dilemma*, which was, like *An African Survey*, the product of several invisible researchers – it considered employing Hailey before it determined to engage Myrdal. See Ellen Condliffe Lagemann, "A Philanthropic Foundation at Work: Gunnar Myrdal's *American Dilemma* and the Carnegie Corporation," *Minerva* 25 (1987): 457.

[101] For example, Lord Hailey, "The Role of Anthropology in Colonial Development," *Man* 44 (1944): 10–15.

[102] See Sir Andrew Cohen to Lord Hailey, 31 December, 1963, in Hailey Papers, OUODP. Cell suggests that Hailey was as much a follower as a leader; see his "Lord Hailey," 505.

for the sake of their knowledge.[103] Hailey became the first chairman of the Colonial Research Council; its subsidiary, the Colonial Social Science Research Council, was organized according to his recommendations.[104] Thus, anthropologists were provided the mechanism and the means to make their discipline increasingly esoteric by a man who wished to put them to work in government service.

Practical anthropology

In 1932, Rockefeller funds supported a project intended to provide a model for applied anthropology. P. E. Mitchell, then secretary for Native Affairs of Tanganyika, arranged a collaboration between G. Gordon Brown, a Malinowski student, and A. McD. B. (later Sir Bruce) Hutt, then commissioner of Iringa District. Mitchell had not repented of the position he had taken in his public debate with Malinowski: he believed that anthropologists left to their own devices would collect detailed, arcane information of no administrative value, so Brown was confined to investigation of specific questions about the Hehe of Iringa, posed to him by the district commissioner.[105] He himself agreed that this was appropriate, that he should avoid doing work that was "scientifically admirable but useless as far as application goes."[106] Because he was not permitted to do a thorough investigation of Hehe social structure, Brown produced a study that might be termed "near-functionalist."

To be sure, Brown's research was conducted in the functionalist manner. It was resolutely ahistorical, declaring that historical inquiries were useful only insofar as they illuminated contemporary practices. But its ahistorical approach was justified in accordance with the conventional wisdom of the Tanganyikan political service: Hehe history was irretrievable, since the German rulers of pre–World War I Tanganyika had deliberately dismantled Hehe political structure. Brown qualified this generalization with the observation that at no point in Hehe history had their society had a stable tradition, for their way of life was always changing, both before the colonial era and after. Answering the district commissioner's questions, the anthropologist considered the unsettling social

---

[103] Lord Hailey to Malcolm MacDonald, May 1940, in Hailey Papers, OUODP.

[104] See the Colonial Office minutes of 18 October, 1943 and 21 October, 1943, in Hailey Papers, OUODP.

[105] P. E. Mitchell, "Introduction," to G. G. Brown and A. McD. B. Hutt, *Anthropology in Action* (London, 1935), iv–xii.

[106] G. G. Brown, "African Research," memorandum for the IAI, n.d., in Perham Papers, Box 8, OUODP.

changes brought by colonialism. He devoted considerable attention to Hehe notions of property, political order, and justice – matters of special interest to the colonial officer attempting to implement the precepts of Indirect Rule. Finally, Brown investigated the features of Hehe culture that the administrator thought were bizarre and possibly dangerous to the Hehe themselves. His analysis of the social impact of Hehe witchcraft beliefs was reassuringly familiar: they played a valuable role in curtailing antisocial behavior and therefore should not be deliberately suppressed.[107]

Because Brown was an anthropologist with credentials that made him a respectable member of the academic community, it might appear that the government of Tanganyika had made a decisive break with administrative tradition in agreeing to work with him. But the government's insistence that he accept the dictates of the district officer preserved the relationship that almost always obtained between colonial regimes and the anthropologists they employed. It was a rare official indeed who welcomed the advice a professional anthropologist could offer with the expectation that "a fresh mind without Government bias was needed" to judge the effectiveness of government policy – as did Sir Douglas Newbold in 1937, when, as governor of Kordofan Province in the Sudan, he arranged S. F. Nadel's investigations of the Nuba (like Brown's inquiries, financed through the IAI).[108] Insofar as Brown's research was not typical colonial anthropology, its peculiarities reflected those of Tanganyikan administration itself. And like virtually every anthropologist colonial governments were prepared to consult, he worked in a rural setting, for during the interwar years this was where governments believed anthropology belonged, not in the areas "into which western capitalism is pressing" – where Malinowski and his fellow organizers of the IAI believed anthropology would be most useful.

Given the colonial services' ingrained habits, however, it is not surprising that political officers resisted experts' recommendations, no matter which colonial policymakers endorsed these recommendations. The field staff of the British Empire, describing themselves as "practical men," frequently declared that colonial policies were in every instance improvised to suit the exigencies of the moment. "The Englishman is an opportunist," they said, "and, unlike the Frenchman, he does not trouble to work out a consistent and logical policy with a clear end in view. Rather, he deals with difficulties as they arise."[109] There was a grain of truth in their claims, for it was often

---

[107] Brown and Hutt, *Anthropology in Action*, 16, 20, 51, 5, 183, 190, and passim.

[108] Major-General Sir Hubert Huddleston, Governor-General of the Sudan, "Forward" to *The Nuba*, by S. F. Nadel (London, 1947), xi.

[109] This specimen statement was made by Major Orde Brown, a sometime prominent official in the Tanganyikan administration, in 1935, and is quoted in C. S. L.

the case that administrative policy did not conform to the directives from the Colonial Office. Colonial policy was remarkably consistent, however, because the tasks of the field staff of the Empire everywhere predisposed them to make similar choices. Among these was a course of action rationalized by evolutionist anthropology – which persisted pace the Colonial Office.

Officials assumed that African societies could be located on the unilinear scale of development toward high civilization, and policies formulated that would encourage their progress to higher stages. It was axiomatic that African societies had regressed to some degree in response to the shock of contact with colonial culture, so administrative action was required to restore them to the status quo ante – as well as to encourage them to advance beyond it. Of particular importance to colonial anthropologists was the evolutionist model of political development: progress was linked to the formation of increasingly larger and increasingly centralized polities, which, by virtue of their organizational structure, were able to enforce universalistic standards of justice and morality. Evolutionist theory cast the development of political organization in a form colonial administrators could translate into prescriptive terms: in the natural course of evolution, clans fused into tribes and tribes into nations. In all of Britain's African territories, colonial officials argued that they were accelerating the natural course of evolution when they undertook to fuse small populations into powerful tribes, and that only if they did so would the peoples in their charge eventually develop a national identity and be capable of self-government.

Colonial officers believed that true Indirect Rule was appropriate only for those peoples who had reached a relatively high stage of evolution. Officials employed the comparative method to determine the state of development that various peoples had attained. From evolutionist indices to developmental stages – religious beliefs, rites of passage, political institutions, and so on – administrators were able to classify whole cultures in the evolutionist taxonomy even when their knowledge of these cultures was very limited, since they assumed that cultures judged in the same stage were virtually identical. Only if societies were considered to be in an advanced stage of evolution would they be ruled in truly indirect fashion; for other societies, colonial anthropologists outlined development plans.[110]

Chachage, "British Rule and African Civilization in Tanganyika," *Journal of Historical Sociology* 1 (1988): 202.
[110] For some analysis and examples, see A. Magid, "British Rule and Indigenous Organization in Nigeria," *Journal of African History* 9 (1968): 299–313; M. G. Smith, "Kagoro Political Development," *Human Organization* 19 (1960): 14–24; Max Gluckman, *Administrative Reorganization of the Barotse Native Authorities with a Plan for*

From the writing of colonial anthropologists such as Talbot, Meek, and Cardinall, we can judge that they also looked to diffusionist work for guidance. What they learned from it, however, did not alter their unilinear developmental scheme – which the diffusionists' historical approach was intended to discredit. They betrayed their diffusionist reading by a propensity to compare African societies with those of ancient Egypt rather than with other classical societies supposedly at the same level of development. Occasionally, they accounted for the character of the societies the British thought especially admirable, such as the Hausa–Fulani kingdoms of Northern Nigeria, as the product of contact with Egypt. Their research on processes of diffusion of culture among peoples was most important because it permitted them to further the colonial strategy legitimated in evolutionist terms: the consolidation of peoples into larger political entities. If they could find similar cultural traits among peoples within a given area, they could argue that the traits had been diffused when these peoples had been in regular contact, and could therefore justify consolidating them. (Conducting such research, they provided material for academic anthropologists in Britain who were concerned to document the diffusion of culture.)[111] But no more than diffusionists, armchair evolutionists would not have approved colonialists' aggressive direction of social change, simply because it was deliberate, and therefore as likely to lead to degeneration as progress.

Government anthropologists accepted a stylized evolutionist theory because it served government needs. First, evolutionism justified the restructuring of traditional societies in a fashion that suited administrators at all levels. Central government directives would be implemented efficiently if colonial subjects were organized into large tribes ruled by chiefs who were advised by district officers, since the consolidation of traditional hierarchies under the authority of a small number of chiefs enabled British rule to be effected by a small number of civil servants. Colonial supervision considerably reduced chiefs' real power. Subject peoples were expected to obey their chiefs, however, thinking their power genuine because their customary trappings of sacred authority had been

Reforming Them (Bulawayo, 1943), 14; P. H. Gulliver, "The Karamajong Cluster," *Africa* 22 (1952): 1; A. W. Cardinall, *The Gold Coast* (Accra, 1931), 9; letter from the Chief Commissioner of Ashanti to Governor Alan Burns, enclosed in Burns's Despatch of 9 December, 1944, in CO 96/780.31458/6, PRO; R.S. Rattray, *Ashanti Law and Constitution* (Oxford, 1929), viii–ix; C. K. Meek, *Law and Authority in a Nigerian Tribe* (London, 1937), 327.

[111] For one illustration of academic analysis of diffusion relying on material supplied by colonial researchers, see A. C. Haddon, "Migrations of Cultures in British New Guinea," *Journal of the Royal Anthropological Institute* 50 (1920): 237–80.

The elaborate hierarchy of colonial authority reproduced in a commemorative photograph: a record of a meeting held in March 1930 in Jos, Nigeria. From the photograph album of Colin Walker. Reproduced with permission of the Bodleian Library, Oxford.

punctiliously preserved. If the chiefs continued to inspire awe and obedience, district officers' interests were served, since colonial rulers relied on local leaders to secure the cooperation of subject peoples. Colonial officers would lose face – not to mention promotion prospects – if they could not effect the instructions that were issued by their superiors. In sum, district officers gained prestige if their chiefs were recognized as powerful figures, able to inspire their subjects to work to become more prosperous and more civilized.[112]

Furthermore, political officers had to maintain order not only in ordinary circumstances but also during times of potential crisis – those occasions when the occupants of chiefly office changed. If there were any doubts about the rightful successors to traditional offices, squabbles over succession could divide populations of subject peoples, making them difficult

---

[112] For one discussion of the precarious authority of the district commissioner, explaining the rationality of conventional administrative tactics from his standpoint, see Max Gluckman, "Inter-hierarchical Roles: Professional and Party Ethic in Tribal Areas in South and Central Africa," in Marc J. Swartz, ed., *Local Level Politics* (Chicago, 1968), 68–93.

to govern. According to evolutionist maxim, progress was associated with the development of hereditary kingship. Therefore, administrators reasoned that when they routinized succession to chiefly offices, they were accelerating evolutionary progress. They were also limiting possible occasions of disorder among their subjects.

The policies government anthropologists sanctioned in the interwar period did not escape the critical attention of functionalist anthropologists. Functionalists argued that the establishment of hereditary rules for chiefly succession eliminated opportunities for the expression of popular desires in the selection of chiefs.[113] Government employees, such as the Nigerian Anthropological Officer R. C. Abraham, were able to appreciate that official policy was expedient: he observed in 1933 that a political officer could rule far more efficiently if he could deal with a few powerful indigenous leaders rather than with many weak ones. Nevertheless, Abraham did not recognize that political officers were abrogating indigenous constitutions, but argued that they were only accelerating inexorable evolutionary trends.[114]

Perhaps under different historical circumstances the altered anthropological views adopted by the Colonial Office staff in the late 1920s might have diffused to – or been imposed upon – colonial administrators. Among political officers in the 1930s there was growing sentiment both for making indigenous leaders more responsive to their subjects' desires and for abrogating what was identified as tradition when better government would result. But the Colonial Administrative Service literally could not afford to abandon evolutionist views during the 1930s, even though they had fallen out of fashion among anthropologists in Britain. Depression retrenchments severely cut the size of colonial regimes' administrative staffs at the lowest level – that of the civil servants who dealt directly with Africans in the districts. Working in depression conditions, political officers were bound to endorse policies that made their negotiations with their subjects more efficient.

With the coming of more prosperous times, the burdens of the rural officer were not lightened, however. The structure of the colonial bureaucracy remained conducive to an administrative strategy rationalized in evolutionist terms. The members of the colonial service had been seriously demoralized by the retrenchments of the depression years, fearful that their opportunities for promotion had been structurally limited. When the colonial service was allowed to grow, it did not do so at the lowest level.

---

[113] See, for example, Lucy Mair, "Chieftainship in Modern Africa," *Africa* 6 (1936): 305–16.

[114] R. C. Abraham, *The Tiv People* (Lagos, 1933), 160–4.

Colonial bureaucracies expanded at the middle-management level, offering junior officers greater prospects for advancement. Service morale improved considerably. But district officers were still obliged to win the approval of their superiors in the manner their predecessors had followed.

Above all, colonial officers were concerned to maintain order. From evolutionist theory they could extrapolate guidelines for the creation of polities that behaved in reassuringly predictable fashion. Functionalist anthropology only presented them starkly contrasting alternatives: societies calmly dealing with changed circumstances, and those in a state of virtual collapse. Referring to the Kenyan African, Malinowski prescribed "re-establish[ing] as far as possible the old tribal system" to prevent the white settler from succeeding in "preparing for his descendents a future similar to that prepared by the Southern slave magnate"; whereas Radcliffe-Brown described Australian cultures as "overwhelmed by the white man's destructive force." But these were extreme cases, and functionalists assumed that in the ordinary course of events traditional cultures would not disintegrate despite challenges to their accustomed ways.[115] By contrast, evolutionist schemes specified indicators of social disintegration. They identified whole culture complexes, remarking upon those beliefs and practices that were incongruous with the cultural patterns characteristic of each stage of development: vestiges of earlier stages of societal maturity or elements imported from higher cultures.

Colonial officials were able to use evolutionist argument to resist whatever innovations they saw as threatening to their authority; primitive peoples would suffer cultural degeneration unless their progress was negotiated very gradually. And officials reasoned that those societies that responded most favorably to Western influences were (paradoxically) the most primitive and the most contemptible because they were the most unstable. These ideas were manifested in two perennial litanies of British colonial rulers: First, Africans had to be made into good community citizens, proud of their traditions and of their tribes, before they could move to a higher stage of development.[116] Second, modernizing innova-

[115] B. Malinowski, "Memorandum on Colonial Research"; A. R. Radcliffe-Brown, "On the Concept of Function in Social Science," reprinted in *Structure and Function in Primitive Society* (New York, 1952 [essay orig. 1935]), 183.

[116] For examples, see Governor of the Gold Coast, letter to the Secretary of the Basel Mission at Akropong, 1898, cited by David Brokensha, *Social Change at Larteh, Ghana* (London, 1966), 16; Neil Wier, a Nigerian District officer, "Nigeria Personal Diary, 1925–36," unpublished manuscript, 41–2, in OUODP; C. G. R. Amory, Assistant District Commissioner, Gonja, the Gold Coast, "Unofficial Diary," 1 May, 1936, in NAG; T. G. Brierly, Nigerian Political Officer, Personal letter, 10 May, 1953, in OUODP. The "Unofficial Diary" quoted in this and other references is a peculiar sort

tions, sure to raise African aspirations and prove administratively unsettling, had to be resisted because they would reduce group cohesion;
immediate gains would prevent ultimate advance.[117] It was generally
understood – by the "man on the spot" as well as by the colonial policymakers active in the foundation of the IAI – that these were the objectives
served by anthropological analyses.

During the interwar period, political officers conducted anthropological
investigations that differed little from those produced by persons formally
employed as government anthropologists. These investigations were part of
routine administrative practice, and they were often termed "intelligence
reports" when they were submitted for official consideration. Political
officers equated political consolidation and the development of hereditary
kingship with evolutionary advance (and political fragmentation with
degeneration); cited classic evolutionist texts such as Frazer's *Golden Bough*;
compared African practices to those of pagan Europe and the ancient
societies of Greece and Rome; talked of "survivals" of practices no longer
appropriate to peoples brought to a higher level of development; cautioned
that superstitions must be tolerated because they were functional in primitive societies, but spoke of the desirability of encouraging higher levels of
rationality among subject peoples when they were ready to accept them.
The collection of random customs, after the fashion encouraged by the
dissemination of *Notes and Queries on Anthropology*, remained an accept-
able pursuit, justified as the recording of disappearing practices. Finally,
anthropological inquiries were undertaken whenever popular social movements appeared to threaten the maintenance of British authority.[118]

of document; political officers were required to write daily records of their activities
to be read by their superiors, but the diary entries were quasi-confidential, not to
be quoted in official papers.

[117] For examples, see W. J. A. Jones, Provincial Commissioner, Central Providence of the
Colony, Gold Coast, "Unofficial Diary," 3 February, 1928, in NAG; an extended
essay by a sometime Nigerian administrative officer, W. R. Crocker, *Nigeria: A Critique
of British Colonial Administration* (London, 1936), 132; Guthrie Hall, District
Commissioner, Gonja, Gold Coast, "Unofficial Diary," 1 April, 1938, in NAG; Derek
Bayley, political officer in the Gambia, Personal Diary, 8 July, 1943, in OUODP; T.
R. Batten, "The Community and the External Agent," *Corona* 4, No. 9 (September
1952), 328.

[118] See, for examples: C. K. Meek, Assistant District Officer, "An Assessment Report on
the Igbedde District," memorandum prepared for the District Officer, Kabba, Nigeria,
Decmber 17, 1917, in MP 84P/1918, PCJ 1453/1918, DCJ, 964/1917 (Okeni), IAI;
N. A. C. Weir, Assistant District Officer, "Intelligence Report on Ado District, Ekiti
Division, Ondo Province [Nigeria]," 20 November, 1933, in WP 10664, IAI; H. A.
Blair, Assistant District Commissioner, Gold Coast, "An Essay upon the Dagomba
Peoples," an essay written by a probationary officer to satisfy requirements preliminary

The professional anthropologists who did research in Africa before the end of World War II were not, in fact, averse to conducting investigations that might have been put to the standard purposes of colonial administrators – if administrators had been prepared to act on them. For example, Meyer Fortes in the Gold Coast and S. F. Nadel in the Sudan (as a government anthropologist) were prepared to find linkages among peoples that might have justified administrative consolidations. But they insisted that the untrained observer could not recognize evidence of relationships among the peoples who might be joined to form the larger political units administrators desired. Indeed, the visible similarities in peoples' cultures that colonial officers might take as indicators of some underlying bond between them – language, religious practices, family structure, and the like – were only superficial traits. What mattered were peoples' subjective perceptions of their identities and the common ideologies underlying divergent social forms that only the professional could discern. [119] The logical implication of their argument – that political officers abandon all delusions that they understood African cultures and cede authority to anthropologists – was clearly unacceptable.

Or, to give another sort of example, when anthropologists undertook to specify the structure of traditional political authority that should be recognized as the vehicle for Indirect Rule, their results could be rejected because they did not fit administrators' preconceptions. So Max Gluckman, a student of Evans-Pritchard and Radcliffe-Brown at Oxford (and sometime participant in Malinowski's seminars), saw his 1943 study of the political structure of the Barotse ignored by the government of Northern Rhodesia (now Zambia) on the grounds that the structure he identified was too complex. Furthermore, it involved an excessive number of hereditary

to confirmation of his civil service status, lent to me by the author; Resident, Benue Province, "Intelligence Report, Ocheku District of Idoma Division [Nigeria], circa 1935, in MP 23,546, PCJ 633, PCJ, IAI; reports by A. B. Matthews and E. A. Leslie on Yangedde District, Idoma Division, Benue Province, Nigeria, May 1937, in MP 20,900, PCJ 564A, DCJ, IAI; H. L. M. Butcher, "Some Aspects of the Obu System of Isa Sub-tribes of the Edo Peoples of Southern Nigeria," *Africa* 8 (1935): 149–62; G. M. Culwick, "New Ways for Old in the Treatment of Adolescent Girls," *Africa* 12 (1939): 425–32; Frank Melland, "Ethical and Political Aspects of African Witchcraft," *Africa* 6 (1935): 495–503; E. Ralph Langley, "The Kono People of Sierra Leone," *Africa* 5 (1932): 61–7; H. H. Palmer, Lieutenant-Governor of Northern Nigeria, Memorandum of 16 February, 1927 on Mah'dism, in CO 583/147.X105A, PRO; D. F. Heath, District Officer, Idoma, Nigeria, "Report on Oturkpo District – August 1938," in MP, 25078, PCJ 550B, DCJ 376, IAI

[119] Fortes, Progress Report to the IAI, May 1936–May 1937; S. F. Nadel, report on "Jebel Tullishi," both in the Perham Papers, Boxes 10 and 554, respectively, OUODP.

office holders, all of whom would have been entitled to salaries if the government had recognized them.[120] Significantly, in this instance as well as the last ones, anthropologists were deviating from the code of behavior prescribed by the IAI no less than were the colonial officials with whom they came in contact. The anthropologist's role as described by Malinowski and internalized by G. Gordon Brown was not to dictate policy but to act as a mediator among all interested parties; when African tradition did not suit administrators' expectations (or convenience), the anthropologist was supposed to facilitate compromise.[121]

By virtue of the form in which anthropologists' advice was offered, when political officers chose to act on professionals' findings they were likely to do so with the clear understanding that they were distorting indigenous constitutions. Hence, F. D. Corfield, a district commissioner in the Sudan who was very helpful to Evans-Pritchard when the latter was doing field-work among the Nuer, concluded that Evans-Pritchard's analysis was correct: notwithstanding other political officers' protests to the contrary, the Nuer had never had a centralized tribal organization that might be reconstructed for administrators to use. If the British wished to encourage development of a political structure appropriate to the conduct of Indirect Rule, they would have to foster greater authority for occupants of a traditional secular office that was relatively minor in the Nuer scheme of things.[122] Similarly, Fortes's determination that the Gold Coast Tallensi had no traditional secular offices whatsoever evidently led to the deliberate transformation of their religious leaders into Native Authorities.[123] In sum, when colonial officers were presented with a clear choice between respecting Africans' modes of self-regulation and deliberately constructing new rural bureaucracies, they chose the latter. But they preferred not to confront evidence that their actions violated tradition, since to do so was to accept that the official doctrine of Indirect Rule was impracticable – and thus to undermine the very justification for the British presence in Africa.

---

[120] Richard Brown, "Passages in the Life of a White Anthropologist: Max Gluckman in Northern Rhodesia," *Journal of African History* 20 (1979): 536.

[121] G. G. Brown, "African Research."

[122] F. D. Corfield, "Notes on the Origins of Native Authority Among the Nuer, with Particular Reference to the Jokany Dor," 22 November, 1935, in Perham Papers, Box 544, OUODP; E. E. Evans-Pritchard, *The Nuer* (Oxford, 1940), viii. Corfield was not the only political officer in the Sudan who attended to Evans-Pritchard's findings and determined to create a political order that somehow blended British and Nuer notions; see Johnson, "Judicial Regulation and Administration Control," esp. 59, 70–2.

[123] Fortes, Progress Report, May 1936–May 1937; Lord Hailey, *An African Survey Revised* (Oxford, 1956), 33.

Praise Be To God The One God

FROM the Representative of HIS MAJESTY THE ENGLISH KING, may God prolong his days, HIS EXCELLENCY SIR DONALD CHARLES CAMERON Knight Commander of the Most Distinguished Order of Saint Michael and Saint George, Knight Commander of the Most Excellent Order of the British Empire, Governor of Nigeria to salutations and peace.

WHEREAS you have in truth sworn to obey the authority of the Representative of HIS MAJESTY THE ENGLISH KING, THE GOVERNOR, now I the GOVERNOR do think proper to establish you firmly in your authority on the conditions which were clearly and explicitly explained to you and the principal conditions are as follows:-

1. AUTHORITY AND DUTIES

Your position and authority is that of the Wakil of the Governor just as the GOVERNOR is the Wakil of HIS MAJESTY THE KING. You have seen how for many years that it is the desire of the Governor to uphold the power and prestige of the Native Rulers over their people and to take measures to ensure that power and prestige be used with wisdom and justice. He wishes to rule through and together with you on condition that you obey the authority of the KING and the orders of his Representative the Governor. When the Governor is not present with you, his orders will be transmitted through the Lieutenant-Governor to the Resident who will explain and enforce them. You must obey all the Laws of Nigeria and see that your people obey them. As the Ruler of your country it behoves you above all to show neither fear nor favour towards great or small and to conceal nothing from the Resident who is your Counsellor and helper. All matters concerning the Government of the land and its people are matters for consultation with the Resident. You may issue orders for the proper control of your people and the Courts will enforce them, but such orders must not be contrary to the Laws of Nigeria.

In any matters of importance or difficulty you can speak with the GOVERNOR himself who will always give full consideration to any matter which you may desire to lay before him and who desires at all times that you and those whom he has raised with you should acquaint him with all things that concern the welfare of yourself and your people.

2. APPOINTMENT OF OFFICIALS OF THE NATIVE ADMINISTRATION

The selection and appointment of District and Village Headmen and of all other officials of your Administration are matters in which you and your Councillors should consult the Resident and make your recommendations to him. In the appointment of higher officials he will seek the approval of the GOVERNOR. It is your duty to see that those set in authority under you, from the highest to the lowest, exercise their powers rightly and eschew corruption and oppression.

3. NATIVE COURTS

In the establishment of Native Courts and in the selection and appointment of the judges and their assistants it is your duty to consult the Resident who will submit your views with his recommendations to the GOVERNOR. It is your duty to see that the Native Courts administer justice impartially and in accordance with the proper procedure and that their orders are obeyed.

4. TAXES

It is only permitted to you to collect such taxes as are authorised by the GOVERNOR and in the assessment of taxes it is your duty to follow the orders of the GOVERNOR, as explained to you by the Resident. The tax which is authorised is laid down in the Laws of Nigeria, and the Governor will set aside such portion of it for your Native Treasury as he considers necessary. In the disposal of this revenue you will consult the Resident. It is for the payment of Native Officials and other purposes of good government.

5. LAND

The disposal of the land is in the hand of the GOVERNOR for the good of the people: it is not the intention of the Government to deprive any man of the land he cultivates or uses for grazing or for residence, except for good cause or unless it is required by the GOVERNOR for public purposes. In that case compensation will be given to the occupier, either in the form of other land or of money. You are not empowered to dispossess any man of his land except in accordance with the Laws or to alienate any land to strangers save with the advice and approval of the GOVERNOR. The GOVERNOR reserves to himself the right to alienate land to strangers for the better development of commerce and industry if occasion therefor should in his opinion arise. The rentals of land so assigned by the GOVERNOR to strangers belong to the Revenue of Nigeria.

6. MINERALS.

All rights in minerals belong to the Government but it is not the intention of the Government to interfere with persons who take iron for making utensils, et cetera.

7. WAR AND SEDITION

If any man should bring evil counsels of sedition or disloyalty, or attempt to create war or disturbance, it is your duty to inform the Resident and to take all the steps in your power to suppress his evil-doing.

8. PROTECTION

And by this letters in the name of King George V (may God prolong his days), I promise you and your people protection against all enemies, so long as you remain loyal to the KING and adhere to the conditions of this letter.

9. RELIGION.

In the matter of Religion every man is free to worship God in his own way, according to his own belief. There shall be no interference with any man's religion so long as it does not sanction cruelty or oppression or acts contrary to good government.

SIGNED by me and SEALED with the Seal of the Government of

Nigeria, in the year   of the Messiah

and the year   of the Hijra.

The bureaucratization of indigenous political order: the formal contract binding indigenous officeholders to their obligations in government service, distributed in Nigeria while it was governed by Sir Donald Cameron. A written contract was not the only means by which colonial regimes ratified the selection of local leaders; the government of the Sudan, for example, distributed "superior clothes," "inferior clothes," and "sashes." Reproduced with permission of the Bodleian Library, Oxford.

The Gold Coast and Tanganyika:
the rule and the exception

To illustrate the function of anthropology in routine administration, I examine in detail the case of the Gold Coast, where patterns established in the interwar period persisted thereafter. R. S. Rattray, the Gold Coast's first government anthropologist, appointed in 1920, established an official anthropological orientation that persisted long after his retirement in 1931. In his anthropological practices, Rattray was closer to the nineteenth century than the twentieth. He based a good deal of his analysis on responses to questionnaires he distributed among the Gold Coast political officers.[124] And like the respondents to armchair anthropologists' questionnaires, he claimed total indifference to theoretical disputes in the discipline, maintaining that he was too busy recording rapidly vanishing customs to bother with theories.[125] He also declared himself a follower of Tylor and Frazer, however, and assumed that the cultures of then-contemporary Gold Coast Africans could be analogized to those peoples of past and present who had been observed in parallel stages of development. His descriptions are full of analogies between African societies and those of Greece, Rome, and feudal Europe.[126] Because he regarded cultural development as a uniform, linear process, he ignored cultural differences among the peoples of the Gold Coast and encouraged policies leading to tribal homogenization (as contemporary historians have recognized).[127] He tested evolutionary hypotheses with his data. In his analysis of Asante law, for example, he found evidence that disconfirmed the model of social evolution from a stage of normative chaos through an era of law enforcement by vendetta.[128]

Like Malinowski, Rattray defended his variant of anthropology by claiming that it was singularly practical.[129] But his position was antithetical to the functionalist one. He argued that there was no point in investigating contemporary practices, since they represented the behavior of peoples who

---

[124] At least some of the responses to Rattray's questionnaires survive in the collections of the RAI, Ms. 101.

[125] R. S. Rattray, *Religion and Art in Ashanti* (Oxford, 1927), vii.

[126] R. S. Rattray, *Hausa Folk-Lore, Customs, Proverbs, Etc.* (Oxford, 1913), xvi.

[127] R. S. Rattray, *Ashanti Law and Constitution*, 6. And see Kimble, *Political History*, 487; T. C. McCaskie, "R. S. Rattray and the Construction of Asante History: An Appraisal," in David Henige ed., *History in Africa* (Los Angeles, 1983), 187–206. Towards the end of the interwar period, some political officers apparently realized that some peoples' customs had been distorted. See, for example, Notes on a Conference of Provincial Commissioners of the Colony, March 24, 1939, in CO 96.760.31352/39, PRO.

[128] Rattray, *Ashanti Law*, 285–6.

[129] Rattray, *Religion and Art*, vii.

had suffered degeneration as the result of culture contact. Instead, historical research was necessary; historical evidence would enable administrators to guide local cultures to restoration of the higher evolutionary conditions they had achieved prior to colonialism.[130] Rattray's work among the Asante peoples was premised on the assumption that it was possible to reconstruct the social order that had obtained prior to the exile of Prempeh as Asantehene in 1896. After 1896, lesser chief had usurped powers they had not enjoyed under the centralized rule of the Asantehene.[131] If the supposedly original tribal structure were reconstituted, the Asante would be once again capable of sustaining the evolutionary course they had been following in the nineteenth century. In theory, the Gold Coast government's "restoration" of the "Ashanti Confederacy" in 1935 served the cause of progress.

The permanent staff of the Colonial Office claimed that Rattray's talents were undervalued, and, indeed, it seemed that they were right, since in 1930 the Gold Coast decided not to replace him after his retirement from government service; "more satisfactory results in anthropological work will be obtained," said the governor, Sir Ransford Slater, "if it is carried on, after some preliminary training, by selected political officers, than if entrusted to a single anthropologist." [132] The historical record suggests, however, that Rattray's plan for the realization of Indirect Rule was implemented. For him, Indirect Rule did not mean indiscriminate preservation of locally reported tribal tradition. Rather, it entailed the encouragement of political centralization. Where tribal states existed, administrators were enjoined to preserve them. Where they did not, officers were instructed to create them. Where tribal centralization had once existed, it was to be reconstructed.[133] This last stipulation left much scope for the realization of historical fictions. But research along these lines clearly suited government needs. No later than 1921, Governor Guggisberg directed that tribes be consolidated throughout the colony.[134]

---

[130] R. S. Rattray, "Memorandum on Anthropology for the Visit of Mr. Ormsby-Gore, Secretary of State for the Colonies," October 1925, in CO 96.662.X7791, PRO.

[131] R.S. Rattray, *Religion and Art*, 86–7.

[132] Minute by A. Bevir, a civil servant in the Colonial Office, 21 January, 1927, in CO 96.662.X7791, PRO. Slater's remarks were addressed to a session of the Gold Coast Legislative Council, February 17, 1930, quoted in J. L. Myres, "Anthropology, Pure and Applied" (See chap. 1, n. 20), xxxviii.

[133] R. S. Rattray, "Memorandum on Anthropology for the Visit of Mr. Ormsby-Gore."

[134] Guggisberg mandated identical policy for peoples with quite different traditions. Not only the Asante but also coastal peoples such as the Ga were to be restored to their hypothetical earlier strength, and progressively extensive alliances were to be formed among such peoples as the Dagombas of the north, who were eventually to be joined in strong states. See his Despatches of 20 September, 1921, CO 96.626, and 10 May,

This policy was sustained. When M. J. Field served the Gold Coast government as its anthropologist from 1938 to 1944, she was specifically commissioned to do research that would lead to "the federation of small native states."[135]

After his retirement from the Gold Coast service, perhaps in consequence of his increased exposure to opinion in Britain, Rattray apparently became quite critical of colonial policy, arguing that autocratic rulers were being installed where formerly responsive democracies had existed. And, betraying some evidence of her diffusionist training, Field objected that the model of Indirect Rule she had been directed to implement was inapplicable to the Gold Coast, having been developed in Northern Nigeria – where autocratic regimes had paradoxically popular legitimacy because they had been forcibly imposed by a conquering people.[136] But such critiques had little effect, even when they might be produced by anthropologists who had been incorporated in the colonial government.

Contemporary historians of Ghana describe the conflicting oral histories repeatedly told by rival factions in traditional polities to justify their claims to power.[137] During the interwar period, colonial officials working at every level of political administration recognized that when they based their decisions on oral histories, they were using politically charged evidence.[138] Nevertheless, they insisted that proven scientific methods enabled them to assess the historical veracity of traditional tales.[139] Obviously, if they could suspend disbelief about the accuracy of some oral historical accounts, they could select versions of the past that suited their purposes. They could invoke oral history to justify the "restoration" of the "Ashanti Confederacy," for example. The confederacy was, however, less a re-creation of the institutions the British deliberately destroyed in the nineteenth cen-

---

1921, CO 96.624.476, PRO. Gold Coast Officers were prone to argue that the administrative style of the particular region for which they worked as distinctive – and superior. But in truth administrative procedures and objectives were substantially the same throughout the colony. See Kimble, *Political History of Ghana*, 328.

[135] See M. J. Field's application for a Colonial Social Science Research Council Grant, 26 July 1955, CRC.

[136] See "Present Tendencies of African Colonial Governments," unpublished paper apparently by R. S. Rattray, 1933; M. J. Field, "Some Problems of Indirect Rule in the Gold Coast," n.d., both in the Perham Papers, Boxes 688 and 390, respectively, OUODP.

[137] See, for example, A. F. Robertson, "Histories and Political Opposition in Ahafo, Ghana," *Africa*, 63 (1973): 41–5.

[138] W. J. A. Jones, Acting Provincial Commissioner, Eastern Province of the Colony, "Unofficial Diary," February 2, 1927, NAG; G. O. Parker, Assistant District Commissioner, Wa, "Unofficial Diary," 16 April, 1924, NAG.

[139] Blair, "Dagomba People," 22–3.

tury than a new colonial construct; only on the eve of Ghanaian independence did the Gold Coast government acknowledge that their "restoration"
was a fiction.[140]

Throughout the colonial period, Gold Coast administrators collected
and applied historical data in a variety of circumstances. Sometimes they
did so in the course of routine touring.[141] More frequently, political
officers invoked history in formulating rules for "proper" selection of
chiefs. Because traditional procedures had often permitted a choice between possible candidates, the administrators' procedures formalized distorted tribal constitutions. Their inquiries often followed chiefly succession
disputes, but sometimes were undertaken systematically in anticipation
of future need.[142] Most important, data were gathered that permitted
colonial officers to establish hierarchies of authority, sanctioning the subordination of some groups to others. In general, political officers usually
concluded from oral histories that fewer chiefs "originally" had independent sovereignty than claimed it, although later district commissioners may
have been more sympathetic to chiefs' historical rationales for autonomy.[143]

Political officers agreed that "the only hope for really effective indirect
rule is amalgamation."[144] Superior officers urged their subordinates to
"get a push on organizing" state formation.[145] When small independent
polities resisted efforts to make them politically subordinate members
of large confederations, their aspirations were declared historically un-

---

[140] Alessandro Triulzi, "The Asantehene-in-Council: Ashanti Politics Under Colonial
Rule, 1935–50," *Africa* 62 (1972): 100; P. H. Canham, "Local Government in
Ashanti," *Corona* 1, No. 5 (May 1949): 17.

[141] S. J. Olivier, Assistant District Commissioner, "Unofficial Diary," 21 January, 1933,
NAG.

[142] See, for examples: E. G. M. Dasent, District Commissioner, Lawra-Tamu,
"Unofficial Diary," 22 August, 1920, NAG; the questionnaire circulated by A. H. C.
Walker Leigh, Chief Commissioner of the Northern Territories, reported in A. J.
Cutfield, Acting Commissioner, Southern Province, Northern Territories, "Northern
Territories," 17 November, 1926, in CO 96.663.X7801, PRO. And see David C.
Davis, "'Then the White Man Came with His Whitish Ideas . . .': The British and the
Evolution of Traditional Government in Mampurugu," *The International Journal of
African Historical Studies* 20 (1987): 627–46, which points out that successive
Ghanaian governments have been no less concerned to establish regularity in chiefly
succession than the British were.

[143] See, for example, John Maxwell, Chief Commissioner of Ashanti, "Unofficial Diary,"
December 1927, NAG; J. C. Anderson, Assistant District Commissioner, Gonja,
"Informal Diary," 17 February, 1945, OUODP.

[144] W. W. Kilby, Acting Commissioner, Central Province of the Colony, "Unofficial
Diary," 30 August, 1931, NAG.

[145] F. W. F. Jackson, Chief Commissioner of the Northern Territories, "Unofficial
Diary," 29 May, 1931, NAG.

justified.[146] Generally, political officers claimed that their charges were "all anxious to *reunite*."[147] Popular enthusiasm served to validate administrative judgment: it indicated that official practices accelerated evolutionary trends, which would have proceeded without administrative intervention in the natural course of events. But colonial civil servants represented themselves as the agents of natural progress even when they allowed that they instigated political consolidation. One administrator confided to his diary, "The more I think of it, the more the idea of a Brong state appeals to me," but he also thought the Brong people welcomed the idea.[148] Moreover, consolidation remained a political ideal throughout the colonial period. In 1943, the administrator of the Saltpond District undertook to persuade his charges to amalgamate.[149] Almost a decade later, his successor in that district was still conducting the same campaign, although its rationale had changed from "restoration" to expediency.[150]

The structure of the colonial bureaucracy gave every political officer a vested interest in enlarging his chief's domain – placing him in competition with other officers seeking the aggrandizement of their chiefs. Behavior characteristic of Gold Coast administrators was observed throughout the colonial service. Thus, Donald Cameron noted that district officers were wont to address one another in tones more appropriate to "states lately belligerent" than to servants of the same regime.[151] Indeed, the prestige of the political officer both in his personal capacity and as the occupant of his office was dependent on the status of the people he adminstered. If he enlarged his chief's authority, he enhanced his own position. If an officer's identification with his people was total, precluding identification with his government, his peers thought him ridiculous.[152] But the very least the administrator expected of his chief was that he be a worthy opponent, not a sycophantic "whiteman's chief."[153] When a tribal leader behaved

---

[146] W. J. A. Jones, Secretary of Native Affairs, Enclosure of 29 November 1929, in Despatch of 6 December, 1929, in CO 96.691.6563, PRO.

[147] W. J. A. Jones, Commissioner of the Central Province of the Colony, "Unofficial Diary," 2 July, 1927, in NAG; the emphasis is his.

[148] Hon. H. W. Amherst, Assistant District Commissioner of Salaga, Informal Diary entries of 16 May, 1933 and 2 January, 1934, in OUODP.

[149] W. H. A. Hanschell, Memo of 16 June, 1943, in OUODP.

[150] W. Peters, "Report for the Quarter Ending 31 March, 1952, on the Saltpond Sub-District," OUODP.

[151] Donald Cameron, *My Tanganyika Service and Some Nigeria* (London, 1939), 317.

[152] See, for example, A. F. E. Fieldgate, Acting Commissioner, Eastern Province of the Colony, "Unofficial Diary," 27 March, 1931, in NAG.

[153] See, for example, C. E. E. Cockey, Acting Commissioner, Southern Province of the Northern Territories, comment in Guthrie Hall, District Commissioner, Gonja, "Unofficial Diary," 18 July, 1930, in NAG.

imperiously, his political officer basked in reflected glory; when a chief did not exert his authority, the officer was ashamed of him, and exhorted him to be forceful.[154]

To be sure, colonial officers did not require texts of evolutionist anthropology to learn their patterns of behavior, but could draw on the resources of their own formative experiences. They themselves frequently analogized the system of colonial administration to the public school prefectorial system, observing that in both the colony and the school management of the governed was effected through delegation of authority to trusted representatives of the population.[155] And the public school rhetoric of house government and team spirit figured in documents of colonial administration everywhere.[156] But it begs the question to debate whether the institution of the public school or evolutionary theory provided the inspiration for the structure of colonial rule, for both the institution and the theory derived from the same cultural matrix. Since the school itself embodied evolutionist notions of the process of individual maturation and the constitution of a stable order, to identify the school as the model for the colony is to conclude that evolutionist assumptions informed both.

Evolutionist theory thus formalized widespread beliefs, and justified the systematic character of colonial rule. If colonial subjects were not "progressive" – as cooperative tribesmen were termed – the district commissioner had a variety of coercive weapons at his disposal. Chiefs were deprived of their perquisites. The victors in tribal elections were not installed if they were unacceptable to the colonial bureaucracy. If all else failed, unsatisfactory chiefs could be threatened with the loss of their jobs.[157] Thus, by persuasion and coercion, the untidy realities of indigenous social systems were pressed to fit the mold of bureaucratic tribal order. And the order that suited the colonial administrator supposedly served evolutionary ends, uniting peoples into tribes that would

---

[154] See, for example, G. O. Parker, District Commissioner, Wa, "Unofficial Diary," 10 February, 1924, in NAG.

[155] For the standard argument that the colonial bureaucracy replicated the hierarchy of the public school, see, for example, Sir Kenneth Bradley, *Once a District Officer* (London, 1966), 15. It was also (no less plausibly) argued that the school was patterned after the colony. See Derek Verschogle, "Indian Innocence, Ltd.," in Greene, ed., *The Old School* (chap. 3, n. 52), 200.

[156] See, for example, J. L. Atterbury, Acting Commissioner, Central Province of the Colony, "Unofficial Diary," 17 July, 1921, and Governor Guggisberg's annotations therein, in NAG.

[157] See, for example, the administrative approach to the political situation in Gonja, Guthrie Hall, District Commissioner, "Unofficial Diary," 17 February, 1937; C. G. R. Amory, Assistant District Commissioner, "Unofficial Diary," 21 July, 1936, NAG.

eventually join to form a nation – at that very remote moment in time at which independence from British rule would be justified.

The colonial administration of Tanganyika, transferred in an extraordinarily bloody conflict during World War I from the German Empire to the British (whose rule was then sanctioned by League of Nations mandate), is the exception that proves the rule, demonstrating the interaction between models of tribal order and bureaucratic interests. The members of the Tanganyika political service were no less evolutionist in their assumptions than the officials of other colonial territories. They, too, assumed that Africans could be made into responsible citizens only if their sense of loyalty to their indigenous polities was reinforced by colonial tactics. As one Tanganyikan civil servant wrote in 1935:

> In a Bantu or Hamitic (i.e. Masai) tribe there is no such thing as an individual as we Europeans understand the term. An English youth who attains his majority can thereafter enter into any contract regardless of his family's wishes. . . . An African never attains to an individual status. Nor can he hold property as an individual right. . . . He is a member of a family, a tribe, a clan, and cares for certain properties only on behalf of the community to which he belongs.[158]

In Tanganyika as elsewhere in the British Empire, political officers linked social order to tribal citizens' belief that traditional leaders had sacred authority, and exhorted their chiefs to preserve the traditional trappings of office in order to mobilize popular assent.[159]

Like their fellows elsewhere, Tanganyikan officials were convinced that the customs of the peoples in their charge reflected their positions on the scale of unilinear evolution. Approvingly, they noted evidence that various Tanganyikan peoples were making progress toward higher evolutionary stages – developing patrilineal rather than matrilineal rules of descent and inheritance; becoming settled agriculturalists rather than migrant pastoralists; acquiring definite notions of private property; moving from clan organization to tribal political structure. Indeed, officials were rather perplexed that their subjects did not rank one another according to the evolutionist prestige hierarchy. "It is a recognized fact," wrote one administrator, "that the pastoralist is a stage behind the agriculturalist in evolu-

---

[158] Assistant District Officer, "Water Conservation," Arusha District Book, 7 February, 1935, TNA.

[159] For example, F. W. C. Morgans, District Officer, "On Enquiries Re: Insignia of Chiefs," Tabora District Book, 1927; W. B. Tribe, "The Death and Replacement of a Divine-King in Uha," Rasulu District Book, January 1938; all in TNA.

tion and progress." Why then, he wondered, did such peoples as the pastoralist Masai look with contempt on settled agriculturalists?[160]

Tanganyika had a peculiar history, however, as a former German colony, and this history lay behind the idiosyncratic features of its administration. Although Tanganyikan officials were to repudiate their original beliefs about the organization of African society before the Germans came, they might well have had a more conventional approach had they not been able to blame the Germans for wreaking havoc in Tanganyika. The administrative system that the Germans had extended over the colony from 1885 had been direct rule: agents alien to the villages they supervised, often men of Arab extraction, had governed according to German principles. Tanganyikan Africans had mobilized considerable resistance to German rule, and the ramifications of resistance contributed to the ecological catastrophe which their country suffered at the turn of the century, largely as the result of German policies. Moreover, they had suffered by being drawn into World War I. Men conscripted to serve as porters by both sides had died in large numbers from disease (and occasionally in battle), while away from the front the population starved both because the military seized foodstuffs and because much of the agricultural economy collapsed. Their experiences had given them good reason to distrust colonial rulers, as the British were obliged to recognize, and had, moreover, prompted many of them to fall in with postwar anticolonialist movements, often led by veterans.[161]

Though many of the artificial chiefs created by the Germans lost power with the advent of British rule, much of the German administrative structure remained intact until 1925, when Donald Cameron arrived to become governor. A West Indian Creole with seventeen years of experience in Nigeria, a man of known liberal convictions appointed by a Labour government, Cameron was determined to institute Indirect Rule in Tanganyika. At the beginning of his administration, he was convinced

---

[160] C. F. Ellaby, Assistant District Officer, "The Wakwavi," Handeni District Book, 7 January, 1932; see also P. E. Mitchell, Acting Provincial Commissioner, "System of Government – Native Administration in Practice," Arusha District Book, 13 April, 1927; O. S. Hopkin, "Tribal History and Legends," Liwali Division of Kilwa District, District Book, 6 October, 1928; R. C. Northcote, "Population-Distribution (General)," Rungwe District Book, 20 October, 1931; N. A., "Tribal Government (Chief, Sub-chiefs, etc.): The Coastal Belt," circa 1931, Handeni District Book; "Laws, Manners and Customs, Wapogoro Tribe," Ulanga District Book, 1935; N. A., "Notes on Hehe History," Iringa District Book, 1938; J. J. Tawney, "Ugabire: A Feudal Custom Among the Waha," Tabora District Book, June 1944. Old intellectual habits died hard; see H. St. J. Grant, "Chiefdom of Berege," Mpwapwa District Book, 12 November, 1957. All of these references in TNA.

[161] See, for example, Iliffe, *Modern History*, 322.

that there were in the country Africans with reliable recollections of pre-German Tanganyika, who might be persuaded to assist the administration in reconstructing the status quo ante, so that normal evolution could proceed on the basis of indigenous custom.[162] Because the traditional order had been suspended for decades, however, this seemed impossible – as Tanganyikan political officers frequently lamented.[163] But some socially integrative system of local government had to be created. Otherwise, Africans unsettled by decades of disruptive influences would turn "into an undisciplined rabble of leaderless and ignorant individuals" susceptible to the appeal of mass movements, turning Tanganyika into another Egypt or India.[164] The form and objectives of Tanganyikan administration were shaped by the urgent need to mollify the population.

This is not to suggest that Tanganyikan administrators were free of aspirations to follow the policies adopted by their colleagues elsewhere. Indeed, throughout the era of British rule in Tanganyika, the territory's officials expressed their preference for administering large, centralized states, often observing that Indirect Rule was most easily established when there was a recognized chiefdom.[165] Thus, in Tanganyika, as elsewhere, administrators, certain that they could reconstruct the past, consolidated peoples under the rule of one chief, disregarding local objections.[166] And efforts were made to homogenize the customs of a population judged to belong to a single culture area, to eliminate those practices dear to the

---

[162] Ibid., 322.

[163] For example, H. J. Rayne, District Officer, Mahenge, "Wambinga Tribe," May 17, 1929, Ulanga District Book; N. F. Burt, "Clans and Clan Lands," 22 August, 1930, Liwali Division of Kilwa District Book; J. O. Lawrence, "Customs and Legends of the Wangindo," Mtwara (Lindi) District Book, March 1932; R. J. Harvey, Assistant District Officer, "Mirambo," Tabora District Book, circa 1937; J. W. Lewis, "Native Custom Regarding Tenure of Land," Mogororo Provincial Book, circa 1940; all in TNA.

[164] The quotation comes from a memorandum written by Cameron in 1925, and the fear that Tanganyika might become like Egypt or India is also his, expressed in a letter he wrote to Joseph Oldham on 18 September, 1925. Both are cited in Chachage, "British Rule and African Civilization in Tanganyika," 206, 218.

[165] N. A., 'Notes on the Structure of Tribal Government in Pare," Handeni District Book, circa, 1931, in TNA; and see Governor E. E. Twining's Despatch, 20 September, 1950, quoted in R. de Z. Hall, *Development of Local Government in Tanganyika* (London, 1951), 7.

[166] P. J. Macmillan, "Tribal History and Legends: Wamatumbi and Wakichi," Rufiji (Utete) District Book, circa 1925; K. H. Coleman, "System of Government, Traditional: Wakwere Tribe," Bagamoyo District Book, 1 January, 1927; L. S. Greening, "Native Administration: The Dissolution of the Kilwa Division of the Wanguu Tribe and Its Absorption by Mgera, Kimbe and Kwekivu," Handeni District Book, 10 February, 1927; all in TNA.

"more conservative" sector of the population.[167] But the colonial canon of sound administrative practice required that historical precedent be found for the social change political officers wished to effect, and the difficulties which they often had in establishing historical rationales for their desired ends led Tanganyikan officials to adopt policies that deviated from the colonial norm.

Unlike interwar administrators elsewhere, Tanganyikan officials frequently recognized the fluidity of ethnic identity and the impossibility of imputing conventional models of tribal organization to many of the peoples they administered. For example, on the basis of sound historical research they concluded that a group might have a very strong ethnic identity that was of recent origin; before the era of German rule, one such population had not been cohesive, but they had been defined as one people by a host of outsiders, and had come to accept others' tribal label.[168] Indeed, when colonial officials undertook to create ethnic loyalties, they were able to acknowledge that they were fabricating new tribal identities.[169]

Furthermore, Tanganyikan officials recognized that they could find no historical justification for arguing that some peoples had ever been organized in centralized states, even prior to the implementation of German policy. As one officer wrote, "A glance at the general history of this part of Tanganyika Territory seems to suggest that the large tribal groups to which we are accustomed are not necessary aspects of native life." Many of the country's peoples were traditionally stateless, living in small, autonomous groups, accustomed to form alliances with their fellows only for the occasional purpose of repelling outside attack.[170] When such peoples talked of political tradition with colonial officials, they portrayed their constitutions as essentially democratic, attributing colonial officials' difficulties in understanding their way of life to the undemocratic nature of European culture; they perceived (accurately) the technocratic ethos of colonial administration, and assumed that the colonial officials had no personal experience of democracy.[171]

Tanganyikan administrators were distinguished from their fellows else-

---

[167] H. H. Mood, "Ngashu Ya Mshitu," Same (Pare) District Book, 1928, in TNA.

[168] A. M. D. Turnbull, Provincial Commissioner, "Tribal History and Legends: Notes on the Ngindo-Ngonde Group of People in the Masia, Tunduru, Liwale and Kibata Divisions of the Lindi Province," Mtwara (Lindi) Provincial Book, 7 July, 1828, TNA.

[169] P. J. Macmillan, "Wamatumbi Native Authority," Rufiji District Book, circa 1928, in TNA.

[170] Smith, District Officer, "Tribal History-Wabena," Njombe District Book, 7 July, 1947, in TNA.

[171] A. T. and G. M. Culwick, "What the Wabena Think of Indirect Rule," Journal of the Royal African Society 36 (1937): 176–93.

where by their democratic sympathies – which may have been engendered by the perception that a restive African population was likely to be placated if provided with genuinely responsive local government. In contradistinction to other colonial theorists, Cameron declared that the peoples of Tanganyika were high on the evolutionary scale because they were democratic rather than feudal, and condemned administrative procedures instituted elsewhere because they benefited the chiefs at the expense of the people. Abandoning the administrative convention that stateless peoples could be brought to a higher stage of evolution under centralized tribal government, Cameron endorsed the creation of conciliar systems of Indirect Rule for them.[172] Echoing his chief's view, Philip Mitchell reported that the typical Tanganyikan "tribal system is as near the ideal of democracy as any human society of which we have knowledge."[173] Thus, an administrative solution that was likely to be seen elsewhere as a compromise was represented as the best one.[174]

Certainly, Tanganyikan officials were willing to grant their colonial subjects only very limited self-government. As late as 1943, Tanganyikan political officers might declare that it would be "hundreds" of years before the African peasant was ready for government based on universal suffrage.[175] Nevertheless, Tanganyikan officials intended the rule of the indigenous leaders they supervised to be responsive to popular demands. They were often prepared to reverse decisions to centralize native authorities, and to suppress the tendencies of some chiefs to elevate themselves at the expense of others, whether or not they could invoke historical precedent for their actions. Indeed, officials were willing to depose a chief of apparently irrefutable historical claims to office, to engineer the election of a chief of irregular pedigree, or to bypass a traditional political structure – such as a council of elders – if customary rulers ignored popular pressures and were not responsive to new needs.[176]

---

[172] Cameron, *Tanganyika Service*, 34; Iliffe, *Modern History*, 323.

[173] Philip Mitchell, *Native Administration* (Dar es Salaam, 1927), 7.

[174] M. W. Parr, Governor of the Upper Nile Province, to F. D. Corfield, District Commissioner, Eastern Nuer, 18 December, 1935, in Perham Papers, Box 544, OUODP.

[175] See G. F. Webster's statement in the Tanganyika Provincial Commissioners' Conference Report for 1943, paragraph 98, in CO 691.184.4297, PRO.

[176] See, for example, N. A., "The Wakimbu" (Chunga District Book, circa 1928), in which the political officer reports declining to revive traditional structure, despite popular requests, since the result might be counterproductive; A. M. D. Turnbull, Provincial Commissioner, "Tribal History and Legends: Matambwe (Makonde)" (Mtwara [Lindi] Provincial Book, 7 July, 1928), reporting the creation of a wholly new government structure; District Officer, Rungwe, report for 1930 (Mbeya [Iringa and Southern Highlands] Provincial Book), describing restoration of traditional checks on

Because the Tanganyikan administration recognized that they could not impute state order to the largely stateless peoples they governed, they welcomed such projects as Brown and Hutt's, which investigated the basis of order effected in the absence of a centralized political system. They encouraged the collection and dissemination of anthropological information through the publication of *Tanganyikan Notes and Records*. They employed the Austrian emigré-turned-anthropologist Hans Cory (before World War II, Koritschoner) to investigate specific problems.[177] With funds available to them after World War II, they engaged four government anthropologists – Cory, H. A. Fosbrooke, Wilfred Whiteley, and P. H. Gulliver – who were called "sociologists," a designation denoting (to British academics as well as the colonial regime) their functionalist, rather than historicist, orientation. Only Gulliver was a formally trained anthropologist, but the others all were granted some measure of professional recognition.

The official plea for the appointment of government anthropologists made in 1945 echoed Malinowski's earlier pronouncements. The anthropologists were intended to serve as Africans' advocates in the administration; the colonial relationship placed Africans in a position of involuntary subordination to the British, and Africans' interests and needs had to be articulated if they were to become active partners in development administration.[178] The government sociologists were, indeed, to portray them-

chiefly powers; F. W. Brett, "Native Administration" (Nzega District Book, 24 January, 1934), describing his efforts to keep a particularly capable chief in an area from establishing himself as paramount over the others; A. V. Hartnoll, "Native Administration" (Rufiji [Utele] District Book, 3 August, 1934), suggesting that the power of the tribal elders be minimal, since they cannot rule, no matter how much traditional lore they know; District Officer, Mbeya, report for 1935 (Mbeya [Iringa and Southern Highlands] Provincial Book), reporting the decentralization of political authority in response to popular demand; N. A., "The Executive Committee of the Tribal Council" (Same [Pare] District Book, circa 1941), on the necessity for giving young men and the "intelligentsia" a place in government; A. Bate, District Officer, "Usmao Succession" (Kwimba District Book, 1942), on the desirability of engineering the election of a chief with no connection to any of the traditional political factions; all in TNA. And see also R. C. Northcote, "The Evolution of Tribal Control," *Africa* 6 (1933): 312–16; T. M. Revington, "Concerning the Banagoma and Basumba Batate Societies of the Bukwimba Wasukuma," *Tanganyika Notes and Records*, No. 5 (April 1938): 60–2; A. T. and G. M. Culwick, "Culture Contact on the Fringes of Civilization," *Africa* 8 (1935): 163–70; R. deZ. Hall, "The Study of Court Records as a Method of Ethnological Inquiry," *Africa* 9 (1938); 412–37.

[177] See, for example, Hans Koritschoner, "The Society of the Bayeye," Mwanza Provincial Book, 1938; Hans Koritschoner, "Report on Nutrition in Uhaga," Bukoba District Book, 1939; both in TNA.

[178] J. P. Moffett, "The Need for Anthropological Research," *Tanganyika Notes and Records*, No. 20 (December 1945): 39–47; see also his "Government Sociologists in Tanganyika: A Government View," *Journal of African Administration* 4 (1952): 100–3.

selves as buffers between the administration and the Africans, acting to prevent government from imposing unwelcome institutions and innovations on colonial subjects.[179]

This is not to suggest, however, that the Tanganyikan government did not equate political amalgamation with evolutionary advance. Officials might not have insisted on the formation of centralized polities, but nevertheless sought to create large ethnic groups through amalgamation of small social units joined in conciliar government. Particularly notable were the administrative consolidations effected among the Chagga, the Nyakusa, and the Sukuma, who were supposedly persuaded that the differences of custom prevailing within ethnic groups that once seemed so important were not very significant after all.[180] Whether justified on the grounds of expediency or explained as the reunion of peoples divided under the Germans, amalgamations were everywhere seen as progressive because they permitted greater efficiency.[181] Government efforts persisted until the eve of independence, and at least one consolidation was accomplished with anthropological assistance, after Cory identified a practice common to several peoples in a culture area (their age–grade system) on which a political order could be based.[182] Peoples were instructed that they had to organize in strong political units, in order to ensure that they received their fair share of national resources.[183] This was a sermon preached to peoples

---

[179] Wilfred Whiteley, "Modern Local Government Among the Makua," *Africa* (1954): 349–58, H. A. Fosbrooke, "The Defensive Measures of Certain Tribes in Northeastern Tanganyika," *Tanganyika Notes and Records*, No. 35 (July 1953): 1–6; H. A. Cory, "Religious Beliefs and Practices of the Sukuma/Nyamwesi Tribal Groups," *Tanganyika Notes and Records*, No. 54 (March 1960): 14–26; R. deZ. Hall and H. Cory, "A Study of Land Tenure in Bugufi, 1935–1944," *Tanganyika Notes and Records* No. 24 (December 1947); 28–45; H. A. Fosbrooke, "Government Sociologists in Tanganyika: A Sociological View," *Journal of African Administration* (1952): 103–8; P. H. Gulliver, "Nyakusa Labour Migration," *Human Problems in British Central Africa* 21 (1957): 32–63.

[180] J. P. Moffett, *Handbook of Tanganyika* (Dar es Salaam, 1958), 320; Iliffe, *Modern History*, 330, 332. And see, for example, Minutes of a meeting of the Sukuma chiefs, 1 November, 1932, in Perham Papers, Box 493, OUODP.

[181] See, for example, N. A., "System of Government in Practice," Rungwe District Book, circa 1934; J. V. Lewis, Acting District Officer, "Native Administration in Practice," Bagamojo District Book, 1938; N. A., "An Appreciation of the Native Authorities of Kahama," Kahama District Book, October 15, 1952; letter from the acting member for local government to the Provincial Commissioner, Western Province, Tabora, October 27, 1955, Kahama District Book, all in TNA.

[182] C. I. Meek, District Officer, "A Practical Experiment in Local Government," Arusha District Book, 1948, in TNA.

[183] See, for example, J. A. K. Leslie, District Commissioner, "Handing Over Notes, Kasulu District," 23 October, 1954, Kasulu District Book, in TNA.

in other parts of the British Empire on the eve of independence.[184] Unquestionably, this sermon on the merits of large ethnic groups was addressed to a responsive audience.

Conclusions

The saga of anthropologists' negotiations with their patrons may seem to exemplify the practice of cynical grantsmanship: over time, anthropologists modified their pleas for support until they finally constructed a justification for their activities that elicited the response they wanted, whereupon they used the funds they were provided for their own ends, confirming the worst fears their patrons had had when they originally resisted anthropologists' entreaties. But there is every reason to believe that when anthropologists from Haddon to Malinowski expressed a desire to reform colonial admin- istrative practices, they were sincere. Haddon, his colleagues, and his students saw colonial regimes as potential employers, to be sure, but they also took an active interest in colonial policy per se. Malinowski and his students examined colonial administrative practices, remarking upon the ways that officials were perverting indigenous custom and suggesting that administrative decisions were violating the very values on which British society rested. No matter how well funded they were, however, academic anthropologists remained suspicious characters to colonial regimes. The leaders of the discipline might have sustained their enthusiasm for applied research had governments taken their advice more seriously, but colonial civil servants were unwilling to relinquish the management of the Empire to scientific experts.

To consider the consequences of anthropology as it was applied by colonial regimes, however, is to move out of the realm of speculation. In specific, the colonial policy of encouraging the shift of individuals' loyalties from small-scale societies to large ethnic groups has left a destructive legacy for new nations. For over half a century, the phenomenon of ethnicity has had considerable interest for Africanists – led by anthropol- ogists. At first, they emphasized the quasi-natural forces that brought together people previously divided by parochial ties: such forces as volun- tary migrations of diverse sorts, facilitated by improved communications and encouraged by growing markets for labor and commodities. During the era in which colonies gained independence, social scientists stressed the positive contributions ethnic groups made to nationalist agitations; par-

---

[184] See, for example, J. C. Britton, Acting President, speech given at the Igala Tribal Meeting at Ajangba, Nigeria, 20 April, 1961, in OUODP.

ticularly in the towns, ethnic voluntary associations formed for the purpose of self-help were active in political protests colonial rulers could not ignore.[185] But it is now clear that fervent ethnic partisanship has impeded the creation of political order in new nations, and, moreover, that the divisive loyalties experienced as primordial are in fact in good measure the products of imperial design.[186] In Africa, as elsewhere in the British Empire, colonial policies exaggerated cleavages within populations. Unfortunately, historical evidence documents the inaccuracy of evolutionist predictions: people whose loyalties have been transferred from small to large ethnic groups are not necessarily in a transitional stage, soon to become loyal citizens of a nation. Strong tribalism has proven difficult to reconcile with national integration, and is likely to surface in virulent – even violent — form in any conflict over the distribution of resources.

---

[185] See, for example, I. Wallerstein, "Ethnicity and National Integration," *Cahiers d'Etudies Africaines* 1 (1960): 129–39.

[186] Mazi Okoro Ojiaki, "European Tribalism and African Nationalism," *Civilisations* 22 (1972): 387–404. For discussion of comparable practices in India, for example, see Heesterman, *The Inner Conflict of Tradition* (chap. 2, n. 14), esp. 180–93.

Chapter 6

Of councillors and kings: images of political authority in British anthropology, 1885–1945

Up to this point, this study has evaluated the significance of anthropological ideas on the basis of their social consequences. It has observed that as a practical enterprise anthropology had by 1945 become quite different from anthropology in 1885. Once, anthropological expertise had been considered relevant in major policy disputes, such as that over Irish Home Rule. By the middle of the twentieth century, anthropologists were assumed competent to offer only specific sorts of technical advice – say, assistance in a campaign to transform Tanganyikan subsistence farmers into commercial coffee growers. When nineteenth-century intellectuals undertook to professionalize anthropology, they projected a demand for just such advice, but they probably did not anticipate that the field's technical purview would be so restricted. To be sure, anthropologists remained concerned to define the fundamental properties of social order, but by the middle of the twentieth century they did so only in the abstract, with little expectation that their conclusions could directly affect public policy. Nevertheless, their deliberations were as much reflections of the national mood as were those of their predecessors; they articulated the values on which practical decisions were predicted. Therefore, to grasp the messages encoded in six decades of anthropological analyses is better to appreciate the direction of political change.

Anthropologists' normative prescriptions for the state fit the conventions of their political culture. Since the revolutionary period of the seventeenth century, the makers of that culture – popular agitators and learned philosophers alike – have assumed that the nation had clear constitutional choices. These choices were contingent on assessments of the state's natural human resources, for the ideal state order was one designed to manage these resources to good effect. If persons reasoned in archetypal conservative mode, their constitutional recommendations derived from their assumption that the capacity for rule – or any significant achievement – was an inborn talent found in only a small fraction of the population. The legitimate state was a centralized polity dominated by a hereditary

242

aristocracy, in which social integration took organicist form: in the service of collective progress, unequal individuals submitted to state discipline and accepted that they were entitled to unequal shares of the nation's wealth and power. Since the maintenance of order ultimately depended on coercion, the ruling class held a monopoly on the use of force.[1] Writ large, the constitution of this state permitted colonial conquest and rule, which forced inferior peoples to conform to a higher behavioral standard than they would have developed naturally – just as state discipline improved the conduct of inferior Britons.

If political thinkers reasoned in classic liberal fashion, their arguments were predicated on the assumption that persons of talent could be found among all types of the human species. The legitimate polity was formed from a contractual union of individuals, each capable of assessing their needs and interests and of recognizing the benefit they would gain from cooperation. No higher good could be served by compelling individuals to act contrary to their own interests or to tolerate a constitution that favored any particular sector of the population. As Mill observed, "Even if a government were superior in intelligence and knowledge to any single individual in the nation, it must be inferior to all of the individuals of the nation taken together." Hence, political leaders should be able to retain their offices only so long as they enjoyed the consent of the governed, and whatever cooperative endeavors individuals undertook should be contracted freely – not based on institutionalized habits of dominance and submission.[2] Extrapolated to the global context, liberal principles precluded colonialism. The state was no more justified in compelling alien peoples to submit to its authority than it was entitled to coerce its own citizens.

Of course, British political debate was not conducted in the abstract. Nor was anthropology a unique cultural product. Arguments over national values were translated into other forms of culture. Of special interest to the historian who would find analogues to anthropological accounts in other sorts of cultural products are two long-sustained national discussions: descriptions of the rural village, and narratives of the origin of the state. The character of the village community was much debated, for it was generally assumed that its social structure embodied an optimal pattern of habitual relationships among individuals that should be extrapolated from

---

[1] For one discussion of this tradition, see Karl Mannheim, "Conservative Thought," in Kurt Wolff, ed., *From Karl Mannheim* (New York, 1971 [orig. 1953]), 132–222.

[2] The Mill quotation is from *Principles of Political Economy* (see chap. 1, n. 7), Vol. II, 553. For one discussion of the differences between ideal-typical liberalism and conservatism see Frank Manuel, "From Equality to Organicism," *Journal of the History of Ideas* 17 (1956): 54–69.

the rural microcosm to the state macrocosm. Different points of origin for the constitution of the state were found in British history, and determinations of the legitimacy of the constitution rested on evaluations of its creators' tactics. British cultural traditions can hardly be appreciated without attention to rival versions of the past – in which the quality of rural life and the nature of the state loom large. And anthropological analyses fit the conventions of mythologized British history.

The village and the state

A national tradition of representing the countryside as the locus of the quintessential virtues of the British character developed from the seventeenth through the nineteenth centuries. As the quality of urban life in Britain became debased by the unpleasant and unhealthy effects of industrialization, the role of the countryside in the popular imagination grew. Perhaps more important, as the British became an increasingly urbanized people, they could the more easily impute the values they cherished to rural life because they had not experienced it themselves.[3] The relevance of such a tradition to the anthropological vision is obvious, and its clear articulation coincides with the emergence of the anthropological enterprise: the remote societies described by anthropologists could be vehicles for projective fantasy just as vanished British rural communities could; and primitives abroad and villagers at home both supposedly enjoyed the benefits of existence close to nature.

To identify anthropology as but one subspecies of British representations of rural life is to beg the question of the moral import of the habitual idealization of the countryside, however, since there was considerable disagreement about the essential virtues of rural communities. Conservative thinkers have portrayed the village community as a benevolent organicist society, necessarily dominated by the landed aristocracy, who fulfill their natural obligations to lead those incapable of governing themselves. Consider, for example, the advice given in 1857 to the hypothetical man of means who is contemplating building a grand country house, and thus, in the social order secure until the late nineteenth century, establishing himself as a member of the national elite.

> Providence has ordained the different orders and gradations into
> which the human family is divided, and it is right and necessary that

---

[3] See, for example, Dewey, "Images of the Village Community" (chap. 3, n. 97), 291; Stone and Stone, *An Open Elite?* (chap. 1, n. 30), 16; Thomas, *Man and the Natural World* (see chap. 2, n. 5), esp. 243–54; Raymond Williams, *The Country and the City* (Oxford, 1973), passim.

it should be maintained. . . . The position of the landed proprietor, be he squire or nobleman, is one of dignity. Wealth must always bring its responsibilities, but a landed proprietor is especially in a responsible position. He is the natural head of his parish or district – in which he should be looked up to as the bond of union between the classes. To him the poor man should look up for protection; those in doubt or difficulty for advice; the ill disposed for reproof or punishment; the deserving, of all classes, for consideration and hospitality; and all for a dignified, honourable and Christian example. . . . he has been placed by Providence in a position of authority and dignity, and no false modesty should deter him from expressing this.[4]

Populist evocations of the rural ideal were very different. Significantly, nineteenth-century conservatives described the optimal village social order in the present tense; evidently those who then cherished this ideal considered its realization still practicable. By contrast, populist evocations of the rural ideal were nostalgic tributes to a way of life obliterated by the forces of history. The vanished folk society of the populists was a non-hierarchical, cooperative order. In it, unalienated individuals were bound together by ties of kinship, loyalty to their particular communities, and shared values that dictated reciprocal rights and obligations.[5]

Nevertheless, radicals and conservatives held substantially identical views on the history of the English village community. All agreed that the development of feudalism had transformed the primeval democratic (or socialistic) order into a hierarchical one. Within the period covered by this study, historical writers debated the merits of this transformation. In the narrative told by relatively conservative thinkers, such as Sir Henry Maine, the primeval order was inherently repressive and stagnant, and progress toward the development of high civilization began with the creation of the feudal system and the creation of private property. To more radical observers, such as John and Barbara Hammond, the premodern village had been democratic and meritocratic, providing "opportunities for the humblest and poorest labourer to rise." In their immensely popular *The Village Labourer* (1911), the Hammonds argued that the trend toward increasing concentration of wealth and power that had begun with feudalism had deprived ordinary villagers of both political rights and prospects for

---

[4] Sir George Gilbert Scott, *Secular and Domestic Architecture* (London, 1857), quoted in Mark Girouard, *The Victorian Country House* (New Haven, 1979), 4–5. Possession of a grand country house was generally agreed to be the sine qua non of membership in the elite, and can be used as an index to elite status; see Stone and Stone, *An Open Elite?* 11.

[5] See, for example, Weiner, *English Culture and the Decline of the Industrial Spirit* (chap. 2, n. 7), 42.

developing their individual talents.[6] Liberals such as E. A. Freeman saw more continuity in history than either conservatives or radicals, and found the basis of modern parliamentary government in the democratic, individualistic values of ancient rural society.[7]

These themes, expressed in qualitative evaluations of the village community, recur in historical narratives of the origin of the state. From the period of constitutional revolution of the seventeenth century, rival origin myths frequently depended on interpretations of the consequences of the Norman Conquest of the Anglo-Saxon people. The conservative image of the village community figured in the conservative account of the Conquest, which was portrayed as an episode essential to the foundation of the English nation. The Conquest made the state a hierarchical organismic society, of which the feudal village community was a derivative part, for the guiding constitutional principles of the state were in fact established with its origin.

Seventeenth-century political theorists who defended the established order saw the Conquest as an event that confirmed a religious principle: submission to conquerors is in accordance with the providence of God, the salvation of a divided and confused people from anarchy.[8] Thus, King James asserted that the imposition of Norman rule had "had a valuable disciplinary effect upon the dissolute Anglo-Saxons."[9] Secularized versions of this argument were to be enunciated in the years to come. In 1762, David Hume wrote that until the Norman Conquest the Saxons had been "very little advanced beyond the rude state of nature."[10] And a number of nineteenth-century historians agreed with Carlyle that without the benefit of alien rule the English would have remained "a gluttonous race of Jutes and Angles, capable of no grand combinations, lumbering about in pot-bellied equanimity; not dreaming of heroic toil, and silence, and endurance, such as leads to high places of this universe."[11]

Because conservatives identified force as the basis of the creation of state order, they argued that the continued legitimacy of the ruling class rested on that class's continued capacity to exercise force, and expected the state

---

[6] J. L. Hammond and Barbara Hammond, *The Village Labourer 1760–1832* (London, 1913 [orig. 1911]), 33; and see also 7–8, 27, 33–41.

[7] See J. R. Burrow, "The 'Village Community' and the Uses of History in Late Nineteenth-Century England," in Neil McKendrick, ed., *Historical Perspectives* (London, 1974), esp. 269–73.

[8] Julian H. Franklin, *John Locke and the Theory of Sovereignty* (London, 1978), 83–4.

[9] Quoted in Christopher Hill, *Puritanism and Revolution* (New York, 1958), 62.

[10] Quoted in Quentin Skinner, "History and Ideology in the English Revolution," *The Historical Journal* 8 (1965): 155.

[11] Quoted in J. W. Burrow, *A Liberal Descent* (Cambridge, 1981), 143.

to conduct its foreign affairs in a manner consistent with its internal constitution. If the aristocracy had won their social position because they possessed the moral qualities engendered by and tested in battle, their authority could be sustained only if they maintained their monopolistic control of military resources and their capacity for conquest; during peacetime, they kept themselves fit to rule by engaging in character-building, quasi-military activities, such as field sports.[12] And the mighty English nation, forged through conquest, was destined to extend its jurisdiction into the territories comprising Great Britain and beyond, using its power to civilize peoples who were as backward as the Anglo-Saxons had been.

At the very beginning of the colonial era, in the early seventeenth century, the subjugation of uncivilized peoples was justified in religious terms. Such peoples as the Native Americans were seen as living in a natural order, resembling the primeval English village community, possessing only communal notions of political order and property ownership. By conquering uncivilized peoples, colonists forced them to submit to the higher laws of formal government and private property. Colonists were obeying the moral imperative to subdue both humankind's base animal instincts and the naturally disorderly plant and animal kingdoms.[13] The Norman Conquest, then, was a paradigm for British colonialism, which could be rendered in entirely secular form; no later than the middle of the nineteenth century, the Conquest became a feature of imperialist rhetoric.[14]

Critics of established order agreed that state formation had been effected through military conquest, and that it entailed elimination of communal notions of government and property. But they did not count the state order an improvement over the antecedent, natural one. They believed that the natural, and hence legitimate, form of government rested on a voluntary

---

[12] The association of aristocratic status with military pursuits and engagement in field sports was behavioral, not merely rhetorical. From the late seventeenth century, when a standing army was created, a military career as an officer – with a purchased rank – was one of the few careers considered appropriate for sons of the landed aristocracy, whether they were older sons waiting to succeed to properties and titles or younger sons whose families could afford to purchase them commissions. And the laws that restricted hunting of game and ownership of certain dogs to men of property – laws in effect from the late seventeenth through the early nineteenth centuries – institutionalized the equation of participation in field sports and elite status, although the cult of fox hunting reached its apogee in the nineteenth century. See Stone and Stone, *An Open Elite?* 228–37; and Thomas, *Man and the Natural World*, 49, 106, 183–4.

[13] See, for example, the views of John Winthrop, Governor of the Massachusetts Bay Colony, 1629–49, quoted in William Cronon, *Changes in the Land* (New York, 1983), 56–7, 130.

[14] Hill, *Puritanism and Revolution*, 120.

compact between autonomous individuals, as Locke wrote in 1689. From his knowledge of primitive peoples, he concluded that a natural society required centralized leadership only during those intermittent occasions when it found itself at war, and if it chose to have a king in times of peace he would be popularly elected and accountable.[15] Portrayed in terms such as Locke's, the government established through the Norman Conquest was illegal, an abrogation of the natural democracy of the Saxons. In this sustained tradition of political argument, Anglo-Saxon precedent was repeatedly invoked by supporters of causes ranging from radical to liberal, from the seventeenth-century Levellers and Diggers, through the followers of Thomas Paine at the turn of the eighteenth century, through advocates of land reform in the 1870s such as John Stuart Mill, to the defenders of Lloyd George's redistributive "People's Budget" of 1909.[16]

To be sure, the declinist narrative of British history did not invariably commence with the imposition of the "Norman Yoke." In one popular version, the villains in the saga of the loss of Anglo-Saxon freedoms were the Tudors and their Stuart successors, whose cumulative efforts led to oligarchic rule. On this interpretation of British history rested the arguments of such figures as the middle-class radicals Richard Cobden and John Bright, so influential in the middle of the nineteenth century, who called for a repudiation of the feudal ideals perpetuated by the landed aristocracy. They believed that their ideal polity was an enlarged, modernized version of ancient society: at home, the state apparatus would be reduced to a minimum, and peaceable relations among the citizenry would be sustained by a host of voluntary activities, most notably the reciprocal exchanges effected by flourishing industry and commerce; abroad, the state would repudiate warfare and imperialist expansion, and international trade would be genuinely free, since foreign traders would not be forced to submit to economic exploitation either by conquest or by indirect pressures.[17]

Members of learned circles often debated political issues in the abstract.

---

[15] Locke, *Of Civil Government, Second Treatise* (see chap. 1, n. 2), esp. chap. 8, paragraphs 102, 105.

[16] Asa Briggs, *Saxons, Normans and Victorians* (Bexhill-on-sea, Sussex, 1966), 708; Hill, *Puritanism and Revolution*, 50–122; J. G. A. Pocock, *The Machiavellian Moment* (Princeton, 1975), 372; E. P. Thompson, *The Making of the English Working Class* (New York, 1966), 96.

[17] See Oliver MacDonagh, "The Anti-imperialism of Free Trade," *Economic History Review* [ser. 2] 14 (1962): 489–501, esp. 492; E. B. Smith, *The Making of the Second Reform Bill* (Cambridge, 1966), 25–81; and, for some randomly selected illustrations of Cobden's constitutional theory, see John Bright and James E. Thorold Rogers, *Speeches on Questions of Public Policy by Richard Cobden, M.P.* (London, 1878), 132, 187.

And, reasoning in the historicist mode beloved by thinkers in the nineteenth century and earlier, they drew examples from their shared knowledge of other national histories, which they judged to hold instructive lessons for the British. From various evaluations of the societies of ancient Rome and Greece, for example, one can also recognize the constitutional theories that informed accounts of British history. Conservatives describing ancient Greece found much to commend in the social organization of Sparta, but little in that of Athens; one writer observed in 1786 that Athenian democracy demonstrated "the incurable evils inherent in every form of Republican polity" and the "inestimable benefits of hereditary kings and the steady operations of a well-regulated monarch."[18] By contrast, liberals saw the same virtues in the societies of ancient Athens and prefeudal England.[19] And nineteenth-century intellectuals were wont to equate the Anglo-Saxon village community with the ancient Teutonic *mark*, however they judged the quality of life of these societies.[20] Nevertheless, the Norman Conquest represents a particularly useful touchstone of political opinion, since it figures in every circle of political debate, in low culture as well as high.

The "Whig" historical tradition of portraying the Conquest exemplifies a moderate reconciliation of conservative and radical normative analyses of the polity. Proponents of the Whig view have stressed the continuity of English history, arguing that the Conquest little altered the pattern of English life. Though the Whig interpretation of history was originally a conservative one, contrived in the sixteenth and seventeenth centuries by those who appealed to the Ancient Constitution in order to resist kings' attempts to innovate, it became an approach particularly congenial to those of liberal temper.[21] Whig thinkers could not deny that the Normans had employed military means to gain their positions of power, but maintained that the Normans were obliged to respect Saxon precedent because they could not sustain their authority without securing the consent of the governed. As one representative thinker of this persuasion suggested in the eighteenth century, William the Conqueror could not have ruled had he not "founded his Right upon the Election of the People."[22] Subsequent scholarship discredited such accounts, but many nineteenth-century historians agreed with Freeman that the Conquest was only a "temporary

---

[18] John Gillies, quoted in Frank M. Turner, *The Greek Heritage in Victorian Britain* (New Haven, 1981), 189.
[19] E. A. Freeman, quoted in ibid., 245.
[20] Burrow, "Village Community," 256–63.
[21] Burrow, *Liberal Descent*, 139.
[22] Quoted in Skinner, "History and Ideology," 174.

overthrow of our national being ... in a few generations we led captive our conquerors."[23]

Whig historians did not invariably celebrate Saxon society and democratic freedoms. Like Sharon Turner, they might allege that Anglo-Saxon society had been no less socially stratified than that of post-Conquest England.[24] Or, like William Stubbs, they might observe that feudalism had been developing in England before the Conquest, and indeed suggest that the Conquest actually halted the erosion of Anglo-Saxon liberties, since England's unusually elastic feudal system was the creation of talented Norman lawyers.[25] Whatever the differences between various Whig narratives, they exemplify a distinct genre because they are predicated on shared assumptions: disjunctive change has never been effected in England by military means; the social conditions structured by England's island environment have made forceful methods impracticable in the regulation of domestic life, although English freemen might be obliged to resort to force in the conduct of foreign affairs.[26]

Playing upon the common themes of British historical narratives, anthropologists used analyses of exotic cultures to render judgments about the optimal social order. Of a piece with their normative political theories were their implicit pronouncements about the legitimacy of colonialism – clearly a matter of particular interest to them. The tenor of political opinion expressed in anthropology changed noticeably in the decades before World War I and again after the war. Evidently, shifts in anthropological views loosely coincided with the diffusionists' assault on evolutionism and the functionalists' subsequent triumph. But at any given time a political consensus obtained in the anthropological community, joining individuals who disagreed about the issues debated within the discipline – the theories and methods anthropologists should employ, and the substantive province they should explore. That is, whatever their views on technical problems, anthropologists were, above all, creatures of their historical moments.

The natural evolution of the polity

Late-nineteenth-century anthropologists were uncertain of the original condition of the human species. Believing that when a people made some sort of progressive innovation they were bound to retain it (barring some

[23] Quoted in Burrow, *Liberal Descent*, 102. See also Parker, "The Failure of Liberal Racialism" (chap. 2, n. 34), 830.
[24] Burrow, *Liberal Descent*, 118.
[25] Collini et al., *That Noble Science of Politics* (see chap. 3, n. 25), 17.
[26] Pocock, *The Machiavellian Movement*, 392, 440.

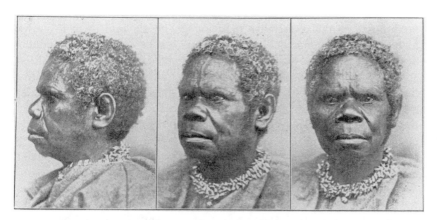

Truganina, who died in June 1876, was generally believed to have been the last full-blooded Tasmanian. To evolutionists, her death confirmed the axiom that truly primitive peoples were doomed to extinction. From H. Ling Roth, "Is Mrs. F. C. Smith a 'Last Living Aboriginal of Tasmania'?" *Journal of the Anthropological Institute* 27 (1898): 451–4.

jarring experience), evolutionists could only assume that contemporary primitives were "at least as far advanced as were our ancestors when they spread over the earth's surface."[27] But evolutionists considered that available evidence was sufficient to indicate a close approximation of the state of nature. It was not an admirable state. It was exemplified by the behavior of a people such as the Tasmanians, the last of whom died in 1876, who were generally believed to have been the most primitive of peoples encountered by contemporary observers. As E. B. Tylor described them:

> Perhaps no people ever had more rudimentary rules of law and government than these savages, with no property in land, but waging war to the death against the trespasser in pursuit of game; with hardly any government over the wandering clan except the undefined authority of "the bully of the tribe," and yet as soon as war broke out following with absolute obedience the chosen war chief.[28]

Nonetheless, evolutionists imputed to backward peoples some of the virtues often attributed to ancient Britons: naturally democratic attitudes, strong family loyalties, and the capacity to withstand all forms of physical adversity. Most importantly, they saw in the self-government of the primi-

[27] John Lubbock, *Pre-historic Times, as Illustrated by Ancient Remains and the Manners and Customs of Modern Savages* (London, 1872), 586.
[28] Tylor, "On the Tasmanians as Representatives of Paleolithic Man" (see chap. 3, n. 23), 150.

tive family evidence that human beings were naturally social creatures, predisposed to the cooperative behavior that would lead them to evolve high standards of morality and rationality. To be sure, these standards depended on the creation of formal government, which institutionalized abstract standards of justice, responsibility, and charity. The primitive family would protect only its own weak and helpless members, and it would exact unrestrained vengeance on those who had somehow wronged its members. But the family was the building block of the future rationally operating nation.

Anthropologists were hardly unique in assuming that the development of high moral standards was associated with the process of state formation. And when they described "the evolution of the state from the family through the tribe," they were relying on a popular historical formula all too familiar to nineteenth-century audiences, as an anonymous contributor to the *Saturday Review* complained wearily in 1896.[29] This formula could be used by adherents of a range of political positions, as should already be clear, but in the hands of the anthropologists it was put to distinctly liberal purposes. Anthropologists plotted the growth of the polity as a function of spontaneous, natural forces. They reasoned that if the state grew from progressive extensions of kinship ties, its motive basis had to be natural— the drive stemming from the biological imperative of reproduction. Following their instinctive inclinations, human beings would enter into kinship alliances that would over time grow more extensive and elaborate, resulting ultimately in the formation of the state. Evolutionist anthropologists' analyses of the dynamics of kinship, then, constituted an explanation of the creation of social order through voluntary acts.

Anthropologists differed over the details of the process of the elaboration of kinship alliances. Some believed that the primordial form of social organization was the nuclear family, whereas others argued that the most primitive peoples lived in promiscuous hordes, which by degrees developed family structures.[30] But whatever the morphological relationship they described between the family and the clan, evolutionists agreed that clans fused into tribes and tribes into nations. Enlarged social structures resulted from the universal practice of exogamy – the custom of choosing marriage partners from outside some basic kinship unit. Exogamy was variously explained as a consequence of the incest taboo invariably engendered in those reared together, the extinction of those peoples that inbred, the

---

[29] Quoted in Collini et al., *That Noble Science of Politics* (see chap. 3, n. 25), 229.

[30] For some discussion of these issues see, for example, G. L. Gomme, "On Evidence for Mr. McLennan's Theory of the Primitive Human Horde," *Journal of the Anthropological Institute* 17 (1887–8): 118–33.

rational decision to act for the good of the community by prohibiting marital unions between close blood relations, or the conscious choice to use enlarged kinship ties to maintain a sense of collective solidarity in a growing population.[31]

Furthermore, the anthropologists' interpretation of the basis of political authority reflected their liberal sentiments. Primitive government was organized to serve popular needs. Its functions were control of natural resources in the interests of collective welfare, realization of collective sentiments, and protection against aggression from without. Selection for political leadership was at first entirely meritocratic. The earliest leaders were popularly selected because they were distinguished by superior skill, wisdom, or strength; and they retained their offices only so long as they remained responsive to popular desires and capable of effective leadership in times of crisis. Those who achieved office by virtue of their personal qualities would make their offices hereditary, but hereditary rulers who proved incompetent in times either of war or peace would be deposed.

When evolutionists described states that were growing in size and power, they observed constitutional changes that seemed to indicate that the natural course of progress led to loss of popular control over government. Yet, they found that these changes were not so significant as they might appear. Certainly, with evolution, elaborate government structures were created to control many spheres of social life, and hereditary succession to office became routinized. But hereditary kings actually became virtually powerless as the state grew. They were constrained by the popular will of the past, embodied in social institutions, and obliged to obey the popular will of the present – not the least because they were creatures of their agents, who controlled the information kings received and were responsible for implementation of instructions. Even in states with pronounced divisions among social classes, kings were not free to act arbitrarily, although they might be directly responsible to the elite alone. The king whose authority seemed supreme – the "divine king," a supernatural figure among men – was in fact the archetypal constitutional monarch: his people irrationally believed that his superior moral and physical condition ensured that the polity's citizens would behave properly and enjoy material prosperity, but the king would be slain when his physical condition weakened;

---

[31] For some discussion of these issues, see A. W. Howitt, "Further Notes on the Australian Class Systems," *Journal of the Anthropological Institute* 18 (1888): 31–70; Andrew Lang, "Edward Burnett Tylor," in R. R. Marett, W. H. R. Rivers, and N. W. Thomas, eds., *Essays Presented to Edward Burnett Tylor* (Oxford, 1907), 5; Tylor, "On a Method of Investigating the Development of Institutions Applied to Laws of Marriage and Descent (see chap. 3, n. 25), 267; E. A. Westermarck, *The History of Human Marriage* (London, 1894 [orig. 1891]), 544.

and because the king could be only a figurehead, his kingdom could be managed by those competent to do so. In sum, the evolution of the state was marked by the progressive growth of institutions for the articulation of the popular will. The democracy of small primitive societies was irreconcilable with progress because it was unsuited either to the mobilization of great military efforts or to the development of the institutions characteristic of high civilization. But great nations transposed the virtues of small democracies into institutions of representative government.[32]

Evolutionists were prepared to grant that compulsion as well as voluntarism figured in the development of the state. Confronted by a common enemy, peoples only loosely affiliated would unite to wage military resistance, forging ties that would persist in peacetime. Successful military campaigns taught that disciplined collective action could serve the common good, conveying a lesson applicable to daily life. Furthermore, the growth of large polities was not always voluntary – the product either of alliances contracted between peoples or of natural population increase. Unions between peoples were often forcibly effected, the result of the conquest of one people by another. Nevertheless, the social organization of a population engaged in combat and the warriors' behavioral code were not ideally preserved in peacetime, for they were dysfunctional for normal evolutionary progress. They thwarted human beings' natural creativity. As Tylor wrote, "Military government in civil affairs is, in fact, despotism."[33]

Nor were forceful methods appropriate means to effect evolutionary advance. Even when a people were conquered by carriers of a superior culture, they would not abandon their customary practices. Rather, they would assimilate only those elements of imported culture appropriate to the level of evolution they had already attained independently. In evolutionist analysis of culture contact, it was presumed "that each successive band of conquerors has its race, language and institutions essentially more or less modified by contact with the race, language and institutions of those whom it has conquered."[34] In fact, military prowess was apt to be negatively correlated with cultural superiority.[35] When peoples were extremely backward, even the most commendable efforts to force them to accept a higher culture were practically doomed. Only relatively advanced peoples

---

[32] See, for example, J. G. Frazer, *The Golden Bough* (2nd ed., London, 1894), Vol. I, 208–10 and passim; Herbert Spencer, "Political Forms and Forces"; and "Political heads – Chiefs, Kings, Etc.," *Fortnightly Review* 35 (1881): 271–84, 521–33, 650–61; Tylor, *Anthropology* (see chap. 3; n. 16), 492–38.

[33] Tylor, *Anthropology*, 431.

[34] John Rhŷs, "1900 Presidential Address," Section H, *Nature* 62 (1900): 519.

[35] For example, Haddon, *The Wanderings of Peoples* (see chap. 4, n. 19), 52.

were "capable of acquiring and *surviving* a higher degree of civilization."[36] Because the modes of life of the most primitive peoples were cumulative products of unconscious adaptation, their social order was precarious, and could become unbalanced after very limited culture contact. At worst, primitives might suffer degeneration so extreme that they became extinct, as the case of the Tasmanians illustrated.

In sum, a middle-class radical message was embodied in evolutionist anthropology. Because evolutionists were obsessed with the definition of natural hierarchies of individuals within societies and among all of the world's cultures, naive readers of their work have sometimes mistaken evolutionist argument for a defense of class privilege in Britain and a justification for British colonialism. But evolutionist anthropologists insisted that societal hierarchies were maladaptive unless they were open to talented individuals, equated progress with the development of responsible government, and considered compulsion to be an appropriate instrument of social progress only in circumstances peculiar to some early phases of evolution – wholly inappropriate in advanced societies such as their own. Moreover, their analysis indicated that sensible foreign policy should not depend on force, even if such worthy objectives as the civilization of primitives might seem unrealizable with peaceable methods.

To some degree, evolutionists' concern for the welfare of backward peoples was irrelevant to their objections to imperialism. They were anxious about their own souls, and they argued that advanced peoples who reorganized their societies for military purposes were themselves degraded. The peoples of ancient Greece and Rome, for example, suffered cultural decline as they fought wave after wave of barbarians.[37] Colonialists lost moral ground as they conquered and subordinated subject peoples.[38] More important, imperialist ventures could never be civilizing missions: perhaps the conquering people would be effectively obliged to accept the culture of those they apparently dominated, following the pattern defined by many Whig historians of the Norman Conquest; or, if subject peoples were truly backward, their cultures would degenerate as the result of colonial rule. Anthropologists' prediction of the extinction of backward peoples was tinged with regret, and not merely because, good natural historians as they were, they mourned the diminution of the world's curio collection of cultures. Evolutionists were hardly cultural relativists, but

---

[36] E. H. Man, "The Nicobar Islanders," *Journal of the Anthropological Institute* 18 (1888): 365.

[37] J. G. Frazer, *Pausanias's Description of Greece* (London, 1898), xxxiv.

[38] E. B. Tylor, *Primitive Culture*, Vol. I; reprinted as the *Origins of Culture* (New York, 1958 [orig. 1871]), 380.

they appreciated the irony in the historical experiences of especially vulnerable societies: they had persisted in backward states because they had achieved perfect adaptation to once stable environments.

Conquest as a civilizing process

Around the beginning of the twentieth century, however, the climate of political opinion in British anthropology changed. The importance of the diffusionist school around the time of the First World War is indicative of the prevailing climate. Like the evolutionists, the diffusionists celebrated the achievement of high civilization, but, as we have seen, they declared that its social forms were "artificial and unnatural," to quote Elliot Smith.[39] Thus, they portrayed the course of development of civilization in the very fashion evolutionists had declared unnatural – in unpredictable, disjunctive leaps, effected under unusual circumstances by especially gifted individuals or peoples.

To be sure, elements of diffusionist argument had figured in the anthropology of the nineteenth century. Archaeologists, in particular, were wont to explain progressive innovations in any given society as the products of contact with superior migrants.[40] A significant minority of folklorists had accounted for cultural change as the result of migration and diffusion.[41] Physical anthropologists, who assumed that the various races of humankind were virtually stable units, linked physical and behavioral traits just as social theorists did, but discounted the effects of the environment on physical evolution.[42] And social theorists' explanation of the spread of high culture seemed to anticipate diffusionist formulations. In 1896, for

---

[39] G. Elliot Smith, "The Influence of Racial Admixture in Egypt," *Eugenics Review* 7 (1915): 167.

[40] Archaeologists continued to portray culture change in this way, even after other members of the anthropological community rejected diffusionism in the post–World War I period. For a very useful review of the nineteenth-century archaeological literature by a contributor to it, see Arthur Evans, "The Eastern Question in Anthropology," *Nature* 54 (1896): 527–35. On the history of twentieth-century archaeology pursued along these lines, see Grahame Clark, "The Invasion Hypothesis in British Archaeology," *Antiquity* 11 (1966): 172–89.

[41] For a near-contemporary account of the place of independent invention and diffusion in folklorists' explanations, see R. R. Marett, "The Psychology of Culture Contact," Presidential address to the Folk-Lore Society, *Folk-Lore* 28 (1917): 24. For a historian's account, see Richard Dorson, *The British Folklorists* (Chicago, 1968), esp. 258–74, 305–15.

[42] See, for example, W. H. Flower, "Presidential Address," Section H, *Nature* 50 (1884): 38. For a general discussion of this issue, see Stocking, "What's in a Name?" (chap. 2, n. 39), 385–6.

example, E. B. Tylor proposed a methodological rule for anthropologists contemplating cultural similarities all over the globe: They should assume that simple practices had been independently invented by each society in which they were found, and that highly complex arts and instituions had been invented in a single place and diffused from there.[43] But because the diffusionists repudiated the evolutionists' assumption that humankind was inherently creative, they constructed an account of the social dynamics of evolutionary progress altogether different from that of their predecessors.

Few anthropologists accepted the diffusionists' account of the origin of modern civilization in ancient Egypt. But many adopted a general model of historical change like theirs. Significantly, even that erstwhile proponent of nineteenth-century evolutionism, J. G. Frazer, enunciated an essentially diffusionist position in 1908:

> The more we study the outward workings of society and the progress of civilization, the more clearly shall we perceive how both are governed by the influence of thoughts which, springing up at first we know not how or whence in a few superior minds, gradually spread until they have leavened the whole inert lump of a community or of mankind. The origin of such mental variations, with all their far-reaching train of social consequences, is as obscure as the origin of those physical variations on which, if biologists are right, depends the evolution of species, and with it the possibility of progress.[44]

Are we to interpret Frazer literally, to conclude that the impetus to paradigmatic change was nothing more than the weight of scientific evidence? Certainly, one of the strengths of the diffusionists' model was that their explanation of cultural change could be reconciled with biological knowledge about the processes of speciation and individual heredity. But it is tautological to argue that anthropologists' views conformed to scientific opinion, for biologists' notions were at least partial functions of the same historical factors that affected anthropologists. However defensible they might have been in abstract scientific terms, new anthropological arguments were products of an era of heightened nationalism. More specifically, the anthropology of the World War I period was serviceable as a defense of colonialism in a period in which British imperialist enthusiasm was exceptionally strong.

The Lamarckist biology of evolutionist anthropologists had suggested reason to doubt the wisdom of colonial ventures other than concern for the welfare of subject peoples. If their environments had shaped the cul-

---

[43] Tylor, "Introduction" to Friedrich Ratzel, *The History of Mankind* (see chap. 1, n. 8), ix.

[44] J. G. Frazer, *The Scope of Anthropology* (London, 1908), 13.

tures of backward peoples, evolutionists argued, these same environments would have injurious effects on European settlers. Removed to thoroughly uncongenial climes, they would succumb to disease (a realistic prediction until the end of the nineteenth century).[45] If Europeans were able to survive in exotic parts, settlers there would come to resemble the indigenous inhabitants in appearance and behavior. With residence in New England, for example, Britons acquired "the hatchet face and thin scraggy beard of the Red Indian" and, happily, found themselves in an environment conducive to the development of democratic virtues (which the Indians, of course, also possessed).[46] Believing that behavior was a causal component of physical evolution, Europeans who were settled in the environments that had fostered primitive cultures thought that they were guaranteed a measure of protection against racial degeneration if they preserved the habits of civilization they brought with them; but they assumed that their children's development was imperiled.[47]

We can easily judge that anthropologists' politics were not dictated by scientific opinion alone, however, for when evolutionists were confronted with biologists' objections to Lamarckism at the end of the nineteenth century, they found reasons to sustain their beliefs with little or no modification. Some suggested that the influence of the environment had in fact been underestimated; the evident incapacity of some races to evolve naturally did not indicate that their inherent capacities were deficient, but that they were settled in environments thoroughly uncongenial to evolutionary progress.[48] Alternatively, some argued that only certain elements of Lamarckist theory required qualification: perhaps some racial types – such as Europeans – were less stable than others; perhaps only some of the human species' physical characteristics – such as skin and eye color – would change when persons were transplanted from one sort of climate to another; perhaps the various characteristics of different races were relatively stable, but a people's failure to prosper in a given environment (or to prevail over another people for control of that environment) indicated only that it was unsuited to that particular area, not that it occupied an inferior position in some evolutionary hierarchy of fixed races; perhaps the racial characters of a people removed from one location to another would eventually change, but the process of environmental adaptation required more time than had previously been imagined; perhaps some

---

[45] See, for example, George Campbell, "Presidential Address to Section H," *Nature* 34 (1886): 457.

[46] William Ridgeway, "The Application of Zoological Laws to Man," Presidential Address to Section H of the British Association, *Nature* 78 (1908): 526.

[47] See, for example, Lubbock, *Pre-historic Times*, 588–93.

[48] See, for example, Ridgeway, "The Application of Zoological Laws to Man," 525–33.

climatic conditions – such as those of the tropics – had greater impact on physical characteristics than others.[49]

Furthermore, when the weight of anthropological opinion shifted during the first decade of the twentieth century, it bore only the partial imprint of new biological orthodoxy. When, for example, Arthur Keith told the Royal Anthropological Institute in his 1916 Presidential Address that the "tribe was nature's evolutionary unit," he seemed to be endorsing the Darwinian view that evolutionary forces operated on populations rather than on individuals as such; but Keith went on to argue that the tribe as an evolutionary unit was impervious even to conquest, thus taking a position distinct from the Darwinian one that the species units of evolution continually changed as the biological boundaries of interbreeding shifted – as they were bound to do when peoples were brought into contact with one another through conquest or other means.[50] And Keith was not alone in imputing extraordinary stability to populations. Reasoning that cultural behavior was a function of biological character, and that biological traits were transmitted unmodified from generation to generation, anthropologists of this era assumed that both cultural stability and change could be explained in racial terms. In the absence of unwonted conditions, a group's culture would not change. Therefore, cultural innovation was typically the result of diffusion. As the president of Section H in 1910, William Crooke argued evolution was almost invariably effected through the "clash and contact of peoples."[51]

[49] To those who would endorse a qualified Lamarckism, Franz Boas's investigations of the changing head forms of European immigrants to the United States provided particularly welcome evidence, not the least because head form had been thought among the most stable of human physical characteristics. See A. C. Haddon, "Environment Versus Heredity," *Nature* 85 (1910): 11–12. The considerable attention Boas's study attracted in Britain is notable, and those who espoused new hereditarian doctrine viewed it with considerable skepticism. See, for example, G. Elliot Smith, *The Ancient Egyptians* (chap. 4, n. 9), 16–17. For other illustrations of efforts to counter new hereditarian doctrine with modified Lamarckist theory, see John Beddoe, "Observations on the Natural Colour of the Skin in Certain Oriental Races," *Journal of the Anthropological Institute* 18 (1888–9): 257–25; Campbell, Presidential Address, 454–7; C. R. Conder, "The Present Condition of the Native Tribes of Bechuanaland," *Journal of the Anthropological Institute* 16 (1887): 76–92; W. H. Flower, "Presidential Address: On the Classification of the Varieties of the Human Species," *Journal of the Anthropological Institute* 14 (1884–5): 378–96; Sir William Ridgeway, "The Influence of the Environment on Man," *Journal of the Royal Anthropological Institute* 40 (1910): 10–22; Sir William Turner, "Some Distinctive Characters of Human Structure," 1897 Presidential Address, Section H, *Nature* 56 (1897): 425–35; Sir William Turner, "1889 Presidential Address," Section H, *Nature* 40 (1889): 526–33.

[50] Arthur Keith, "On Certain Factors Concerned in the Evolution of Human Races," Presidential Address, *Journal of the Royal Anthropological Institute* 46 (1916): 32.

[51] William Crooke, "The Scientific Aspects of Folklore," *Folk-Lore* 23 (1912): 31.

The study of migrations became a crucial problem for anthropological inquiry, no less important to those who doubted the new formulation of the relationship between biological nature and cultural behavior than to those who accepted it.[52]

The diffusionist scheme was characteristic of the anthropology of this era because it explained social change as a function of the contact of races. For example, although Elliot Smith was to repent of his earlier position after World War I, in his original formulation behavioral traits were associated with racial groups: thus, the Archaic Civilization would not have spread if the Armenoids had not been a restless people; the Archaic Civilization would not have provided the basis for European culture if the Nordic race had not been inherently capable of elaborating it.[53] To Rivers, on the other hand, it was social structure that determined which innate human characteristics would be expressed (an argument Elliot Smith evidently also made when it suited him). But Rivers conceived the social structure of a people to be extraordinarily persistent, capable of withstanding considerable changes in material culture, so that his judgment of the probable stability of the character of a people was in practical terms no different from that of Elliot Smith.[54]

Moreover, the diffusionists' scheme accounted for data that violated evolutionist assumptions. Peoples of strikingly different appearance and behavior could be found in virtually identical environments, even residing side by side. Furthermore, cultural similarities could be observed among peoples separated by great distances – among peoples whose social systems could not be categorized in the evolutionists' taxonomy, since they gained livings from their lands by practices that ranged from hunting to migrant pastoralism to settled agriculture. These findings seemed to indicate that various forms of culture were highly stable and specific to distinct racial groups who, even if they migrated to areas quite different from their original habitats, would remain recognizably themselves.[55] Therefore, it

---

[52] See J. L. Myres, "The Influence of Anthropology on the Course of Political Science," Presidential Address to Section H, *Nature* 81 (1909): 379–84.

[53] Elliot Smith, *Ancient Egyptians*, esp. 154–7, 182; for his later views, see, for example, Sir Grafton Elliot Smith, "The Place of Thomas Henry Huxley in Anthropology," The Huxley Memorial Lecture for 1935, *Journal of the Royal Anthropological Institute* 65 (1935): 202.

[54] Rivers, "The Ethnological Analysis of Culture" (see chap. 4, n. 35).

[55] Ibid. See also A. C. Haddon, *The Decorative Art of British New Guinea* (Dublin, 1894), 266–7; W. H. R. Rivers, "An Address on the Aims of Ethnology," in *Psychology and Politics and Other Essays* (London, 1923 [essay orig. 1919]), 112–3; Charles Gabriel Seligman, "Physical Anthropology and Ethnology of British New Guinea," The Hunterian Lectures of the Royal College of Surgeons, *The Lancet* 1906 (1): 422, 506–7.

seemed reasonable to assume that whatever cultural similarities obtained among peoples were products of migration and diffusion, and that peoples would accept significant changes in their accustomed habits only if forcibly obliged to do so.[56]

Because anthropologists of diverse persuasions accepted the proposition that each race had an inherent behavioral character, which would be manifested in recognizably identical form no matter where in the world the race was found, they assented to general propositions about the relationship between race and culture: cultural diversity within an area was prima facie evidence that its inhabitants were a racially diverse collection of migrant settlers; particular environments were not particularly suitable for particular races, but the global pattern of distribution of races reflected the inherent migratory propensities of different stocks.[57] And, unlike their predecessors, anthropologists now argued that whenever two peoples came into contact, the superior group would inevitably establish dominance over the inferior, forcing the latter to adopt a more civilized mode of behavior.

In the racist construction given to diffusionist argument by many members of the anthropological community, available evidence indicated that inferior peoples' habits could never be thoroughly eradicated. Therefore, the success of forcible civilization was limited by a population's inherent potential, and a people forcibly cvilized would remain so only so long as it remained subordinate. This pattern obtained everywhere – in the ancient societies of Greece, Rome, and Egypt; in prehistoric Europe; and among contemporary primitives.[58] When Rivers formulated his generalizations about the results of culture contact, he claimed that they described behavior based

---

[56] For example, Elliot Smith, *Ancient Egyptians*, 180; Haddon, "Migrations of Cultures in British New Guinea" (chap. 5, n. 111).

[57] See, for examples: John Beddoe, "Colour and Race," *Journal of the Anthropological Institute* 35 (1905): 219–50; D. J. Cunningham, "Right-Handedness and Left-Brainedness," *Journal of the Anthropological Institute* 32 (1902): 273–96; F. G. Parsons, "Anthropological Observations on German Prisoners of War," *Journal of the Royal Anthropological Institute* 49 (1919): 20–35; Haddon, "Migrations of Cultures in British New Guinea" (chap. 5, n. 111); C. G. Seligman, "Anthropology and Psychology: A Study of Some Points of Contact" (chap. 4, n. 34).

[58] See, for examples: Elliot Smith, "The Influence of Racial Admixture in Egypt," 163–83; H. H. Johnston, "A Survey of the Ethnography of Africa," *Journal of the Royal Anthropological Institute* 43 (1913): 375–421; Arthur Keith, "On Certain Factors Concerned in the Evolution of Human Races," 33; F. W. H. Migeod, "The Racial Elements Concerned in the First Siege of Troy," *Man* 17 (1917): 45–6; Edouard Naville, "The Origin of Egyptian Civilisation," *Journal of the Royal Anthropological Insitute* 37 (1907): 201–14; Harold Peake, "The Racial Elements Concerned in the First Siege of Troy," *Man* 17 (1917): 80; W. H. R. Rivers, "Report on Anthropological Research Outside America," in A. Rivers, E. Jenks, and S. G. Morley, *Reports upon the Present Condition and Future Needs of the Science of Anthropology* (Washington, D.C., 1913), 17; C. G. Seligman and Brenda Z. Seligman, "Note on the

on wholly subjective perceptions of cultural superiority, not on absolute differences between the cultures of peoples in contact. Nevertheless, his behavioral laws could be and were interpreted as manifestations of a natural racial hierarchy: the higher the culture of the host population, the less likely this population was to be influenced by contact with other peoples; and the greater the superiority of migrant to indigenous culture, the smaller the number of migrants that would suffice to impress the host population.[59]

Like their fellow countrymen, anthropologists of the early twentieth century were extremely anxious about the capacity of the British population to withstand competition against the other races of the world.[60] The non-sectarian diffusionism of many members of the anthropological community was a product of their nationalist concerns. And their views were clearly compatible with imperialist enthusiasm. First, they indicated that the British had no reason to fear that they would themselves suffer degeneration when they undertook civilizing missions. Such a fear had been institutionalized in the regulations of tropical colonies: for example, until 1916 the British employees of the Gold Coast had been forbidden to have their children reside there, but afterwards the regime recognized that officials' children could mature into proper Europeans in a tropical environment.[61] Second, they suggested that backward peoples could not advance unless they were forced to do so. This was a proposition particularly attractive to those who wished to settle in climates that seemed ideal for Europeans, such as that of Southern Africa. The indigenous inhabitants of this region were pro-nounced congenitally incapable of achieving any sort of high culture on their own, and evidence that they were capable of great accomplishments, such as the stone ruins that attested to the existence of a powerful city-state in Zimbabwe (once Southern Rhodesia) during the early modern period, was dismissed as the leavings of a racially superior people long departed from the area.[62]

History and Present Condition of the Beni Amer (Southern Beja)," *Sudan Notes and Records* 9 (1930): 83–97; Alice Werner, "The Akikuyu." *Journal of the African Society* 10 (1911): 447–58.

[59] W. H. R. Rivers, "The Contact of Peoples," in Quiggin, ed., *Essays and Studies Presented to William Ridgeway* (chap. 4, n. 72), 475–7. The documentation Rivers provided for his argument rather belied his ostensive cultural relativism, however, since the societies that he identified as unaffected by contact with other peoples were the high cultures of India and China, whereas he described the primitive peoples of America, Africa, and Oceania as extremely vulnerable to outside influence.

[60] See, for example, Donald MacKenzie, *Statistics in Britain* (chap, 3, n. 2); esp. 51–72.

[61] See my *Imperial Bureaucrat* (chap. 2, n. 14), 124.

[62] See my "Contested Monuments: The Politics of Archaeology in Southern Africa," in Stocking, ed., *Colonial Situations* (chap. 5, n. 36).

Significantly, even such persons of liberal temper as Haddon and Rivers represented cultural progress as the consequence of interracial contact and conquest. The so-called Aryan conquest of India, said Haddon, exemplified the process of cultural change; because the Aryans were superior in "moral and intellectual" terms, they were able to impress superior habits on the aboriginal population.[63] To be sure, liberals' justification of colonialism suggested that subject peoples practically assented to subordinate status – although they did not necessarily do so consciously. Rivers evidently believed that the psychological dynamics of culture contact favored voluntary submission to peoples of superior culture. And Haddon observed that peoples became vulnerable to conquest because they had somehow degenerated prior to contact, as, for example, the ancient Romans had before they were overcome by barbarians.[64] This was the argument that the British had used to justify their rule over peoples whom they acknowledged as the creators of high culture, such as the peoples of India.[65]

If the bearers of superior culture were racially distinct, it followed that all over the world class distinctions coincided with racial divisions within populations, and were legacies of migrations and/or military pacifications.[66] Indeed, the social structure deriving from the relationship between conquerors and conquered peoples was the organization basic to every Indo-European society.[67] Thus, working on the assumption that each successive band of migrants could only partially obliterate the life-styles of the people or peoples they conquered, anthropologists could translate the class structure of contemporary Britain into racial terms and, by doing so, also account for the apparent rigidity of the British class system, which was a part of their generation's social experience.

The triumphant Normans, ancestors of the dominant class, had sustained their culture's integrity; their original way of life could be recognized in the upper class's wine-drinking habits, kinship structure, and Catholic religion (superficially disguised as Anglicanism). The Anglo-Saxons conquered by the Normans became socially subordinate; they modified their kinship structure to fit the form imported by the Normans, but they retained

---

[63] Haddon, *The Wanderings of Peoples*, 27.
[64] Ibid., 43.
[65] See Cohn, "Representing Authority in Victorian India" (chap. 3, n. 42), 166.
[66] William Crooke, "Presidential Address," Section H, *Nature* 89 (1910): 418; F. W. Migeod, "Some Observations on the Physical Characters of the Mende Nation," *Journal of the Royal Anthropological Institute* 49 (1919): 265–70; L. Torday and T. A. Joyce, "Notes on the Ethnography of the Ba-Yaka," *Journal of the Royal Anthropological Institute* 36 (1906): 39–59; Perry, *The Children of the Sun* (chap. 4, n. 9), 326, 489; Rivers, *The History of Melanesian Society* (chap. 4, n. 8), Vol. II, 556–64.
[67] G. L. Gomme, "Sociology, The Basis of Inquiry into Primitive Culture," *The Sociological Review* 2 (1909): 323.

kinship nomenclature that testified to Anglo-Saxon modes of reckoning family relationships, and also retained their preference for beer over wine. Of the Celtic culture obliterated by the Anglo-Saxons, few traces remained, save the whiskey-drinking habits of some of the lower classes.[68] Moreover, different racial types predominated in different British occupational groups. The typical artisan came of long-headed stock, whereas figures of considerable accomplishment – from William Shakespeare to Charles Darwin – had round heads, as did most civil servants, squires, and professional men.[69]

Like nineteenth-century evolutionists, then, early twentieth-century anthropologists constructed formulae that comprehended the histories of all varieties of humankind, but they were very different formulae: peoples had usually made progress toward a more civilized mode of existence when they had been forced to do so by superior peoples; conquest was the basis of the creation of the state, which was the social organizational form essential to the achievement of high civilization; and the class system of a polity represented a natural hierarchy, for each of its strata had a distinct racial character, and each of its races had inherent endowments that enabled it to perform certain of the tasks society required for the good of the whole. With little difficulty, these generalizations can be translated into the conservative British folk model of the state. Indeed, some anthropologists – among them such figures as Frazer and Rivers – explicitly referred to the Norman Conquest and its aftermath to illustrate the phenomena of state formation and the creation of a social hierarchy.[70]

The glorification of innocence

The political orientation of British anthropology changed after World War I. Emblematic of the shift in anthropological opinion was the functionalist scheme variously articulated by Bronislaw Malinowski, A. R. Radcliffe-Brown, and their associates. In technical terms, functionalism constituted a dramatic departure from earlier styles of anthropological practice, but the political message conveyed in functionalist accounts was also present in postwar evolutionist and diffusionist works. That is, the majority of anthropologists no longer presumed that conquering peoples were culturally

---

[68] W. H. R. Rivers, *History and Ethnology* (London, 1922), 17–24.

[69] Arthur Keith, "The Bronze Age Invaders of Britain," *Journal of the Royal Anthropological Institute* 45 (1915): 15; Arthur Keith, "Address to the Royal Institution," 20, February, 1914, reported in *Nature* 93 (1914): 66.

[70] For a summary of the use of the Norman analogy in this period, see Lord Raglan, "The Class Society," *Journal of the Royal Anthropological Institute* 86 (1956): 2–3.

superior, that culture must be some function of race, that the state was the highest and best form of political organization, and that the current character of Western civilization represented an evolutionary yardstick by which to measure the developmental level of all other cultures. Most important, they no longer assumed that the most technologically advanced and politically organized societies would adhere to the highest moral standards. Hence, postwar anthropology became a vehicle for liberal criticism of Western society in general and colonialism in particular.

Postwar anthropologists of every theoretical persuasion took as proven the causal relationship explicated in both evolutionist and diffusionist analysis: the development of a strong state and an elaborated status hierarchy required technological sophistication and material wealth.[71] But after the war, anthropologists stressed the negative features of high civilization. Elliot Smith, for example, had never described the development of civilization as a natural process, but after the war he mourned the "Golden Age" before the development of settled agriculture. Then "Natural Man" lived in monogamous families, enjoying "idyllic conditions of happiness and contentment" and "a higher type of morality and social probity." Afterwards, states were based on social inequality, which led to "hardship and injustice," and conflicts between states had "been responsible for an infinity of suffering."[72] And the intellectual eccentric A. M. Hocart, loosely identified with the diffusionists, said of ostensibly undeveloped peoples: "True it is that such societies cannot form big nations, maintain disciplined armies, lay networks of roads and railways, or suffer economic crises on a colossal scale; but they can exist, and quite successfully too, if success consists in surviving with happiness." [73]

Anthropologists who remained committed to the evolutionist standpoint, as well as those who embraced the new functionalist one, uttered much the same litany. R. R. Marett, who anachronistically practiced nineteenth-century armchair anthropology in the first third of the twentieth century, argued that many primitive peoples were so morally exemplary that the anthropologist was obliged to wonder "whether it is possible to be both

---

[71] This was one of the findings to emerge clearly from a quantitative analysis of available ethnographic data which, if it relied on some data that might be judged questionable, nevertheless exhaustively surveyed anthropological opinion; see Hobhouse, Wheeler, and Ginsburg, *The Material Culture and Social Institutions of the Simpler Peoples* (chap. 1, n. 33), esp. 48–59.

[72] Elliot Smith, *Human Nature* (London, 1927), 13, 22, 35, and passim. Throughout this book, Smith cites Perry as his ally in argument. And see also Smith's *Human History* (London, 1930), xviii, 256; and his "The Study of Man," *Nature* 112 (1923): 440–4.

[73] A. M. Hocart, *Kings and Councillors* (Chicago, 1970 [orig. 1936]), 128; see also his "Early Fijians," *Journal of the Royal Anthropological Institute* 49 (1919): 42–51.

civilized and good."[74] The functionalist Meyer Fortes, accounting for the harmonious social relationships of the Tallensi, observed that their society was distinguished by "the almost complete absence of economic differentiation, by occupation or by ownership of resources, and, in particular, the absence of both material or technological possibilities for capital accumulation or for technological advance."[75]

If Western civilization had defects primitive cultures lacked, did it have some compensatory virtues? Denial of the special character of Western society was basic to functionalist anthropology, which was premised on the assumption that all societies were essentially alike, that all were organized to fulfill the "necessary conditions of existence"; the values and habitual practices of societies varied considerably, but each society's institutions in the aggregate effected an orderly social environment in which it was possible to satisfy humankind's fundamental biological needs to survive and reproduce.[76] When functionalists based their theory on "the principle of mental uniformity of all races and varieties of man," they relied on a model of human nature much like that denoted by the evolutionist axiom of the psychic unity of humankind, presuming that all varieties of the species were inherently creative and capable of making appropriate adaptations to their circumstances; and functionalists transposed the individual's needs and drives onto societies, which they analogized to organisms.[77]

By the logic of functionalist reasoning, then, the material trappings of civilization that had seemed so significant to prewar anthropologists were superficial, and progress was an illusion. By treating every society as an organism, a harmonious complex of integrated and mutually reinforcing institutions, the functionalists rendered nonsensical the questions evolutionists had asked about the direction of social change. Functionalists did not expect that environmental factors could imperil the survival of a people, for as an "automatic result" of their unconscious drives they would develop both a coordinated social system and adequate adaptation to the material constraints of their environment.[78] Just as evolutionists had done, functionalists anticipated that culture contact would not necessarily lead to social change; diffused practices would be so thoroughly modified to suit

[74] R. R. Marett, *Head, Heart and Hands in Human Evolution* (New York, 1935), 21; see also his "Presidential Address: The Psychology of Culture Contact," *Folk-Lore* 28 (1917): 19.

[75] Meyer Fortes, *The Dynamics of Clanship Among the Tallensi* (London, 1945), x.

[76] A. R. Radcliffe-Brown, "On the Concept of Function in Social Science," reprinted in *Structure and Function in Primitive Society* (New York, 1952 [essay orig. 1935]), 178.

[77] Malinowski, "New and Old in Anthropology" (see chap, 4, n. 18), 299.

[78] Malinowski, *Argonauts* (see chap. 4, n. 2), 11.

indigenous culture that they would be virtually "reinvented."[79] Unlike evolutionists, however, functionalists did not predict that societies' internal dynamics were likely to generate qualitative social changes. By definition, innovations represented functional equivalents of previous practices, and did not alter social character in any fundamental way.

In certain respects, functionalism was more like diffusionism than evolutionism, for functionalists represented the natural condition of society as static, not dynamic. They also characterized the stable social order in organicist terms. The ideal-typical functionalist man was not an individualist banding together with his fellows to pursue common purposes, but was the creature of his social system, with a personality structure shaped by his culture.[80] Nevertheless, the functionalists' model of organic social integration was very different from the diffusionist one. Individuals' various roles in service of the social order were defined primarily by age and sex. Unequal measures of power and status were allocated to occupants of these roles, but as individuals aged they might rise in the social hierarchy. By contrast, the diffusionist model of social stratification presumed that individuals suffered lifelong inequities – or enjoyed lifelong privileges – by virtue of their membership in social classes. Functionalist man was motivated by sentiments of group solidarity. But, at least in his Malinowskian guise, he had some of the individualism of evolutionist man, for his calculations included his own needs, as well as those of his society; he manipulated social rules to gain personal advantage, so that his conformity to collective norms was "partial, conditional, and subject to evasions."[81]

Functionalists' representation of the quality of life in the ideal society was no different from their predecessors'. To evolutionists, progress meant increasingly harmonious social relationships, as individuals grew ever more altruistic in nature and voluntarily cooperated with their fellows to serve the interests of society as a whole. Diffusionists such as Rivers also maintained that the ideal society was one in which there was harmony between individuals' desires and social ideals.[82] When functionalists such as Rivers's student Radcliffe-Brown spoke of progress, they did not point to advances in material culture, as evolutionists and diffusionists had done; neverthe-

---

[79] Malinowski, "The Life of Culture," in Smith et al., *The Diffusion Controversy* (see chap. 1, n. 12), 37–41.
[80] See, for examples, Malinowski, *Argonauts* (see chap. 4, n. 2), 23.
[81] Malinowski, *Crime and Custom in Savage Society* (chap. 2, n. 81), 15; and see also *Argonauts*, esp. 513–16.
[82] W. H. R. Rivers, "Inaugural Address" to the Medical Section of the British Psychological Society (chap. 4, n. 1), 891.

less, functionalists looked for the same behavioral result – higher levels of social integration.[83]

A disregard for material goods was the distinguishing mark of postwar anthropologists, not merely the functionalists. They assumed that the best approximations of their social ideal were to be found in simple societies, to which functionalists restricted their scholarly attentions. Functionalists analyzed such societies in organicist terms because they saw little (if any) conflict between primitive man and his culture, a position they reached by defining individual psychology as a derivative of social structure. In their work, then, simple societies are described in terms that evoke the lost Anglo-Saxon village community beloved of centuries of British radicals.

Certainly, there were anthropologists whose work contravened prevailing trends. The most important of these was C. G. Seligman, who absorbed anthropological innovations at a conspicuously slow rate, and came to an essentially diffusionist position only after the war. (In his 1915 Presidential Address to Section H of the British Association, he propounded a model of social change that blended evolutionist and diffusionist elements, describing an initial diffusion of a culture complex over a broad area, which culture was subsequently elaborated in parallel fashion by diverse peoples whose continued resemblance to one another thus depended on independent invention.)[84] Even in the 1930s, Seligman continued to equate race with culture, and military success with cultural superiority. In his "Hamitic hypothesis" he elaborated a point Haddon had made in 1911, and explained evolution in Africa in diffusionist terms:

> The history of Africa South of the Sahara is no more than the story of the permeation through the ages, in different degrees and at various times, of the Negro and Bushman aborigines by Hamitic blood and culture. The Hamites were, in fact, the great civilising force of black Africa...[85]

In the late 1930s, Malinowski's student Margaret Read adopted a similar approach in her analysis of the Ngoni: their superior moral qualities had been tested and shaped through their conquest of inferior peoples; they became the hereditary rulers of the state they formed through combat.[86]

---

[83] A. R. Radcliffe-Brown, "The Social Organisation of Australian Tribes," *Oceania* 1 (1913): esp. 411–52.

[84] C. G. Seligman, "Presidential Address," Section H, *Reports of the British Association for the Advancement of Science* 85 (1915): 651–65.

[85] C. G. Seligman, *Races of Africa* (London, 1939 [orig. 1930]), 18; and see his *Pagan Tribes of the Nilotic Sudan* (London, 1932), 4.

[86] Margaret Read, "Tradition and Prestige Among the Ngoni," *Africa* 9 (1936): 453–83; "The Moral Code of the Ngoni and Their Former Military State,"*Africa* 11 (1938): 1–24; "Native Standards of Living and African Culture Change," Suppl. to *Africa* 11 (1938).

Significantly, though, Read became an academic but made her career as a professor of education. By the time of World War II, anthropologists had rejected the argument that the origin of the state lay in the conquest of one ethnic group by another, the conventional wisdom of the era of World War I.[87] Indeed, for a time British anthropologists did not entertain speculations about the origin of the state, perhaps out of reluctance to conclude that compulsion was necessary to political organization.

Anthropologists of the 1920s and 1930s turned for preference to the study of simple, "acephalous" (i.e., stateless) societies. A number of factors conspired to direct anthropologists' attention to such societies. They were the ideal subjects for a group then anxious to distinguish itself from its amateur predecessors, for trained expertise was necessary to discern the routinized patterns of behavior that sustained their social order. Acephalous societies constituted a new research topic; they had not been investigated by previous anthropologists because they were likely to be found in the possibly perilous areas remote from colonial authority – both because political consolidation was common among indigenous peoples who were resisting colonial conquest and because colonial officials encouraged state formation in thoroughly pacified areas. Finally, the investigation of stateless societies represented new employment opportunities for anthropologists. Colonial officials unable to determine how to manage the indigenous authority structure of such peoples as the remote, barely pacified Nuer of the Sudan were prepared to finance research by academic anthropologists such as Evans-Pritchard. In sum, in investigating stateless societies anthropologists served several of their professional interests. Nevertheless, the anthropologists' selection of research problems also represented normative judgment, for it entailed recognition of sources of social stability and personal satisfaction ignored by previous generations of anthropologists. And anthropologists' judgments were cast in conventional form; acephalous polities were portrayed as societies that fit the mold of the folk model of Anglo-Saxon democracy.

Fortes and Evans-Pritchard's *African Political Systems*, published in 1940, summarized the approach of this era in anthropology. It is generally agreed that this book heralded and inspired a generation of anthropologists.[88] But

---

[87] See, for example, S. F. Nadel, "The Kede," in Meyer Fortes and E. E. Evans-Pritchard, eds., *African Political Systems* (London, 1940), 193.

[88] See John Middleton and David Tait, "Introduction," to J. Middleton and David Tait, *Tribes Without Rulers* (London, 1958), 1–3. More recent appraisals of *African Political Systems* have acknowledged its influence in a rather more critical spirit. See Talal Asad, *The Kababish Arabs* (New York, 1970), 2; Louis Dumont, "Preface to the French Edition of Evans-Pritchard's *The Nuer*," in J. H. M. Beattie and R. G. Lienhardt, eds., *Studies in Social Anthropology* (Oxford, 1975), 328–44; Lucy Mair, "How Far Have We

it also constituted the culmination of a previous trend. Post–World War I anthropologists typically portrayed the simplest societies as the realization of a cultural ideal. In economically undeveloped societies, only minimal differences of power and status existed, and in them social order was maintained through informal cooperation and consensus. In simple societies such as that of the Andaman Islands as described by Radcliffe-Brown, community leaders were selected on the basis of talent, not inherited status.[89] Indeed, functionalists postulated that political authority affected only a limited sphere of social life.[90]

Hence, domination based on force or inherited status could not be conceptualized or described in functionalist terms.[91] By definition, persistent relationships between individuals and groups were inherently egalitarian, for they rested on cooperation and reciprocal obligations. Institutionalized relationships between different groups within a society might appear to rest on mutual antagonism, but close inspection would reveal that these relationships effected mutual interdependence.[92] Even those political structures resulting from invasion and subsequent domination of one group by another did not necessarily breach the norm of consensual government, for different peoples could be integrated as virtual equals in the same social system, and a government framework created by a conquering people as an instrument of subordination could become irrelevant in these terms.[93] Such a denial of the importance of force evokes the Whig interpretation of the Norman Conquest.

Anthropologists could not deny the existence of centralized states, or of aristocracies, but they emphasized the democratic features of traditional centralized polities. Their observations were consistent with their assumptions about the necessary relationship between peoples and their environments: a surviving culture was by definition one that tolerated, if not embraced, meritocratic standards, because these standards were an adaptive trait that permitted a people to reach accommodation with their environment. Even in a society pervaded by consciousness of class distinctions,

Got in the Study of Politics?" in Meyer Fortes and Sheila Patterson, eds., *Studies in African Social Anthropology* (London, 1975), 8–9, 14–5; Joan Vincent, *Anthropology and Politics* (Tucson, Ariz., 1990), 227, 255–60.

[89] A. R. Radcliffe-Brown, *The Andaman Islanders* (Cambridge, 1922), 45.

[90] A. R. Radcliffe-Brown, "Preface" to *African Political Systems*, viii–xix.

[91] This is a frequent criticism of functionalist analysis. For one example, see Edmund Leach, "Models of Man," in William Robson, ed., *Man and the Social Sciences* (London, 1972), 152.

[92] Raymond Firth, *We the Tikopia* (Boston 1963 [orig., 1936]), 57; Fortes, *The Dynamics of Clanship*, 182–3; Malinowski, *Crime and Custom*, 25.

[93] E. E. Evans-Pritchard, *The Nuer* (Oxford, 1940), 125; Fortes, *The Dynamics of Clanship*, 6.

dominated by a hereditary aristocracy, the ruling class was effectively required to grant some measure of authority to persons of talent and achievement.[94] Even in centralized tribal societies, leadership was evaluated by performance standards; however explicitly they were articulated, contractual obligations governed the relationship of a ruler to his subjects, and indigenous tribal constitutions incorporated checks on chiefly power. A ruler who failed to fulfill his obligations would certainly cease to compel popular obedience, and might well be deposed. Nevertheless, the constitutional ideal that functionalists implicitly endorsed was most fully realized in a society with minimal distinctions of power and without centralized political leadership.

A case in point: the Nuer

The degree to which this normative political theory was manifested in anthropological analysis can be best documented by the diverse interpretations of a single people who have been repeatedly studied. No people have received more scholarly attention than the Nuer. Indeed the debate about the Nuer continues (although recent arguments are irrelevant to the issues considered here, because they are framed rather differently). The classic work on the Nuer is, of course, that done by E. E. Evans-Pritchard. Writing in 1954, Evans-Pritchard suggested that the sustained interest in the Nuer was a "tribute to the Nuer themselves. Twenty years ago they were not so highly regarded, but little by little we have learnt...that they are a people whose values are worth handing down to posterity."[95] Thus, his landmark study, *The Nuer*, published in 1940, may legitimately be interpreted as a brief for the Nuer way of life. An appreciation of Evans-Pritchard's differences with his fellow students of the Nuer requires review of the salient features of his exposition of their political system.

The Nuer live in a "segmentary society," composed of equivalent, autonomous units, which are not joined in a centralized hierarchy but act together in situation-specific alliances against common enemies. The largest stable unit, which Evans-Pritchard rather confusingly calls the "tribe," does not include all people who consider themselves Nuer and follow the practices of Nuer pastoral culture, but is the largest group of distinct communities that "affirm their obligation to combine in warfare

---

[94] Evans-Pritchard, *Witchcraft, Oracles and Magic Among the Azande* (chap. 4, n. 27), 203, 343.
[95] E. E. Evans-Pritchard, "Forward" to P. P. Howell, *A Manual of Nuer Law* (London, 1954), v–vi.

against others and acknowledge the rights of their members to compensate for injury." The critical feature of Nuer political organization is its relative character. Loyalties are determined in the mode that is common to all Nuer culture; "a political group . . . is a group only in relation to other groups. . . . The political system is an equilibrium between opposed tendencies towards fission and fusion, between the tendency of all groups to segment, and the tendency of all groups to combine with segments of the same order." Conflict is, paradoxically, a basis of social integration. "The function of the feud" is "to maintain the structural equilibrium between opposed tribal segments which are, nevertheless, politically fused in relation to larger units"; for the "feud has little significance unless there are social relations of some kind which can be broken off and resumed, and, at the same time, these relations necessitate eventual settlement if there is not to be complete cleavage."[96]

The Nuer are fiercely democratic. What status distinctions they make are slight. Each tribe has a dominant clan, and each includes captured Dinka, people from the ethnic group habitually preyed upon by the Nuer, who constitute at least half of the total population. Nevertheless, the Dinka are incorporated as equals in Nuer society; the relations between men and women, young and old, are as egalitarian as those found anywhere; and barely significant distinctions separate the social classes.

> No man recognizes a superior. Wealth makes no difference. A man with many cattle is envied, but not treated differently from a man with few cattle. Birth makes no difference. A man may not be a member of the dominant clan of his tribe, he may even be of Dinka descent, but were another to allude to the fact he would run a grave risk of being clubbed.[97]

Hence, the Nuer have virtually no tradition of institutionalized leadership, no social roles whose occupants can expect obedience by virtue of the authority inherent in their offices. Figures become leaders when they command respect both because they fulfill the culture's behavioral ideals and because they articulate the popular will. Typically, a powerful local figure is distinguished by the attributes of "lineage, age, seniority in the family, many children, marriage alliances, wealth, in cattle, prowess as a warrior, oratorical skill, and often ritual powers," but "leadership in a local community consists of an influential man deciding to do something and the people of other hamlets following suit at their convenience." As descendents of the original settlers of the area, the dominant clan of a tribe

---

[96] Evans-Pritchard, *The Nuer*, 5, 147–8, 159.
[97] Ibid., 181.

One of the photographs taken for Evans-Pritchard's book *The Nuer* in which
one can see the idealization of non-Western cultures. Evans-Pritchard on the
Nuer: "They strut about like lords of the earth, which, indeed, they consider
themselves to be." *The Nuer* (1940), 182. Reproduced by permission of the
Pitt Rivers Museum, Oxford.

may be recognized as "owners of the land," but they have "prestige rather
than rank and influence rather than power."[98]

The men known as "leopard-skin chiefs" are only "ritual experts,"
being persons from outside the dominant clan whose power to mediate
disputes is restricted to "specific social situations." The Nuer never "treat
a chief with more respect than they treat other people, or speak of them
as persons of much importance," and a chief will be unsuccessful in me-

---

[98] Ibid., 179–80, 215, 173–6, 189.

diating a dispute unless the conflicting parties have already determined to resolve it peacefully and recognized "that the other side has a good case." In the colonial period, prophets arose among the Nuer to lead raids against the Dinka and mobilize resistance to Arab and European aggression. Prophets "personified the structural principle of opposition in its widest expression, the unity and homogeneity of Nuer against foreigners." To a nineteenth-century anthropologist, the prophets would have appeared to be agents of future political consolidation, aborted by colonial rule, for never before had "a single person symbolized . . . the unity of a tribe." But to Evans-Pritchard, the prophets were ritual rather than political figures.[99]

From the nineteenth-century anthropological viewpoint, the Nuer are a lawless people, akin to the Tasmanians. Fighting is their typical mode of conflict resolution. The reparations exacted for homicide depend on the kinship and territorial relationship between the murderer and the victim; and the greater the social distance between the murderer and the victim, the greater is the probability that the victim's kin will be dissatisfied with their compensation and will pursue their grievance aggressively. "There are conventional compensations for damage, adultery, loss of limb, and so forth," but "there is no authority with power to adjudicate on such matters or to enforce a verdict." But Evans-Pritchard insisted that among the Nuer antisocial behavior is punished fairly, according to collectively established and accepted norms. The Nuer system of justice is fair because it operates democratically – because every man is entitled to use force to redress wrongs. Collective pressures prevent abuse of force, for though the "threat of violence is the main sanction for payment of compensation," when a man wishes to act on his threat his "kinsmen will only support him if he is right."[100]

Evans-Pritchard's portrait of the Nuer is different from others in several ways: it minimizes the importance of status distinctions in Nuer society; it eliminates strong leaders from their political life, even as occasional figures; it minimizes those features of their society that reflect their history as a people who have expanded their territory by preying upon others. Certainly, there are common elements in all descriptions of Nuer culture: their democratic values, and also the absence of a centralized, coordinated political system, in which authority inheres in established offices rather than charismatic figures. But other anthropologists have argued that the Nuer have a tradition of strong leadership, particularly evident in times of crisis. And other anthropologists have seen the "leopard-skin chief," a

[99] Ibid., 173–6, 189.
[100] Ibid., 162, 171. For a summary of Evans-Pritchard's work similar to mine, see Vincent, *Anthropology and Politics*, 256–7.

constant character in Nuer society, as having more power than Evans-Pritchard was willing to grant.[101] Indeed, counterevidence to Evans-Pritchard's theses may be recognizable in his own material, although he did not draw out these implications of his findings.[102]

In some part, Evans-Pritchard's interpretations were strategic, designed to counter the views and objectives of the Sudan Political Service, who were attempting to establish an administrative structure for the recently pacified Nuer. Like other members of his professional generation, he was determined to prevent colonial rulers from subverting indigenous institutions to serve their own ends.[103] Like British colonial officials everywhere, those in the Sudan were eager to find in traditional Nuer political institutions an orderly system of leadership which they could employ, and they were disappointed with Evans-Pritchard's findings, however useful they found them.[104] Furthermore, Evans-Pritchard might have provided a mandate for the colonial pacification of the Nuer, had he represented them as another anthropologist has – as a people with an insatiable appetite for conquest whose society is structured to make it a "successful predatory organization in conflicts with other tribes."[105] Even the most vehement critic of imperial rule could not fault the Pax Britannica it brought.

No tactical purpose was served by another distinctive feature of Evans-Pritchard's analysis, however. Why did he insist that everywhere in Nuerland there existed egalitarian relations among social classes, instead of observing systematic variation? That is, why did he not observe that in those areas recently acquired by the Nuer through military conquest there is considerable social distance between aristocrats and commoners and between commoners and incorporated Dinka?[106] Evans-Pritchard had cast his description of the Nuer in the stylized form of the archetypal democratic polity envisioned in the British tradition of political argument. Perceived in the terms of this tradition, Nuer society is the democratic order of natural

[101] P. P. Howell, *A Manual of Nuer Law*, 28–34; Ray Huffman, *Nuer Customs and Folk-Lore* (London, 1931), 1; C. G. Seligman, *Egypt and Negro Africa* (London, 1934), 23–34.

[102] Kathleen Gough, "Nuer Kinship: A Reexamination," in T. O. Beidelman, ed., *The Translation of Culture* (London, 171), 79–112.

[103] Hortense Powdermaker, *Stranger and Friend* (New York, 1966), 43.

[104] Howell, *A Manual of Nuer Law*, 28–9. Not all colonial officers were willfully deluded; see H. C. Jackson's lament that the Nuer "lack chieftains in whom to repose confidence or regard" and are a people among whom "each man is a law unto himself." "The Nuer of the Upper Nile Province," *Sudan Notes and Records* 6 (1923): 61.

[105] Marshall Sahlins. "The Segmentary Lineage: An Organization of Predatory Expansion," *American Anthropologist* [n. s.] 63 (1961): 323, 335, 343.

[106] Gough, "Nuer Kinship," 89–90.

man, akin to that of the ancient Anglo-Saxons. Furthermore, Evans-Pritchard's Nuer are as admirable as Locke's Native Americans.

The conventions of traditional conservative British political argument suit the social pattern in recently acquired areas of Nuerland, for this pattern fits the mold of the archetypal aristocratic polity, incorporating the elements that have been seen as essential features of aristocratic government: one, military pacification; two, inherited, not achieved, characteristics as requisites for political leadership; and three, exaggerated divisions among social classes. To admit of this range of variation in Nuerland, however, is to accept that the same cultural matrix can support antithetical social forms, a position difficult to reconcile with the generalization that Nuer culture is animated by values of egalitarian individualism. Nor does this range of variation in Nuerland make sense in the terms of British folk political theory, for a people accustomed to consensual social relationships and willing to engage in collective action only to repel outside aggressors should not find it natural to become the oppressors of subject peoples.

To put the least attractive face on it, Evans-Pritchard's rendition of the relations between dominant Nuer and subordinate Dinka in the language of mutual consent and benefit constitutes an apology for British colonial power, cast in the standard formula of Whig liberalism. Evans-Pritchard and other anthropologists would not rationalize colonial rule as necessary to the improvement of subject peoples. But by denying that a conquered people could be forcibly compelled to follow an unwonted way of life, they denied the reality of colonial domination. If the consent of the governed was essential to the maintenance of authority, by definition colonized peoples had accepted only those British colonial directives they recognized as legitimate, practicing various forms of subterfuge in order to sustain cultural practices they cherished.[107]

Nevertheless, it seems likely that anthropologists' understanding of political order was in some measure a function of their field experience. Living for long periods among their research subjects, anthropologists came to identify with them. Thus, anthropologists came to appreciate that colonial subjects had many means of evading colonial authority – as, indeed, subordinates in any social system are capable of subverting the directives of their superiors, at least to some degree. And anthropologists imputed to the peoples they had come to admire the values they themselves held dear. Thus, their idealization of stateless societies is better interpreted as an appreciation of the virtues of egalitarian democracy than as an apology for colonial power.

---

[107] See, for example, Lucy Mair, *Native Administration in Central Nyasaland* (London, 1952), 1.

Perhaps most important, the celebration of the virtues of simple societies in *The Nuer* and other works of this period was an exercise in nostalgia. Anthropologists suggested that Western societies can never completely recapture the idyllic innocence of primitive peoples, although by contemplating the merits of exotic cultures Westerners may be inspired to improve their own. The message of interwar anthropology, then, was that progress was an illusion, at least insofar as it was defined in material terms. In this regard, British anthropology was typical of the intellectual culture of its period. And some of the most celebrated works of the interwar years reveal the same general attitudes expressed in anthropology.

Indeed, some of the most obvious illustrations of postwar disenchantment with contemporary culture relied on anthropological material. T. S. Eliot's long poem "The Waste Land," first published in 1922, used pessimistic Frazerian imagery of social disorder and natural decay. In their immensely influential *The Meaning of Meaning*, the first edition of which appeared in 1923, C. K. Ogden and I. A. Richards reached conclusions through philosophical analysis of language that they saw corroborated by the empirical research of Malinowski (whom they enrolled as an author of a supplement to their book). Ogden and Richards exposed the emotional element in apparently rational discourse, suggesting that the nature of human communication itself precluded purely objective judgments of fact.[108] Another significant intellectual manifesto, Herbert Butterfield's *The Whig Interpretation of History*, repeatedly reissued after its first publication in 1931, represented for historians the same ideological shift that the repudiation of evolutionism had signified for anthropologists – a loss of faith in the inevitability of progress. Butterfield debunked the long tradition of portraying British history as the chronicle of centuries of slow but steady, conflict-free progress toward realization of the ideals of justice and liberty.[109]

Conclusions

The disenchantment with progress which intellectuals, and others, felt after World War I was not peculiar to Britain. It was a commonplace of European and American culture. Similarly, the attitudes expressed in earlier British anthropology have analogues – if not exact equivalents – elsewhere. Meritocratic reformers campaigned to increase their social

---

[108] C. K. Ogden and I. A. Richards, *The Meaning of Meaning* (London, 1938 [orig. 1923]), ix–x, 10–19, and passim.
[109] Herbert Butterfield, *The Whig Interpretation of History* (London, 1931).

influence in Europe and the United States during the late nineteenth century, although in the United States, for example, their campaign did not have to be framed as a repudiation of the legitimacy of aristocratic privilege. All of the parties to World War I were consumed by nationalistic fervor, but the extrapolation of this emotion to imperialist enthusiasm in Britain was particularly notable, since Britain was suffering especially intense anxiety over its relative loss of status as a world power. By recognizing that British anthropological analyses have fit conventional genres of historical narrative and political argument, however, we have been able to contextualize anthropology within the national culture. We more readily apprehend the successive political messages of British anthropology because we hear them as familiar refrains. And appreciating the national tradition of political debate permits us to discern the peculiarities of Britain's responses to a changing world order.

Chapter 7
The politics of perception

Throughout this book, the subjects of enthnographies have been treated as nearly inert – little capable of modifying Westerners' propensities to cast exotic cultures in familiar forms. Indeed, anthropologists themselves, recognizing that they take their own cultures' obsessions into the field, have identified the solipsistic element in their work: the French find everywhere peoples who are prone to flights of philosophic speculation; the Americans show how interpersonal conflicts are eliminated in societies structured differently from our own; the British explore the limits of individual liberty and equality in the face of the obligations of citizenship.[1] Furthermore, in Britain, as elsewhere, ethnographic evidence can be appreciated only if it is translated into local terms, as is invariably the case whenever some novel cultural element – be it a technological innovation, a behavioral practice, or an idea (including an anthropological theory) – is appropriated from abroad. In the context of local use, it makes no difference if anthropological accounts are complete fabrications. They are believed accurate if they can be reconciled with direct experience, and if they are believed they can serve to justify both specific courses of action and general self-examination – critical as well as congratulatory. Hence, the qualitative character of the relationships between anthropologists and their subjects has been practically irrelevant to consideration of the significance of anthropological ideas in Britain.

In the colonies, systematic misunderstanding of indigenous cultures had obviously significant consequences for colonial subjects, and it was often promulgated by anthropological investigators employed by colonial regimes. Their work was used to restructure traditional polities into manageable form, and because colonial rulers held the balance of power their subjects' capacity to resist was often fairly minimal – unless officials themselves

---

[1] See, for example, Adam Kuper, "Regional Comparison in African Anthropology," *African Affairs* 78 (1979): 108–9; Derek Freeman, *Margaret Mead and Samoa* (chap. 1, n. 18); Louis Dumont, "Preface to the French Edition of Evans-Pritchard's *The Nuer*," in J. H. M. Beattie and R. G. Leinhardt, eds., *Studies in Social Anthropology* (chap. 6, n. 88), 338.

were terrified by the results (and prospect) of popular revolt in the absence of prudent regard for indigenous sentiment. To understand the consequences of colonial rule for its subjects, however, it is more important to appreciate the consistent pattern of official action than the occasional deviations from it prompted by considerations of expediency. And this pattern suggests relatively minimal consideration for colonial subjects' views.

The subjects of anthropological inquiry have not been inert, however. In varying degrees at various times they have themselves shaped Westerners' perceptions of their cultures. Before and after the period analyzed in this study, non-Westerners have participated in individual cross-cultural encounters that have been defined by large-scale political relationships. Thus, ethnographies are historical documents. However explicitly, they convey the quality of personal encounters between alien Europeans and sometime colonial subjects at particular moments. As such, ethnographies illustrate the changing culture of colonial societies. I now turn to consideration of the history of colonial social relations, and the connection of that history with ethnographic representation. Observed trends indicate that early – and recent – anthropologists were – and are – highly conscious of the possibilities of mutual misunderstanding inherent in cross-cultural encounters. A lack of anthropological self-doubt has been correlated with a clearly established relationship of political domination.

Colonial situations

At the outset of the age of colonialism, the outcome of the encounters between imperialists and exotic peoples was by no means foreordained. To be sure, some negative opinions about non-Western cultures were formed prior to any contact with them. Explorers expected to find extraordinarily backward peoples in the remote regions of the Antipodes, where deprived and depraved societies had been imagined from ancient times. And settlers were prone to label as irredeemable savages the peoples resident in areas they wished to claim for themselves, thus justifying their cruel treatment of such unhappy victims of colonialism as the Tasmanians, Native Americans, and the Khoikiho (whom they called Hottentots). As the differences of opinion about Native American societies that obtained between men such as Daniel Gookin and John Locke indicate, Europeans' ideas about indigenous cultures were usually products of their interests – and actions – and ranged from condemnation to glorification.

Nevertheless, on the colonial frontier, relationships between Europeans and indigenous peoples were as egalitarian as they would ever be. They

The inchoate idea of the savage presented to the British public in the relatively early days of colonialism: the inhabitants of Tierra del Fuego, pictured at the top of the page, and the Khoikhoi, as represented in Banks's *New System of Geography* (1792). The Fuegans, shortly to be fixed in the human hierarchy as the most primitive of beings, are here seen as capable of creating the rudiments of civilized shelter from natural materials, and are portrayed in attitudes that evoke images of the classical ancients. The Khoikhoi, to be judged only slightly less harshly, are witnessed performing a marriage ceremony in the solemn attitudes of Christian iconography.

Cultural accommodation in the early stages of colonialism: until the middle of the eighteenth century it was common among European residents in India to adopt some form of Indian dress. William Fielding, first Earl of Denbigh, wearing modified Indian dress, being led about by an Indian guide. Painted c. 1633–4 by Sir Anthony van Dyck. Reproduced by courtesy of the Trustees, the National Gallery, London.

were so of necessity, for Europeans depended on local good will for their very survival, and had to respect indigenous standards. Everywhere that British traders advanced into areas that they did not control – in North America, Asia, Oceania, and Africa – they became integral members of local societies. In order to ingratiate themselves with their trading partners, they adopted local dress, technology, protocol, and other customs, and frequently took local wives, often drawn from the powerful families who became their business associates. The progressive extension of colonial authority was correlated with declining degrees of accommodation to indigenous practices, although such accommodation could be essential to the very process of colonial conquest. The process of pacification of subject peoples proceeded unevenly, however, as, indeed, did the process of recognition of colonial subjects' aspirations. Remember, for example, that at the end of the First World War Britain was both obliged to make formal concessions to Indian nationalism and establishing its rule of Tanganyika. And some parts of the British Empire remained virtually untouched by colonial authority throughout the period covered by this study, despite formal annexation. Hence, to a degree frontier conditions persisted in some areas, shaping cross-cultural social relationships there.

For example, when British domination of North America was insecure, colonial settlers were relatively respectful of local cultures. Indeed, the British treated as virtual equals those indigenous peoples they enrolled as their allies in their fight to drive the French off the continent. To wit, Benjamin Franklin came to admire the League of the Iroquois while negotiating their military assistance, and later urged American revolutionaries to imitate their federal constitution. In the latter part of the eighteenth century, the British in India admired the artistry, spiritual values, and scientific achievements of Indian society; many of them believed that their presence would remove the blight on India that had been cast by oriental despotism, so that Indians could eventually achieve full equality with Englishmen. In the middle of the nineteenth century, the British required knowledge of the New Zealand Maori's mythology and poetry both to defeat them in battle and to negotiate terms for peace with them. When in the nineteenth century the British encountered the formidable Asante Kingdom, which once encompassed much of present-day Ghana, they were obliged to learn enough about its social organization to turn its divisions to their own advantage, and evidenced considerable regard for its culture and power.

With the imposition of formal British rule, however, colonialists' respect for indigenous culture diminished considerably. When the British assumed sovereignty over India after the widespread civil and military revolt of 1857–8, they became dubious about the prospect that Indians might eventually become thoroughly acculturated to British norms, and they altered entirely the ritual as well as the practical aspects of their relations with the Indian nobility; previously they had been more respectful of traditional modes of expressing power relationships (even though they misunderstood, and therefore changed them). After the annexation of Asante in 1896, the British evidently managed to forget what they had once known about the Asante Kingdom, and set about inventing a new tradition for the Asante that suited their own administrative purposes. These attitude and policy reversals were emblematic of a widespread pattern.

Moreover, on the individual, as well as the collective, level, the outcome of encounters between colonists and local peoples was shaped by highly variable local conditions. For example, even though the white settler societies of Southern Africa were to become rigidly segregated, in the frontier societies that developed there some European settlers became fully incorporated members of African societies. Clearly, had a substantial proportion of Europeans chosen to assimilate to indigenous societies, the historical trajectory of developing relationships between Europeans and non-Western peoples would have been very different. But thorough assimilation was an eccentric response to frontier conditions. And by their complete identification with local peoples, Europeans became powerless to determine the outcomes of colonial encounters.

Nevertheless, it is by looking at the quality of individual lives in colonial areas that we can judge the general character of the colonial situation at a particular time and place. Relations between colonists and indigenous populations changed dramatically with the growth of European populations sufficiently large to permit their communities to take on a distinctive, inward-looking behavior pattern. This happened even in those tropical areas considered unsuitable for large-scale, permanent British settlement, although there were obvious differences between these areas and those that became the white Dominions. Britain acquired tropical colonies in order to profit economically from exploitation of their natural resources, and it was assumed that Britain could not extract maximum value from these tropical possessions until European experts could be sent there in numbers adequate to the managerial tasks of Empire. This became possible with the consolidation of the Pax Britannica and the development of a repertoire of medical therapeutics and public sanitation measures that promised to protect the health of Europeans living in the tropics.

When Europeans in sizable numbers took up prolonged (if ultimately temporary) residence in Britain's tropical territories, there were recognizable signs of the altered relationships between colonists and indigenous peoples. The management of Empire became a distinctly British prerogative – so that the representation of local peoples in important colonial administrative positions declined significantly. And colonists removed themselves from indigenous peoples in segregated residential and recreational areas – sometimes justifying spatial segregation in military terms and sometimes rationalizing it on medical grounds. In their special preserves, colonists were able to sustain European-centered social lives, not the least because their communities now included European women in significantly enlarged proportions.

It is a cliché of the colonial literature – memoirs, novels, histories – that the life of the colonial station changed dramatically with the advent of wives. Old colonial hands mourned the passing of the unrestrained good old days. And the residents of the station undertook to live their lives according to metropolitan standards, although, in fact, they were living very differently from the way they would have at home; persons of middle-class origins presiding over households of local servants and offices of locally recruited subordinates, they were frequently enacting near-parodies of upper-class British behavior, following a pattern so obvious and so widespread that it is a stock element in colonial fiction (a highly conventionalized genre). When European women became a substantial portion of the colonial population, the last vestige of the era of cultural accommodation – public tolerance of interracial sexual liaisons – disappeared. Certainly, by this time such relationships usually constituted a particularly personal variant of colonial domination, but they were personal relationships nonetheless. Thus, it is possible to mark the emergence of self-contained colonial societies by an official act: on January 11, 1909, the colonial secretary, Lord Crewe, warned all of the colonial employees within his jurisdiction that any of them who had sexual relations with local women would suffer "disgrace and official ruin."

Certainly, these historical generalizations require qualification. Colonial social relationships admitted individual variations about the mean. Officials, soldiers, settlers, commercial agents, and missionaries came to the colonies from different backgrounds and with different agendas. These traits affected their relations with one another and with indigenous peoples – as Malinowski observed at the end of the imperial era – although colonial demographics tempered initial attitudes. If the colonies presented individuals opportunities to reinvent themselves – tolerating, especially on the frontier, social types who ranged from extravagantly self-indulgent adventurers to the self-styled unadulterated British gentlemen who donned formal jacket to dine alone in the wild – even extreme forms of behavior were linked to individuals' metropolitan identities. Yet, changing colonial demographics did effect a changing social mean. And, for the most part, by

World War I an order had been created in which colonial rulers and subjects had each learned to play highly conventionalized roles.[2]

The colonial context of ethnographic observation

When A. C. Haddon was preparing to make his first field trip to the islands of the Torres Straits, he was urged by Alfred Russel Wallace to go instead to the West Indies, where he would have been "able to work in a comfortable house and with civilized surroundings."[3] Evidently, naturalists were generally loath to venture into areas where Europeans were not well established, and, indeed, it seems extraordinary that Wallace doubted the

---

[2] The literature substantiating these generalizations is enormous. For examples, see Axtell, *The European and the Indian* (chap. 1, n. 1), George D. Bearce, *British Attitudes Toward India, 1784–1858* (London, 1961); James A. Boutilier, "European Women in the Solomon Islands, 1900–1942: Accommodation and Change on the Pacific Frontier," in Denise O'Brien and Sharon W. Tiffany, eds., *Rethinking Women's Roles: Perspectives from the Pacific* (Berkeley, 1984), 173–200; Kenelm Burridge, *Encountering Aborigines* (New York, 1973), 117–18; John W. Cell, "Anglo-Indian Medical Theory and the Origins of Segregation in West Africa," *American Historical Review* 91 (1986): 307–35; Cohn, "Representing Authority in Victorian India" (chap. 3, n. 42), 165–209; Philip D. Curtin, *The Image of Africa: British Ideas and Actions, 1780–1850* (Madison, Wis., 1964), esp. 343–87; Johansen, *Forgotten Founders* (chap. 1, n. 5), 87 and passim; Howard Lamar and Leonard Thompson, eds., *The Frontier in History* (New Haven, 1981), esp. (1) Robert F. Berkhofer, Jr., "The North American Frontier as Process and Context," 44–6; (2) Ramsay Cook, "The Social and Economic Frontier in North America," 201; (3) Hermann Giliomee, "Processes in Development of the Southern African Frontier," 78; (4) Lamar and Thompson, "Introduction," 12; (5) Christopher Saunders, "Political Processes in the Southern African Frontier Zones," 151–62. See also my *Imperial Bureaucrat* (chap. 2, n. 14), 103, 122; Mary McCarthy, *Social Change and the Growth of British Power in the Gold Coast: The Fante States, 1807–1874* (Lanham, Md., 1983). Adrian C. Mayer, "The King's Two Thrones," *Man* [n.s.] 20 (1985): 211, 216–17; Arthur T. Porter, *Creoledom* (London, 1966), esp. 67–8, 106–15; Marshall Sahlins, "Others Times, Other Customs: The Anthropology of History," *American Anthropologist* [n.s.] 85 (1983): 517–44; Sheehan, *Savagism and Civility* (chap. 1, n. 5); Stokes, *The English Utilitarians and India* (chap. 5, n. 30), 282–8; Pauline Turner Strong, "Fathoming the Primitive: Australian Aborigines in Four Explorers' Journals, 1697–1845," *Ethnohistory* 33 (1986): 176–9; R. E. S. Tanner, "European Leadership in Small Communities in Tanganyika Prior to Independence," *Race* 7 (1965): 289–302; Ivor Wilks, *Asante in the Nineteenth Century* (Cambridge, 1975). A similar sequential pattern of relationships between colonizers and colonized can be seen in colonial empires other than the British. For an example on the French, see William B. Cohen, *The French Encounter with Africans* (Bloomington, Ind., 1980).

[3] Alfred Russel Wallace's letter of 28 November, 1887, is quoted in Quiggin and Fegan, "Alfred Cort Haddon, 1855–1940" (chap. 3, n. 9), 99.

wisdom of Haddon's trip to an area that so many other Europeans had visited. When Haddon chose to make the islands the site of his revolutionary expedition, he did so because he knew from previous experience "of the willingness of the Torres Straits islanders to impart information and to render personal assistance," whereas some unknown people might have "prove[n] to be suspicious and refractory."[4] Not until after World War I, when colonial authority seemed secure in most parts of the Empire, did it become routine for anthropologists to go into the field to collect their own data for analysis, and the discipline's altered methodology was at least a partial function of political change, for anthropologists could be reasonably confident that peoples accustomed to defer to colonial rulers would be cooperative subjects. In the prewar era, scholarly anthropological analyses based on extensive field experience were written, but they were produced by men who were themselves colonial agents – missionaries and colonial administrators.

In the post–World War I era, anthropologists were to congratulate themselves on the virtues of their techniques of participant observation, rendering themselves the heroes of their own narratives because they had managed to endure prolonged periods of residence among alien peoples. Malinowski was to describe the research style of the prewar era with palpable disdain, suggesting that his predecessors' research methods did not admit of accurate assessments of indigenous cultures.

> The anthropologist must relinquish his comfortable position in the long chair on the veranda of the missionary compound, Government station, or planter's bungalow, where, armed with pencil and notebook and at times with a whisky and soda, he has been accustomed to collect statements from informants, write down stories, and fill out sheets of paper with savage texts.[5]

But in at least one respect the field reports of the prewar era were often more honest than later ones: they described the relationships between colonialists and subject peoples explicitly.

After the framework of colonial rule was established, the character of relationships between colonists and subject peoples might never again be so plainly seen as it was in the late sixteenth century, the dawn of the imperial era, when a man such as Thomas Harriot, sent by Sir Walter Raleigh to investigate conditions in the first Virginia colony, could both sympathetically describe Native American culture and recognize that this culture

---

[4] A. C. Haddon, "Preface" to Vol. V of *Reports of the Cambridge Anthropological Expedition to Torres Straits* (Cambridge, 1904), v.
[5] Bronislaw Malinowski, *Myth in Primitive Psychology*, the Frazer Lecture of 1925 (New York, 1926), 92.

must be subverted if local inhabitants were to become willing colonial subjects.[6] Yet, a fully routinized colonial system was not to develop in most parts of the Empire until much later. Recall that in 1890, H. H. Risley faulted armchair anthropologists because, without the experience of colonial conditions, they were ignorant "of the extraordinary fluidity and mutability of custom."[7] And note that Risley was speaking from the vantage point of a man who had joined the Indian Civil Service only fifteen years after the Mutiny. Because frontier conditions persisted in the remote regions of formally colonized areas, anthropologists who worked there were able to observe colonial societies in the making, to recognize that when colonizers and local peoples dealt with each other, the conditions of their associations were effectively negotiated by both parties, although each party was capable of setting only some of the terms of its negotiations.

Thus, when at the turn of the century academic anthropologists went to do field research in various parts of the Empire, they recognized what W. H. R. Rivers described as the "strong hybrid [cultural] growth which has come into existence between the people and their rulers." Habitual patterns of behavior had been developed that sustained orderly relations between colonizers and colonized, and these were peculiar to the colonial situation, neither wholly indigenous nor imported.[8] Anthropologists were bound to observe that under colonial conditions the culture they would record was precarious. Writing of the Veddas of (then) Ceylon in 1911, C. G. and B. Z. Seligman confessed that they often had no alternative but to rely on the testimony of the informant who had "assumed the role of professional primitive man" – who dressed himself in outmoded costume for his interviews with anthropologists, and described to them a way of life he no longer followed – whose information the anthropologists both welcomed and questioned.[9]

During the formative period of colonial culture, some of its "hybrid" features were shaped by local populations. For example, Pidgin English, the lingua franca of European–local relationships in Oceania, was developed when colonists were few in number. It was the creation of indigenous inhabitants, who taught the language to Europeans.[10] Indigenous peoples

---

[6] Stephen Greenblatt, "Invisible Bullets: Renaissance Authority and Its Subversion," *Glyph* 8 (1981): esp. 44–53.

[7] Risley, "The Study of Ethnology in India" (chap. 5, n. 38), 238.

[8] W. H. R. Rivers, "The Government of Subject Peoples," in A. C. Seward, ed., *Science and the Nation* (Cambridge, 1917), 309.

[9] C. G. Seligman and Brenda Z. Seligman, *The Veddas* (Cambridge, 1911), vii.

[10] Gunnar Landtman, *The Kiwai Papuans of British New Guinea* (London, 1927), 453. Landtman was a Finnish disciple of A. C. Haddon. Note that the fieldwork on which this study was based was done between 1910 and 1912.

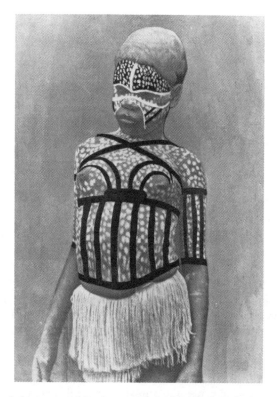

A contrived document, this photograph is frankly described in the Torres
Straits Expedition reports. Not only does the caption acknowledge that lines
have been drawn on the photograph to highlight features of the body painting
traditionally applied to a woman who has just passed through her puberty
rites (which are so obvious that they could not pass unnoticed), it also reveals
that the costume she is wearing was especially made to suit C. G. Seligman's
photographic requirements.

came to have less power in setting the terms under which their political
negotiations with Europeans were conducted, however. And the active
modification of local power structures was clearly visible to longtime
resident observers of colonial frontier conditions. Acting on the assumption
that "savage people are always ruled by chiefs," wrote R. H. Codrington, a
missionary-anthropologist working in Melanesia at the end of the nineteenth century, the "trader or other visitor looks for a chief, and finds such
a one as he expects; a very insignificant person in this way comes to be
called, and to call himself, the king of his island, and his consideration

among his own people is of course enormously enhanced by what white people make of him."[11]

Because anthropologists of the interwar period themselves valued – and were encouraged to value – analysis of heretofore unexamined peoples, they were likely to do field research in areas under only nominal colonial rule. There, they worked in circumstances that possessed many of the elements characteristic of the earliest colonial encounters, and responded to their situations much as the earliest colonists had done. Living in a remote area of the Australian territory of New Guinea in the early 1930s, Gregory Bateson observed that in their relations with each other, Europeans and indigenous peoples both were obliged to behave according to the stereotyped notions each had of the other.[12] At roughly the same time, Evans-Pritchard described the difficulties he had in eliciting any information from the Nuer of the Sudan, who had just been brutally defeated by British Government forces. So frustrated did he become in his efforts to persuade the Nuer to cooperate with him that he shamelessly described himself as afflicted with "Nuerosis." In order to work with the Nuer, he was obliged to accept all of the conditions they effectively imposed on the way he lived his life among them.[13] The high regard Evans-Pritchard came to have for the culture of the Nuer can, at least in part, be explained as a consequence of the relationship he had with them.

Anthropologists worked under very different conditions in those areas where colonial domination was secure. If the subjects of their research failed to recognize them as somehow allied to the agents of colonial rule, they might unabashedly use the threat of official action as a means to elicit information. When Margaret Mead and Reo Fortune had trouble persuading the New Guinean Arapesh to help them begin their research, Mead wrote from the field in 1932, Fortune "went about from one village to another, unearthed their darkest secrets which they wished kept from the government, and then ordered them" to do what the couple wished.[14] Because anthropologists working in pacified societies could depend – however directly – on the authority of government to ensure their subjects' cooperation, they presented their findings as unproblematic. The typical ethnographies of the interwar period included little (if any) description of

[11] R. H. Codrington, *The Melanesians* (Oxford, 1891), 46.
[12] Bateson, *Naven* (chap. 4, n. 59), 184–5.
[13] Evans-Pritchard, *The Nuer* (chap. 6, n. 93), 11–15.
[14] Mead described Fortune's coercive tactics in a letter to an unidentified recipient, dated 15 January, 1932. Commenting on this saved document decades later, she apparently found no reason to repent of her imperious behavior. See her "Fieldwork in the Pacific Islands, 1925–67," in Peggy Golde, ed., *Women in the Field* (Berkeley, 1986), 308, 295.

the anthropologists' progressive immersion in local cultures, since anthropologists' ability to comprehend these cultures and to extract accurate information from their informants was assumed.[15]

Secure colonial rule brought more than the enforced cooperation of research subjects, however. It obviously also shaped the societies anthropologists studied. It is not surprising that interwar anthropologists often wrote of routinized relationships in the "anthropological present" tense. Colonial rulers had worked to stabilize the behavior of their subjects, to fit the structure of indigenous polities into predictable – and hence manageable – patterns. The stable orders anthropologists described were not natural but, at least in some measure, engineered. The ahistorical character of the ethnographies of the interwar period derived from many factors, not the least of them literary convention; but the quality of the colonial situation was among the most important of these factors, probably more important, for example, than the paucity of written records available for the peoples (largely African) who were then the usual subjects of anthropological inquiry – which anthropologists have been wont to represent as the limiting constraint on their inquiries.[16] As the letters and reports they sent from the field during this period show far more clearly than do their published accounts, anthropologists were certainly aware of conflict and change in the colonial situation. When their work dealt with social change, however, it often "treated the native as a passive recipient in a non-reciprocal situation," a person whose society had no history of managing to cope with changing conditions.[17] Indeed, indigenous peoples themselves relinquished title to their own history, and were observed deferring to anthropologists' accounts of their own traditions when disputes required them to invoke precedents.[18]

To be sure, colonial societies were not totalitarian regimes. There were considerable limits to colonial authority, "secrets" subject peoples could guard (although an anthropologist like Fortune might ferret them out). And colonial rulers did not thoroughly transform indigenous cultures. It was in

[15] James Clifford, "On Ethnographic Authority," *Representations* 12 (Spring, 1983): 124.

[16] For one argument that the functionalist anthropology of the interwar period was ahistorical because its African subjects had no written histories, see Needham, "Introduction" to the reissue of Hocart, *Kings and Councillors* (chap. 6, n. 73), lxxxi. With the benefit of hindsight, we can recognize the possibility of historically informed ethnographies of Africans, since it is evidently possible to write them by using oral histories and previously unexploited written records. See Jan Vansina, "Towards a History of Lost Corners in the World," *Economic History Review* [n.s.] 35 (1982): 165–78.

[17] Nash, "Nationalism and Fieldwork" (see chap. 5, n. 25), 230.

[18] See, for example, Allan Hanson, "The Making of the Maori: Culture Invention and Its Logic," *American Anthropologist* 91 (1989): 890–902.

the political institutions of colonial regimes that the "hybrid growth" of colonial culture became most clearly defined and routinized. Anthropologists working in stabilized colonial societies were not necessarily blind to this phenomenon; Max Gluckman, for example, observed it in Zululand in the late 1930s.[19] But when anthropologists working in the colonial era dealt with tractable subjects, they were able to do so because indigenous peoples had learned to be deferential to persons they saw as representatives of colonial political authority.

Those contemporary anthropologists who work among non-Western peoples (a diminishing fraction of practitioners) are supplicants. Their research subjects may be predisposed to regard them with hostility, indifference, or friendliness. Whatever attitude subjects bring to their meeting with the ethnographer, however, they cannot be coerced to volunteer information, and researchers themselves approach cross-cultural encounters warily. They are fearful that they will succumb to the moral perils to which practitioners of their discipline are heir – the dangers of "objectifying" their subjects, of extracting their secrets through duplicity, and of publishing information that can be turned against them. They assure their subjects that they recognize that Western culture is not superior, and that the anthropological encounter should be one in which the researcher and the subject will each learn something; each will come to see the advantages and disadvantages of the other's way of life. They defer to their subjects' interpretations of tradition, correcting in print the points they have made in their writings with which their subjects have taken issue, and securing permission to mount museum displays of traditional artifacts – indeed, returning sacred artifacts to the peoples who cherish them. Evidently, anthropologists do not always succeed in persuading their subjects of their sincere intentions to learn from them. Contemporary ethnographies sometimes suggest that travel is broadening – to the traveler, who has gained in self-understanding – but that true communication with peoples of other cultures is impossible.[20] Anthropologists of European extraction who study the indigenous peoples of nations created by colonialism – Australia, Canada, New Zealand, the United States – have often internalized the guilt of colonialism, not the least because they often confront fellow citizens who

[19] Max Gluckman, "Analysis of a Social Situation in Modern Zululand," *Bantu Studies* 14 (1940): 1–30, 147–74; Gluckman did the fieldwork on which this was based between 1936 and 1938.

[20] See, for example, Hanson, "The Making of the Maori," 895–7; Rena Lederman, "The Return of Redwoman: Fieldwork in Highland New Guinea," in Golde, ed., *Women in the Field*, 367–8. For one illustration of an ethnographic encounter filled with self- and other-imposed frustrations, see Paul Rabinow, *Reflections on Fieldwork in Morocco* (Berkeley, 1972).

have become political activists. But their colleagues who work elsewhere have obligations that differ only in degree, not in kind.

Conclusions

Clearly, the character of anthropological accounts reflects the character of the social situations in which anthropologists have produced them. What relationship obtains between the quality of ethnographic evidence and the uses to which it is put? There is little difficulty in relating the contexts of observation and use in consideration of the work of anthropologists employed by colonial regimes, since the two contexts were effectively identical. Anthropologists conducting inquiries under government auspices could expect to get the sort of information they wanted, since they had the weight of official authority behind them. And because government anthropologists – as opposed to those anthropologists who came to the colonies to do research with the aid of government subvention – were themselves usually drawn from the ranks of colonial officials, the information they sought was of the sort the government wished. To be sure, colonial officials were somewhat suspicious of those of their company who carved out niches for themselves as anthropological experts within the colonial government hierarchy. Most officials assumed that those of their colleagues who developed considerable enthusiasm for investigating local culture had "gone native," had become excessively sympathetic with indigenous peoples' objections to government policy. To a degree, conventional colonial administrators' suspicions of government anthropologists were well founded. But within colonial regimes government anthropologists were members of the loyal opposition, not subversives.

If the contexts of anthropological observation and use are not the same, however, it seems impossible to decipher some systematic relationship between them. One can see ethnographies as historical documents that are, as such, aids to understanding the quality of social life in a particular place at a particular time. One can identify the situations in which readers of ethnographies found themselves, and explain how their circumstances conditioned the constructions they placed on anthropological evidence, the impact their reading had on their understanding of themselves and of their society. But there need be no interpretative agreement between the writers of ethnographies and the readers of them, if the two groups lead their lives in different social milieux. Can one do more than say that anthropological texts are like other sorts of cultural products, susceptible to a range of interpretations?

Consider, for example, T. S. Eliot's interpretation of W. H. R. Rivers's

report on Melanesian society. Reading Rivers in 1914, Eliot found analogues between the behavior of Melanesians and that of Britons. Recall
that when Rivers observed the effects of colonialism on Melanesians he
reported that they were failing to reproduce because they had lost the will
to live; the vital moral center of their culture had been destroyed by the
onslaught of Europeans. Modern materialism was destroying British culture, according to Eliot, eradicating those features of public life that
embodied and perpetuated the virtues that gave moral significance to
individuals' private lives. If present trends continued, Eliot wrote, "it will
not be surprising if the population of the entire civilized world rapidly
follows the fate of the Melanesians."[21]

Clearly, there was a certain elective affinity between Rivers's observations and Eliot's. Not alone, Eliot felt himself to be in the midst of a
collapsing social order. Rivers, of course, went to Melanesia from Britain,
bearing the concerns of his own culture. Indeed, given his own understanding of the operations of human psychological mechanisms, Rivers
would not have denied that he was bound to understand Melanesian
society in terms that were shaped by his prior experiences. Nevertheless,
Rivers did observe a people undergoing the unhappy process of colonial
subjugation. The message Eliot derived from Rivers's work was unambig-
uously stated, and it was formulated in the context of a particular sort of
colonial situation. Eliot and Rivers were both witnesses to societies in flux,
and the causes of fluctuation in each of the societies they witnessed were,
at least to some degree, the same; both the breakdown of Melanesian social
order and the changing character of British society reflected a reconfiguration of international relations.

Although there is no necessary relationship between the character of an
ethnographic text and the construction that may be placed upon it, this
single case suggests that widespread historical forces may shape a common
outlook for authors and readers. To be sure, individuals rarely respond
directly to broad historical circumstances. Individuals' responses are distinguished by variations in temperament and politics, by the attitudes they
share with fellow members of social groups whose experiences differentiate
them from other groups coexisting in place and time, and by outlooks
deriving from ecological variations within the world system – as this book
has shown. Nevertheless, at the dawn of the imperial era, when the world
order was changing and the terms of cross-cultural encounters were still

---

[21] Eliot, "Marie Lloyd" (see chap. 4, n. 113), 408. This essay was originally published in
1923, but in a vaguely worded footnote to it, Eliot indicates that the section in which
he discusses the implications of Rivers's work – if not the entire essay – was written in
1914.

provisional, Europeans at home and abroad were provoked by revelations of the unexpected behaviors of exotic peoples to question their own institutions. The social turmoil of the World War I era ushered in another period of global reconfiguration, of which the repudiation of colonialism was but one element. When anthropologists relinquished the comfortable assumptions of Western moral superiority, they were responding to changing world conditions. And their response attests to the fundamental character of social knowledge: it represents considered analysis of palpable experience and, because it is grounded in the actual, offers realizable visions of the possible.

Appendix 1

Statistical analysis of the membership of the Royal Anthropological Institute

Table A1.1 *Sometime presidents of Section H and the RAI among the Anthropological Institute's officers and council*

	No. of presidents, Section H	No. of presidents, RAI	Total No. officers and council
1883	5	9	29
1893	8	12	32
1900	10	12	32
1910	14	16	36
1920	10	13	32
1930	10	10	32
1938	8	11	32

	Other anthropology[a] (%)	Civic/Professional[b] (%)	Natural history[c] (%)	Policy sciences[d] (%)	Biomedical[e] (%)	Other social[f] (%)	Info. avail. (N)	Total (N)
1883								
Amateurs	44	37	30	26	7	4	21	27
Professionals	50	0	0	0	0	0	2	2
1893								
Amateurs	48	37	30	22	11	4	20	27
Professionals	80	0	0	20	0	0	5	5
1900								
Amateurs	46	25	25	25	25	4	20	24
Professionals	62	0	13	25	0	0	5	8
1910								
Amateurs	76	36	16	32	24	8	22	25
Professionals	82	0	9	18	9	9	11	11
1920								
Amateurs	38	24	5	29	38	10	19	21
Professionals	73	9	9	27	9	0	11	11
1930								
Amateurs	45	30	10	20	15	0	17	20
Professionals	75	8	8	8	8	0	12	12
1938								
Amateurs	38	23	8	15	15	0	10	13
Professionals	74	16	5	21	5	0	19	19

[a] Archaeology, antiquities (including numismatics), folklore, Section H, and any other anthropological society, domestic or foreign.
[b] Societies devoted to public affairs per se, and to nonacademic professional activities.
[c] Geology, botany, zoology.
[d] Geography, statistics, area studies (e.g., the Royal African Society, the International African Institute, the Hellenic Society, the Royal Asiatic Society, etc.).
[e] Medicine, surgery, anatomy.
[f] Psychology, sociology.

Table A1.3 *Scholarly publications, Anthropological Institute elite*

	Amateurs (N)	Professionals (N)	Total (%)
1883			
Published anthropology	16	2	62
Other scholarship	21		72
1893			
Published anthropology	17	5	69
Other scholarship	22	1	72
1900			
Published anthropology	14	8	69
Other scholarship	18	2	63
1910			
Published anthropology	19	10	81
Other scholarship	19	4	64
1920			
Published anthropology	19	9	88
Other scholarship	16	5	66
1930			
Published anthropology	15	11	81
Other scholarship	12	4	50
1938			
Published anthropology	9	18	84
Other scholarship	8	4	38

Table A1.4 *Higher education, Anthropological Institute, officers and council*

	1883	1893	1900	1910	1920	1930	1938
Universities							
Oxbridge	5	7	9	16	10	14	14
London	5	5	4	5	3	2	2
Scottish U.	3	4	4	1	1		
Manchester				1	1	1	
Dublin	1	1	2	3	1		
Wales					1		1
Foreign U.	4	2	3	3	1	2	3
Professional							
Hospital/Med. schl.	3	3	3	8	5	5	2
Sandhurst/Woolwich	2	1	1			1	1
Read law	1	2	2	3	1	2	
Total individuals	15	16	20	28	20	21	22
All institute elite, median age in years	51	53	50	57	57	58	58

Table A1.5 *Achieved distinctions, Anthropological Institute Ordinary Fellows*

	1883	1893	1900	1910	1920	1930	1938
Titles conferred (%)	4	6	6	6	0	10	2
F.R.S.[a] (%)	2	2	6	4	4	2	0

[a] F.R.S. = Fellow of the Royal Society.

Table A1.6 *Occupations, Anthroplogical Institute Ordinary Fellows*

	1883	1893	1900	1910	1920	1930	1938
Anthropologists	1	2	1	4	4	3	6
Other university/museum posts	3	2	8	6	7	5	10
Professional class (physicians, barristers/solicitors, engineers, clergymen, military officers, schoolmasters, home civil servants, accountants, dentists, architects)	16	23	17	16	13	7	8
Commercial class (in business, finance, manufacture)	2	4	6	2	3	3	1
Arts and letters (journalists, authors, publishers, artists; poets, art dealers)	2	4	3	3	0	2	1
Colonial figures (missionaries, civil servants)	7	6	0	10	9	8	11
Government (diplomats, politicians)	4	2	2	1	1	0	1
Leisured gentlemen	2	2	3	2	2	1	1
Women, not employed	2	3	3	2	3	7	4
Miscellaneous[a]	1	3	0	1	0	0	1
No information	19	10	16	12	13	18	10
Sample size	50	50	50	50	50	50	50

[a] In 1883, an Indian traditional notable; in 1893, two subjects of British India – a notable and an antiquarian book dealer; in 1910, a subject of British India; and in 1938, a farmer.

Note: For each year, sample size = 50.

Appendix 2
Selected brief biographies

In this appendix, I summarize the (public) lives of thirty-five persons who figured in the anthropological community during the period covered by my study. I intend these data to document the historical trends in career patterns I extrapolated from the quantitative analysis of Royal Anthropological Institute (RAI) members presented in Chapter 2, so I have arranged my biographies by the date of birth of their subjects. These figures are exemplary rather than representative – unlike the population of 453 RAI members (a number of whom appeared several times in my samples), whose careers I analyzed quantitatively. All of them played prominent roles in the RAI, although three of them – Malinowski, Richards, and Fortes – did not appear in any of the samples of RAI leaders and Ordinary Fellows that I compiled. They are outstanding specimens of their particular types: learned amateurs, colonial figures-cum-anthropologists, diverse sorts of professionals, and one distinguished scholar (Hocart) who did not win the recognition he deserved. On the whole, this group constitutes an acclaimed lot, and academics are overrepresented among them. These sketches are partial, for two reasons: First, the public records of anthropologists' lives – *Who's Who* entries, obituaries, and the like – are often incomplete. (I have added supplementary data gleaned incidentally.) Second, many of these persons figured prominently in so many learned societies and were such prolific writers that I can only present samples of their activities. Nevertheless, these biographies illustrate the increasingly standardized character of scholarly lives, and show some of the relationships members of the anthropological community had with one another and with other segments of the intelligentsia that defy quantification.

1820 Augustus Henry Pitt-Rivers (originally Lane-Fox), d. 1900
  Family: son of W. A. Lane-Fox of Hope Hall and the daughter of the 18th Earl of Morton (took the name Pitt-Rivers in 1880 as stipulated by the will of his great-uncle, the 2nd Baron Rivers); married daughter of the 2nd Lord Stanley of Alderly.

Education: Sandhurst.

Career: military officer, ultimately lieutenant-general; served in the Crimean War; inspector of ancient monuments in Great Britain.

Learned society activities: president of the (R)AI and of the Society of Antiquaries.

Publications: *On the Development and Distribution of Primitive Locks and Keys* (1883); J. L. Myres, ed., *The Evolution of Culture and Other Essays* (1906).

Honors: Fellow of the Royal Society.

1822   **Francis Galton**, d. 1911

Family: son of Francis T. Galton, banker, and grandson of Erasmus Darwin.

Education: King Edward's, Birmingham; Medical School of King's College, London; Trinity College, Cambridge (pass degree).

Career: independently wealthy after the death of his father in 1844; traveled in the Middle East and Southern Africa and undertook diverse projects, including the establishment of his anthropometric laboratory in 1884.

Learned society activities: secretary of the BAAS; president of the Geographical Section of the BAAS, of Section H, and of the (R)AI; Council of the Royal Geographical Society; member of the Meteorological Council; chairman of the Committee of Management of Kew Observatory of the Royal Society.

Publications: *The Art of Travel* (1855); *Hereditary Genius* (1869); *Fingerprints* (1893); *Essays in Eugenics* (1909).

Honors: knighthood; Fellow of the Royal Society and recipient of its Gold and Darwin medals; (R)AI Huxley Medal; Darwin Wallace Celebration Medal, Linnean Society; Honorary Fellow, Trinity College, Cambridge.

1825   **Thomas H. Huxley**, d. 1895

Family: son of Georgy Huxley, teacher of math and assistant headmaster of Ealing School (which the son briefly attended), and manager of Coventry Saving Bank.

Education: Charing Cross Hospital; University of London (M.B.), gold medalist for anatomy and physiology.

Career: assistant surgeon in the Royal Navy, including service on *Rattlesnake*, which cruised in Torres Straits, 1846–50; lecturer on natural history at the School of Mines, 1854–81; naturalist to the Geological Survey, 1854–82; Hunterian professor, Royal Institution, 1863–7; between 1862 and 1884, service on ten royal commissions on education, fisheries, and vivisection; professor of biology, Royal College of Science, 1881–95; trustee, British Museum; member, London School Board.

Learned society activities: president of the Royal Society, the Geological Society, of the Ethnological Society, and of BAAS; vice-president of the (R)AI

Publications: *Evidence as to Man's Place in Nature* (1863); *Science and Culture* (1881); *Evolution and Ethics* (1893).

Honors: Fellow of the Royal Society and recipient of its Royal, Copley, and Darwin medals; privy councillor; Civil List pension.

1831 William H. Flower, d. 1899

Family: son of E. F. Flower, brewer.

Education: University College, London; Middlesex Hospital.

Career: assistant-surgeon of the 63rd Regiment during Crimean War; assistant-surgeon, lecturer on comparative anatomy, and curator of museum, Middlesex Hospital, 1858–61; conservator of museum, Royal College of Surgeons, 1861–64; Hunterian professor of comparative anatomy, 1870–84; director of natural history departments, British Museum, 1884–98.

Learned society activities: Council of the Royal Society; president of the Zoological Society, of the Anthropological Institute, and the BAAS.

Publications: *Introduction to the Study of Mammals, Living and Extinct* (1891); *Essays on Museums* (1898).

Honors: knighthood; Fellow of the Royal Society and recipient of its Royal Medal; numerous honorary degrees.

1832 Edward Burnett Tylor, d. 1917

Family: son of Joseph Tylor, brass founder.

Education: Grove House, Tottenham (a school run by the Society of Friends).

Career: entered father's foundry at age 16, but left it in 1855 for the sake of his health; accompanied Henry Christy on an ethnological expedition to Mexico in 1856; at Oxford – keeper of the university museum, 1883; reader in anthropology, 1884; professor of anthropology, 1896 (emeritus 1909); justice of the peace.

Learned society activities: led movement resulting in formation of Section H of the BAAS and was its first president; president of the (R)AI

Publications: *Anahuac, Mexico and the Mexicans* (1959); *Researches into the Early History of Mankind* (1865); *Primitive Culture* (1871).

Honors: knighthood; Fellow of the Royal Society; doctorate in civil law, Oxford University, 1875.

1834 John Lubbock (Lord Avebury), d. 1913

Family: eldest son of Sir John William Lubbock, third baronet, a banker and a notable amateur astronomer and mathematician who was treasurer of the Royal Society for many years. Married Alice Fox-Pitt-Rivers, daughter of A. H. Pitt-Rivers, after the death of his first wife.
Education: Eton.
Career: left Eton at fourteen to join father's firm, Roberts, Lubbock, and Co.; first president of the Institute of Bankers, 1879–83; Liberal MP for Maidstone, 1870–80, and for the University of London, 1880–1900 (sponsor of over two dozen bills, including the Bank Holidays Act of 1871, Wild Birds Protection Act of 1880, Open Spaces Act of 1882, Act for Preservation of Ancient Monuments of 1882, and the Early Closing Act of 1904); president of London Chamber of Commerce, 1888–93; member and chairman of London County Council, 1890–2; member of the Senate and vice-chancellor of London University, 1872–80; chairman of the Society for the Extension of University Teaching, 1894–1902; principal of the Working Men's College in Great Ormond Street, 1883–98; trustee of the British Museum; rector of St. Andrew's University; member of Royal Commissions on the Advance of Science, the Public Schools, International Coinage, and others.
Learned society activities: president of a range of associations, including the BAAS, the Entomological Society, the Linnean Society, the Ray Society, the Statistical Society, the African Society, the Society of Antiquaries, the Royal Microscopial Society, the International Institute of Sociology, the International Association of Prehistoric Archaeology, the International Association of Zoology, and the (R)AI; vice-president of the Royal Society.
Publications: *The Origin of Civilisation* (1871); *Ants, Bees, and Wasps* (1882); *On the Senses, Instincts, and Intelligence of Animals* (1888).
Honors: elevation to the peerage; Fellow of the Royal Society; privy councillor.

1839 Edward William Brabrook, d. 1930.

Education: private school; read law.
Career: assistant registrar of Friendly Societies, 1869; chief registrar, 1891–1904.
Learned society activities: president of the (R)AI, of Section H, of the

Folk-Lore Society, of the Sociological Society, of Section F of the BAAS (Economic Science and Statistics).

Publication: *The Law Relating to Trades Unions* (1871); *The Royal Society of Literature of the United Kingdom* (1897); *Building Societies* (1906).

Honors: Companion of the Bath; knighthood.

1844 Alexander Macalister, d. 1919

Education: Trinity College, Dublin (M.D.).

Career: demonstrator of anatomy, Royal College of Surgeons of Ireland, 1860; at the University of Dublin – professor of zoology, 1860 (while still an undergraduate); professor of comparative anatomy and Zoology, 1872–83; professor of anatomy and chirurgery, 1877–83; Cambridge University – professor of anatomy, 1883–1919; Fellow of St. John's College, Cambridge; for a time chief acting editor, *Journal of Anatomy and Physiology*.

Learned society activities: president of the Geological Society of Ireland, of the RAI, and of Section H; Council of the Royal Society.

Publications: *Introduction of Animal Morphology* (1876); *Text Book of Human Anatomy* (1889); essays on Egyptology and archaeology in the *Proceedings of the Society of Biblical Archaeology*, *Encyclopaedia of Religion and Ethics*, and the *Dictionary of the Bible*.

Honors: Fellow of the Royal Society; honorary degrees from Edinburgh, Glasgow, Montreal, Cambridge, Dublin; Robert Boyle lecturer.

1848 William Crooke, d. 1923

Family: son of a physician.

Education: Tipperary Grammar School; Trinity College, Dublin.

Career: Indian Civil Servant, 1871–95, working throughout the United Provinces of Agra and Oudh; upon retirement, pursued scholarly life and was especially active in folklore circles, serving as editor of *Folk-Lore*, 1915–23.

Learned society activities: president of Section H and of the Folk-Lore Society; member of Council of the RAI.

Publications: *The Tribes and Castes of the North-Western Provinces* (1896); *Observations on the Mussalmans of India* (1916); *Islam in India* (1922).

Honors: Commander Order of the Indian Empire; Hon. D.Sc., Oxford; Hon. Litt.D., Dublin.

1848 E. Sidney Hartland, d. 1927

Family: son of Rev. E. J. Hartland, Congregational minister.

Education: read law.

Career: solicitor at Swansea, 1871; clerk to Swansea School Board,

1872–90; mayor of Gloucester, 1902; Registry County Court, Gloucester, and District Registrary of the High Court, 1889–1923; District Probate Registrary, 1918–24.

Learned society activities: president of the Folk-Lore Society, of Section H, and of Section I (Religions of the Lower Culture) of the BAAS; Council of the RAI.

Publications: *Primitive Paternity* (1910); *Ritual and Belief* (1914); *Primitive Law* (1924).

Honors: Hon. LL.D., St. Andrews; Hon. D. Litt., University of Wales; RAI Huxley Medal; first Frazer lecturer, Oxford, 1922.

1850   Richard Carnac Temple, d. 1931.

Family: eldest son of Sir Richard Temple, first baronet.

Education: Harrow; Trinity, Cambridge.

Career: ensign to lieutenant-colonel between 1871 and 1877 with the Royal Scots Fusiliers and the Bengal Staff Corporal afghan Campaign, 1878–9; Burma War, 1887–9; cantonment magistrate, Punjab, 1879; Assistant-commissioner, Burmah and cantonment magistrate, Mandelay, 1887; deputy commissioner, 1888; Rangoon municipality and port commissioner, Rangoon, 1891; chief commissioner, Andaman and Nicobar Islands, and superintendent, penal settlement at Port Blair, 1894; justice of the peace; chairman, Worcester Territorial County Association, 1907–22; chairman, Standing Council of the Baronetage, 1910–24; founded and edited *Punjab Notes and Queries*, 1883–7; editor and proprietor of *The Indian Antiquary* from 1884.

Learned society activities: president of Section H, of the Jubilee Congress of the Folk-Lore Society, and of the Bombay Anthropological Society; hon. vice-president, Royal Asiatic Society; member of the Council of the RAI, of the Philological Society, of the Asiatic Society of Bengal, and of the Royal Society of Arts; Fellow of the Royal Geographical Society.

Publications: *Andamese Language* (1877); *Legends of the Punjab* (1883–90); *Government of India* (1911); *Anthropology as a Practical Science* (1914).

Honors: Companion of the Bath; Companion of the Order of the Indian Empire; Fellow of the British Academy; Honorary Fellow, Trinity College, Cambridge.

1851   Arthur J. Evans, d. 1941

Family: son of (Sir) John Evans, paper manufacturer and prominent member of the anthropological community.

Education: Harrow; Brasenose College, Oxford (First Class in Modern History); Göttingen.

Career: At Oxford: keeper of Ashmolean Museum, 1884–1908, and Extraordinary professor of prehistoric archaeology; a founder of the British School at Athens; explorations included travel in Finland, Lapland, the Balkans during 1873 to 1875 and imprisonment by the Austrian government on charge of complicity in the Crivoscian Insurrection in South Dalmatia 1882 – perhaps a manifestation of the same love of adventure that made him a committed patron of the Boy Scouts – as well as excavations in Crete 1900–8, which resulted in the discoveries of the Palace of Knossos and pre-Phoenician script.

Learned society activities: president of the BAAS; vice-president of the RAI.

Publications: *Prehistoric Tombs of Knossos* (1906); *The Palace of Minos*, 4 vols. (1921–35); *The Earlier Religion of Greece in the Light of Certain Discoveries* (1931).

Honors: knighthood; Fellow of the Royal Society and recipient of its Royal and Copley medals; Petrie Medal; Frazer lecturer; honorary degrees from Oxford, Edinburgh, Dublin, Berlin.

1853 William Ridgeway, d. 1926

Family: son of Rev. John Ridgeway.

Education: Portarlington School; Trinity College, Dublin; St. Peter's College, Cambridge and Gonville and Caius College, Cambridge (scholarship); ranked fifth in classical tripos.

Career: fellow, Gonville and Caius, 1880; chair of Greek at University College, Cork; Disney chair of archaeology at Cambridge and reelection to Gonville and Caius fellowship, 1892; Brereton readership in classics at Cambridge, 1907.

Learned society activities: president of the RAI, of the Classical Association, of Section H, of the Cambridge Philological Society, of the Cambridge Anthropological Society; Fellow of the Zoological Society.

Publications: *The Origin of Metallic Currency and Weight Standards* (1892); *The Early Age of Greece* (1901); *The Origin and Influence of the Thoroughbred Horse* (1905); *The Dramas and Dramatic Dances of Non-European Races, in Special Reference to the Origin of Greek Tragedy* (1915).

Honors: knighthood; Fellow of the British Academy; RAI Huxley Medal; honorary degrees from Dublin, Aberdeen, Edinburgh, Manchester.

1854 James George Frazer, d. 1941

Family: son of Daniel F. Frazer, partner in Glasgow firm of chemists.

Education: Larchfield Academy; Glasgow University (M.A.); scholarships to Trinity College, Cambridge (placed second in the First Class of the classical tripos of 1878); read law and called to the Bar by the Middle Temple.

Career: fellowship, Trinity College, 1879; chair in social anthropology, University of Liverpool, 1907–22 (although remained in residence in Liverpool for only one session).

Learned society activities: member, Council of the RAI.

Publications: *The Golden Bough* (1890, 2 vols.; 1900, 3 vols.; 1911–5, 12 vols.); *Pausanias's Description of Greece*, 6 vols. (1898); *Totemism and Exogamy*, 4 vols. (1906).

Honors: knighthood; Order of Merit; Civil List pension; Fellow of the Royal Society; Original Fellow of the British Academy; numerous honorary degrees from British and foreign universities; lecture series established in his honor and given in turn at the universities of Oxford, Cambridge, Glasgow, and Liverpool.

1855 Alfred Cort Haddon, d. 1940

Family: son of John Haddon, head of firm of type founders and printers and proprietor of produce business dealing with Africa and the South Seas.

Education: various schools; evening classes at King's College, London; Christ's College, Cambridge (First Class in natural sciences tripos); grant for study at Stazione Zoologica at Naples.

Career: curator of Zoological Museum at Cambridge, and university demonstrator in zoology, 1879; professor of zoology at Royal College of Science and assistant naturalist to the Science and Art Museum in Dublin, 1880–1901; at Cambridge – part-time lectureship in physical anthropology, 1894–8; leader, Cambridge Anthropological Expedition to Torres Straits, 1898; university lecturer in Ethnology, 1900 (with a stipend of £50 a year); fellowship at Christ's College, 1901; readership in ethnology, 1909–26 (with a stipend of £200 a year; he did considerable extra teaching and writing in order to earn more money); frequently deputy curator of the Cambridge Museum of Archaeology and Ethnology, and honorary curator of the New Guinea collections (his Cambridge retirement dinner was the first occasion on which women dined in Christ's College); lecturer in ethnology at the University of London 1904–9. Fieldwork in Torres Straits, New Guinea, and Borneo, as well as fleeting visits among some indigenous peoples of Canada and the United States.

Learned society activities: president of Section H, of the RAI, of the Folk-Lore Society, of the Cambridge Antiquarian Society; member of the Council of the Royal Dublin Society; Fellow of the Cambridge Philosophical Society.

Publications: *Introduction to the Study of Embryology* (1887); *Evolution in Art* (1895); editor of and contributor to the *Reports of the Cambridge Expedition to Torres Straits*, 6 vols. (1901–35); *History of Anthropology* (1910); *The Races of Man and Their Distribution* (1912).

Honors: Fellow of the Royal Society; Conway Memorial lecturer; Herbertson Memorial lecturer; Frazer lecturer; Huxley and Rivers medals from the RAI, honorary doctorates from the universities of Manchester and Perth.

1863   Henry Balfour, d. 1939

Family: son of Lewis Balfour, silk broker.

Education: Charterhouse; Trinity College, Oxford (Second Class degree in Natural Science).

Career: all at Oxford – curator of Pitt-Rivers Museum, 1891–1939; taught courses in technology and prehistoric archaeology from 1904; elected a research fellow of Exeter College, and entitled professor, 1935.

Learned society activities: president of the RAI, of the Folk-Lore Society, of the Oxford Ornithological Society, and of the Royal Geographical Society; Fellow of the Zoological Society and of the Society of Antiquaries.

Publications: *The Evolution of Decorative Art* (1893); *The Natural History of the Musical Bow* (1899); *Spinners and Weavers in Anthropological Research* (1938).

Honors: Fellow of the Royal Society; Frazer lecturer.

1864   William Halse Rivers Rivers, d. 1922

Family: son of Rev. H. F. Rivers.

Education: Tonbridge; St. Bartholomew's Hospital (M.D.).

Career: lecturer on psychology, Guy's Hospital; lecturer on physiological and experimental psychology, University of Cambridge; member, Cambridge Expedition to Torres Straits; temporary captain, RAMC; psychologist, Central Hospital, RAF; fellow and praelector in natural sciences, St. John's College, Cambridge; founding editor (with James Ward) of the *British Journal of Psychology*.

Fieldwork: in Oceania and India.

Learned society activities: president of Section H, of the Folk-Lore

Society, of the RAI, and of the Psychology Section of the BAAS (but died before assuming office).

Publications: *The Todas* (1906); *A History of Melanesian Society*, 2 vols. (1914); *Instinct and the Unconscious* (1922).

Honors: Fellow of the Royal Society and recipient of its Royal Medal; Croonian lecturer, Royal College of Physicians; Fitzpatrick lecturer, Royal College of Physicians; honorary degrees from St. Andrews and Manchester.

1866   Arthur Keith, d. 1959

Family: son of John Keith, a farmer.

Education: Gordon College, Aberdeen; Marischal (medical) College (with highest honors): Aberdeen University (M.D.)

Career: medical officer to mining company in Siam, 1889–92; senior demonstrator in anatomy at the London Hospital Medical School, 1894; conservator of Royal College of Surgeons and director of Hunterian Museum, 1908; Fullerian professor of physiology, Royal Institution, 1917–23; rector of Aberdeen University, 1930; retired to live at Buckston Browne Research Institute in Down, 1933.

Learned society activities: president of the BAAS and of the RAI; secretary of the Anatomical Society of Great Britain.

Publications: *Human Embryology and Morphology* (1902); *The Antiquity of Man* (1915); *Nationality and Race* (1920); *Darwin and His Critics* (1935); *A New Theory of Human Evolution* (1948).

Honors: knighthood; Fellow of the Royal Society; Robert Boyle lecturer; Conway Memorial lecturer; honorary degrees from Durham, Manchester, Birmingham, and Oxford.

1866   Robert Randulph Marett, d. 1943

Family: son of (Sir) Robert Pipon Marett, attorney general and then bailiff and president of the legislative assembly of Jersey.

Education: Victoria College, Jersey; Balliol College, Oxford (First Class in Literae Humaniores), Chancellor's Prize (Latin verse) and Green Prize (essay on primitive ethics); studied philosophy at the University of Berlin; read law (Inner Temple) and called to the Jersey Bar.

Career: at Exeter College, Oxford, Fellow and tutor in philosophy from 1891 to 1928, and rector from 1928 to 1943; university reader in social anthropology, Oxford, 1910–36.

Learned society activities: president of the Sociological Institute, the Folk-Lore Society, and Section H; Council member of the RAI; principal founder of the Oxford University Anthropological Society.

Publications: *Anthropology* (1912); *Psychology and Folklore* (1920); *Head, Heart and Hands in Human Evolution* (1935).

Honors: Fellow of the British Academy; RAI Huxley Medal, Oxford D.Litt.; St. Andrews, LL.D.

1869 John L. Myres, d. 1954

Family: son of Rev. W. M. Myres.

Education: Winchester scholarship; New College, Oxford on scholarship (First Class in Literae Humaniores); fellow at Magdalen College, Oxford, 1892–5; Craven travelling Fellow, 1892–4; Burdett-Coutts geological scholar, 1892; student and tutor of Christ Church College, 1895–7; winner of Arnold Essay, 1897.

Career: lecturer in classical archaeology, University of Oxford, 1903–7; secretary to the Oxford Committee for Anthropology, 1905–7; Gladstone professor of Greek, and lecturer in ancient geography, University of Liverpool, 1907–10; Wykeham professor of ancient history, Oxford, 1910–39; fellow and librarian of New College, Oxford; chairman of the British School at Athens, 1934–47; editor of *Man*, 1901–3 and 1931–46.

Fieldwork: traveled and did excavations in Greece and Asia Minor.

Learned society activities: president of the RAI, of the Folk-Lore Society, and of the Hellenic Society; vice-president of the Society of Antiquaries; general secretary of the BAAS; Fellow of the Royal Geographical Society.

Publications: *The Dawn of History* (1911); *The Ethnology and Primitive Culture of the Nearer East and the Mediterranean World* (1934).

Honors: knighthood; officer, Order of the British Empire; Fellow of the British Academy; RAI Huxley Medal; Royal Geographical Society Victorian Medal; honorary degrees from Wales, Manchester, Witwatersrand, and Athens; Frazer lecturer.

1871 Grafton Elliot Smith, d. 1937

Family: born in Grafton, New South Wales, the son of Stephen Smith, a schoolmaster.

Education: student at his father's school in Sydney; University of Sydney (M.B. and Ch.M.); gold medal for his M.D. thesis; came to England and undertook research at Cambridge supervised by Alexander Macalister.

Career: first professor of anatomy at the Egyptian Government Medical School at Cairo, 1900–09; helped begin Archaeological Survey of Nubia, including excavation of 20,000 burials; professor of anatomy, Manchester, 1909; professor of anatomy, University College, London,

1919; General Medical Council, 1913–9; Fullerian professor, Royal Institution, 1933.

Learned society activities: president of the Anatomical Institute of Great Britain and Ireland, of the Manchester Literary and Philosophical Society, and of Section H; vice-president of the Royal Society and of the RAI.

Publications: *The Ancient Egyptians* (1911); *The Evolution of Man* (1924); *Human History* (1930).

Honors: knighthood; Fellow of the Royal Society and recipient of its Royal Medal; Hon. Gold Medal of the Royal College of Surgeons; *Prix Fauvelle* of the Anthropological Society of Paris; Aris and Gale lecturer (twice); Croonian lecturer.

1873   Charles S. Myers, d. 1946

Family: son of Wolf Myers, a London merchant; married Edith Seligman.

Education: City of London School; Gonville and Caius College, Cambridge (First Class in both parts of the natural sciences tripos); Arnold Gerstenberg Student; M.B.

Career: on Cambridge Anthropological Expedition to Torres Straits; house physician, St. Bartholomew's Hospital, 1899–1900; returned to Cambridge to assist Rivers in 1902 and became demonstrator, lecturer, and (in 1921) reader in experimental psychology; concurrently professor in psychology at King's College, London, 1906–9; lieut.-col., RAMC during World War I, including consulting psychologist to the British Army in France; helped found the National Institute of Industrial Psychology in 1921, and left Cambridge for full-time work there in 1922; member of the Home Office Factory Lighting Council and Industrial Health Research Board; editor of the *British Journal of Psychology*, 1911–24.

Learned society activities: president of Section J (psychology) of the BAAS, of the British Psychological Society (its first), and of the International Congress of Psychology; Council member of the RAI.

Publications: *An Introduction to Experimental Psychology* (1911); *Mind and Work* (1920); *Shell-Shock in France* (1940).

Honors: Commander Order of the British Empire; Fellow of the Royal Society; Honorary Fellow of Gonville and Caius College, Cambridge; Herbert Spencer lecturer; Hobhouse lecturer; honorary degrees from Cambridge, Manchester, Calcutta, Pennsylvania.

1873   Charles Gabriel Seligman, d. 1940.

Family: son of Hermann Seligman, London wine-merchant; married

Brenda Z. Salamon, who joined him in anthropological work – and proved more theoretically adventurous than he.

Education: St. Paul's School; St. Thomas's Hospital (M.D.); awarded Bristowe medal in pathology.

Career: house physician, St. Thomas's; went on Torres Straits Expedition; resumed pathological research at St. Thomas's and appointed superintendent of clinical laboratory, 1901; led Daniels Expedition to New Guinea, 1904; chair of ethnology, University of London, 1913–34; military service during World War I; Hunterian professor and Aris and Gale lecturer, Royal College of Surgeons; Lloyd-Roberts lecturer, Royal College of Physicians, 1935.

Fieldwork: in Ceylon, 1906; in Sudan, 1909.

Learned society activities: president of Section H and of the RAI, member of the Executive Council IAI.

Publications: *The Melanesians of British New Guinea* (1910); with B. Z. Seligman, *The Veddas* (1911) and *The Pagan Tribes of the Nilotic Sudan* (1932); *The Races of Africa* (1930).

Honors: Fellow of the Royal Society; Rivers and Huxley medals of the RAI; Annandale Memorial Medalist of the Asiatic Society of Bengal; Frazer lecturer.

1876 (Rev.) Edwin W. Smith, d. 1957

Family: son of Rev. John Smith, sometime missionary in South Africa and president of the Primitive Methodist Church.

Education: Blundell College, York.

Career: missionary of the Primitive Methodist Church, Southern Africa, 1898–1915; chaplain of Forces, 1915; worked for the British and Foreign Bible Society from 1916 to 1939, starting as the secretary at Rome and eventually becoming editorial superintendent; visiting professor, Hartford Seminary, 1939–43; head, School of African Studies, Fisk University, 1943; editor, *Journal of the Royal African Society*, 1938–40; editor, *Africa*, 1944–8.

Learned society activities: president of the RAI; member of the Executive Council, IAI.

Publications: with A. M. Dale, *The Ila-Speaking Peoples of Northern Rhodesia* (1920); *The Golden Stool* (1926); *African Beliefs and Christian Faith* (1936).

Honors: hon. doctoral degree, Wesley College, Winnipeg.

1878 Thomas A. Joyce, d. 1942

Education: Dulwich; Hertford College, Oxford.

Career: British Museum: entered, 1902; deputy keeper in Department of Ethnography, 1921; subkeeper, 1930; retired, 1938; military service in World War I (gaining rank of Captain); led archaeological expeditions to British Honduras, 1925, 1927, 1929, 1931.

Learned society activities: president of Section H and of the RAI.

Publications: editor, with N. W. Thomas, *Women of All Nations*, 2 vols. (1908); with E. Torday, *Notes ethnographiques sur des populations, habitant les bassins du Kasai et du Kwango Oriental* (1922); *Report on the British Museum Expedition to British Honduras* (1927).

Honors: Officer Order of the British Empire.

1881   Alfred Reginald Radcliffe-Brown (born Brown), d. 1955

Education: King Edward's High School, Birmingham; a year of premedical science at Birmingham; scholarship to Trinity College, Cambridge (First Class degree in mental and moral science); twice Anthony Wilkin student in ethnology (in 1906 and 1909).

Career: Fellow at Trinity College, Cambridge, 1908–14; reader in ethnology at the London School of Economics, 1909–10, and at the same time gave a course of lectures in comparative sociology at Cambridge; gave course of lectures at the University of Birmingham in 1913–14 academic year; taught in a Sydney grammar school; director of education in Tonga, 1916–19 (invalided out of service); ethnologist to the Transvaal Museum in Pretoria; professor of anthropology, University of Cape Town, 1921–5; professor of anthropology, University of Sydney, 1925–31, during which time he presided over the creation of the journal *Oceania*; professor of anthropology, University of Chicago, 1931–7; fellow of All Souls College and professor of social anthropology, Oxford University, 1937–46; professor of sociology, Farouk I University (Egypt) 1947–9; visiting professorships at Manchester, Rhodes (South Africa), Yenching (China), Sao Paulo (Brazil).

Fieldwork: in the Andaman Islands, Australia, Basutoland (his was not intensive fieldwork, however, and, lacking facility for languages, he relied on interpreters).

Learned society activities: president of the RAI; life-president of the Association of Social Anthropologists; IAI Executive Council.

Publications: *The Andaman Islanders* (1922); *The Social Organization of Australian Tribes* (1931); *Taboo* (1939); *Structure and Function in Primitive Society* (1952).

Honors: Fellow of the British Academy; Rivers and Huxley medals of the RAI; Henry Myers lecturer; Frazer lecturer.

1881   Richard Sutherland Rattray, d. 1938 (in a gliding accident)
   Family: son of Arthur Rattray, ICS; grandson of Robert Haldane Rattray, chief justice of Bengal.
   Education: Stirling High School; Exeter College, Oxford; on study leaves from colonial service employment, enrolled as student of R. R. Marett at Oxford in 1909 and earned a Diploma in Anthropology; also read law and was called to the Bar.
   Career: trooper in South African War; employed by the African Lakes Corporation, British Central Africa, 1902–7; entered the colonial service, first as a member of the Customs Department in 1907, transferring to the political service in 1911; served European War (Togoland) earning the rank of captain and becoming a district officer in the Anglo-French occupation of Togoland, 1914–17; acting assistant colonial secretary and clerk to the Legislative Council, Gold Coast, 1920; appointed to head of the Gold Coast Anthropology Department, 1921; after retirement from colonial service taught Hausa to colonial service probationers at Oxford.
   Learned society activities: member, RAI Council.
   Publications: *Religion and Art in Ashanti* (1927); *Ashanti Law and Constitution* (1929); *The Tribes of the Ashanti Hinterland* (1932); *The Leopard Princess*, a novel (1934).
   Honors: member, Order of the British Empire; commander order of the British Empire; Palmes d'Officier d'Academie (France); D.Sc., Oxford; Rivers Medal of the RAI.

1883   Arthur Maurice Hocart, d. 1939
   Family: son of Rev. James Hocart (originally Wesleyan, later Unitarian minister).
   Education: Athenee d'Ixelles, Brussels; Elizabeth College, Guernsey; scholarship at Exeter College, Oxford (Second Class in Literae Humaniores); Richards Prize; studied psychology and philosophy at the University of Berlin; senior studentships from Exeter and Jesus colleges took him on the Percy Sladen Trust Expedition to the Solomons; graduate research scholarship from Oxford took him to Riji, Rotorua, Wallis Island, Samoa, and Tonga; studied Sanskrit at Oxford.
   Career: headmaster of school on Fiji, 1909–12; delivered lectures at Oxford on "problems of anthropology," 1915; 1915–19 fought in France, reaching the rank of captain; appointed archaeological commissioner in Ceylon, assuming charge of his department, 1921; invalided from Ceylon service, 1929; lectured and examined in

anthropology at University College, London, 1929–34; elected to the chair of sociology at Fuad I University of Cairo in 1934.

Fieldwork: in Egypt, later in life.

Learned society activities: member, RAI Council.

Publications included: *The Progress of Man* (1933); *Kings and Councillors* (1936); Lord Raglan, ed., *The Life-Giving Myth* (1952).

Honors: RAI Rivers Medal.

1884   Bronislaw Malinowski, d. 1942

Family: son of Lucjan Malinowski, professor of slavonic philology at the Jagiellian University of Cracow; married Elsie Masson, daughter of (Sir) David Masson, professor of chemistry at the University of Melbourne, and herself the author of *An Untamed Territory* (1915), in which she describes various features of life in the remote Northern Territory of Australia – including the life of the Aborigines.

Education: Ph.D., Philosophy of Science, Cracow, 1908; three semesters of study at Leipzig attending lectures in economics and psychology (including Karl Bucher's, Wilhelm Wundt's and Felix Kruger's); D.Sc., London School of Economics, 1913, after study at the LSE with Westermarck and Seligman; Robert Mond studentship, 1914–17.

Career: at the London School of Economics – first appointed lecturer, 1913; reader in social anthropology, 1924; professor, 1927 (the first full-time chair in anthropology at the University of London); took leave for the duration of hostilities from London in 1939, and from then until his death was visiting professor of anthropology at Yale.

Fieldwork: worked intensively in Australian territories, chiefly in the Trobriand Islands; also passed briefly through other research areas, visiting the Pueblo Indians in 1926, some South and East African peoples (Swazi, Bemba, Chagga, Bantu Kavirondo) in 1934, and the Valley of Oaxaca, Mexico in 1940 and 1941.

Learned society activities: member, Council of the RAI and of the IAI.

Publications: *The Family Among the Australian Aborigines* (1913); *Argonauts of the Western Pacific* (1922); *The Father in Primitive Psychology* (1927); *Coral Gardens and Their Magic* (2 vols., 1935).

Honors: Hon. D.Sc. Harvard; honorary member, numerous foreign societies; Frazer lecturer.

1888   Jack Herbert Driberg, d. 1946 (buried in Muslim cemetery, as a convert to Islam).

Family: born Assam, son of an Indian Civil Service family.

Education: Lancing; Hertford College, Oxford; after retirement from colonial service, studied with B. Malinowski, Graham Wallas, M. Ginsburg, and G. Childe.

Career: political officer, serving in Uganda, 1912–21, and in the Sudan, 1921–5 (invalided out); lectured at University College, London, and the London School of Economics, 1927–9; began lecturing at Cambridge, 1931; appointed full-time lecturer, 1934; left Cambridge to work with the Middle East Section of the Ministry of Information, 1942.

Learned society activities: member, Council of the RAI.

Publications: *Poems* (1908); *The Longo* (1923); *The Savage as He Really Is* (1929); ed., with I. Schapera *The Ethnology of Africa* (1930).

Honors: Wellcome Gold Medal of the RAI.

1889   Gertrude Caton-Thompson, d. 1985

Family: daughter of William Caton-Thompson, solicitor, and the former Ethel Gertrude Page, the daughter of a physician.

Education: Miss Hawtrey's Eastbourne; earned no formal degrees, but studied surveying, zoology, paleontology, geology, prehistory, and anthropology in preparation for a career in archaeology; studied particularly at University College, London and the British School of Archaeology in Egypt with (Sir) Flinders Petrie, and at Cambridge with A. C. Haddon and Miles Burkitt.

Career: Ministry of Shipping, 1915–19; Paris Peace Conference, 1919; governor of Bedford College for Women and of the School of Oriental and African Studies, both of the University of London: Fellow of Newnham College, Cambridge. Never held a teaching position, although it was credibly reported that she declined the Disney chair of archaeology at Cambridge.

Fieldwork: excavated Abydos, Oxyrhychos, Malta, Qau, Badari, Northern Fayum, 1921–6; field director, RAI, 1927–8; appointed by the British Association to conduct Zimbabwe excavations and investigations of other Rhodesian sites, 1929; excavations in Kharga Oasis, 1930–3; excavations in South Africa, 1937–8.

Learned society activities: member, Council of the RAI.

Publications: *The Zimbabwe Culture* (1931); *The Kharga Oasis in Prehistory* (1952).

Honors: Fellow of the British Academy; the Cutherbert Peek Medal of the Royal Geographical Society; the Rivers and Huxley medals of the RAI; the Burton Medal of the Royal Asiatic Society; Hon. Litt.D., Cambridge.

1895 Wilfred Edward Le Gros Clark, d. 1971

Family: son of Rev. Travers Clark.

Education: Blundell's School, Tiverton; St. Thomas's Hospital (M.D.).

Career: Captain, RAMC; principal medical officer of Sarawak, Borneo, 1920–3; reader in anatomy, University of London, 1924–7; professor of anatomy, St. Bartholomew's Hospital, 1927–9; professor of anatomy, St. Thomas's Hospital, 1929–34; at Oxford – professor of anatomy, 1934–62, and director of research on clinical and working efficiency, 1948–62; Hunterian professor, Royal College of Surgeons, 1934 and 1945; member of Medical Research Council, 1950–4.

Learned society activities: president of Section H, of the International Anatomical Congress, of the Anatomical Society, and of the BAAS; vice-president of the Zoological Society and of the RAI; Council of the Royal Society.

Publications: *Man: A Morphological Study of the Evolutionary Origin of the Primates* (1934); *The Tissues of the Body* (1939); *History of the Primates* (1949); with J. S. Weiner and K. P. Oakley, *The Solution of the Piltdown Problem* (1953).

Honors: knighthood; Fellow of the Royal Society and recipient of its Royal Medal; other prizes, including the Doyne and Viking medals and the Triennial Prize of the Royal College of Surgeons; honorary degrees from Durham, Manchester, Edinburgh, Witwatersrand, Melbourne, Oslo, and Malaya; distinguished lectureships, including the Robert Boyle, Ferrier, Maudsley, and Edridge-Green; various honors from foreign societies.

1899 Audrey Richards, d. 1984

Family: daughter of (Sir) Henry Richards, Chichele professor of international law, Oxford, and legal member of Viceregal Council, granddaughter of Spencer P. Butler, barrister and public servant.

Education: Downe House School; Newnham College, Cambridge (Natural Science); Ph.D. in anthropology, London School of Economics, 1931; IAI fellowship.

Career: lecturer in social anthropology, LSE, 1931–3 and 1935–7; senior lecturer in social anthropology, University of Witswatersrand, 1939–41; principal, Colonial Office, 1942–5; reader in social anthropology, University of London, 1946–50; director, East African Institute of Social Research at Makerere College, Uganda 1950–6; director, Centre for African Studies, Cambridge University, 1956–7; Smuts reader in anthropology at Cambridge, 1961–7. Member of the Colonial Research Committee, 1944–7; Colonial Social Science Research Council, 1944–50 and 1956–62; Committee for Scientific Research in Africa South of the Sahara, 1954–6.

Fieldwork: in Northern Rhodesia, 1930–1 and 1933–4; in Northern Transvaal, 1939–40; in Uganda, 1950–5; and in Elmdon (England).

Learned society activities: president of the RAI (its first woman president) and of the African Studies Association; IAI Executive Council.

Publications: *Hunger and Work in a Savage Tribe* (1932); *Land, Labour and Diet in Northern Rhodesia* (1939); *Chisungu* (1956); *The Changing Structure of a Ganda Village* (1966).

Honors: Commander Order of the British Empire; Fellow of the British Academy; Rivers and Wellcome medals of the RAI.

1902   Edward Evan Evans-Pritchard, d. 1973

Family: son of Rev. Thomas Evans-Pritchard.

Education: Winchester (Commoner); Exeter College, Oxford (Honorary Scholar); Ph.D. in anthropology, London School of Economics, 1928; Leverhulme fellowship.

Career: professor of sociology, Fuad I University, 1930–3; research lecturer, Oxford University, 1935–40; hon. research assistant, UCL; military service, 1940–5 (mentioned in despatches); reader, Cambridge University, 1945–6; professor of social anthropology and fellow of All Souls College, Oxford University, 1946–70; chairman, Committee on Anthropology and Sociology of the Colonial Social Science Research Council.

Fieldwork: six major and several minor anthropological expeditions to Central, East, and North Africa, 1926–39.

Learned society activities: president of the RAI; life president of the Association of Social Anthropologists; member, IAI Executive Council.

Publications: *Witchcraft, Oracles and Magic Among the Azande* (1937); *The Nuer* (1940); *The Sanusi of Cyrenaica* (1949); *Kinship and Marriage Among the Nuer* (1951); *Nuer Religion* (1956); *The Position of Women in Primitive Societies* (1965); *The Azande: History and Political Institutions* (1971).

Honors: knighthood; Chevalier, Legion of Honor (France); Fellow of the British Academy; Rivers Medal of the RAI; honorary degrees from Chicago, Bristol, and Manchester.

1906   Meyer Fortes, d. 1983

Family: born Britstown, South Africa, the son of Russian immigrants, Bertha (Kerbel) and Nathan Fortes, a businessman.

Education: University of Cape Town (English and Psychology); Ph.D. in psychology from University College, London, 1929 (thesis entitled "A New Application of the Theory of Noegenesis to the Problem of

Mental Testing"): LSE Ratan Tata Student, 1930–1; Rockefeller Fellow, 1933–4; IAI support, 1934–8.

Career: lecturer, London School of Economics, 1938–9; research lecturer, Oxford 1939–41; National Service, West Africa, 1942–4; head of the Sociological Department, West Africa Institute, Accra, Ghana, 1944–6; reader in social anthropology, Oxford 1946–50; William Wyse professor at Cambridge 1950–73.

Fieldwork: worked extensively in Ghana.

Learned society activities: president of the RAI and of Section H; chairman, Association of Social Anthropologists; Executive Committee, British Sociological Association.

Publications: *The Dynamics of Clanship Among the Tallensi* (1945); *The Web of Kinship Among the Tallensi* (1949); *Marriage in Tribal Societies* (1962); *Time and Social Structure and Other Essays* (1970).

Honors: Fellow of the British Academy; Rivers and Wellcome Medals of the RAI; honorary degrees from Chicago and Belfast.

Index

Abraham, R. C., 203, 221
Acephalous societies, 236, 238, 269, 271–6
Adult education, 46, 108
Advisory Committee on Education in the Colonies, 205–8
African Political Systems, 270
Agricultural depression, 35, 52
American Revolution, 3
Ancient Egyptians, 84, 125–7, 146, 149, 150, 153, 181, 219, 261
Ancient Greeks, 19, 84, 146, 223, 227, 249, 255, 261
Anglo-Saxons, 246, 247, 248, 249, 250, 263–4, 268
Anthony Wilkin Studentship, 135
Anthropological Institute, *see* Royal Anthropological Institute
Anti-Semitism, 57
Archaic Civilization, 125–7, 260
Armstrong, W. G., 49, 131
Asante, 227–8, 229, 283, 284
Association of Social Anthropologists, 10, 14, 57
Australian Aborigines, 154
Australian colonial policy, 48–9, 55, 209
Avebury, Lord, *see* John Lubbock

Balfour, Henry, 199, 309
Barotse, 224
Bartlett, F. C. (Sir Frederick), 136, 138, 139, 153, 158, 163, 164
Bateson, Gregory, 17, 131, 135, 153
Bateson, William, 17
Beddoe, John, 115, 151
Bennett, Arnold, 180
Biometricians, 150–1
Boer War, 22, 23, 133, 152, 172
Booth, Charles, 140
Booth, William, 101
Brabrook, E. W. (Sir Edward), 92, 110, 111, 115, 304–5
Brace, William, 173
Brain structure and function, 157–8, 163

British Association for the Advancement of Science, 6, 14, 18, 43, 46, 53, 58–9, 64, 101, 114–15, 130, 135, 196
Brong, 231
Brown, G. Gordon, 216, 217, 225, 238
Burt, (Sir) Cyril, 136, 137, 207
Butterfield. Herbert, 277

Cambridge Anthropological Expedition to Torres Straits, 15, 49, 132, 133–49, 170, 174, 287
Cambridge University, 5, 8, 16, 21, 27–8, 38–9, 40–1, 51–3, 56, 131
Cameron, (Sir) Donald, 203, 231, 234, 237
Cannibalism, 103
Cardinall, A. W., 203, 219
Carlyle, Thomas, 246
Carnegie Corporation, 56, 207, 210, 215
Carter, R. Brudenell, 147
Caton-Thompson, Gertrude, 317
Celts, 264
Chagga, 239
Childe, V. Gordon, 71
Chinnery, E. P., 49
Churchill, Winston, 24
Civil services reform, 20, 33–4, 37, 38, 48, 95
Clark, (Sir) Wilfred Edward LeGros, 318
Codrington, R. H., 289
Colonial Administrative Service, *see* Colonial services
Colonial anthropology, British Empire, 13–14, 49–50, 54, 93–4, 95, 182–241, 279, 293
Colonial Development and Welfare Act, 215
Colonial Education Service, 207
Colonial Office, 182, 199, 200, 203, 213, 214–15, 218, 221, 228
Colonial Research Council, 14, 191, 216
Colonial Secretaries, 199, 205, 215, 285
Colonial services, 47–8, 182, 196, 198, 202, 221–2

321